C000118775

Segment Reporting under IFRS 8

MÜNSTERANER SCHRIFTEN ZUR INTERNATIONALEN UNTERNEHMENSRECHNUNG

Herausgegeben von Peter Kajüter

Band 13

Zu Qualitätssicherung und Peer Review der vorliegenden Publikation

Die Qualität der in dieser Reihe erscheinenden Arbeiten wird vor der Publikation durch den Herausgeber der Reihe geprüft.

Notes on the quality assurance and peer review of this publication

Prior to publication, the quality of the work published in this series is reviewed by the editor of the series.

Martin Nienhaus

Segment Reporting under IFRS 8

Reporting Practice and Economic Consequences

Bibliographic Information published by the Deutsche Nationalbibliothek
The Deutsche Nationalbibliothek lists this publication in the Deutsche
Nationalbibliografie; detailed bibliographic data is available in the internet at
http://dnb.d-nb.de.

Zugl.: Münster (Westfalen), Univ., Diss., 2015

Library of Congress Cataloging-in-Publication Data
Nienhaus, Martin, 1986-
Segment reporting under IFRS 8 : reporting practice and economic
consequences / Martin Nienhaus.
    pages cm. – (Münsteraner Schriften zur Internationalen
Unternehmensrechnung, ISSN 1868-7687 ; Band 13)
    ISBN 978-3-631-66458-2
    1. Accounting–Standards. 2. Financial statements–Standards. I. Title.
    HF5626.N54 2015
    657.02'18–dc23
                                            2015025231

                            D 6
                    ISSN 1868-7687
              ISBN 978-3-631-66458-2 (Print)
              ISBN 978-3-653-05653-2 (E-Book)
                DOI 10.3726/978-3-653-05653-2

                    © Peter Lang GmbH
            Internationaler Verlag der Wissenschaften
                    Frankfurt am Main 2015
                    All rights reserved.
        PL Academic Research is an Imprint of Peter Lang GmbH.

        Peter Lang – Frankfurt am Main · Bern · Bruxelles · New York ·
                    Oxford · Warszawa · Wien

            This publication has been peer reviewed.

                    www.peterlang.com

Preface

The adoption of IFRS 8 represented a major change to the segment reporting requirements under IFRS. The IASB adopted the US segment reporting rules following
SFAS No. 131 and the risk-and-reward approach was replaced by the management approach. Consequently, firms now have to report segment information "through the management's eyes". This change was heavily criticized by academics and practitioners since it
led to less uniform segment reporting. Critics feared that IFRS 8 would also allow substantial management discretion and decrease comparability. In contrast, proponents argued that the management's perspective would lead to more useful information.

To date, however, the consequences of IFRS 8's adoption are barely known. The Post-
Implementation Review by the IASB also revealed an extensive research gap in this regard.
This thesis is the first provide an empirical analysis of the adoption of IFRS 8 with a particular focus on the usefulness from a capital market's perspective. Martin Nienhaus conducts four sub-studies to provide a thorough investigation of IFRS 8. First, the change in
segment reporting practice is documented based on a content analysis of segment reports
before and after the adoption of IFRS 8. The descriptive results are subsequently used for
three further sub-studies on how IFRS 8's adoption affected investors, preparers and financial analysts.

Martin Nienhaus exploits a natural experiment in a unique setting with a quasi-
experimental research design. This research strategy allows him to draw causal inferences –
which is generally very challenging in empirical disclosure research. The study provides
evidence that the adoption of IFRS 8 helps to mitigate information asymmetries. Moreover, firms can reduce their cost of capital through the disclosure of segment information
from the management's perspective. Finally, the precision of the common and private
information sets of financial analysts increases. Analysts use the segment information under IFRS 8 to generate more private information which leads to less consensus. In summary, Martin Nienhaus finds that the adoption of IFRS 8 impacted investors, preparers
and financial analysts in a positive way.

The study's findings greatly contribute to the existing literature since it is the first analysis
to document the economic consequences of IFRS 8's adoption. The results have several
implications. Most importantly, the findings directly add to the literature on IFRS 8 and
help the IASB to assess IFRS 8's consequences. Moreover, implications for users of financial statements such as investors and financial analysts, preparers as well as auditors and
enforcement institutions are discussed.

Given the importance of segment reporting, the rigor in the empirical analyses as well as
the contribution of the findings, I am convinced that this thesis will gain a lot of attention
and enjoy popularity among academics and practitioners.

Münster, January 2015   Prof. Dr. Peter Kajüter

Acknowledgement

I have written this thesis during my time as a PhD-student at the Chair of International Accounting of the University of Münster. The Münster School of Business and Economics accepted this thesis as a dissertation in January 2015.

First, I sincerely thank my academic teacher and supervisor Prof. Dr. Peter Kajüter. He devoted a lot of time and energy helping me to improve my work. His ability to set and demand high standards of himself and those around him create a very fruitful research environment. Moreover, his constant support and advice helped me to become a better researcher. Much of my academic achievements, I owe to him. I also thank Prof. Dr. Christoph Watrin and Prof. Dr. Mark Trede for reviewing my study as the second and third referee.

My sincere thanks are further given to Prof. Dr. Steven Huddart and Prof. Dr. Dan Givoly, who accepted me as a visiting scholar at the Accounting Department of the Pennsylvania State University. I am very grateful for all the fruitful discussions with faculty members and PhD-students at Penn State, which helped me to improve my research projects and also to develop a critical thinking about good research. I also thank Prof. Dr. Stephen A. Zeff for our inspiring discussions at the 2014 AAA Annual Meeting in Atlanta. He is undoubtedly the most interesting person in academia I have ever met and I have received great motivation from our encounter.

I am also very grateful for my dear friends and colleagues at the Chair of International Accounting. First, let me say that I could not have wished for a better team. We have had a lot of fun outside of the university – particularly at late hours. You guys made my time here very enjoyable. It has been a pleasure to share my office for almost two years with Stefan Hannen, who is one of the most relaxed officemates I have ever had. He also tried improving my soccer skills, which was a challenging task. I was lucky having Dr. Christina Voets and Daniela Peters on my side sharing the responsibility for our AccountingTalents student development program. Without their care and cleverness, I would have been hopelessly swamped. I also thank Stephanie Eckerth for her continuous help and support. She has not only proofread parts of my thesis, but also challenged my thinking and helped me to sharpen my work. Special thanks go to Marcel Baki, whose sympathy and sometimes crazy ideas enlightened many of my days. Furthermore, Gregor Hagemann helped me to overcome all technical hurdles in a very professional and nice way and also proofread parts of my thesis. I very much appreciate the help of Florian Klassmann, who streamlined the entire empirical analysis of my dissertation. He was always there when I needed his comments and feedback on numerous other research issues. I am also very grateful for having had Dr. Maximilian Saucke and Dr. Moritz Schröder on my team. I appreciate working with you two since your reasonable care and selflessness as well as critical thinking made life at the chair so much easier. My particular thanks go to my former colleagues Dr. Kristian Bachert, Dr. Daniel Blaesing, Julius Hannemann, Dr. Martin Merschdorf, Dr. Matthias Moeschler, Dr. Christian Reisloh and Dr. Thomas Poplat. All of you and in particular Daniel helped me to get off on the right foot in my PhD-life. Now, I am looking forward to the common times with my "newer" colleagues Friedrich

Kalden, Max Meinhövel, Matthias Nienaber, Alexander Schulz and Martin Vogelpohl. I am sure that those will be as enjoyable as it has been so far.

In addition, I want to thank Leila Prousch, Ashly Bills and Tobias Langehaneberg for helping me with the all the administrative issues of the chair work. Moreover, I greatly appreciate the help of my student assistants Ina Gährken, Theresa Jording and Mareike Schlöter, who supported me in the final stage of my dissertation. You made life easier for me during a very stressful time.

Outside of my university, I thank my dear friends Florian Diesner, Stanislaus Hergert, Dmitrij Spolwind, Gleb Spolwind, Dustin Werk, Lars Wolters, Simon Hellenkamp and Fabian Nohse. I have known you guys for a very long time and your friendship means a lot to me. I hold many dear memories of us growing up together and becoming adults. Certainly, there are many more worthwhile moments ahead of us.

Finally, I would not be here today if it wasn't for my family. I owe my deepest gratitude to my wife Dorothee. We have gone through so much together and she willingly sacrificed a lot so that I could pursue my ambitions. Her endless love, understanding and self-less patience helped me through all difficult times. She was also willing to listen to all my crazy research ideas and proofread my dissertation. Words won't do justice to express the way I feel about you.

My parents, Christel and Gerd, have supported and inspired me my entire life. Their love and dedication to their children are unmatched. I am deeply grateful for their trust, un-conditional support and love. Your example has set high standards for me to achieve once I become a parent myself. I am also very thankful for the endless support of my parents-in-law Irene and Georg. You have welcomed me into your family with such ease and always had my back. Last and surely not least, I thank my sister and brother, Margit and Ralf, as well as my sisters-in-law, Kornelia, Daniela and Stefanie, and my almost-brother-in-law Pascal, for standing me by and helping us in so many ways. I have shared wonder-ful and unforgettable times with you!

To them, my family, I dedicate this thesis.

Münster, January 2015   Martin Nienhaus

Contents overview

Contents

List of figures

List of tables

List of abbreviations

AAER	Accounting and Auditing Enforcement Releases
Adj.	Adjusted
AICPA	American Institute of Certified Public Accountants
AIMR	Association for Investment Management and Research
AG	Aktiengesellschaft
BC	Basis for Conclusion
BTM	Book-to-Market
Cf.	Confer
C.p.	Ceteris paribus
CAPM	Capital Asset Pricing Model
CEO	Chief Executive Officer
CFA	Chartered Financial Analyst
CODM	Chief Operating Decision Maker
CMAC	Capital Markets Advisory Committee
CPA	Certified Public Accountant
CSEF	Center for Studies in Economics and Finance
DAX	Deutscher Aktien Index
DJIA	Dow Jones Industrial Average
E.g.	Exempli gratia
EBIT	Earnings Before Interest and Taxes
EBITA	Earnings Before Interest, Taxes and Amortization
EBITDA	Earnings Before Interest, Taxes, Depreciation and Amortization
EBITDAR	Earnings Before Interest, Taxes, Depreciation, Amortization and Rent
EBT	Earnings Before Taxes
ED	Exposure Draft
Ed.	Edition
Eds.	Editors
EFFAS	European Federation of Financial Analysts Societies
EFTA	European Free Trade Association
EPS	Earnings Per Share
Et al.	Et alii
Etc.	Et cetera
EU	European Union
E-DRS	Entwurf Deutscher Rechnungslegungs Standard

FASB	Financial Accounting Standards Board
FREP	Financial Reporting Enforcement Panel
FTSE	Financial Times Stock Exchange
GICS	Global Industry Classification Code
GLS	Generalized Least Squares
HGB	Handelsgesetzbuch
http	Hypertext Transfer Protocol
I.e.	Id est
IAS	International Accounting Standards
IASB	International Accounting Standards Board
IASC	International Accounting Standards Committee
I/B/E/S	Institutional Brokers' Estimate System
IFRS	International Financial Reporting Standards
IPO	Initial Public Offering
KonTraG	Gesetz zur Kontrolle und Transparenz im Unternehmensbereich
KPI	Key Performance Indicator
Market Cap	Market Capitalization
MD&A	Management Discussion and Analysis
NASDAQ	National Association of Securities Dealers Automated Quotation System
NYSE	New York Stock Exchange
No.	Number
OECD	Organisation for Economic Co-operation and Development
OLS	Ordinary Least Squares
p.	Page
PDF	Portable Document Format
PE	Price/Earnings Ratio
PEG	Price/Earnings to Growth Ratio
PIR	Post-Implementation Review
pp.	Pages

QC   Qualitative Characteristics

RFI   Request for Information
ROCE   Return on Capital Employed
ROS   Return on Sales
R&D   Research and Development

SEC   Securities and Exchange Commission
SFAS   Statement of Financial Accounting Standard
SME   Small and Medium-Sized Entities
SIC   Standard Industrial Classification Code
Sqm   Square Meter
Std. Dev.   Standard Deviation
Suppl.   Supplementary

U.S.   United States
UK   United Kingdom
US-GAAP   United States Generally Accepted Accounting Principles

Vs.   Versus
VIF   Variance Inflation Factors

www   World Wide Web

List of symbols

α	Constant Regression Term
β	Regression Coefficient
ε	Error Term
*	Significance Level
&	And
€	Euro
F	F-value of the F-Test
H	Hypothesis
i	Item in the Company Index
N	Number of Observations
P	Proposition
t	Item in the Time Index
Σ	Sum

1 Introduction

1.1 Research questions and objectives

Understanding the business of multinational and diversified entities is challenging for users of financial statements, especially in light of ongoing globalization and the associated growth of foreign operations. Until the 1970s and early 1980s, investors and other users of financial reporting had to subsist on aggregated financial statements. Considering that firms engage in business activities in different industries and that multinational entities face diverse economic and political environments, aggregated financial disclosures as a single source of information may conceal important facts and prevent a thorough financial analysis. **Segment reporting** – which can be defined as the disaggregation of financial information of an entity's business operations by business lines, geographical areas or major customers – can help to overcome the shortcomings of financial statements.

On the one hand, segmental disclosures assist users to take the varying profitability, growth opportunities and risk of different business operations into account. This potentially enhances the users' ability to assess an entity's future development. In fact, empirical research has shown that segmental disclosures lead to **improved earnings forecasts** (e.g., *Kinney* (1971); *Kochanek* (1974); *Collins* (1975); *Emmanuel/Pick* (1980); *Silhan* (1983); *Baldwin* (1984); *Roberts* (1989); *Balakrishnan et al.* (1990); *Swaminathan* (1991); *Berger/Hann* (2003); *Ettredge et al.* (2005)). Moreover, numerous studies provide evidence that the availability of segment information affects investors' **risk assessments** and leads to a reduction in systematic risk (e.g., *Collins/Simonds* (1979); *Ajinkya* (1980); *Prodhan* (1986); *Prodhan/Harris* (1989); *Dupnik/Rolfe* (1990)). Furthermore, there is plenty of evidence that segment reports yield **value relevant** information that is incremental to financial statements (e.g., *Berger/Hann* (2003); *Hossain* (2008); *Hope et al.* (2008); *Hope et al.* (2009); *Kajüter/Nienhaus* (2013)). Finally, the *IASB* (2013a) also noted the importance of segment information as "*a key input into most investors' modelling of future results and cash flows*" (*IASB* (2013a), p. 8).

On the other hand, researchers and particularly preparers have voiced **concerns** that the disclosure of segment level information may be competitively harmful. For instance, *Elliott/Jacobson* (1994) posit that revealing detailed information of very successful segments attracts competitors that might enter the market to get a share of excess profits. Moreover, it is questionable if segment information is useful at all as differences in inter-segment transfer pricing policies, arbitrary cost allocations among segments and inconsistent segment definitions across firms may mislead users of financial statements (*Collins* (1975), p. 125).

Given the relevance and potential benefits as well as the concerns raised by opponents of segment disclosures, financial accounting standard setters such as the IASB and FASB have always regarded segment reporting as a **contentious topic**. Consequently, segment reporting requirements have undergone constant adjustments and amendments since the issuance of the first segment reporting standard for US-GAAP in 1976[1] and for IFRS in 1981. As there are different fundamental approaches to segment reporting, the two standard setters tried to find a **common approach** for the preparation of segmental disclosures during the 1990s. The FASB was convinced that the management approach was best suited whilst the IASC, the predecessor of the IASB, favored the risk-and-reward approach. Eventually, they went different paths. The FASB introduced Statement of Financial Accounting Standard Number 131 (SFAS No. 131) "Disclosures about Segments of an Enterprise and Related Information" in 1997 and the IASB introduced International Accounting Standard 14 revised[2] (IAS 14R) "Segment Reporting" in the same year. However, in 2006, as part of the **short-term convergence** project with US-GAAP, the IASB reconsidered its decision and adopted International Financial Reporting Standard 8 (IFRS 8) "Operating Segments", which was obligatory for financial years commencing on or after January 1, 2009. IFRS 8 is identical to the US-GAAP segment reporting requirements of SFAS No. 131 except for some marginal differences. Overall, the introduction of the management approach to segment reporting was considered a major step:

> "*IFRS 8 Operating Segments was to some extent a ground-breaking standard, as it represented the IASB's first foray into the territory of requiring companies to disclose information 'through the eyes of management' ...*"

> (*Crawford et al.* (2012), p. 1)[3]

The **management approach** requires preparers to define segments and disclose segment information the same way as they are reported internally for performance evaluation and resource allocation purposes. This means that a company which calculates its segmental profits based on, for instance, imputed costs has to disclose **non-IFRS** profits. This is in contrast to IAS 14R which requires segment information to be in line with the same measurement principles used for financial statements.

However, there has been a lot of **criticism** towards the introduction of the management approach. For example, IASB board members Gilbert Gélard and James J. Leisenring voted against IFRS 8 because they thought that segment data should be in line with IFRS. Moreover, the French economist Nicholas Véron criticized that:

> "*...the change from IAS 14 to IFRS 8 can be described as a decision taken solely for the sake of convergence with US GAAP, in spite of the criticism emanating from users which see it as a poor move from the point of view of standards' quality.*"

> (*Véron* (2007), p. 38)

---

[1] The Securities and Exchange Commision (SEC) already required information on segment income and revenues for publicly traded firms since 1969 in the U.S.

[2] The first segment reporting standard under IFRS from 1981 was already labeled IAS 14 ("Reporting Financial Information by Segment"). Since this standard was substantially revised and relabeled in 1997, the post 1997 version is referred to as IAS 14R in the following.

[3] However, there have already been other standards which incorporate some elements of the management approach, for instance, IAS 11 or IAS 36. But IFRS 8 is the first standard that makes use of the management approach in such an extensive manner.

Additionally, the European Parliament raised concerns about the adoption of a U.S. standard without further analysis of the implications for EU law as well as about potential managerial discretion and lack of comparability of segment information (*European Parliament* (2007*a*)). Therefore, the **endorsement** process was delayed for almost a year. As the findings of the introduction of the management approach to segment reporting in the U.S. (SFAS No. 131) cannot simply be transferred to IFRS 8, the European Parliament asked the European Commission to conduct an impact assessment of IFRS 8 by 2011 (*European Parliament* (2007*b*)). In addition, the IASB launched a post-implementation review (PIR) in 2012 to assess the effect of IFRS 8's adoption.

However, until today, several questions regarding the consequences of the introduction of IFRS 8 **remain unanswered**: It is unclear whether the view "*through the management's eyes*" (*Martin* (1997), p. 29) helps users of financial statements to facilitate better decisions or if the potential flexibility and discretion of the management approach impair the decision usefulness of segment reporting. The IASB points out a substantial **research gap** in this regard:

> "*At this time, there is no academic evidence that application of IFRS 8 has reduced information asymmetry or the cost of capital. Evidence of improvements in analysts' information environments is generally absent.*"

> (*IASB* (2013), p. 7)

Although there is already some **research** on the introduction of the management approach to segmental information in the U.S., the impact in a German setting may be entirely different for several reasons. First, the **preceding standard** Statement of Financial Accounting Standard Number 14 (SFAS No. 14) is different from IAS 14R. SFAS No. 14 required far less extensive disclosures. Hence, the introduction of SFAS No. 131 increased the number of segment disclosures. In contrast, IAS 14R was already a well-developed standard and the adoption of IFRS 8 did not change much to the required quantity of disclosures. This allows isolating the effect of a change in underlying concepts (risk-and-reward approach to management approach) instead of analyzing a mere increase in disclosures. Moreover, there are substantial differences in the **accounting tradition** and **capital market structures** between Germany and the U.S. Finally, **cultural differences** may also influence the perception of information based on the management approach.[4] Therefore, findings from U.S. studies should not simply be transferred to the introduction of IFRS 8. Furthermore, some prior U.S. studies **lack an identification strategy** that would allow them to draw causal inferences on the impact of introducing the management approach to segment reporting. Hence, there is a need for further empirical evidence in this field as indicated by the IASB.

The relevance and contention of segment information, the substantial changes induced by the introduction of IFRS 8 and the controversy about adopting the management approach together with the lack of research build the foundation for the main **research question** of this study. The implications of introducing IFRS 8 are empirically analyzed by conducting two comprehensive studies that shed light upon two different aspects. First,

---

[4] Refer to section 3.3 for a detailed discussion of the reasons.

it is analyzed how **segment reporting practices** have changed after the adoption of IFRS 8 compared to the disclosures under its predecessor IAS 14R. This allows to grasp a basic understanding of the changes that are visible at first sight and to analyze whether introducing IFRS 8 induced an increase or decrease in segmental disclosures overall. Second, **economic consequences** of the adoption of the new standard are investigated. To capture a broad understanding of the impact, the perspectives of three different capital market participants are assumed: investors, the reporting firm and financial analysts. All three should be affected if the adoption of IFRS 8 led to the disclosure of previously undisclosed useful information.

For **investors** this notion builds on a fundamental link in economic theory: improved disclosures of a firm should increase the amount of useful information available and thus decrease inequality in its distribution among investors (*Verrecchia* (1983)). This in turn mitigates the risk to deal with a superiorly informed investor and the related adverse selection problem when trading stock (*Glosten/Milgrom* (1985); *Venkatesh/Chiang* (1986)). Reduced information asymmetries should then be reflected in an increased liquidity of the stock (*Leuz/Wysocki* (2008)).

From the **firm's** perspective, one key concern is to raise capital at low cost. Improved disclosures can also affect the cost of an entity's capital, both through an indirect and a direct link. Better disclosures have an implicit effect on the cost of capital through the information asymmetry component as elaborated above (*Verrecchia* (2001); *Lambert et al.* (2007); *Stulz* (2009)). Furthermore and in a more direct relation, enhanced disclosures reduce estimation risk as well as parameter uncertainty (*Barry/Brown* (1985); *Coles et al.* (1995)) and increase investors' recognition and thus improve risk sharing due to a larger investor base (*Merton* (1987)). Moreover, monitoring costs of investors can be reduced due to enhanced disclosures and thus reduce the returns they require, which again lowers the cost of capital (*Lombardo/Pagano* (2002)). Hence, if the adoption of IFRS 8 improved the quality of disclosures it should be reflected in reduced cost of capital.

Finally, **financial analysts** have often stressed the importance of segmental disclosures to their work (e.g., *Knutson* (1993); *Brown* (1997)). Hence, an improvement in these disclosures should also be reflected in the outcome of analysts' forecasts. However, analysts' forecast accuracy can be affected in two (potentially opposite) ways. Analysts can use costly private information as well as less costly market-wide public information to facilitate forecasts. If the adoption of IFRS 8 improves public information and analysts discard more expensive private information in favor of public information, it is unclear how overall forecast accuracy will change. The effect depends on how informative the two sets of information are (*Botosan/Stanford* (2005)). However, to gauge the two effects separately, an approach that allows measuring the change in precision in idiosyncratic information and common information is used in this study (*Barron et al.* (1998)).

Taken together, the analysis from **three different perspectives** facilitates a comprehensive understanding of the economic consequences of introducing IFRS 8 and the management approach to segment reporting. Although the measures used to capture the effects for the three different capital market participants are neither mutually exclusive nor collectively exhaustive, they cover a great deal of what other studies usually analyze separately. Jointly analyzing the three different perspectives can yield complementary effects to better interpret the individual perspectives as well as to draw more comprehensive conclusions about the overall effect.

The two studies require different **research methods**. First, a content analysis of segment reports for a large sample of German listed firms prior and post IFRS 8 adoption is conducted. This allows to thoroughly and systematically investigate the **changes in segment reporting practices** induced by the adoption of IFRS 8. For instance, differences in key features of segment reports such as basis of segmentation, number of reported segments, measurement basis and type of segment information are analyzed descriptively. The key challenge in this study is to distinguish between differences in segment reporting practice caused by the standard change and differences due to changes in the business structures from the pre to the post IFRS 8 period of an entity resulting from acquisitions or divestures. To ensure that findings can be attributed to the change in reporting requirements, segment reports of the last year of IAS 14R (historical year) are compared to restated segment reports in the first year of IFRS 8 for the previous financial year (lag-adoption year) and thus reports for the same year and firm under different standards are compared.

Second, different measures of information asymmetry, cost of capital and analysts' forecasts prior and post IFRS 8 adoption are examined to analyze the **economic consequences** and whether the adoption of IFRS 8 increased the decision usefulness of segment information and thus improved the information environment of firms. According to prior research, many firms did not change their segment reporting practice since they already reported segment information consistent with IFRS 8 and the management approach under IAS 14R (e.g., *Crawford et al.* (2012); *Nichols et al.* (2012)). This study exploits this setting by sub-dividing the sample into "change-firms" (treatment group) and "no-change-firms" (control group). This approach allows a difference-in-differences design that inherently controls for confounding time effects and other events that might have changed from the pre-IFRS 8 period (2008) to the post-IFRS 8 period (2009). For instance, in case of an overall increase in capital market transparency due to changes in stock market regulations or changes in other accounting standards, information asymmetry, cost of capital and forecast properties would improve for all firms. If one would simply gauge changes in these measures from the IAS 14R to the IFRS 8 period, the effect would falsely be attributed to the standard change. However, if the change is different between the treatment and the control group, this difference is caused by the treatment effect, namely the adoption of IFRS 8 and the management approach. Thus, the research design employs the unique setting that some firms had already reported segmental information consistent with IFRS 8 and the management approach before the introduction whereas others had to change their reporting to comply with IFRS 8. Furthermore, to strengthen confidence that results are in fact driven by changes in segment reporting, cross-sectional variations in the changes sample are exploited. Specifically, change firms that show an increase in segment disclosures should experience a positive impact in contrast to those disclosing less than under IAS 14R.

To summarize, Figure 1-1 provides an overview of the main research fields and the respective research approaches.

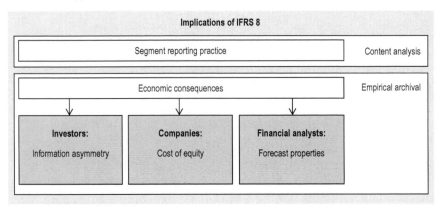

Figure 1-1: Research fields of the study

This study aims to analyze the impact of introducing IFRS 8 for segment reporting practice and the respective economic consequences for capital market participants. To achieve this goal, the **research objective** is divided into two sub-objectives:

- The first sub-objective is to facilitate a basic understanding how segment reporting practice changed upon the adoption of IFRS 8 by descriptively analyzing to what extent reporting practice differs from IAS 14R.

- The second sub-objective is to investigate capital market implications from three different perspectives:

  ➢ consequences for shareholders in terms of stock liquidity and information asymmetry;

  ➢ implications for reporting entities with respect to the cost of capital; and

  ➢ the impact on financial analyst's information environment.

Finally, **implications** for the IASB (and potentially the FASB and other standard setters), users of financial statements such as investors and financial analysts, preparers as well as auditors and enforcement institutions are derived based on the results.

This study largely **contributes to the literature** since it is the first to analyze the consequences of IFRS 8 in every of the three capital market perspectives. Additionally, it exploits the unique setting that a large fraction of German firms already reported segmental disclosures in line with IFRS 8 under IAS 14R. This allows for a difference-in-differences research design which strengthens the confidence in the causality of the findings. Furthermore, it adds to a growing stream of literature that analyzes the link between disclosure, investor information and the cost of capital, which is far from conclusive (*Leuz/Schrand* (2009)). Finally, this study provides descriptive evidence on the change in segment reporting practice that goes beyond prior literature.

The next section outlines the study and section 1.3 describes its scientific positioning.

1.2 Outline of the study

The study is subdivided into seven chapters. The **first chapter** motivates the topic and underlines its relevance. Moreover, it introduces the research question as well as the research objectives. Next, the scientific positioning is outlined to derive the research method based on a methodological grounding.

In the **second chapter**, the conceptual grounding of the study is developed. First, the role of segment reporting in financial accounting is described to facilitate an understanding of its purposes and users as well as benefits and costs. Different fundamental concepts of segment reporting are introduced to classify the management approach. Second, the historical development of segment reporting rules and the concurrent debate accompanying the introduction of IFRS 8 are discussed. Finally, the reporting requirements under IFRS 8 and IAS 14R with regard to the core principle, scope, segment definition, measurement and disclosures are presented.

The **third chapter** reviews the literature in the area of segment reporting. The review distinguishes between descriptive and economic consequences studies on the one hand and studies on SFAS No. 131 and IFRS 8 on the other hand. Based on the findings and limitations of prior research, the research gap is identified and the contribution is outlined.

The **fourth chapter** builds the theoretical foundation for the study. First, fundamental theories such as the principal agent theory and the efficient market hypothesis are briefly introduced since they provide the theoretical basis. Subsequently, a detailed theoretical framework for each of the three capital market perspectives is developed. Based on this framework, hypotheses are derived using the fundamental link between disclosures and information asymmetries, the cost of capital as well as financial analysts.

The **fifth chapter** empirically analyzes the change in segment reporting practice. After introducing the key features of a content analysis, the chapter presents the sample selection procedure as well as general descriptive statistics for the final sample. The main content analysis in this chapter is structured around five key pillars: general information, segmentation, measurement, disclosures and reconciliation. For each of the pillars, an in-depth analysis of segment disclosures under IAS 14R and under IFRS 8 is conducted. The chapter closes with a discussion of the findings.

The **sixth chapter** deals with the empirical analysis of the economic consequences for investors, firms and financial analysts. First, some preliminary considerations about causal inferences in accounting research are presented. Next, the research design and the variables used within the regressions are described in detail. Finally, the three main studies of this thesis are reported. Each sub-study starts with some preliminary descriptive statistics and univariate analyses. Subsequently, the main results of the difference-in-differences design and further robustness tests are presented. The chapter concludes with a discussion and synthesis of the different capital market perspectives.

The **last chapter** summarizes the main results and discusses limitations as well as implications for standard setters, users of financial statements such as investors and financial analyst, preparers, auditors and enforcement institutions. Finally, potential avenues for future research are presented.

Figure 1-2 depicts the outline of the study:

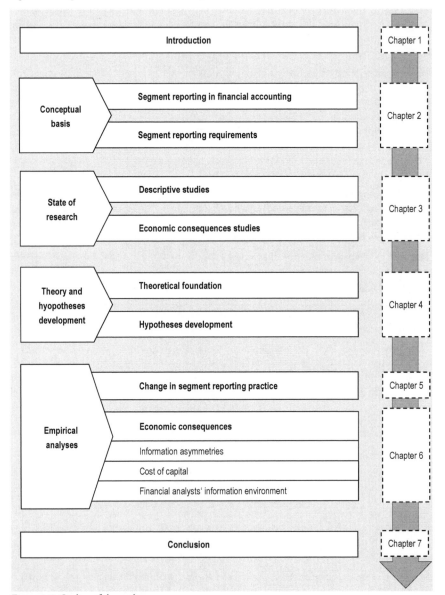

Figure 1-2: Outline of the study

1.3 Scientific positioning

Science is the process of a systematic gain in knowledge (*Kornmeier* (2007), p. 4). Knowledge requires justification or verification of specific notions or positions and thus differs from belief or intuition (*Kornmeier* (2007), p. 4). The objective of science is the advance and accumulation of knowledge (*Fülbier* (2004), p. 267). The **philosophy of science**, as a meta-science, develops approaches how to achieve this objective (*Kornmeier* (2007), p. 8).

There are different objectives of science. *Schweitzer* (1978), pp. 3–9, distinguishes between four **scientific objectives**. First, descriptive science documents and defines real phenomena in a systematic way. Second, the explanative objective goes beyond description and explains causal relationships. Third, for the pragmatic objective, these causal relations are used for predictions and decision-making. Finally, the normative objective aims for value judgments and derives recommendations and suggestions.

Concurrent business economics research is dominated by two scientific approaches: critical rationalism and constructivism (*Fülbier* (2004), p. 268). The **critical rationalism** goes back to *Popper* (1935). The basic idea behind this approach is the general fallibility of human knowledge. Knowledge is only temporary as it can be falsified any time (*Lingnau* (1995), p. 124). Hence, there is no ultimate verification of notions or positions. Popper does not consider this a problem as one learns from the falsification of a notion or position and thus approximates "true" knowledge (*Popper* (2005), pp. 16–19). The critical rationalism suggests the following approach to gain knowledge (*Fülbier* (2004), p. 268): Hypotheses are developed (solution) for an observable phenomenon with a need for explanation (problem). Subsequently, one empirically tests these hypotheses and eliminates them upon falsification. Hypotheses or theories are temporary valid until they are falsified (*Bartel* (1990)).

The **constructivism** follows a different approach. A gain in knowledge is achieved by argument. Based on a theoretical framework, one attempts to draw conclusions through deductive argumentation (*Fülbier* (2004), p. 269; *Kornmeier* (2007), p. 40). The constructivism, however, also recognizes the fallibility of human reasoning. Hence, knowledge is never considered as ultimately true (*Fülbier* (2004), p. 269).

Although the majority of recent business economics research uses the scientific approach suggested by the critical rationalism, one should not neglect the importance of the constructivism (*Fülbier* (2004), p. 269). Solely relying on the critical rationalism seems questionable in light of the limitations of empirical research (*Frank* (2003), p. 283). In general, both approaches can **complement** each other. For instance, regarding financial reporting research, the effect of particular accounting standards on capital market participants can be empirically analyzed in a positive vein. On the other hand, the development of accounting standards can benefit from the deduction of worthwhile rules based on the objectives of a specific set of accounting standards (such as the IFRS Conceptual Framework).

In relation to the choice of the scientific approach, the **research strategy** must be chosen. There are three dominant research strategies in business economics (*Grochla* (1978), p. 71):

- factual analytical;
- formal analytical; and
- empirical.

The **factual analytical** research strategy uses logical reasoning to analyze a problem and derives implications based on plausibility. Derived implications or statements are rather descriptive and their empirical validity is not considered within this research strategy (*Grochla* (1978), pp. 72–78).

The **formal analytical** research strategy analyzes a particular problem by abstract modeling (*Grochla* (1978), pp. 85–93). Based on the model, solutions for the problem are derived. The formal analytical research does not claim to entirely depict reality. It rather focuses on a specific problem, which distinguishes this strategy from the other two.

The **empirical** research strategy confronts theory with reality to support or reject it (*Grochla* (1978), pp. 78–85). This confrontation can either be a description of reality or empirical-cognitive explanations of causal relationships.

The **study at hand** follows the **critical rationalism** as the underlying scientific approach. It does not intend to deductively derive recommendations with regard to the introduction of IFRS 8. The study rather posits hypotheses about the effect of introducing the management approach to segment reporting and its economic consequences and empirically tests them. Hence, an **empirical research strategy** is used employing both a **description** of reality (segment reporting practice) and an empirical-cognitive **explanation** of causal relationships (impact of introducing the management approach to segment reporting on capital market participants). Based on the objectives of description and explanation, implications for standard setters, users of financial statements such as investors and financial analysts, preparers as well as auditors and enforcement institutions are derived. It is not intended, however, to give normative recommendations with regard to the research questions.

2   Conceptual basis

2.1   Segment reporting in financial accounting

This section presents the role of segment reporting in financial accounting by describing its purposes and users. Furthermore, the benefits and costs associated with segment reporting as well as its general concepts are described. Finally, this section details on the management approach in IFRS in general and its use for segment reporting in particular. This allows to get a general understanding of the role segment reporting in financial accounting which helps to better understand the potential consequences of the introduction of IFRS 8.

2.1.1   Objectives and users of segment reporting

Segment reporting is the disaggregation of financial information of an entity's business operations by business lines, geographical areas or major customers. In financial accounting, segment reporting is one instrument among others of general purpose financial reporting. Due to its disaggregated nature, however, it can be particularly useful for fundamental valuation analysis (*Alvarez* (2003), p. 7).

The **objectives** of segment reporting are derived from the objectives of general purpose financial reporting. Following the IFRS Conceptual Framework, the objective of IFRS

> "...is to provide financial information about the reporting entity that is useful to existing and potential investors, lenders and other creditors in making decisions about providing resources to the entity. Those decisions involve buying, selling or holding equity and debt instruments, and providing or settling loans and other forms of credit."

> (IFRS Conceptual Framework.OB2)

Hence, the primary **users** to whom financial reporting and thus segment reporting under IFRS is addressed are potential investors, lenders such as banks or other creditors. To make decisions about providing resources in form of equity or debt, these users need information about future net cash flows of an entity to gauge its repayment capabilities. The IASB believes that financial statements prepared to address the needs of potential investors, lenders and other creditors will meet the common needs of most other users (IFRS Conceptual Framework.A20). For instance, regulators and other members of the public may also use this information to determine taxation policies, to regulate the activities of entities or to prepare national income statistics. Moreover, suppliers or employees may use financial statements to evaluate the stewardship or accountability of management or to assess the ability of the entity to pay wages and to provide other benefits to its employees (IFRS Conceptual Framework.A20). Yet, those other parties are not primary users to whom financial reporting is predominantly directed (IFRS Conceptual Framework.OB10).

Segment information is particularly useful for (professional) investors, analysts and other financial intermediaries due to its significance for fundamental valuation analysis (*Alvarez* (2003), p. 7). The disaggregation of financial information by sub-units allows a differentiated analysis by business lines or geographical areas. Cash flow prospects of sub-units may differ due to **diverse economic environments** so that segment reporting can enhance the estimation of total future net cash flows.

Beyond that, the **particular accounting standards** provide further information about the objectives of segment reporting. For instance, IFRS 8.1 states that segment reporting shall:

> "...enable users of its financial statements to evaluate the nature and financial effects of the business activities in which it engages and the economic environments in which it operates."

Alternatively, the objective of **IAS 14R** is to help users of financial statements to better understand the entity's performance and assess its risks and returns (IAS 14R Objectives).[5]

Hence, the **main objective** of segment information is to provide users of financial statements with useful information to facilitate economic decisions. In that regard, the objective is in line with the aim of general purpose financial reporting. The disaggregated nature of segment information, however, makes it particularly useful for that purpose as it can help to better estimate future cash flows.

2.1.2 Benefits and costs of segment reporting

The benefits and costs of segment reporting can be analyzed from different perspectives. There is a wide range of stakeholders that are concerned with an entity's financial disclosures. However, based on the objective of segment reporting as described in the previous section, the following analysis only focuses on the entity's interests as the preparer of segment information and its users – in particular (potential) investors, lenders and financial intermediaries.[6]

Benefits

Under the assumption that segment disclosures fulfill their objective and yield informative disclosures that are decision useful, an entity will benefit from a lower cost of capital. The total cost of capital comprises three components: the risk-free rate of return, the economic risk premium and the information risk premium (*Elliott/Jacobson* (1994), pp. 81–82). Figure 2-1 illustrates the relationship of the three cost of capital components and the informativeness of disclosures at a given point-in-time. The risk free rate and the economic risk premium only vary over time and do not depend on the level of disclosure. When making investment decisions, investors attempt to assess the economic risk of the entity. With no or insufficient information about the underlying properties of the investment, investors will charge a high price for the risk (information risk premium).

---

[5] Section 2.3.2 provides a description of the objectives of the particular segment standards in detail.
[6] Regulators or national interests are not considered since they are not primary addressees of segmental disclosures (IFRS Conceptual Framework.OB10).

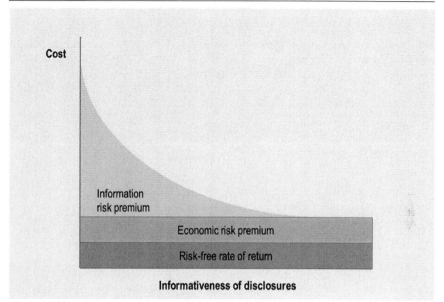

Figure 2-1: Cost of capital components and informativeness of disclosures
(Following *Elliot/Jacobson* (1994), p. 81)

Segment reports can **improve** the **informativeness** of financial disclosures. Aggregation leads c.p. to a loss of information. The Business lines or geographical areas of diversified companies are exposed to different environmental influences such as macro-economic situation, technology and innovation speed, market restrictions, exchange rates or political stability (*Alvarez* (2003), p. 21). Financial statements present information for a firm in a homogenized way and thus cannot sufficiently take account of the differences among the units. The aggregation for the financial statements may **average out** the risk and returns of different business units. For instance, future net cash flows are of primary interest for investors. General growth trends may differ between different business lines or areas. When estimating the future cash flows to assess the economic risk of the entity, investors can use information for the different lines of business and thus improve their estimations' precision. Hence, segmental disclosures can help users to better gauge the economic risk of an investment and thus help investors with their assessment. In **summary**, both reporting firms and users of financial statements can benefit from an improvement of disclosures through the availability of segment information. The former will experience lower cost of capital and the latter will be exposed to less uncertainty and information risk about the underlying economic properties of an entity.

Moreover, segment information increases **overall transparency** of an entity. This helps investors to better evaluate management performance (**stewardship**) (*OECD* (1990), *Anderson/Epstein* (1995)). The availability of segment information facilitates investors to judge managements' decisions on a finer level. Without segment information, investors would be unable to tell whether there is cross-subsidization from well to poorly performing segments. *Hope/Thomas* (2008) show that without segmental disclosures and thus sufficient scrutiny, managers tend to engage in empire-building activities that involve un-profitable growth strategies or expansions. Furthermore, business line managers are ex-posed to scrutiny and thus to more pressure from investors when financial data about the performance of their units is available (*Alvarez* (2003), p. 23). Hence, segment reporting induces incentives for the top-level management as well as second-tier managers to behave in the interest of shareholders.[7]

In **summary**, segment information increases transparency which reduces information risk and facilitates better monitoring. Both is desirable from an investor's perspective and should consequently lower the cost of capital.

Costs

Preparers and users of segment information also face **direct and indirect costs**. Direct costs comprise any costs that are immediately linked to the preparation and publication of segment reports. Indirect costs involve any adverse or negative reactions induced by the publication of segment information (*Alvarez* (2003), p. 24).

Direct costs

Firms bear the direct costs of developing and presenting financial disclosures. These costs comprise gathering and processing of information, in some cases auditing and finally dis-seminating (*Elliott/Jacobson* (1994), p. 83). If information is already prepared for man-agement purposes, the gathering costs can be omitted. Packaging, auditing and dissemi-nating, however, are still relevant.

In terms of segment reporting, these direct costs can be **substantial** (*Alvarez* (2003), p. 25). For instance, *Gray et al.* (1990) find in a survey analysis of 220 U.S. and 195 British CFOs of multinational listed firms that the gathering and preparation of segmental disclo-sures is among the most costly items of financial disclosures. However, there are cross-company differences in the direct costs of disclosures (*Benston* (1984), pp. 127–135). Re-garding segment reporting, determinants of the direct costs of disclosure encompass (*Hacker* (2002), p. 107):

- the degree of congruence between internal reporting structure and segmentation for financial reporting (*Radebaugh et al.* (2006), pp. 226–227);
- the development status of internal reporting systems and availability of segmental data; and
- size (*Salamon/Dhaliwal* (1980), pp. 560–561).[8]

There are also direct costs for **users** of segment reporting. They need to gather and process the information and spend time and resources on analyzing and interpreting it (*Pacter* (1993), p. 24). Poorly presented data or information overload may impose additional di-rect costs on the users (*Alvarez* (2003), p. 24).

---

[7] One could also consider the "compliance value" of segment reports, that is, the avoidance of negative reactions and penalties which an entity would face in the case of non-disclosure if segment reports are mandatory items of financial reporting.

[8] *Salamon/Dhaliwal* (1980) report that the average out-of-pocket costs of disclosure in relation to the size of an entity decreases for large firms.

Indirect costs

With the disclosure of segment information, **entities** can face adverse reactions by other parties which may create **competitive disadvantages**. In fact, *Gray et al.* (1990) show in their survey study that disclosure of information that *"weaken[s] a company's ability to generate future cash flows by aiding its competition"* (*Elliott/Jacobson* (1994), p. 84) is the most important cost factor related to financial disclosure for their sample of U.S. and UK multinational firms (*Gray et al.* (1990), p. 607). While the threat of a competitive disadvantage is a general effect of corporate disclosures, it is particularly prevalent with segment reports: (potential) competitors may get insight to the business activities that they can use to enhance their own operational and strategic decision making. For instance, they may increase or decrease the production output or potential competitors may consider engaging or expanding their business activities in a certain field if there are abnormally high profit margins (*Hacker* (2002), pp. 108–110).

Moreover, there may be adverse reactions upon the disclosure of segment information by other parties as well. **Suppliers** and **customers** of an entity can use segment information to gauge whether there is room to negotiate prices or other conditions and use this information to their advantage (*Miller/Scott* (1980), p. 10). **Employees** or **trade unions** may use segment information for wage bargaining (e.g., *Boersema/van Weelden* (1992), p. 36). In case of poorly performing segments, qualified employees may consider to change jobs at an early stage. Furthermore, **national authorities** may use segmental disclosures for competition policy purposes. For instance, high abnormal returns in certain fields may stir the attention of authorities and cause them to take actions such as implementing price mechanisms, imposing monopoly restrictions or other statutory requirements. Moreover, geographical segment disclosures may help foreign tax authorities to check the plausibility of actual taxes paid in that country (*Hacker* (2002), pp. 113–114). Finally, there are other groups such as **environmental organizations** which may take actions that negatively affect firms that are doing business in certain segments.

Hacker (2002) argues that entities can also face an increase in the **cost of capital** due to the disclosure of segment reports. The demanded return of an investor depends on the risk of an investment. If segment reports reveal previously unknown information that indicate a higher risk of the investment than initially expected, investors will update their beliefs and demand a higher return which in turn will increase the cost of capital:

> *"If managers manipulated, or simply did not publish adverse financial data to hide poor performance from investors, subsequent disclosure of such information due to the passage of some regulation might result in a lower market price for the related shares and a higher cost of equity capital."*

(*Dhaliwal* (1978), p. 76)

This line of arguments, however, is only valid if investors would not impose an information risk premium for the obscure or **vague set of information** in the initial state. Assuming rational investors, there will at least be an information risk premium to some extent. Whether this risk premium outweighs the increase in cost of capital induced by the disclosure of adverse financial data depends on the perceived uncertainty in the initial state and the extent of "hidden risk" which is subsequently disclosed and leads to an update in the beliefs of investors. In some constellations, it may be that disclosure of segment reports causes an increase in the cost of capital.

Individual **users** of segment reports can also face indirect costs due to reactions by management or other capital market participants. **Management** may feel to be under more scrutiny and thus engage in less risky projects. While this may be in line with the objectives of lenders and other creditors, it also limits the returns to be earned by equity investors. Moreover, **individual investors** with less ability to take advantage of segment information may suffer from losses compared to more trained and educated investors who are able to incorporate segment information in their decision making process to facilitate more informed decisions.

In **summary**, the disclosure of segment information entails certain benefits and costs for preparers and users of financial information. The magnitude and importance of these benefits and costs depend on the specific circumstances of the entity and the users. In a setting without mandatory segment reporting, entities will disclose segment information if the benefits outweigh the costs.[9]

2.1.3 Fundamental concepts and characteristics of segment reporting

While the previous sections discussed segment reporting in general, the following sections briefly introduce the two **fundamental concepts** of segment reporting. Subsequently, these concepts are further characterized in light of the three general areas of segment reporting, that is, **definition of segments, measurement** and **disclosures** (*Alvarez* (2003), p. 46; *Haller/Park* (1999), pp. 61–62).

2.1.3.1 Fundamental concepts

The two most fundamental and common concepts of segment reporting are the **management approach** and the **risk-and-reward approach** (*Alvarez* (2003), p. 45). These approaches are ideal-type concepts which do not always occur in their pure form in reality.[10] There are some other suggestions, in particular by the Special Committee on Financial Reporting of the American Institute of Certified Public Accountants (AICPA) from 1994 (The Jenkins Report), how segment information should be prepared. These suggestions, however, are closely related to the management approach and the risk-and-reward approach and can rather be considered as modifications of the former two. Moreover, this study analyzes the consequences of a change from the risk-and-reward approach to the

---

[9]   Also see *Watrin* (2001), pp. 68–79, for a general discussion why firms would voluntarily provide more information in the absence of a mandatory reporting regime.

[10] For instance, the German Accounting Standard No. 3 "Segment Reporting" (GAS 3) is a compromise between the management approach and the risk-and-reward approach (*Kajüter/Barth* (2007), p. 428). The definition of segments is primarily based on the management approach (GAS 3.10), but it also includes elements of the risk-and-reward approach (GAS 3.11). The measurement of segment items follows the risk-and-reward approach which is consistent with the measurement principles for the financial statements.

management approach. Hence, the following analysis solely focuses on these two concepts.

2.1.3.1.1 Management approach

The **concept** of the management approach originated in the 1990s with the Jenkins Report and the discussion of the US-GAAP standard SFAS No. 131 (*Merschdorf* (2012), pp. 21–23; *Kajüter* (2013), p. 8). Although the approach is primarily mentioned in association with segment reporting, it is a much broader concept for financial accounting in general, which is applied in several other IFRS standards as well.[11] However, note that the management approach is not a fundamental concept of the IFRS Conceptual Framework.[12]

The basic idea behind the management approach is that the management of an entity implements management and reporting systems that provide **custom-fit information** to make value maximizing decisions (*Fey/Mujkanovic* (1999), p. 63; *Maier* (2008), p. 12). As the enterprise value is also one of the key concerns of equity investors, it is assumed that the information used by management is also useful for equity investors (*Weißenberger/Maier* (2006), p. 2077). This basically facilitates users of financial statements to see the entity "*through the management's eyes*" (*Martin* (1997), p. 29). This is also in line with the suggestion of the Jenkins Report that "*high-level operating data and performance measurement that management uses to manage the business*" should be part of external financial reporting (*AICPA* (1994), p. 25).

The main objective of the management approach is to provide decision useful information from the management's perspective. However, introducing the management approach to IFRS is also a step towards the **convergence and harmonization** of management and financial accounting. For a long time, the literature discussed harmonization from the perspective of financial accounting. This means that financial reporting instruments or measurements are used for management accounting purposes (*Küting/Lorson* (1998), p. 483;

---

[11] For instance, the costs of goods sold in IAS 2 ("Inventories") are determined based on the management approach. Moreover, the accounting for construction contracts in IAS 11 ("Construction Contracts") under the percentage-of-completion method requires the estimation of the stage of completion, which is based on internal analyses. IAS 12 ("Income Taxes") compels the estimation of future profits to assess the recoverability of deferred tax assets. The impairment test in IAS 36 ("Impairment of Assets") requires data from internal analyses for determining the object of impairment as well as its valuation (*Wulf et al.* (2011), pp. 96–103; *Reinke* (2009)). Moreover, applications of the management approach can also be found in IAS 16 ("Property, Plant & Equipment"), IAS 24 ("Related Party Disclosures"), IAS 38 ("Intangible Assets"), IAS 39 ("Financial Instruments"), IAS 40 ("Investment Properties"), IFRS 3 ("Business Combinations"), IFRS 5 ("Discontinued Operations"), IFRS 13 ("Fair Value Measurement") and particularly in the IFRS Practice Statement Management Commentary. For a detailed discussion refer to *Weißenberger/Maier* (2006), pp. 2077–2079; *Maier* (2008), pp. 15–98; *Merschdorf* (2012), pp. 40–90; and *Kajüter* (2013), pp. 13–23.

[12] The old IFRS Conceptual Framework before the revision in 2010 included the reference that "*published financial statements are based on the information used by management*" (F.11). This reference was eliminated upon revision of the framework (phase A). *Kajüter* (2013), however, uses the term "*implicit principle*" since the management approach became increasingly important for the development of new standards and the revision of old standards in recent years (*Kajüter* (2013), pp. 7–8).

Melcher (2002), p. 81). The management approach, however, induces harmonization from the internal management accounting perspective. Management accounting data or measurements are either directly used for recognition, measurement or disclosure or indirectly used as a basis to derive information for financial reporting (*Blase* (2011), p. 10; *Kajüter* (2013), p. 11). A direct transfer of management accounting data entails that internal information and numbers are used for financial reporting without any adjustments as it is the case for segment reporting under IFRS 8 (*Kajüter* (2013), p. 11). An indirect transfer means that management accounting data is used as a basis which is adjusted and reconciled.[13] The only premise is that data is primarily obtained for management purposes and subsequently re-used for financial reporting (*Weißenberger/Maier* (2006), p. 2077; *Maier* (2008), p. 7; *Kajüter* (2013), p. 10).

In the context of **segment reporting**, the management approach requires segments to be constructed the same way as they are structured internally by the management for resource allocation and performance evaluation purposes. It is based on the notion that management should possess the best information which segmentation is the most adequate (*Albrecht/Chipalkatii* (1998), p. 49).

2.1.3.1.2 Risk-and-reward approach

The risk-and-reward approach is based on the similarity of the **risk-and-reward structure** of segments. First, an entity's business activities are analyzed with regard to returns and their riskiness (*Böcking/Benecke* (1998), p. 97). Subsequently, business activities that show similar risks and returns are aggregated to segments. Hence, a segment's activities should be homogeneous while different segments of an entity should be heterogenous in terms of returns and risks (*Haller/Park* (1994), pp. 510–511).

This approach sheds light on the **potential opportunities and risks** of each segment, which facilitates easier forecasting of future returns and cash flows (*Alvarez* (2003), p. 45). Investors can, for instance, apply different discount rates according to the riskiness of segments when valuing an entity based on discounted cash flow methods. Moreover, structuring according to similar returns may enhance the forecastability of returns and cash flows (*Fey/Mujkanovic* (1999), p. 261). Additionally, the risk-and-reward approach should facilitate comparability between different companies as segments are constructed according to the same criteria (*Wagenhofer* (2005), p. 471).

There is some **discretion** involved in determining similar risks and returns when aggregating business activities to segments (*Emmanuel/Garrod* (1992), p. 34). This is particularly the case if the internal organisation is not based on risks and returns and segments are solely constructed for reporting purposes. It is difficult for users of financial statements or even an auditor to judge the neutrality or arbitrariness of the segmentation in these cases (*Alvarez* (2003), p. 49). Moreover, risks and returns of certain activities may **change over**

---

[13] This is, for instance, the case for impairment testing under IAS 36 when financial budgets used to determine future cash flows include future restructurings (to which an entity is not yet committed (IAS 36.44)). Restructuring expenses must be excluded when determining the value in use for financial reporting purposes (see *Kajüter* (2013), p. 11, for a more detailed discussion and a further example).

time. This requires constant adaption of the segmentation, which can be costly for entities (*Fröhling* (2000), p. 13).

With regard to the measurement of segment information, the risk-and-reward approach is considered as a "*financial accounting approach*" (*Ulbrich* (2006), pp. 21–22). This means that all financial information disclosed in the segment report is based on the **same measurement principles** as used in the financial statements, which should also promote intercompany comparability and understandability of segment disclosures (*Naumann* (1999), p. 2290).

In the following, the definition of segments, measurement and disclosures are discussed for the management approach and the risk-and-reward approach.

2.1.3.2 Definition of segments

The definition of segments under both approaches can follow **different segmentation criteria**. Most companies structure and organize their activities along business lines or geographical areas. In rare cases, companies may use major customers, legal units or regulated/non-regulated markets as segmentation criteria. The vast majority of companies, however, use either business lines or geographical areas (see section 3.1.2).

Segmentation according to **business lines** shows the different markets and industry sectors of a company's business activities. According to the Jenkins Report, "*industry segment information most frequently provides the greatest insight into the opportunities and risks a company faces.*" (*AICPA* (1994), p. 20). Business line segmentation can vary in depth (*Bernards* (1994), pp. 95–97):

- product or service level;
- group of products or services; or
- sectors or industrial branches.

Segmentation on the **product or service level** may not be suitable for large companies with a lot of different products. For instance, users of financial statements would be unable to cope with the information overload if a company such as Henkel or Volkswagen disclosed segment information on the product level. Moreover, such a detailed disclosure might yield competitive disadvantages for firms since competitors gain insights about the profitability of single products which may be exploited by aggressive pricing.

To address this, some entities aggregate similar products or services to **groups**. Entities face the trade-off between the loss of information due to aggregation and information overload. Defining meaningful groups and allocating products to these groups can be challenging for some entities (*Haase* (1974), pp. 74–75).

Segmentation according to **sectors or industrial branches** is the broadest definition category. Allocating particular products or group of products to industry sectors is rather easy in most of the cases (*Haase* (1974), p. 76). Moreover, there are official industry classifications available such as the Global Industry Classification Code (GICS), Standard Industrial Classification Code (SIC) or classifications of stock exchanges which are easily applied. These classifications, however, may be too broad for some entities.

There is **no rule** which depth in the classification of business line segmentation is preferable. The decision depends on the particular case and the business model of the entity, the information needs of investors as well as the direct and indirect costs of segmentation (*Köhle* (2006), p. 96).

The segmentation according to **geographical areas** is also often applied by companies. Yet, the Jenkins Report notes that "*Segmentation based on geographic location also provides insight, although it often is of less interest to users than is industry segment information.*" (*AICPA* (1994), p. 20). Empirical evidence also shows that geographical segmentation is used less by preparers.[14] The literature, however, argues that business line segmentation does not dominate geographical segmentation in terms of decision usefulness, particularly when taking the increasing internationalization of businesses into account (*Nichols et al.* (2000), p. 60; *Peskes* (2004), p. 213).

The geographical segmentation can also vary in depth. Some entities just distinguish between domestic and foreign activities. Others report areas on a continental basis, groups of countries or based on single countries (*Peskes* (2004), p. 214). The trade-off between decision usefulness and information overload is similar to the discussion above about the depth of business line segmentation. When using geographical segmentation, entities have to further decide how to **classify geographical regions** (*Blase* (2011), p. 57):

- based on the location of production facilities; or
- on the location of the sales market.

A geographical classification according to the location of **production facilities** can be preferable if the production part of an entity's business model and in particular its costs are the critical factor of success (*Bernards* (1994), pp. 107–108; *Haller* (2000), p. 770; *Blase* (2011), p. 58). For these companies, setting up production sites often entails substantial investments. Examples are natural resource extraction companies such as oil drilling or mining. Allocating assets, liabilities, and expenses to the different segments is rather easy in this classification (*Baumann* (1987), p. 14).

In contrast, if the distribution part of an entity's business model predominantly determines the success, a classification according to **sales markets** can be desirable (*Bernards* (1994), p. 102; *Haller* (2000), p. 770). These companies rather depend on the demand of customers. Examples are retail or wholesale companies. The allocation of revenues to the different segments is simple. However, assets and liabilities as well as expenses are usually allocated pro rata (*Baumann* (1987), p. 14).

The definition of segments under the **management approach** compels that the internal segmentation is used for external reporting as well. Management usually receives disaggregated financial information about separate business units for planning and monitoring purposes. The separation of business activities used in these internal reports has to be

---

[14] See section 3.1 for findings of other studies and section 5.2.2 for the findings in this study.

adopted for external segment reports (*Böcking/Benecke* (1998), p. 97; *Haller* (2000), p. 768).

Under the premise that management is superiorly informed about which segmentation suits best, this insight in the internal organization and management structure allows users of financial statements to better assess an entity's **future development** and to judge the quality of organization and management systems (*Haller/Park* (1999), pp. 62–63).

Critics, however, argue that the reliance on internal segmentation does not necessarily yield the best information as the internal segmentation may be influenced by a certain historical development of the entity or particular management structures, which may not cater to investors' information needs in an optimal way (*Boersema/van Weelden* (1992), p. 137).

As elaborated above, the optimal definition of segments in terms of segmentation as well as depth of segmentation depends on the individual characteristics and situation of an entity. Under the **management approach**, the definition that management perceives to be optimal and thus deliberately chooses for their internal organization is made available to users of financial statements. Under the **risk-and-reward approach**, management is obliged to define segments according to risks and returns, even if this contrasts the optimal internal segmentation.

2.1.3.3 Measurement

Measurement deals with the basis of measurement for segment line items. This is very different under the management approach and the risk-and-reward approach:

To fulfill the requirements of the "*full management approach*" (*Baetge/Haenelt* (2008), p. 45; *Fink/Ulbrich* (2006), p. 243), the measurement of segment information shall also be the same as the internal amounts prepared for planning and monitoring purposes. Measurements for management accounting often comprise imputed costs such as depreciation based on replacement cost or imputed interest on equity capital, or they exclude neutral expenses such as transitory or extraordinary items (*Schildbach* (1997), p. 263). These **internal measurements** have to be reported externally, even if they are not in line with the measurement principles for the financial statements (*Müller/Peskes* (2006), p. 822; *Haller/Park* (1999), p. 62). This implies that entities may, for instance, disclose earnings that differ from those in the financial statements.

Again, the literature presumes that information prepared for resource allocation and performance evaluation purposes is also useful for users of financial statements. The decision usefulness of measurements under the management approach, however, may be **impaired** due to the manipulation and the circularity effect (*Blase* (2011), p. 75).

Management may receive biased or erroneous information from lower management levels as these lower-tier managers may have incentives to manipulate information to achieve their own goals such as the maximization of compensation (**manipulation effect**) (*Weißenberger/Maier* (2006), p. 2083; *Weißenberger/Franzen* (2011), p. 332). Under the management approach, this information is subsequently used for external reporting.

Moreover, top management itself may manipulate internal reporting systems to avoid the disclosure of certain items or to achieve the presentation of particular items to the outside (**circularity effect**) (*Himmel* (2004), p. 138; *Weißenberger/Franzen* (2011), p. 332). This, however, comes at the cost of less than optimal internal reporting systems (*Blase* (2011), p. 32).

Measurement under the **risk-and-reward approach** follows the "*financial accounting approach*" (*Ulbrich* (2006), pp. 21–22) and therefore measurement is consistent with the measurement principles for the financial statements. Hence, the risk-and-reward approach is by definition less prone to the manipulation and circularity effect.

Another aspect that needs to be taken into consideration regardless whether an entity prepares segment information under the management approach or risk-and-reward approach is the **underlying assumption** how segments are related to each other. The literature distinguishes between the following two concepts for the measurement of segment information (*Alvarez* (2003), p. 54):

- the autonomous entity approach; and
- the disaggregation approach.

The **autonomous entity approach** considers segments as stand-alone and independent units (*Himmel* (2004), p. 145). This means that all interdependencies between segments such as synergies are eliminated for measurement purposes (*Husmann* (1997), pp. 353–354; *Küting/Pilhofer* (1999), p. 603; *Alvarez* (2003), p. 54). For instance, cost savings due to a bundled supply system for several segments may not be considered when determining the profit of single segments (*Haller/Park* (1994), pp. 511–512; *Haller* (2000), p. 767). Moreover, intersegment-transactions have to be measured based on the arm's length principle. The more the segments are integrated, the higher is the discrepancy between segment and total earnings under the autonomous entity approach (*Alvarez* (2003), p. 55).

This approach allows a better **comparison** of segments with other non-diversified companies in the same industry (*Husmann* (1997), p. 353; *Küting/Pilhofer* (1999), p. 603). Additionally, measuring transactions based on the arm's length principle allows a better judgment of the "true" segment performance (*Blase* (2011), p. 77). In contrast, assuming independent business units requires estimations how the segment would perform on a stand-alone basis. This may impair the reliability and understandability of segment information (*Haller* (2000), p. 768).

The **disaggregation approach** considers segments as parts of the entity as a whole (*Fröhling* (2000), p. 14). Segment amounts are measured by disaggregating and allocating total GAAP amounts to segments (*Haller/Park* (1994), p. 511; *Husmann* (1997), p. 353). In contrast to the autonomous entity approach, interdependencies and synergies between segments are considered. The key challenge is to find an appropriate way of disaggregating the entity (*Pejic* (1998), pp. 116–117).

The **measurement** of segment amounts under the disaggregation approach is generally in line with the measurement principles for financial statements as there is no need for estimating the "as-if stand-alone" performance of segments. GAAP amounts are simply broken down to segmental level, which should yield an easy understandability (*Haller/Park*

(1994), pp. 511–513). Moreover, (potential) investors are rather interested in the entity as a whole than in simulated stand-alone segments (*Blase* (2011), p. 79). In contrast, the inter-company comparability is lower than under the autonomous entity approach.

It depends on the specific situation of an entity whether the autonomous entity or the disaggregation approach is **preferable**. In general, measurement based on the disaggregation approach yields a higher understandability as the reported amounts are in line with the measurement principles of financial statements and no estimates are necessary (*Haller/Park* (1994), p. 512). However, if segments are highly independent from each other and from the parent company, the autonomous entity approach will provide a more consistent picture of the performance on segment level (*Alvarez* (2003), p. 58). Moreover, the less interdependencies between segments exist, the less differences will be between the measurements under both approaches.

The autonomous entity and the disaggregation approach are both applicable under the management approach. However, due to the nature of the autonomous entity approach that requires "as-if" estimations, only the disaggregation approach can be used under the risk-and-reward approach (*Alvarez* (2003), p. 58). Hence, there is more **flexibility** for the measurement of segment information under the management approach compared to the risk-and-reward approach.

2.1.3.4 Disclosures

Once segments are defined and a basis for measurement is chosen, companies have to determine which items to disclose. **Segment items** can comprise financial and non-financial information. The focus of most segment reports, however, is on the disclosure of financial items.[15]

A firm can potentially choose between **full disclosure**, which means a segmentation of every item in the financial statements, and **non-disclosure** (*Blase* (2011), p. 67). Both ends of the continuum are rather theoretical and of less practical relevance (*Alvarez* (2003), p. 65). Full disclosure may be very costly and may produce too much information (*Haller* (2000), p. 776; *Alvarez* (2003), p. 65). Non-disclosure, however, will not fulfill any information needs of users of financial statements and may even violate legal requirements.

It is difficult to determine an optimal degree of disclosures. Companies face a **trade-off** between catering to information needs of users of financial statements and the direct as well as indirect costs of disclosures (*Blase* (2011), p. 65). Under the **management approach**, this trade-off is somewhat addressed by the requirement that only information which is primarily generated and used for internal purposes needs to be disclosed.[16] This means that c.p. direct costs can be ignored. Under the **risk-and-reward approach**, there is usually a pre-defined list of items that constitute minimum disclosures regardless of the

---

[15] See section 5.2.4 for an overview of line items disclosed by the firms in this study's sample.
[16] See section 2.2.5.1 for a detailed description of the reporting requirements under IFRS 8.

costs of an entity.[17] In the practical application of the management approach under IFRS 8 and SFAS No. 131, the standard setters also set a minimum requirement that segment profits need to be disclosed even if not reported to the Chief Operating Decision Maker (CODM), to ensure a minimum degree of disclosures.

Under both approaches, the management approach and the risk-and-reward approach, entities may **voluntarily** disclose additional items that are either not reported to the CODM (management approach) or exceed the minimum requirements (risk-and-reward approach). In general, the disclosures under the management approach are more flexible and consider the particular circumstances of an entity in a better way as they directly address the direct costs of disclosures.

Overall, disclosing the same items that are used by management for decision making purposes (management approach) should be more relevant than the disclosures of predetermined items deemed relevant by the standard setter (risk-and-reward approach). The possibility to voluntarily disclose more items, however, will lead to the general trade-off between the benefits and costs of disclosures (as elaborated in section 2.1.2) under both approaches.

2.2 Segment reporting requirements

The following sections describe the segment reporting requirements of IFRS 8 and IAS 14R. Based on a brief description of the historical development, section 2.2 is structured around the core principle and scope, definition of segments as well as measurement and disclosure requirements for both standards.

2.2.1 Historical development

The **first segment reporting accounting standard** in financial reporting was released in the U.S. by the FASB in 1976. SFAS No. 14 "Financial Reporting for Segments of a Business Enterprise" mandated the disclosure of segment revenues, earnings, assets, depreciation and capital expenditures for business lines and geographical segments as well as major customers. Before that, however, the SEC already required filing entities to disclose revenues and earnings by business line segments in their 10Ks since August, 1969.

Under IFRS, the first segment standard IAS 14 "Reporting Financial Information by Segment" was issued in August 1981 and became effective for financial years beginning January 1, 1983. IAS 14 was similar to SFAS No. 14 and stipulated the disclosure of segment revenues (external and internal), result and assets by business lines and geographical areas. In the 1990s, IAS 14 was criticized for vague guidance on the definition of segments and measurement of line items and the emerging alternative practices that impaired the understandability and comparability of segment reports (*Street/Nichols* (2002), p. 92). Hence, the IASC decided to revise the standard to address these issues. At the same time, the FASB and the Canadian Accounting Standards Board jointly revised their segment reporting rules. Despite considerable efforts to converge segment reporting rules, the

---

[17] Under the risk-and-reward approach in IAS 14R, for instance, there is a list of eight items that every firm has to report (see section 2.2.5.2).

North American standard setters and the IASC eventually went different paths and issued utterly different standards in 1997 – SFAS No. 131 and IAS 14R.[18]

In October 2002, the IASB and FASB reached a general agreement ("Norwalk Agreement") to eliminate differences between IFRS and US-GAAP and thus to converge international accounting rules. As part of this **convergence project**, the IASB and FASB identified segment reporting as an area where differences between the two accounting standard sets could be reduced in a short period of time (ED IFRS 8.BC2). Based on a review of academic research on the implementation of SFAS No. 131 and meetings with users of financial statements, the IASB decided that adopting the management approach is preferable to the risk-and-reward approach under IAS 14R.

Hence, in January 2006 the **exposure draft** of IFRS 8 was published and open for comments until May 2006. In total, 182 comment letters were received which showed different views about potential benefits and disadvantages of introducing the management approach.[19] IFRS 8 received support by the majority of respondents to the exposure draft. Some remarked that it would allow users to assess an entity's operations from a management's perspective (IFRS 8.BC10). Moreover, although segment reports under IAS 14R would be more comparable among different entities, the disclosures might not be used for decision making and thus be less relevant. Hence, the majority considered IFRS 8 superior to IAS 14R (IFRS 8.BC10).

Other respondents to the exposure draft argued, however, that a **convergence** of US-GAAP to IAS 14R would be preferable as IAS 14R facilitates comparability due to the definition of key segment line items. Some supported the management approach for the identification of segments, but disagreed with the measurement of segmental disclosures. These respondents questioned whether internally reported measures and amounts would be of much use for investors if they are different from IFRS amounts (IFRS 8.BC12). The IASB (2013a, p. 10) summarized the views of the comment letters about expected benefits and disadvantages as follows:

---

[18] Since IAS 14 was substantially revised and relabeled in 1997, the post 1997 version is referred to as IAS 14R.

[19] 182 comment letters is a relatively high number of respondents. For instance, amendments to IAS 23 ("Borrowing Costs") received 90 letters in 2007, amendments to IFRS 3 ("Business Combinations") received 72 letters in 2008 and ED IFRS 10 ("Joint Arrangements") received 110 letters in 2008 (also see *Crawford et al.* (2013)).

Benefits	Disadvantages
• Achieves convergence with US-GAAP. • "Management eyes" perspective would improve users' ability to predict future results and cash flows. • Highlights risks that management considers to be important. • Use of management reporting would result in increased interim reporting, because the information would be readily available.	• Inconsistent segments may be reported between entities, because the internal organization of each entity might differ. • Frequent internal reorganizations would result in a loss of trend data. • Geographical analyses would not be available because IFRS 8 does not require that a separate geographical analysis is presented. • IFRS 8 requires that the segment information disclosed is measured on the basis used for management reporting. Non-IFRS measures used by management may not be understood.

Figure 2-2: Expected benefits and disadvantages based on the comment letters
(*IASB* (2013), p. 10)

With the issuance of the new standard, the IASB hoped to achieve that (IFRS 8.BC9):

a. entities will report segments that correspond to internal management reports;
b. entities will report segment information that will be more consistent with other parts of their annual reports;
c. some entities will report more segments; and
d. entities will report more segment information in interim financial reports.

Additionally, the IASB expected that IFRS 8 would reduce the **direct costs** of preparing segment information as it is already available.

However, the board members (at that time) Gilbert Gélard and James J. Leisenring expressed opinions dissenting from the issuance of IFRS 8: They **criticized** that IFRS 8 does not mandate a defined measure of profit or loss. Moreover, they disapproved that the reported measure of profit or loss need not be consistent with the allocation of assets to the reported segments (IFRS 8.DO1). Due to the missing definition of the profit or loss measure, they believed that IFRS 8 would fail to meet its objective. Additionally, in their view *"proper external reporting of segment information should not permit the use of non-GAAP measures because they might mislead users"* (IFRS 8.DO4).

Nonetheless, the final standard was issued on November 30, 2006. In April 2009, the IASB further released Annual Improvements to IFRSs 2009, which required minor **amendments** to the standard to clarify that segment assets only have to be disclosed if they are reported internally to the CODM. These changes were effective for financial years commencing on or after January 1, 2010. Board member Stephen Cooper dissented from the amendments. He argued that allowing an entity not to disclose segment assets, just because they are not reported internally, may prevent the disclosure of important information which might help to understand the financial position of an entity. However, the amendment was a necessary step to actually achieve convergence with US-GAAP as segment reporting practice in the U.S. did not consider the disclosure of assets as mandatory. Although SFAS No. 131.27 explicitly mandates the disclosure of assets (independent on whether they are reported to the CODM), SFAS No.131.28 and SFAS No.131.29 can be interpreted so that the disclosure of segment assets is CODM-conditional (*Haller/Park* (1999)).

Finally, after implementing IFRS 8, a **PIR** was conducted during 2012-2013. The PIR is a new instrument of the IASB for the maintenance of IFRS that was used for the first time on IFRS 8. The goal is to review new standards or major changes two years after the initial application. Figure 2-3 shows the timeline of the steps undertaken during the PIR of IFRS 8 (*IASB* (2013), p. 4):

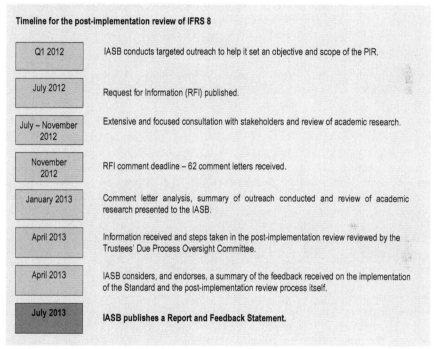

Timeline for the post-implementation review of IFRS 8

Q1 2012	IASB conducts targeted outreach to help it set an objective and scope of the PIR.
July 2012	Request for Information (RFI) published.
July – November 2012	Extensive and focused consultation with stakeholders and review of academic research.
November 2012	RFI comment deadline – 62 comment letters received.
January 2013	Comment letter analysis, summary of outreach conducted and review of academic research presented to the IASB.
April 2013	Information received and steps taken in the post-implementation review reviewed by the Trustees' Due Process Oversight Committee.
April 2013	IASB considers, and endorses, a summary of the feedback received on the implementation of the Standard and the post-implementation review process itself.
July 2013	**IASB publishes a Report and Feedback Statement.**

Figure 2-3: Timeline for the post-implementation review of IFRS 8
(*IASB* (2013), p. 4)

The PIR began with an initial assessment of potential issues in early 2012. In July 2012, the main **information-gathering** phase started which comprised three major sources:

- public consultation through a Request for Information (RFI);
- outreach activities; and
- review of academic literature.

The **RFI** included five open questions and was due by November 16, 2012.[20] 62 comment letters from all over the world were received.[21] The largest group of respondents were preparers and industry organizations followed by standard setters and accounting firms as well as investors. Moreover, during 2012, 36 **outreach** events were held in the form of discussion forums, conferences, webcasts and individual meetings with a particular focus on investors and financial analysts[22]:

> "*Investors and financial analysts are primary users of segment information and were therefore important sources of input to the post-implementation review process. [...] Because of the importance of investors and financial analysts [...] we developed more focused alternatives for engaging with them.*"

> (*IASB* (2013), p. 14)

Finally, the IASB conducted a **review of academic literature** including 30 studies on the effect of IFRS 8. Only five studies, however, were published papers at that time and the rest comprised working papers at different stages. Based on this experience, the IASB concluded for future PIRs that they plan to signal topics for research earlier "*to encourage academics to contribute to [...] standard setting*" (IASB (2013), p. 15).

As a result of the PIR, the **IASB concluded** that their expectations with issuing IFRS 8 were largely confirmed: The management approach makes management's communication with investors easier and implementation costs of IFRS 8 were low. Moreover, convergence with US-GAAP was achieved. Auditors, accounting firms, standard setters and regulators are at large content with IFRS 8. However, they also see some room for improvements in the application of the standard. Investors, however, have a mixed perception. On the one hand, some investors appreciate when different parts of an entity's financial disclosures such as financial statements, management commentary and analyst presentations align. Moreover, there is a spill-over effect to the credibility of other sources of consistent segment information since IFRS 8 information is audited. On the other hand, investors fear that managers may use the flexibility of the management approach to conceal the entity's "true structure" or to hide unprofitable business areas (*IASB* (2013), p. 5). In **summary**, IFRS 8 mostly achieved its objectives, but the PIR also highlighted the need for further clarification or guidance in some areas. These more detailed aspects are discussed in light of the empirical findings of this study.

The next sections elaborate on the specific reporting requirements of IFRS 8 and IAS 14R.

---

[20] The questions in the RFI were rather vague and left room for a broad discussion of major issues. For instance, Question 2 asked "*What is your experience of the effect of the IASB's decision to identify and report segments using the management perspective?*" (IASB 2012, p. 13).

[21] The majority of responses came from Europe (53 per cent). Other geographical regions were Asia-Oceania (18 per cent), Latin America (8 per cent), North America (7 per cent), Africa (3 per cent) and Other (11 per cent).

[22] Among the investors and financial analysts were representative groups such as the European Federation of Financial Analysts Societies (EFFAS), the Japanese Investors Forum, the Capital Markets Advisory Committee (CMAC), the CFA Society of the UK and the Users Advisory Council of Canada.

2.2.2 Core principle and scope

2.2.2.1 IFRS 8

The **core principle** of IFRS 8.1 stipulates that the disclosures of an entity shall "*enable users of its financial statements to evaluate the nature and financial effects of the business activities in which it engages and the economic environments in which it operates.*" The IASB does not particularize this further. However, the core principle is consistent with the general objectives of the IASB's Conceptual Framework for Financial Reporting which requires financial information to help existing and potential investors, lenders and other creditors to assess future net cash flows of an entity (IFRS Conceptual Framework.OB3).

Application of IFRS 8 is compulsory for individual and consolidated financial statements of an entity or a group whose debt or equity instruments are publicly traded or in the process of being filed with a security or any other regulatory commission. According to IFRS 8.2 (a) (i) and IFRS 8.2 (b) (i), a public market is specified as a domestic or foreign stock exchange or an over-the-counter market, including local and regional markets. If an entity falls out of the scope of this standard and chooses to disclose segment information that is not in conformity with IFRS 8, it may not label the information as segment information (IFRS 8.3). Additionally, in case the financial report of an entity comprises both the consolidated and the separate financial statements of the parent, segmental disclosures are only required for the consolidated financial statements (IFRS 8.4).

During the due process of IFRS 8, the IASB deliberated to **expand the scope** of the standard to all entities that have public accountability. The board decided that the adoption of a term that was by that time part of the on-going project on small and medium-sized entities (SMEs) was too early (IFRS 8.BC18). They agreed that this should be decided within the context of IFRS for SMEs. When the IFRS for SMEs was issued in 2009, the term public accountability included all firms with publicly listed equity or debt instruments and firms that hold assets in a fiduciary capacity for a broad group of outsiders as one of their primary businesses such as banks, insurance companies or funds (IFRS for SMEs 1.3).[23] The scope of IFRS 8, however, was not expanded to firms holding assets in a fiduciary capacity. Moreover, segment reporting was also not required for firms that do not have public accountability (i.e., SMEs) in the IFRS for SMEs (IFRS for SMEs 3.25).

2.2.2.2 IAS 14R

The **objective** of IAS 14R is to help users of financial statements (IAS 14R.Objective) to:

a. better understand the entity's past performance;
b. better assess the entity's risks and returns; and
c. make more informed judgments about the entity as a whole.

---

[23] IFRS for SMEs are geared towards firms that do not have public accountability (IFRS for SMEs 1.2 (b)).

Segment disclosures under IAS 14R provide information about a firm's different types of products or services and geographical operations which is helpful in evaluating the risk-and-return structures of diversified firms (IAS 14R.Objective).

Similar to IFRS 8, IAS 14R has to be **applied** by entities that prepare complete sets of financial statements under IFRS (IAS 14R.1) and *"whose equity or debt securities are publicly traded and [...] entities that are in the process of issuing equity or debt securities in public securities markets."* (IAS 14R.3). Entities that fall out of this scope are encouraged to voluntarily provide segment information (IAS 14R.4). However, if entities choose to do so, they have to fully comply with all requirements of IAS 14R (IAS 14R.5). In case a firm reports consolidated as well as separate financial statements of the parent in its financial report, segment information has only to be provided in the consolidated financial statements (IAS 14R.6).

In **summary**, IFRS 8 and IAS 14R have a similar scope and their core principles are also substantially comparable. Both standards aim to provide users of financial statements with information that helps them to better judge and evaluate the entity as a whole. Hence, the scope and core principle of segment reporting did not change much upon adoption of IFRS 8.

2.2.3 Definition of segments

2.2.3.1 IFRS 8

The definition of segments under IFRS 8 is a two-step process. First, **operating segments** are identified when they meet the definition criteria of IFRS 8.5-10. Second, identified operating segments are classified as **reportable** if they meet the quantitative thresholds as set out by IFRS 8.13.

Pursuant to IFRS 8.5, an operating segment is defined as a component of an entity:

a. that engages in business activities from which it may earn revenues and incur expenses (including revenues and expenses relating to transactions with other components of the same entity);

b. whose operating results are regularly reviewed by the entity's chief operating decision maker to make decisions about resources to be allocated to the segment and assess its performance; and

c. for which discrete financial information is available.

These criteria have to be met **cumulatively**. It is not necessary that an operating segment earns revenues. For instance, start-up operations may be classified as an operating segment before generating sales. In addition, it is not required that the majority of revenues of an operating segment stems from external sales. However, it is explicitly stated that neither corporate headquarters nor an entity's post-employment benefit plan are operating segments, since they do not earn revenues at all or earn revenues that are solely supplementary to an entity's business (IFRS 8.6).

The view of the **CODM** plays an essential role within the segment identification process. According to IFRS 8.7, the term "chief operating decision maker" refers to a function, not to a specific manager with a particular title. The function "*is to allocate resources and assess the performance of the operating segments of an entity*" (IFRS 8.7). IFRS 8.7 further suggests that the chief executive officer or the chief operating officer are often the CODM of an entity. Yet, the term CODM is relatively vague. This is not surprising given that IFRS are applied worldwide in numerous countries which show different corporate governance structures (*Böckem/Pritzer* (2010), p. 615). The IASB had to implement rules that take account of this international variability in corporate governance structures. In the German context, *Heintges et al.* (2008) propose that the executive board, the chairman or other executive committees can be CODMs (*Heintges et al.* (2008), pp. 2773–2774). For German public corporations, the CODM is generally the executive board (*Rogler* (2009), p. 501; *Böckem/Pritzer* (2010), p. 615). Hence, in general only reports that are regularly reviewed by the entire executive board are relevant for the definition of segments. If single board members receive further reports about specific business units or geographical regions, these reports should not be used for the definition of segments (*Kajüter* (2013), p. 19). It is evident that the term CODM, which was first introduced to IFRS in IFRS 8, is a vague concept that leaves room for managerial discretion (*Rogler* (2009), p. 501).

The third criterion regarding the **availability of discrete financial information** is rather clarifying and will presumably be met if the first two criteria hold true (*Sandleben/Schmidt* (2010), p. 49).

If the attributes detailed in IFRS 8.5 a.-c. are **not sufficient** to identify the operating segments because the CODM uses several sets of segment information, IFRS 8.8 suggests to use factors such as the nature of business activities, the existence of manager responsibility or the information presented to the board of directors to identify operating segments.

In the second step of segment definition process, an operating segment is deemed **reportable** if it meets *any* of the following quantitative thresholds (IFRS 8.13):

a. its reported revenue, including both sales to external customers and intersegment sales or transfers, is ten per cent or more of the combined revenue, internal and external, of all operating segments; or
b. the absolute amount of its reported profit or loss is ten per cent or more of the greater, in absolute amount, of (i) the combined reported profit of all operating segments that did not report a loss and (ii) the combined reported loss of all operating segments that reported a loss; or
c. its assets are ten per cent or more of the combined assets of all operating segments.

Management may **separately disclose segments** that do not meet the quantitative criteria if they consider the information to be beneficial to users of financial statements (IFRS 8.13).

Furthermore, management may **aggregate** economically similar segments[24] – that do not meet the quantitative thresholds – to create reportable segments (IFRS 8.14). Segments can only be aggregated if aggregation is consistent with the core principles and if the segments are similar in each of the following dimensions (IFRS 8.12):

---

[24] IFRS 8.12 refers to similar long-term average gross margins as an indication of economically similar segments.

a. the nature of the products and services;
b. the nature of the production processes;
c. the type or class of customer for their products and services;
d. the methods used to distribute their products or provide their services; and
e. if applicable, the nature of the regulatory environment, for example, banking, insurance or public utilities.

Given that the core principle is rather general and only requires segment information to be helpful in evaluating the nature of a firm's business activities, management will easily find arguments supporting that an aggregation is consistent with the core principle (*Rogler* (2009), p. 502). Moreover, *Rogler* (2009) argues that long-term average gross margins are based on future expected values and thus provide room for **managerial manipulation**. The similarity criteria listed above (IFRS 8.12) also leave room for interpretation (*Rogler* (2009), pp. 502–503). This is supported by anecdotal evidence for segment reports under the management approach in the U.S. Sony and Enron used the aggregation criteria in SFAS No. 131, which are identical to IFRS 8, to hide the losses of an important segment by combining it with a profitable segment. Subsequently, the SEC issued several Accounting and Auditing Enforcement Releases (AAER) to punish these practices (*SEC* (1998a, b); *SEC* (2004a, b, c)).

In case the total external revenue of the reportable segments comprises less than 75 per cent of the entity's total revenue, **additional segments** have to be classified as reportable, even if they do not meet the criteria mentioned above (IFRS 8.15). This ensures that all reportable segments together comprise a substantial amount of a firm's total revenue. Segments that are not reportable must be combined in an "all other segments" category, which is to be disclosed separately (IFRS 8.16).

If a segment that was reportable in the preceding period does no longer meet the criteria in IFRS 8.13, management shall **continue to disclose** the segment in the current period if the segment is deemed to be of lasting significance (IFRS 8.17). In a similar vein, segments that are classified as reportable in the current period for the first time have to be restated to represent a separate segment in the prior year for comparison unless the information is not available or costs to obtain the information are excessive (IFRS 8.18). To inhibit too detailed segment information, IFRS 8.19 suggests a **practical limit** of ten reportable segments.

In the guidance on implementing IFRS 8,[25] the IASB presents a decision tree that summarizes the whole process of identifying reportable segments:

---

[25] Implementation guidance on IFRS standards usually provides illustrative examples or helpful explanations. However, they are only supplemental material and should not be interpreted as altering or adding to IFRS requirements.

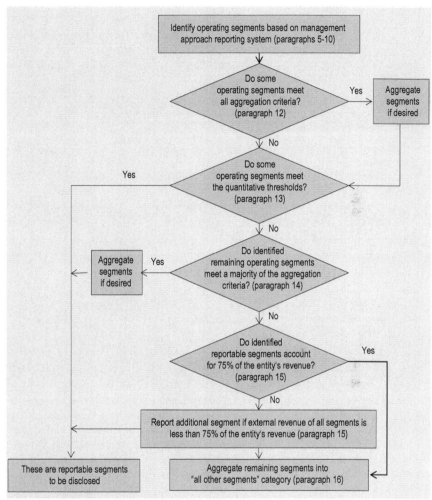

Figure 2-4: Diagram for identifying reportable segments
(IFRS 8.IG 8)

2.2.3.2 IAS 14R

The definition of segments under IAS 14R also follows a two-step process in which segments are first **identified** and then deemed as **reportable** if they meet certain size-related criteria.

For the **identification** of segments, IAS 14R uses a two-tier-segmentation (*McConnell/Pacter* (1995), p. 34) based on a firm's operating business lines and its operating geographical activities. According to IAS 14R.9, a segment is defined as follows:

A business (*geographical*) segment is a distinguishable component of an enterprise that is engaged in providing an individual product or service or a group of related products or services (*within a particular economic environment*) and that is subject to risks and returns that are different from those of other business segments (*operating in other economic environments*).

Analogous to the similarity criteria for the aggregation of segments under IFRS 8.12, the following factors need to be taken into account to determine whether products and services of a **business segment** are related (IAS 14R.9):

a. the nature of the products or services;
b. the nature of the production processes;
c. the type or class of customer for the products or services;
d. the methods used to distribute the products or provide the services; and
e. if applicable, the nature of the regulatory environment, for example, banking, insurance, or public utilities.

Regarding **geographical segments**, factors that need to be taken into consideration to identify geographical segments are (IAS 14R.9):

a. similarity of economic and political conditions;
b. relationships between operations in different geographical areas;
c. proximity of operations;
d. special risks associated with operations in a particular area;
e. exchange control regulations; and
f. the underlying currency risks.

Hence, business and geographical segments showing different risks and returns are identified (IAS 14R.11-12).

Following the risk-and-reward approach, the set of segments, either business or geographical, which primarily determines the dominant source and nature of a firm's risks and returns is considered as the **primary segment reporting format** and the other as **secondary** (IAS 14R.26). IAS 14R.27-28 implicitly assume that management uses the same approach for internal purposes. However, if the internal organisational structure leads to the definition of segments with risk-and-reward characteristics that oppose IAS 14R.11 and IAS 14R.12, segmentation has to be adjusted according to the risk-and-reward structure (*Street/Nichols* (2002), p. 94). Therefore, the literature commonly refers to IAS 14R's underlying concept as "*a management approach with a risks-and-rewards safety net*" (*McConnel/Pacter* (1995), p. 36).

Identified segments are classified as **reportable** if they meet certain quantitative thresholds. These quantitative thresholds (IAS 14R.35) as well as the guidance on the aggregation of segments (IAS 14R.36) are essentially identical to the current requirements of IFRS 8. Hence, the aggregation criteria provide comparable room for discretion under both standards when combining reportable segments. In contrast to IFRS 8, IAS 14R.35 requires that the majority of a reportable segment's sales stem from external customers. However, IAS 14R.39-40 encourage to voluntarily report vertically integrated business activities as single segments even if they do not fulfill the requirements of IAS 14R.35.

2.2.4   Measurement

2.2.4.1   IFRS 8

IFRS 8.25-27 stipulate the **basis of measurement** for the reported line items of the reportable segments. Segment information amounts do not necessarily have to comply with the measurement principles under IFRS. The reported amount of each line item has to be the same as the amount reported to the CODM for resource allocation and performance evaluation purposes. Hence, in case an entity uses imputed costs (e.g., imputed depreciation based on replacement costs or imputed interest on equity) and omits neutral items (e.g., extraordinary costs or income), these measures have to be reported in the segment report (*Kajüter/Barth* (2007), p. 432). However, if the CODM makes use of more than one measure for an entity's profit or loss, assets or liabilities, the amount reported shall be the one which is most consistent with the measurement principles used under IFRS (IFRS 8.26).

Since the measurement of segment items does not have to be consistent with general IFRS measurement principles, management can decide whether they use the autonomous entity approach or the disaggregation approach.[26] Both approaches leave substantial room for **managerial interpretation** (*Rogler* (2009), pp. 504–505). Under the autonomous entity approach, synergies between the segments must be eliminated and transactions between segments have to be measured at hypothetical market prices. The disaggregation approach requires a distribution of total amounts to segments. For instance, if some assets or liabilities are used by multiple segments, they have to be allocated to segments on a reasonable basis. The exact allocation of total amounts is left to management's discretion. The choice between the autonomous entity approach and the disaggregation approach as well as the discretion within both approaches provide management with room for earnings management.

2.2.4.2   IAS 14R

In contrast to IFRS 8, segment information under IAS 14R has to be prepared according to IFRS measurement principles. Hence, the **measurement basis** does not differ from an entity's financial statements. However, IAS 14R.46 allows preparers to disclose additional segment information that is not based on IFRS measurement principles, if the information is reported to key management personnel for resource allocation and performance evaluation purposes and if the measurement basis is clearly described (IAS 14R.46).

Since the general IFRS measurement principles have to be applied for the measurement of segment items under IAS 14R, management should **not have particular discretion** to manipulate segment numbers as it is the case for segment reporting under the management approach in IFRS 8.

---

[26]   See section 2.1.3.3 for a description of both approaches.

2.2.5   Disclosures

2.2.5.1   IFRS 8

The core principle of IFRS 8 states that information disclosed in the segment report shall help users of this information to assess the nature of an entity's business activities and the economic environment (IFRS 8.20).

To meet this principle, IFRS 8.21 requires **threefold disclosures**: General information, conditional and unconditional line items as well as reconciliations.

General information such as the factors used to identify segments, the basis of organization and types of products and services of each reportable segment have to be disclosed (8.22). Moreover, IFRS 8.27 requires an entity to report:

- the basis for inter-segment pricing of transactions (a);
- any differences between the entity's and the segments' measures of profit or loss before tax, assets and liabilities (if not explained by the reconciliation) (b) (c) (d);
- any deviations from prior periods in the measurement basis of segment profits and (if any) its effect on segment profit or loss (e); and
- the nature and effect of any asymmetrical allocations (f).

With regard to the **segment line items**, a measure of profit or loss is the only item that has to be disclosed even if not reported to the CODM (**unconditional disclosure**) (IFRS 8.23). In the initial version of IFRS 8, segment assets also had to be disclosed. However, this requirement was removed in the annual improvements project (AIP) 2009.

A measure of assets and liabilities and several other measures[27] have to be reported for each segment if they are regularly reviewed by the CODM (IFRS 8.23) (**conditional disclosure**). Moreover, in case an entity changes its internal organization structure and thus changes its segmentation, the information for the previous year has to be restated accordingly. An entity can refrain from restating if the respective information is not at hand and the collection would cause excessive costs (IFRS 8.29).

Entities must also provide **reconciliations** of total segment revenue, total segment profit or loss or every other material item disclosed in accordance with IFRS 8.23 to the corresponding GAAP amounts (IFRS 8.28). Material reconciling items, for instance due to different accounting policies, need to be described separately. Some respondents on the exposure draft favored the reconciliation of individual segments between the segment amounts and equivalents measured based on IFRS. However, the IASB noted in the basis for conclusion that this would lead to two complete segment reports – one based on internal measures and the other based on IFRS measures. The IASB decided that the costs would outweigh the benefits and did not address the proposal (IFRS 8.BC42).

---

[27] These other measures are external and internal revenue, interest revenue and expense, depreciation and amortization, material items of income and expense disclosed in accordance to IAS 1.97, an entity's interest in the profit or loss of associates and joint ventures accounted for by the equity method, income taxes, material non-cash items, amount of investment in associates and joint ventures accounted for by the equity method and the amount of additions to non-current assets (IFRS 8.23-24).

In addition, every entity – even those that only have a single reportable segment – must provide certain **entity-wide disclosures** (IFRS 8.31-34) in case this information is not already provided in the segment report (IFRS 8.31). These disclosures comprise:

- revenues from external customers for each product and service (IFRS 8.32); and
- revenues from external customers and non-current assets for geographical areas – at least at the domicile/foreign level whilst individual foreign countries need to be disclosed separately (IFRS 8.33).

In contrast to the idea of the management approach, these entity-wide disclosures have to be reported based on the **measurement principles** used to prepare the financial statements.

Moreover, an entity must provide revenues with **major single external customers** if these exceed ten per cent of the entity's total revenue (IFRS 8.34). However, IFRS 8.34 does not require reporting the identity of these customers.

IFRS 8 only defines a few unconditional disclosures and many conditional disclosures. Management, however, has some **flexibility** with regard to the conditional disclosures. For instance, by influencing the periodicity of internal reporting, management can avoid the disclosure of conditional items as it is required that items are reported on a regular basis. Hence, there is room for management to avoid the disclosure of specific items.

2.2.5.2 IAS 14R

IAS 14R.50-67 specify the reporting requirements for the primary segment reporting format and IAS 14R.68-72 do the same for the secondary reporting format. Although the requirements are substantially less for the secondary format, entities are encouraged to present all primary-segment disclosures as well for the secondary segments (IAS 14R.49). Mandatory line items that need to be reported for each **primary segment** comprise:

- segment revenue; segment revenue from sales to external customers and segment revenue from transactions with other segments shall be reported separately (IAS 14R.51);
- segment result; segment results from continuing operations and segment results from discontinued operations shall be reported separately (IAS 14R.52);
- total carrying amount of segment assets (IAS 14R.55);
- segment liabilities (IAS 14R.56);
- total cost incurred during the period to acquire segment assets that are expected to be used during more than one period (property, plant, equipment and intangible assets for each reportable segment) (capital expenditures)[28] (IAS 14R.57);
- segment depreciation and amortization expenses (IAS 14R.58);
- significant non-cash expenses, other than depreciation and amortization, that were deducted in measuring segment result (IAS 14R.61); and

---

[28] To fulfill this requirement, companies usually report this item as "capital expenditures" or "capital additions". However, IAS 14R.57 stresses that measurement of this category has to be on an accrual basis, not on a cash basis. For practicability, this category is referred to as "capital expenditures" in the following.

- investments in associates, joint ventures, or other investments accounted for under the equity method and the net profit or loss of these investments (IAS 14R.64 and IAS 14R.66).

An entity must also provide **reconciliations** between segment amounts of primary reportable segments and the GAAP amounts for the following items (IAS 14R.67):

- segment revenue to entity revenue from external customers;
- segment result from continuing operations to a comparable measure of entity operating profit or loss from continuing operations;
- segment result from discontinued operations to entity profit or loss from discontinued operations;
- segment assets to entity assets; and
- segment liabilities to entity liabilities.

Moreover, IAS 14R **encourages** but does not require the following disclosures for each segment:

- other measures of segment profitability or profitability ratios with an appropriate description of the measure (IAS 14R.53);
- other material items of segment revenue and segment expense (IAS 14R.59); and
- segment cash flows and significant non-cash revenues (IAS 14R.62).

The required disclosures for the **secondary reporting format** are identified in IAS 14R.68-72. If an entity's primary reporting format is based on business lines, IAS 14R.69 requires the disclosure of the following items by **geographical areas**:

a. segment revenue from external customers based on the geographical location of its customers, for each geographical segment whose revenue from sales to external customers is ten per cent or more of total entity revenue sales to all external customers;

b. total carrying amount of segment assets by geographical location of assets, for each geographical segment whose segment assets are ten per cent or more of total assets of all geographical areas; and

c. segment capital expenditures during the period to acquire non-current segment assets by geographical location of assets, for each geographical segment whose segment assets are ten per cent or more of total assets of all geographical areas.

IAS 14R.70 stipulates the disclosure of the same items for business segments if the primary segment format is geographical segments.

Other disclosure matters for all entities are regulated in IAS 14R.74-83.

In contrast to IFRS 8, there are numerous mandatory line items. Hence, there is **no room for management** to avoid the disclosure of these items.

2.2.6   Remaining differences to SFAS No. 131

One objective of introducing IFRS 8 was to bring about convergence of US-GAAP and IFRS. As laid out in the basis for conclusion of IFRS 8, the IASB decided that making use of the exact text of SFAS No. 131 – expect for differences in terminology to ensure consistency with other IFRS standards – would be the best way to ascertain convergence (IFRS 8.BC12). However, **differences** between the two standards remain (IFRS 8.BC60). The definition of **non-current assets** as part of the entity-wide disclosures differs from SFAS No. 131. Under SFAS No. 131, the term "long-lived assets" is used instead. The term also implies a different scope as it only refers to hard assets that cannot be readily removed. However, the IASB could not see the reason why intangible assets should not be included in this definition and changed the definition (IFRS 8.BC15).

Unlike in SFAS No. 131, IFRS 8 requires the disclosure of segment **liabilities** if it is regularly reported to the CODM (IFRS 8.BC60 (b)). Such a disclosure was not included in the initial exposure draft. Some respondents, in particular users of financial statements, viewed this information as helpful. Hence, the IASB decided to require the disclosure of segment liabilities if they are regularly used by the CODM for internal decision making and performance evaluation (IFRS 8.BC36-38).

Moreover, under SFAS No. 131 firms with a **matrix organisation** must determine their operating segments based on business lines. The IASB initially followed this approach. Respondents to the exposure draft, however, noted that this would be incoherent with the management approach and the IASB agreed (IFRS 8.BC27). Hence, IFRS 8 requires operating segments to be identified according to the core principle of the standard.

2.2.7 Summary

As illustrated in the prior sections, there are **substantial differences** between the reporting requirements under IFRS 8 and IAS 14R. The core principle and scope of both standards are comparable. However, the definition of segments, measurement and disclosures differ considerably.

These differences also lead to different levels of **managerial discretion** that are inherent in the two standards. While the risk-and-reward approach under IAS 14R is closely related to the general measurement principles of IFRS, the management approach under IFRS 8 leaves more room for managerial interpretation and manipulation. Whether management exploits this room to report less segment information will be investigated in the analysis of segment reporting practice in chapter five.

Table 2-1 summarizes the main findings of section 2.2 and presents the key differences between IFRS 8 and IAS 14R.

Comparison of the requirements under IFRS 8 and IAS 14R		
	IFRS 8 **Management approach**	**IAS 14R** **Risk-and-reward approach**
Core principle and scope	Enable users of an entity's financial statements to evaluate the nature and financial effects of the business activities in which the entity engages and the economic environments in which the entity operates.	Help users of financial statements to better understand the entity's past performance; better assess the entity's risks and returns; and make more informed judgments about the entity as a whole.
Definition of segments	A segment is a component of an entity that engages in business activities from which it may earn revenues and incur expenses; whose operating results are regularly reviewed by the entity's CODM to make decisions about resources to be allocated to the segments and assess their performance; and for which discrete financial information is available.	A segment is a distinguishable component of an enterprise that is subject to risks and returns that are different from those of other business segments.
Measurement	The amount of each segment item reported shall be the measure reported to the CODM. Segment information amounts do not necessarily have to comply with the measurement principles under IFRS.	Segment information has to be prepared according to IFRS measurement principles.
Disclosures	General information: Factors used to identify segments, the basis of organization and types of products and services of each reportable segment have to be disclosed. Operating segments: Segment result is mandatory. Segment assets, segment liabilities, segment external and internal revenue, interest revenue and expense, depreciation and amortization, other material income/expense items, amount and result of equity method investments, income taxes, material non-cash items and capital expenditures have to be reported if regularly reviewed by the CODM. Entity-wide disclosures: Certain entity-wide disclosures (based on the measurement principles used to prepare the financial statements) must be provided if this information is not already available in the segment report. These disclosures comprise revenues from external customers for each product and service and revenues from external customers as well as non-current assets for geographical areas. Additionally, an entity must provide revenues with major single external customers if these exceed ten per cent of the entity's total revenue.	Primary format: Mandatory disclosures comprise segment revenue with external customers, segment revenue with other segments, segment result, segment assets and liabilities, capital expenditures, depreciation and amortization, significant non-cash expenses, amount and result of equity method investments. Secondary format: Mandatory disclosures comprise segment revenue with external customers, segment assets and capital expenditures.

Table 2-1: Reporting requirements under IFRS 8 and IAS 14R

3 State of research

In general, there is plenty of empirical research on segment reporting and there is also a variety of different research approaches. In a broad sense, the empirical literature on segment reporting can be distinguished in descriptive studies and studies on the economic consequences. This study conducts both approaches and, thus, both research streams are introduced in the following.

There is a lot of early research on the general benefits of segment reporting. This study, however, analyzes the impact of introducing the management approach to segment reporting. Therefore it predominantly focuses on studies that deal with the introduction of SFAS No. 131 and IFRS 8. Figure 3-1 presents the classification of the related empirical literature discussed in this chapter. The literature on the economic consequences is further sub-divided into different fields which analyze segment reporting from different angles.

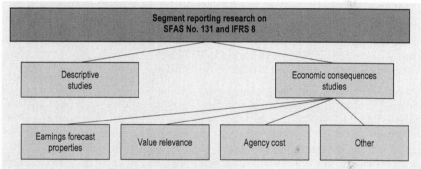

Figure 3-1: Classification of the related empirical literature

3.1 Descriptive studies

Descriptive studies describe the current state of reporting practice. Some descriptive studies on corporate disclosures also try to find determinants of increased voluntary disclosures or high quality disclosures: For instance, whether larger companies publish more or better information. Regarding segment reporting, this has, however, not been the case yet. Hence, the following studies comprise descriptive evidence on segment reporting practice. This study focuses on the literature about SFAS No. 131 and IFRS 8 which yield relevant insights for the research question at hand.

3.1.1 Studies on the introduction of SFAS No. 131

Herrmann/Thomas (2000) obtain segment information from the largest 100 Fortune 500 list U.S. firms as of 1998 for the last year under SFAS No. 14 and the first year under SFAS No. 131. They find that 68 per cent of the sample changed the definition of segments upon the introduction of the new standard. This change led to an increase in the average number of reported segments from 3.4 to 3.8. Moreover, the number of reported line items increased as well from an average of 5.5 under SFAS No. 14 to 6.3 under SFAS No. 131 (*Herrmann/Thomas* (2000), pp. 291–295). However, the authors also note that although the fineness of geographical segment disclosures has in general increased, fewer companies report geographical earnings (*Herrmann/Thomas* (2000), p. 301). Hence, the introduction of SFAS No. 131 led to an **overall increase** in segmental disclosures.

Nichols et al. (2000) assess the impact of introducing SFAS No. 131 on geographical segment disclosures for a sample of 158 U.S. companies listed on the Business Week Global 1000 for 1997 and 1998 (*Nichols et al.* (2000), pp. 64–65). They find that only 22 per cent of their sample firms report segments based on geographical areas (*Nichols et al.* (2000), p. 66). Most geographical segment information is disclosed under the entity-wide disclosures. Although the introduction of SFAS No. 131 resulted in the disclosure of more country-specific data compared to SFAS No. 14, one third of the sample still reports highly aggregated geographical information based on a U.S./Other countries classification (*Nichols et al.* (2000), pp. 70–71). Moreover, under SFAS No. 14, 85 per cent disclosed income on a geographical level compared to the 15 per cent under SFAS No. 131 (*Nichols et al.* (2000), pp. 76–77). Finally, the authors also find an increase in the consistency of segment data with other parts of the annual report (*Nichols et al.* (2000), pp. 78–79). They conclude that financial analysts would welcome most of the changes induced by the introduction of SFAS No. 131 (*Nichols et al.* (2000), p. 80). However, they also note that there is **still room for improvement** of segmental disclosures.

Street et al. (2000) also analyze segmental disclosures in 1997 and 1998 under SFAS No. 131 and SFAS No. 14 for a sample of 160 large listed U.S. firms of the Business Week Global 1000 list. Similar to *Herrmann/Thomas* (2000), they find a significant increase in the number of reported business line segments from 2.7 to 3.7. Notably, 38 entities that maintained to operate in only one business segment under SFAS No. 14 started to report multiple segments under SFAS No. 131. The number of reported line items, however, did not change significantly upon the adoption of SFAS No. 131 (*Street et al.* (2000), pp. 267–275). Moreover, the authors note that the consistency of segment reports with other parts of the annual reports improved considerably as 25 per cent report segment information that was inconsistent with the Management Discussion and Analysis (MD&A) in 1997 and only 8 per cent in 1998 (*Street et al.* (2000), pp. 279–280). They conclude that **segment reporting generally improved** due to the introduction of SFAS No. 131 (*Street et al.* (2000), p. 281). However, despite of controlling for major changes in the business structure, results of both previously described studies (*Herrmann/Thomas* (2000) and *Street et al.* (2000)) might be driven by other economic events as two different years are compared. Hence, the change in segment reporting might not entirely be due to the change in reporting requirements. In contrast, this study uses a research design that controls for this.

Based on a small sample of 30 Dow Jones Industrial Average (DJIA) companies, *Paul/Largay III* (2005) also analyze the change in segmental disclosures from 1997 under SFAS No. 14 to 1998 under SFAS No. 131. They find an increase of the number of reported segments upon the introduction of the management approach (*Paul/Largay III* (2005), p. 307). Although findings indicate a compliance gap for both standards, the extent of standard compliance increased under SFAS No. 131 (*Paul/Largay III* (2005), p. 309). The authors subjectively judge the quality of segmental disclosures with a simplified scoring system for the disclosure of line items and find **no significant difference** in the "quality" of disclosures between SFAS No. 131 and SFAS No. 14 (*Paul/Largay III* (2005), p. 309).

In **summary**, empirical evidence signals an increase in the extent and fineness of segment information upon adoption of the management approach in the U.S. However, note that the disclosure requirements under the old standard SFAS No. 14 were rudimentary and mandated far less disclosures. Hence, the improvement in segmental disclosures should not solely be attributed to the change in underlying principles. It may rather be driven by stricter reporting requirements that are independent of the management approach.

Table 3-1 presents an overview of the descriptive studies on the impact of SFAS No. 131.

Descriptive studies on the impact of SFAS No. 131		
Reference	**Sample**	**Findings**
Herrmann and Thomas (2000)	100 U.S. firms, 1997-1998	Increase in the number of reported segments and reported line items, but less geographical earnings reported.
Nichols et al. (2000)	158 U.S. firms, 1997-1998	More country-specific data and disclosures are more consistent with other parts of the annual report. However, a significant proportion of the sample still reports highly aggregated geographic segment data.
Street et al. (2000)	160 U.S. firms, 1997-1998	Increase in the number of reported segments and no change in the number of reported line items. Improvement in consistency of segment information with other parts of the annual report.
Paul and Largay III (2005)	30 U.S. firms, 1997-1998	Increase in the number of reported segments and an increase in standard compliance. No change in the "quality" of disclosures measured by the number of line items.

Table 3-1: Overview of descriptive studies on the impact of SFAS No. 131

3.1.2 Studies on the introduction of IFRS 8

Blase/Müller (2009) are one of the first to empirically analyze the implementation of IFRS 8 of 13 German DAX, MDAX and SDAX companies that adopted the new standard early in 2009. However, they primarily focus on the **degree of accounting integration** (financial versus management accounting) by investigating the reconciliations. They find that accounting systems are largely integrated and segments are generally evaluated based on IFRS numbers (*Blase/Müller* (2009), p. 544). *Matova/Pelger* (2010) conduct a similar analysis based on an extended sample of 43 early adopters (DAX, MDAX, SDAX and TecDAX) from 2007 and 2008. They also provide evidence that accounting systems of more than 50 per cent of their sample firms are fully integrated while the other half only shows minor reconciliation differences. No entity discloses imputed costs or gains (*Matova/Pelger* (2010), p. 500). Results of these two studies, however, have to be interpreted with caution as the sample firms only represent the largest listed German companies and the analysis of early adopters suffers from a self-selection bias.

Meyer/Weiss (2010) analyze the change in segment reporting practice from 2008 (IAS 14R) to 2009 (IFRS 8) based on a sample of 116 listed Swiss companies. They find that 21 per cent of their sample firms **increase the number of reported segments** while seven per cent show a decrease. Hence, 72 per cent did not change the number of reported segments at all upon adoption of IFRS 8 (*Meyer/Weiss* (2010), p. 850). With regard to the disclosed line items, they find that the introduction of IFRS 8 induces a **decrease in reported items per segment** (*Meyer/Weiss* (2010), p. 852). Moreover, 49 per cent of the sample firms explicitly state that internal measurement is based on the same measurement principles that are used for external financial reporting. No company reports a deviation of reported numbers due to non-IFRS measurements such as imputed costs or gains. Reconciliations, however, are provided by almost all firms (98 per cent) as items such as financial instruments or taxes are usually not allocated on segmental level (*Meyer/Weiss* (2010), p. 853). *Meyer/Weiss* (2010) conclude that – at least with regard to the increase in number of reported segments – IFRS 8 has fulfilled its objective.[29]

KPMG (2010) conducts a content analysis of a sample of 81 companies of the 2009 Fortune Global 500 list from 17 different IFRS-applying countries of different industries. Early adopters and companies with financial year end other than 31 December are excluded from the sample. The final sample selection is somewhat arbitrary as there is no randomized process but rather a subjective selection of companies that are – according to the authors – supposed to reflect a good mixture of countries and industries (*KPMG* (2010), pp. 6–7). The authors find an **increase in the average number of reported segments** from 4.6 under IAS 14R to 5.2 under IFRS 8 (*KPMG* (2010), pp. 17–18). Moreover, almost 25 per cent of the sample adopt a mixed approach and use products or services combined with geographical areas as the basis of segmentation upon adoption of IFRS 8. Two-thirds of the sample, however, disaggregate by products or services (*KPMG* (2010), pp. 19–20). Finally, they find that the **measurement** basis of segment line items is generally **based on IFRS**. The authors conclude that internal management reporting is probably based on IFRS numbers.

Weißenberger/Franzen (2011) conduct a disclosure survey of segment reports of 72 nonfinancial and non-early adopting German HDAX and SDAX entities as of 2009. They find an average number of reported segments of 3.2 and 13.8 reported line items for each segment. The predominant basis for segmentation is business lines (78 per cent) while 11 per cent report segments on a geographical basis and eight per cent use a matrix format (*Weißenberger/Franzen* (2011), p. 343). They conclude that **segment reporting practice has not changed** considerably compared to IAS 14R. Additionally, standard compliance has slightly improved but remains fragmentary for some entities (*Weißenberger/Franzen* (2011), pp. 345–347). However, the authors draw all conclusions based on a comparison of their IFRS 8 findings to other studies on the reporting practice under IAS 14R and do not obtain IAS 14R data for their sample firms.

Crawford et al. (2012) investigate a sample of 150 UK companies (99 of the Financial Times Stock Exchange 100 index (FTSE 100) and 51 of the FTSE 250 index) in the first

---

[29] The dissertation of *Weiss* (2012) is based on a very similar sample and shows comparable results (*Weiss* (2012), pp. 52–92).

year of IFRS 8's adoption to gauge the consequences of introducing the new standard on segment reporting practice for UK blue-chip and midcap entities. They find an **increase in the mean of reported segments** from 3.3 under IAS 14R to 3.6 under IFRS 8 (*Crawford et al.* (2012), pp. 17–18). However, the authors also provide evidence for a **decrease in the number of reported line items** per segment. Moreover, most entities do not use non-IFRS measures (*Crawford et al.* (2012), pp. 22–23). Finally, they report that the word count of segmental narratives generally increases (*Crawford et al.* (2012), pp. 23–24). The authors highlight the finding that even under the management approach there is inconsistency for many companies between the business structure shown in the segment report and in other parts of the annual report narratives (*Crawford et al.* (2012), p. 27).

Nichols et al. (2012) also analyze the impact of introducing IFRS 8 on 335 blue chip companies from the main stock indices of 14 European countries. On average, the **number of reported segments increased** significantly (with Switzerland being the only country showing a decrease) (*Nichols et al.* (2012), pp. 91–93). Furthermore, *Nichols et al.* (2012) confirm the findings of other studies and provide evidence for a **decrease in the number of reported line items**. Particularly the disclosure of segment liabilities, equity method income, equity method investments and capital expenditures decline significantly upon adoption of the new standard (*Nichols et al.* (2012), pp. 93–95). Contrary to the expectation, the **consistency** of the segmentation in the segment report with other parts of the annual report **does not change** significantly. However, this is due to the fact that companies have already shown highly consistent segmentations under IAS 14R (97 per cent under IFRS 8, 96 per cent under IAS 14R) (*Nichols et al.* (2012), pp. 87–88). Moreover, they also find an **increased fineness of geographical segment disclosures**. While companies under IAS 14R generally use rather broad geographical segments, the geographical disclosures as part of the entity-wide disclosures for firms reporting line-of-business as reportable segments are on average much finer under IFRS 8 (*Nichols et al.* (2012), pp. 97–98). The authors conclude that their results may not be generalized to smaller European companies as blue ship companies are subject to more scrutiny and face different regulatory forces. Moreover, they highlight the need for an analysis of different countries in the world (*Nichols et al.* (2012), p. 99).

Kang/Grey (2012) conduct a comparative analysis of segment disclosures of an Australian sample of 189 ASX companies' segment reports in 2008 (IAS 14R) and 2010 (IFRS 8). They find a significant increase in the average number of reported segments from 3.2 to 3.7 (*Kang/Grey* (2012), pp. 14–15). However, the authors also maintain that the disclosed **segment information has not changed** to a great extent (*Kang/Grey* (2012), p. 16). Their results further indicate that there is a notable **increase in the narrative descriptions** of reportable segments (*Kang/Grey* (2012), pp. 17–19). A drawback of the study is that the authors make no attempt to isolate the effect of the standard change from real economic changes such as growth, mergers and acquisitions, or divestures.

The study of *Pisano/Landriana* (2012) mainly focuses on **proprietary costs** associated with segment disclosures under IFRS 8 and IAS 14R for a sample of 122 listed **Italian firms**. However, they also provide some descriptive information about the number of segments and segment line items. *Pisano/Landriana* (2012) document that about 85 per cent of their sample use business lines as the predominant basis for segmentation under both IFRS 8 and IAS 14R (*Pisano/Landriana* (2012), pp. 123–130). The average **number of segments increased** from 3.71 to 3.85. 14 per cent (11 per cent) of all firms show an increase (a decrease) while 71 per cent do not change the number of reported segments.[30] In terms of **segment line items, there is an increase** from an average of 8.47 items under IAS 14R to 10.33 under IFRS 8. Their results also reveal some **compliance issues** under both standards. Except for eliminating firms from their sample that were involved in mergers or major acquisitions, the authors do not isolate the effect of the standard change from other concurrent developments.

Mardini et al. (2012) take a different approach and consider the effect of IFRS 8 on firms from an **emerging economy**: They analyze segmental disclosures of 109 listed **Jordanian firms** in 2008 and 2009. Interestingly, there is a **compliance issue** under both standards because almost 20 per cent of all firms do not categorize segments as primary/secondary or as operating segments. A sub-sample of 70 firms that provides sufficient segment data reports an **increase in the mean number of reported segments** from 2.4 under IAS 14R to 2.7 under IFRS 8. Moreover, there was an **increase in the mean number of segment items** from 6.4 to 10.4 upon adoption of the new standard. Furthermore, geographical locations show an increased fineness. In summary, the authors conclude that the introduction of IFRS 8 **improved the disclosure** of segment information for Jordanian companies. However, they also note that other factors beyond the introduction of IFRS 8 may have impacted their findings.

In **summary**, there is some evidence that IFRS 8's introduction led to a change in segment reporting practice. However, there are also a lot of firms that were unaffected by the new standard. Most of the studies focus on the major aspects such as number of segments or number of line items. In contrast, this study uses a more thorough approach and also analyzes several areas of segment reporting that have been unaddressed thus far.

Table 3-2 presents an overview of the descriptive studies on the impact of IFRS 8.

Descriptive studies on the impact of IFRS 8		
Reference	**Sample**	**Findings**
Blase and Müller (2009)	13 German firms, 2007	Accounting systems of early adopters are largely integrated and segment reports generally include IFRS-conform numbers.
Matova and Pelger (2010)	43 German firms, 2007-2008	Accounting systems of early adopters are largely integrated and firms only report IFRS-conform numbers.
Meyer and Weiss (2010)	166 Swiss firms, 2008-2009	A majority of firms (77 per cent) does not change the number of reported segments upon adoption of IFRS 8. The number of reported line items decreases. Firms only report IFRS-conform numbers.
-Table is continued on the next page-		

---

[30] The remaining four per cent change the segmental structure without changing the number of segments.

KPMG (2010)	81 European firms (15 European countries + Hong Kong and Israel), 2008-2009	Increase in the number of reported segments. Measurement of line items is generally based on IFRS-conform numbers.
Weißenberger and Franzen (2011)	72 German firms, 2009	Mean of reported segments is 3.2 and mean of line items is 13.8. Predominant basis of segmentation is business lines.
Crawford et al. (2012)	150 UK firms, 2008-2009	Increase in the number of reported segments and a decrease in the number of line items. Increase in the word count of segment narratives. Most firms use IFRS-conform measures. Still some inconsistency of segment reports with other parts of the annual report.
Nichols et al. (2012)	335 European firms (14 countries), 2008-2009	Increase in the number of reported segments and decrease in the number of line items. Increased fineness of geographical segments. No change in the consistency of segment reports with other parts of the annual report.
Kang and Gray (2012)	189 Australian firms, 2008/2010	Increase in the number of reported segments and no substantial change in the information disclosed in the segment reports.
Pisano and Landriani (2012)	122 Italian firms, 2008-2009	Small increase in the number of reported segments and also an increase in the number of reported line items.
Mardini et al. (2012)	109 Jordanian firms, 2008-2009	Increase in the number of reported segments and in the number of reported line items.

Table 3-2: Overview of descriptive studies on the impact of IFRS 8

3.2 Economic consequences studies

Studies on the economic consequences analyze the impact of segment information on various parties. Most studies compare the usefulness of segment information under two different standards. For the purpose of this study, only research on the introduction of SFAS No. 131 and IFRS 8 is considered. Moreover, the economic consequences studies comprise earnings forecast properties studies, value relevance studies, agency cost studies and other studies. This provides a broad picture of the economic consequences of introducing the management approach to segment reporting.

3.2.1 Studies on the impact of SFAS No. 131

Earnings forecast literature

Venkataraman (2001) is the first to analyze the impact of introducing SFAS No. 131 on the information environment of financial analysts. His sample comprises 566 U.S. firms. He obtains data for the pre-adoption period in the first quarter of 1998 and for the post-adoption period in the first quarter of 1999. Similar to the research design of this study, *Venkataraman* (2001) exploits the fact that 256 of his sample firms did not change the number of reported segments upon SFAS No. 131's adoption. Hence, he controls for economic wide changes from 1998 to 1999 that may affect the information environment of financial analysts of all companies (*Venkataraman* (2001), p. 20). His findings indicate that the individual **forecast accuracy increases** for the treatment sample of firms that changed their segmentation to comply with SFAS No. 131 (*Venkataraman* (2001), pp. 42–43).

Behn et al. (2002) analyze whether the introduction of SFAS No. 131 improved the **predictive ability of mechanical earnings forecast models** based on geographical segment disclosures. They use a sample of 172 U.S. companies listed in the Business Week Global 1000 for the years 1996-1997 (*Behn et al.* (2002), p. 35). The authors exploit the fact that firms adopting SFAS No. 131 in 1998 have to provide segment data for the prior two years. Hence, they have access to segment reports under both standards for 1997 and 1996 (*Behn et al.* (2002), p. 32). They find a **significant increase in the accuracy** of earnings forecasts for models based on geographical segment data under the new standard SFAS No. 131 (*Behn et al.* (2002), pp. 39–40). Moreover, findings indicate that this is due to the new requirement for companies to report geographical sales for the domicile country as well as any other material countries (*Behn et al.* (2002), pp. 41–43). However, results also indicate that the geographical forecasts do not differ from consolidated forecast models. Moreover, one should bear in mind that the mechanical models are not comparable to the models used by financial analysts. Financial analysts also rely on business line data (*Behn et al.* (2002), p. 43).

Berger/Hann (2003) explore whether information that was newly released under SFAS No. 131 and not previously available under SFAS No. 14 was already known to financial analysts. Based on a sample of 2,589 companies and an **analysis of mechanical forecast models and analysts' forecasts**, they show that analysts had access to some of the SFAS No. 131 information before it was disclosed in the annual report (*Berger/Hann* (2003), p. 165). However, they also find a significant **increase in forecast accuracy** for 514 firms that changed the number of reported segments upon SFAS No. 131's adoption compared to 2,046 firms that did not change anything (*Berger/Hann* (2003), pp. 196–197). *Berger/Hann* (2003) interpret this as evidence that the reporting requirements under the new standard mandated some disclosures that are useful for financial analysts, and which they could not obtain through private information channels before (*Berger/Hann* (2003), pp. 211–212).

Botosan/Stanford (2005) investigate a similar research question. They also focus on the effect of the introduction of SFAS No. 131 on **financial analysts' information environment**. *Botosan/Stanford* (2005) use a similar research design as *Venkataraman* (2001). Based on a sample of 615 firms that changed from being a single-segment firm to report multiple segments and a matched control sample of no-change firms, they find that overall **accuracy of analysts' forecasts decreased** from the pre-SFAS No. 131 to the post-SFAS No. 131 period for the change firms (*Botosan/Stanford* (2005), pp. 766–769). *Botosan/Stanford* (2005) suggest that this result is driven by analysts relying more on publicly available information. The results, however, are attributable to the general initiation of segment reporting rather than a change in underlying principles to segment reporting as in this study.

Hope et al. (2006) address the issue that SFAS No. 131 no longer requires the disclosure of geographical earnings if operating segments are based on business lines. Some critiques of SFAS No. 131 argued that this would lead to a loss of valuable information. However, *Hope et al.* (2006) find for a sample of 688 multinational U.S. firms that the **forecast accuracy of financial analysts increased** after the adoption of the new standard (*Hope et al.* (2006), pp. 332–335). Moreover, they find that the change in forecast accuracy is not different for a sub-sample (74 per cent) of firms that ceased to report geographical earnings upon SFAS No. 131's adoption (*Hope et al.* (2006), pp. 336–337). The authors conclude that the decision of the FASB to no longer mandate geographical segment earnings is appropriate (*Hope et al.* (2006), pp. 343–344). Their study, however, is subject to a major caveat: The findings could be driven by the possibility that financial analysts do not use geographical earnings although they *should* use them. Hence, the nondisclosure shows no significant effect but just due to the failure of financial analysts to use this information and not due to the insignificant incremental information content of these disclosures. Other users of financial statements such as investors may very well use geographical information. This study avoids this caveat by analyzing IFRS 8 from three different perspectives.

Instead of focusing on forecasts of financial analysts, *Ettredge et al.* (2005) analyze the **capital markets' ability to predict future earnings**. They use a metric based on *Collins et al.* (1994) that relates current stock returns to future earnings. If the market's future earnings expectations and the actual realizations are closely aligned, it can be assumed that market participants are able to predict future earnings. The authors build on a sample of 6,827 U.S. firms from 1995-2002 (*Ettredge et al.* (2005), p. 781). They compare the markets' ability to predict future earnings in the pre-adoption period (1995-1998) with the post-adoption period (1999-2002) (*Ettredge et al.* (2005), pp. 787–791). Findings indicate that multi-segment firms that also were multi-segment firms under SFAS No. 14 and firms that started to report multiple segments upon SFAS No. 131's adoption experienced an **increase in the predictability** of their earnings. However, single-segment firms that kept on reporting a single segment and thus did not undergo any changes due to the SFAS No. 131 introduction were not affected. The authors conclude that SFAS No. 131 improves the disclosure of information that helps market participants to assess future earnings (*Ettredge et al.* (2005), p. 801).

Park (2011) extends the study of *Ettredge et al.* (2005) by separating annual earnings innovation into firm-specific and industry-wide components. He finds that firms which increase the number of segments upon adoption of SFAS No. 131 exhibit a significant increase in the **incorporation of future earnings information into security prices**. This increase, however, is largely driven by the industry-wide information component. The market's ability to predict future firm-specific performance remains unchanged upon the adoption of SFAS No. 131 (*Park* (2011), p. 605). The author concludes that this may be due to the reduction of geographical earnings disclosures that firms show. Therefore, he suggests that mandating geographical earnings would enhance the predictive ability of the stock market. However, it is unclear whether the degree of statistical association between current stock returns and future earnings (as used in *Ettredge et al.* (2005) and *Park* (2011)) is a desirable criterion to evaluate a change in accounting standards that only affects disclosures and not recognized amounts. Moreover, it is also questionable how this concept relates to decision usefulness in general. This study overcomes these shortcomings by the joint analysis from different perspectives which do not solely rely on stock price data or future earnings.

Value relevance literature

Hossain/Marks (2005) are the first to analyze the information content of newly released geographical quarterly segment sales data based on SFAS No. 131 in the period from 1999-2001 based on a sample of 78 multinational U.S. entities. They show that **interim segment disclosures yield value relevant information content** (*Hossain/Marks* (2005), pp. 114–117). Yet, they do not compare the value relevance of SFAS No. 131 with disclosures under the predecessor. *Hossain* (2008), however, extends the study with a comparison of the two standards: He analyzes the information content of geographical quarterly segment sales data under SFAS No. 131 and SFAS No. 14 from 1996-2001 of 127 U.S. entities (*Hossain* (2008), pp. 9–10). The findings indicate that the general **value relevance of quarterly segment sales increased** for all firms upon SFAS No. 131's adoption (*Hossain* (2008), pp. 15–18). He also finds higher segment sales response coefficients for a subsample of firms that changed the basis of segmentation under the new standard (*Hossain* (2008), p. 18). Although this cross-sectional variation in the value relevance of segment sales supports the notion that results are driven by the introduction of the new standard, the research design cannot entirely isolate the standard effect from other confounding time effects. Hence, results have to be interpreted cautiously.

Hope et al. (2009) conduct a **value relevance study** of geographical segment disclosures after the introduction of SFAS No. 131. They analyze 719 multinational U.S. firms from 1998-2004. *Hope et al.* (2009) document an **increase in the pricing of foreign earnings** for firms that increased the fineness of geographical segmentation and firms that report geographical earnings measures upon adoption of SFAS No. 131. The authors do not compare their results with the previous standard SFAS No. 14. This shortcoming is addressed by *Hope et al.* (2008) as they investigate the foreign earnings pricing before and after the adoption of SFAS No. 131. They use a sample of 2,187 U.S. multinational firms from the period 1992-2004 (seven years under each standard) and find a significant **increase in the foreign earnings response coefficient** after the introduction of SFAS No. 131. The authors interpret this as evidence for a correction of underpricing of foreign earnings that might have occurred due to poorer disclosures under SFAS No. 14. Although *Hope et al.* (2008) employ a number of features to control for the effect of confounding time events, their research design does not fully capture all other factors that might drive the results. Hence, empirical findings should be interpreted with caution.

Agency cost literature

In addition to the analysis of the financial analyst information environment as described above, *Berger/Hann* (2003) also analyze the effect of SFAS No. 131 on the **monitoring environment**. Based on the same sample, they investigate whether the new standard facilitates better disclosures about firm diversification and inter-segment resource transfers. Prior literature has shown that diversified firms show systematically lower stock prices compared to non-diversified firms (*Berger/Ofek* (1995)) and that the extent of this "diversification discount" is related to agency problems (*Denis et al.* (1997)). Additionally, *Berger/Hann* (2003) argue that inter-segment transfers of funds are found to be inefficient (*Lamont* (1997); *Shin/Stulz* (1998)). Hence, if SFAS No. 131 facilitates users to **better judge diversification and inter-segment transfer**, it should help them to discover potential agency problems and thus enhance monitoring. In fact, the authors find that firms which turn from single-segment to multi-segment under SFAS No. 131 experience a **significant decrease in the diversification discount** in the period following the adoption of the new standard. *Berger/Hann* (2003) conclude that these results support the notion that SFAS No. 131 improved the monitoring environment of firms.

Botosan/Stanford (2005) also analyze agency cost aspects next to the analysis of financial analysts' information environment as discussed above. They investigate whether 615 U.S. firms that reported a single segment under SFAS No. 14 and became multi-segment firms under SFAS No. 14 used the flexibility under the old standard to conceal disclosures of highly profitable or poorly performing segments. However, they only find evidence for potential **proprietary costs as managers try to hide profitable segments in less competitive industries** rather than obscuring poorly performing segments to avoid agency problems. Hence, they conclude that SFAS No. 131 led to the disclosure of information that was withheld by managers under the old regime.

Hope/Thomas (2008) empirically investigate whether the removal of the mandatory disclosure of geographical earnings is potentially exploited by managers by engaging in **value-destroying foreign investments** ("empire building"). The authors argue that mangers – when not appropriately monitored – conduct more foreign investments that are motivated by self-interests as they try to "build up an empire" which can be detrimental to shareholders' interests. In fact, they find for a sample of 502 U.S. multinational firms over a ten year period around the introduction of SFAS No. 131 in 1997 that firms which stop to report geographical earnings show more foreign sales and lower foreign profit margins in the post-adoption period. They interpret their findings as evidence that geographical segment disclosure requirements under SFAS No. 131 **adversely affect monitoring** mechanisms of shareholders and thus induce agency costs.

Other literature

Maines et al. (1997) take a different approach and analyze the impact of SFAS No. 131 in an **experiment with 56 financial analysts**. In this experiment, financial analysts receive segment reports that are either congruent or not congruent with internal reporting systems. The authors factorially cross the congruence dimension with another dimension which reflects whether segments are clustered in an either similar or dissimilar way in terms of products or customers. They examine the analysts' confidence in forecasts and the analysts' perceived reliability of segment information in this 2x2 setting. *Maines et al.* (1997) document more confidence and higher perceived reliability if internal and external segmentation are congruent. In these cases, the perception of analysts does not change along the similarity dimension. However, if internal and external segmentation are incongruent, analysts are more confident and deem segment information as more reliable when similar instead of dissimilar segments are clustered. *Maines et al.* (1997)'s results signal that **congruence in internal and external segmentation** (management approach) enhances segment reporting and support the decision of the FASB to introduce SFAS No. 131.

Table 3-3 presents the studies on the economic consequences of introducing SFAS No. 131.

Studies on the economic consequences of SFAS No. 131			
	Reference	**Sample**	**Findings**
Earnings forecast properties	Venkataraman (2001)	566 U.S. firms, 1998-1999	Forecast accuracy improves for firms that change their segmentation upon SFAS No. 131's adoption.
	Behn et al. (2002)	172 U.S. firms, 1996-1997	Predictive ability of mechanical forecast models based on geographical segment data improves after the introduction of SFAS No. 131.
	Berger and Hann (2003)	2,589 U.S. firms, 1997-1998	Some information under SFAS No. 131 was already known under the old regime. Still, there is a significant increase in forecast accuracy for firms that changed the number of segments upon SFAS No. 131's adoption.
	Botosan and Stanford (2005)	1,230 U.S. firms, 1997-1998	Overall forecast accuracy decreases upon SFAS No. 131's adoption, which could be driven by financial analysts more relying on publicly available information.
	Hope et al. (2006)	688 U.S. firms, 1997-1999	Overall forecast accuracy increases after the adoption of SFAS No. 131. Firms that cease to report geographical earnings under the new standard also show increased forecast accuracy.
	Ettredge et al. (2005)	6,827 U.S. firms, 1995-2002	The introduction of SFAS No. 131 improves the market's ability to predict future earnings.
Value Relevance	Hossain and Marks (2005)	78 U.S. firms, 1999-2001	Interim geographical segment disclosures under SFAS No. 131 are value relevant.
	Hossain (2008)	127 U.S. firms, 1996-2001	General value relevance of quarterly geographical sales increases upon SFAS No. 131's adoption.
	Hope et al. (2008)	2,187 U.S. firms, 1992-2004	Increase in the foreign earnings response coefficient after the adoption of SFAS No. 131.
	Hope et al. (2009)	719 U.S. firms, 1998-2004	Foreign earnings are value relevant under SFAS No. 131.

-Table is continued on the next page-

	Berger and Hann (2003)	2,589 U.S. firms, 1997-1998	Firms that turn from single-segment to multi-segment under SFAS No. 131 experience a significant decrease in diversification discount.
Agency cost	Botosan and Stanford (2005)	1,230 U.S. firms, 1997-1998	Before the introduction of SFAS No. 131 firms tried to hide profitable segments in less competitive industries.
	Hope and Thomas (2008)	502 U.S. firms, 1992-2002	Geographical segment disclosure requirements under SFAS No. 131 adversely affect monitoring mechanisms of shareholders.
Other	Maines et al. (1997)	Experiment with 56 financial analysts	Financial analysts are more confident in their forecast and deem segment information as more reliable if the internal and external segmentation are congruent.

Table 3-3: Overview of economic consequences studies of SFAS No. 131

3.2.2   Studies on the impact of IFRS 8

Since IFRS 8 became effective in 2009, only a few studies analyze the **economic consequences of its adoption** to this point. There are some working papers that were quoted in the review of academic literature of the PIR. As of now, however, most of these papers are not publicly available. The only study is *Kajüter/Nienhaus* (2013) which is the first to analyze the impact of IFRS 8's adoption on the **value relevance of segment reporting**. *Kajüter/Nienhaus* (2013) investigate segment reports under IAS 14R and IFRS 8 of the 160 largest listed German firms (H-DAX and SDAX) for the period from 2007 to 2010. They find that while there is a decrease in the value relevance of consolidated financial statements from the IAS 14R period (2007-2008) to the IFRS 8 period (2009-2010), the value relevance of segment reports increases. Moreover, they exploit the unique setting that some firms did not have to change their segment reporting practices upon IFRS 8's adoption as they already reported segment information in compliance with the management approach under IAS 14. Hence, they employ a difference-in-differences design to isolate the effect of the IFRS 8's adoption from other confounding time effects. Results show that only firms that had to change their segment reporting upon adoption of the new standard experienced a significant **increase in value relevance of segment reports**. Furthermore, they use a unique sample of segment reports for the same year and the same company but different standards and find a superior value relevance of segment reports under IFRS 8.

Studies on the economic consequences of IFRS 8		
Reference	**Sample**	**Findings**
Kajüter and Nienhaus (2013)	160 German firms, 2007-2010	Segment reports under IFRS 8 are more value relevant compared to segment reports under IAS 14R.

Table 3-4: Overview of economic consequences studies of IFRS 8

3.3   Summary and research gap

In essence, the **descriptive** studies on the impact **SFAS No. 131's** adoption show that the fineness of segmentation increased while the information available for each segment did not change substantially. All results, however, have to be interpreted carefully as changes in segment reporting might be driven by other factors than the change in reporting requirements. In addition, results should not be compared to studies on the impact of IFRS 8, as SFAS No. 14 is entirely different from IAS 14R. A further drawback is that the studies only focus on the largest of U.S. companies.

In a similar vein, most of the **descriptive** studies indicate that the introduction of **IFRS 8** led to an increase in the number of reported segments while findings for the number of reported line items show a decrease. There is also a fair number of companies that did not change their segment reporting upon adoption of the new standard. Moreover, results from different studies show that the impact does not seem to be similar in each country. However, some of the studies suffer from weak research designs that cannot separate the effect of the standard change from other influences. Additionally, evidence for German firms is restricted to early adopters (*Blase/Müller* (2009); *Matova/Pelger* (2010)) or lacks a sufficient comparison with IAS 14R (*Weißenberger/Franzen* (2011)). Hence, this study adds to the literature by providing comprehensive evidence on the impact of IFRS 8 on segment reporting practice for the largest sample of German firms thus far, based on a research design that is capable of isolating the effect of the standard change from other concurrent developments. Moreover, this study provides very detailed descriptive information in different areas of segment reporting that goes beyond what other studies have investigated thus far.

Studies on the **economic consequences of SFAS No. 131's** introduction indicate an improvement in forecast accuracy, value relevance and better monitoring for shareholders. However, similar to the descriptive studies, these results cannot simply be transferred to the introduction of IFRS 8 for several reasons. First, the standard preceding SFAS No. 131 in the U.S. (SFAS No. 14) is utterly **different from IAS 14R** as it required far less extensive disclosures. Thus, it is difficult to attribute the findings of U.S. studies to the introduction of the management approach or merely to an increase in disclosures or maybe to both.

Second, many of these prior studies on SFAS No. 131 suffer from **weak research designs**. For instance, *Behn et al.* (2002) use mechanical forecast models to draw inferences on the predictive ability of segment data. These models, however, are not comparable to the work of financial analysts who use more information than historical earnings time series data. Moreover, several studies rely on the relationship between stock returns and current as well as future earnings (e.g., *Ettredge et al.* (2005); *Hope et al.* (2008); *Hope et al.* (2009); *Park* (2011)). They use the extent of statistical association between stock data and accounting data to conclude whether the adoption of SFAS No. 131 improved the market's predictive ability (*Ettredge et al.* (2005); *Park* (2011)) or the value relevance of segment information (*Hope et al.* (2008); *Hope et al.* (2009); *Kajüter/Nienhaus* (2013)). It is, however, questionable how these concepts map into the objective of IFRS to provide decision useful information. Furthermore, *Holthausen/Watts* (2001) argue that mere statistical associations have limited implications or inferences for standard setting (*Holthausen/Watts* (2001), p. 3). This study circumvents these shortcomings by analyzing the effect of IFRS 8 from multiple perspectives. Moreover, the proxies used in this study provide a more direct test of IFRS 8's economic consequences compared to the traditional association studies.

Third, the accounting history in Germany is based on the **duality of books**. Traditionally, German firms have one set of books for financial accounting and another for management accounting whilst U.S. firms usually employ just one set of books for both purposes (*Kaplan/Atkinson* (1998); *Haller/Park* (1999)). In Germany, managerial accounting data often incorporates imputed costs and omits neutral expenses (*Schildbach* (1997); *Wagenhofer* (2008)). Although there has been a recent tendency for German multinational firms to employ an integrated accounting system with one set of books (*Jones/Luther* (2005)), this development has not yet affected all German firms and non-IFRS figures might still be used a lot more than in other countries. These non-IFRS figures have to be reported in the segment report under the management approach.

Fourth, there are substantial **cultural differences** between Germany and the U.S. This is particularly important with respect to the perception of segment information based on the management approach. For instance, Germans tend to be more uncertainty avoidant (*Hofstede* (2001); *House et al.* (2004)) and thus prefer more uniform and consistent accounting practices among different firms (*Gray* (1988)). Contrastingly, the management approach allows for more flexibility and potentially managerial discretion. This might lead to an entirely different reaction upon the introduction of the management approach in Germany (and similar countries) compared to the U.S.

Finally, the **German capital market differs** substantially from the U.S. market (*Glaum/Street* (2003), p. 65). In the past and still for smaller and medium-sized German entities, the main source of debt financing is bank loans (*Alexander/Nobes* (2007)). Contrastingly, in the U.S. capital markets are more frequently used even by smaller firms to raise funds. Moreover, in Germany, users of capital markets are rather institutional investors such as pension funds or insurance companies than plenty of small private investors which is more often the case in the U.S. (*Alexander/Nobes* (2007)). Hence, it is questionable whether the introduction of segmental disclosures based on the management approach will induce the same impact in Germany (or similar countries) as markets that have a more pronounced institutional investor base might process and use new information differently.

Hence, there is rather **need for research** on the economic consequences of IFRS 8's adoption. This view is supported by the findings of the academic staff paper prepared for the post-implementation review process from January 2013, which underlines that there is no academic evidence on the economic consequences of IFRS 8's adoption in terms of information asymmetry, cost of capital, and analysts' information environment (*IASB* 2013, p. 7).

This study directly addresses these three **gaps** in the literature. The analysis from three different perspectives sheds light on the implications for information asymmetry, cost of capital and financial analysts' information environment. Moreover, in contrast to U.S.

research that analyzes the effect of SFAS No. 131, this study isolates the effect of a change in fundamental concepts from a mere increase in segment disclosures. Hence, this study contributes above and beyond extant literature.

4 Theory and hypotheses development

This chapter lays the theoretical foundation of this study and derives hypotheses. First, the principal agent theory and the efficient market hypothesis are introduced. They provide the underlying framework and justification for the subsequent discussion of the link between disclosures and the three capital market perspectives. Second, the impact of introducing the segment report to the decision usefulness of segment information is discussed. Based on this, hypotheses for the expected change in segment reporting practices and the economic consequences are derived.

4.1 Theoretical foundation

4.1.1 Fundamental theories

4.1.1.1 Principal agent theory

The principal agent theory was developed by *Jensen/Meckling* (1976). It is part of the **new institutional economics**[31] and deals with the relationship in which one party (i.e., the principal) delegates work to another party (i.e., the agent), who carries out that work (*Eisenhardt* (1989), p. 58).

There are two branches in the agency theory literature. First, **positivist agency literature** identifies constellations in which principals' and agents' objectives are incompatible and derives mechanisms to limit potential malbehavior of agents with a particular focus on the shareholder management relationship. This branch is more empirically-focused. Second and in contrast, **normative principal agency literature** is broader, more abstract as well as mathematical. It is based on microeconomics and deals with the maximization of individual utility functions. Normative principal agency literature is non-empirical (*Richter/Furubotn* (2010), p. 176). This study is based on the positivist agency literature since it uses a positive and empirically-focused research strategy in the context of the shareholder management relationship.

Jensen/Meckling (1976) define an agency relationship as:

> "... a contract under which one or more persons (the principal(s)) engage another person (the agent) to perform some service on their behalf which involves delegating some decision making authority to the agent."

> (*Jensen/Meckling* (1976), p. 308)

The principals entrust the agent with an **assignment**, for instance, shareholders hire a management to govern the company. It is assumed that there are **information asymmetries** and partially **conflicting objectives** among principals and agents (*Spremann* (1990), pp. 562–563; *Pfaff/Zweifel* (1998), p. 184). With regard to the shareholder management

---

[31] The term "new institutional economics" was first established by *Williamson* (1975). It also builds on work by *Coase* (1937); *Coase* (1960); *Demsetz* (1967); *Demsetz* (1969); *Cheung* (1970); *Cheung* (1973) and *North* (1990). The new institutional economics also includes the property rights theory and the transaction cost theory. For a comprehensive review refer to *Richter/Furubotn* (2010).

example, it is apparent that management is superiorly informed as it has plenty of inside information that is unknown to shareholders.[32] Moreover, while shareholders are interested in maximizing the return on their investment through stock value or dividends (total shareholder return), management may pursue different objectives such as compensation maximization or empire building. Although shareholders can evaluate the outcome of the assignment (profit, shareholder value or another measure of interest), it is difficult for them to disentangle in how far the outcome is determined by the management's efforts or exogenous events that are out of the management's control.

This constellation allows the agent **room for discretion** and **opportunistic behavior** (*Meinhövel* (2005), p. 65; *Ross* (1973), pp. 134–139 and *Hartmann-Wendels* (1989), pp. 716–718). In the following, potential problems and means to mitigate those are presented in detail and discussed in light of segment reporting.

Agency problems, agency costs and means of mitigation

Problems that arise due to agency relationships with information asymmetries and conflicting objectives can be classified as **pre and post contract conclusion** problems (e.g., *Hart/Holmström* (1987), p. 76; *Watrin* (2001), pp. 39–40).

Before contract conclusion, it is difficult for the principal to evaluate the agent's characteristics. This problem is often referred to as **hidden characteristics** (*Göbel* (2002), p. 101; *Breid* (1995), p. 824). Due to information asymmetries, the actual quality of the agent's services is unknown to the principal and, thus, he only pays an average compensation (*Horsch* (2005), p. 86). This causes the adverse selection problem as illustrated by *Akerlof* (1970): Agents with above average quality will cease to offer. This reduces the average quality of offered services and principals will adjust the average compensation downward. As a result, this will finally lead to a breakdown of the market.

After contract conclusion, the agent can take advantage of information asymmetries to engage in actions that are unobservable for the principals, a problem which is referred to as **hidden actions** (*Hartmann-Wendels* (1989), p. 714). Agents may reduce their efforts (shirking) as this is not directly apparent for principals (*Decker* (1994), p. 20). Moreover, agents may consume resources provided by the principals for own purposes (consumption on the job).

Although principals may be able to observe the actions of agents after contract conclusion, they are unable to assess them (*Stiglitz/Weiss* (1981), pp. 393–398; *Arrow* (1985), pp. 38–39). With **hidden information**, principals cannot evaluate whether the agents' actions are beneficial to them or motivated by the agents' own self-maximizing interests (fringe benefits). Hence, the principals face moral hazard (*Arrow* (1985), p. 38).

Jensen/Meckling (1976) define the costs that arise in agency relationships as **agency costs**, which comprise three different components (*Jensen/Meckling* (1976), p. 308): First, principals supervise the agents' behavior or incentivize them to make the agents behave in the principals' interest. This supervision, however, causes **monitoring costs**. Second, there are

---

[32] Examples of principal agency relationships are manifold: For instance, employer and employee, citizen and state, voters and politicians, patient and doctor.

bonding costs for agents that are incurred for actions that mitigate information asymmetries or harmonize objectives (such as signaling or reporting). The third component is the **residual loss**, which reflects the loss in welfare due to the deviation of the agents' actual behavior based on an optimal bonding and monitoring from the welfare maximizing optimum from the principals' perspective (*Göbel* (2002), p. 125; *Meinhövel* (2005), p. 73).

Agency costs are the sum of all three components. The magnitude of agency costs is increasing with the size and complexity of firms as bigger and more complex firms likely show more information asymmetries (*Jensen/Meckling* (1976), p. 305). One approach to mitigate information asymmetries is suggested by the signaling theory: Before contract conclusion, principals may carefully observe and screen the agents' behavior (**screening**) (*Stiglitz* (1975); *Kräkel* (2007), pp. 29–31). After contract conclusion, principals may supervise the actions of the agents or establish supervision bodies (**monitoring**) (*Göbel* (2002), p. 112).

Agents can also undertake actions that mitigate agency problems. For instance, before contract conclusion, the agents may attempt to credibly signal their characteristics (**signaling**) to avoid problems arising from hidden characteristics (e.g., *Spence* (1973), p. 357). After contract conclusion, the agents may have incentives to regularly report about their activities and thus provide transparency (**reporting**) (*Spence* (1973), p. 355; *Breid* (1995), p. 824).

With regard to the shareholder management relationship, **financial reporting** can be an instrument to reduce agency costs and to make the agents act in the principals' interests. In particular, financial statements and other financial disclosures are signaling and reporting means. Management can signal potential investors that their firm is a good investment (**signaling**) or confirm current investors in their investment decision (**reporting**).

Segment reports are a part of financial disclosures and thus also a way to mitigate problems arising from principal agent relationships. Moreover, segment reports are particularly suited to help investors in estimating future cash flows and thus in assessing a potential investment (signaling). Furthermore, segment reports provide a detailed picture of the company's and managers' performance which helps investors to better assess the managers' performance (reporting): For instance, managers cannot easily conceal unprofitable segments by cross-subsidization. Hence, this study considers segment reporting as an instrument of the principal agent theory that is used for signaling and reporting purposes to reduce agency costs.

4.1.1.2 Efficient market hypothesis

The efficient market hypothesis is the foundation for capital market-based research. The theory was developed by Eugene Fama (*Fama* (1965); *Fama* (1970); *Fama* (1991)). He defines an **efficient market** as:

"*A market in which prices always 'fully reflect' available information.*"

(*Fama* (1970), p. 383)

Fama (1970) derives three conditions that contribute to the efficient adjustments of security prices (*Fama* (1970), pp. 387–388): First, there are **no transaction costs**. Second, **information is costlessly** available. Third, there is a **consensus** in the belief of the implications of current information for future stock prices. It is obvious that real life markets fall short in one or more of these aspects. Therefore, *Fama* (1970) defines three different categories of market efficiency (*Fama* (1970), p. 388):

- Under the **weak form** efficiency, the only information set relevant for pricing is current or historical prices (*Wagenhofer/Ewert* (2007), p. 92). Stock prices or successive price changes are serially independent and thus follow a random walk. This implies that an analysis of stock price patterns will not generate excess returns.

- Under the **semi-strong form** efficiency, all publicly available information is instantaneously impounded into prices. The relevant information set, for instance, comprises historical price data, financial disclosures, media releases and other publications of a firm. Trading strategies based on this information set do not yield excess returns. Solely insider-based trading may generate abnormal returns ((*Schildbach* (1986), p. 11).

- Under the **strong form** efficiency, all information – private and public – is impounded into prices. This implies that even insider-based trading strategies do not generate excess returns (*Lindemann* (2004), p. 14).

Following *Fama* (1970), the strong form efficiency is a rather theoretical construct (*Fama* (1970), p. 414):

> "*One would not expect such an extreme model to be an exact description of the world, and it is probably best viewed as a benchmark against which the importance of deviations from market efficiency can be judged.*"

Empirical findings also support the notion that capital markets are not strong form efficient (e.g., *Jaffe* (1974); *Möller* (1985); *Laffont/Maskin* (1990)). Furthermore, empirical research has shown that stock prices reflect financial information, which contradicts the weak form efficiency. In general, the **semi-strong** form efficiency is **widely accepted** in the literature (e.g., *Beaver* (1972), pp. 418–420).

This study also assumes semi-strong efficient capital markets. This assumption **provides the justification** for using capital market data for the analysis of a change in the information environment. Segment reports are publicly available and thus they are impounded in stock prices under the efficient market hypothesis. Therefore, an analysis of bid-ask prices is a legitimate approach to gauge the impact of a change in the public information component.[33] Moreover, the semi-strong efficiency assumption also provides justification for **using financial analyst data**. Under the strong-form efficiency, financial analysts would be redundant as all information is already impounded in prices and there is no

---

[33] The efficient market hypothesis does not detail the use of bid-ask prices, it is rather a theory that supports the use of stock price data in general. There is, however, evidence that shows how characteristics of stock price data such as bid or ask prices can be used to draw more meticulous inferences on the general information environment. Section 4.1.3.1 describes this in more detail.

need for information intermediaries (*Henze* (2004), p. 9). Hence, this assumption is a necessary requirement for studying financial analysts.

The following sections build on the principal agent theory, which considers segment reporting as a reporting and signaling instrument, and on the efficient market hypothesis, which provides justification for analyzing capital market data. First, it is analyzed how the adoption of IFRS 8 affects the quality of segment disclosures. Subsequently, the effect of a change in the quality of segment disclosures for each of the three different capital market perspectives is delineated in a theoretical framework.

4.1.2 Theoretical assessment of the impact of the management approach on the quality of segment disclosures

This study defines high quality disclosure as information that is decision useful. Similarly, the purpose of financial reporting under IFRS is to provide **decision useful** information to (potential) investors, lenders and other creditors (IFRS Conceptual Framework.OB2). Decisions by these parties largely depend on the expected future returns of an entity. Hence, information that helps to gauge the amount, timing and uncertainty of future net cash flows to the entity is decision useful (IFRS Conceptual Framework.OB2). In particular, the IASB describes six qualitative characteristics for information to be decision useful. The two fundamental qualitative characteristics are relevance and faithful representation (IFRS Conceptual Framework.QC5). Comparability, verifiability, timeliness and understandability are enhancing qualitative characteristics supporting the decision usefulness of financial information (IFRS Conceptual Framework.QC19). The following sections discuss the impact of introducing the management approach to segment reporting on the qualitative characteristics of decision usefulness.

4.1.2.1 Relevance

According to the conceptual framework, information is relevant if it "*is capable of making a difference in the decisions made by users*" (IFRS Conceptual Framework.QC6). Moreover, to be capable of **making a difference** in decisions, information must have predictive or confirmatory value (IFRS Conceptual Framework.QC7). Information has predictive value if users of financial statements can use it as an input for predicting future outcomes (IFRS Conceptual Framework.QC8) and it has confirmatory value if it provides feedback about previous predictions (IFRS Conceptual Framework.QC9).

The **key characteristic** of segment information based on the management approach is that it is the same information which is used by management. In general, information prepared for financial reporting is influenced by national or international regulations and thus may not be sufficient for management purposes (*Müller et al.* (2005), p. 2121). Hence, most entities implement internal management and reporting systems that provide information helping management to make value-maximizing decisions. (*Haller/Park* (1999), pp. 62–63). In terms of relevance and information content, the information used by management should yield more relevant information than the information solely prepared for external reporting. Hence, if internal information is disclosed due to the adoption of the management approach, it should increase the relevance of segment information.

Findings of the Jenkins Report indicate that information based on the management approach facilitates better **monitoring** by users of financial statements and thus decreases information asymmetries (*AICPA* (1994)). Additionally, *Maines et al.* (1997) find that financial analysts show more confidence in their forecast if internal and external segment definitions are congruent. Furthermore, *Ernst & Young* (1998) claim that segment reports under the management approach enhance the evaluation of future cash flow prospects, which signals an improved **predictive value**.

However, not every piece of information used by the management must be relevant for users of financial statements. Hence, users might face an **information overload problem** if too much information, which is solely relevant for the management, is communicated to them (*Blase* (2011), p. 27). Moreover, if internal measurements such as inter-segment transfer prices are set to incentivize sub-level managers in a specific way, it may be that these measurements are not optimal for the decision making of users of financial statements (*Blase* (2011), pp. 28–29).

In **summary**, however, the introduction of the management approach to segment level information should increase the relevance of segment information compared to segment information based on the risk-and-reward approach.

4.1.2.2   Faithful representation

"To be useful, financial information must not only represent relevant phenomena, but it must also faithfully represent the phenomena that it purports to represent."

(IFRS Conceptual Framework.QC12)

The IASB defines three criteria for information to be faithfully represented: it has to be complete, neutral and free from error. A **complete** representation entails that users receive all necessary descriptions and explanations for understanding the process of determining the numerical or verbatim depiction of particular information (IFRS Conceptual Framework.QC13). **Neutrality** demands that the depiction is unbiased in the selection or presentation of information (IFRS Conceptual Framework.QC14). **Free from error** requires that the information is described without errors or omissions (IFRS Conceptual Framework.QC15). In total, faithful representation entails that information is not biased or manipulated to influence the perception of users of financial statements.

When the management approach was introduced to segment level information in IFRS, it was **criticized** for offering more room for discretion compared to the risk-and-reward approach (*European Parliament* (2007*a*)). Moreover, as discussed in section 2.1.5.2, segment reporting under the management approach is more prone to the circularity and manipulation effect, which impair the faithful representation of segment information. For instance, firms can potentially avoid the disclosure of a specific (finer) segmentation if they introduce another (more aggregated) reporting level and deem this as the CODM-level. Additionally, firms could just add IFRS-conform numbers to their pro-forma measures in the internal reports and thus avoid disclosures of the pro-forma measures as IFRS 8.26 requires reporting the number which is most consistent with IFRS. The extent to which entities may be able to use this discretion, however, is limited by the auditor's engagement.

Moreover, *Hartle* (1984) argues that the reliability of financial disclosures is not only driven by the potential room for managerial discretion, but also by the management's **incentives** to exploit this room (*Hartle* (1984), pp. 77–85). In the context of the management approach, *Kirsch et al.* (2010) note that the management may have fewer incentives to manipulate internal measures since they rely on these measures for resource allocation and performance evaluation purposes. Hence, manipulation may impair the management's own decision making.

On the one hand, there is more room for managerial discretion. On the other hand, management has fewer incentives to exercise this discretion. Thus, the impact of introducing the management approach to segment reporting on the faithful representation of segment information is **unclear.**

4.1.2.3 Enhancing qualitative characteristics

The enhancing qualitative characteristics comparability, verifiability, timeliness and understandability are used to decide between two ways to depict financial information if both are equally relevant and faithfully represented (IFRS Conceptual Framework.QC19).

Comparability means that users can compare the information with other entities (intercompany) or with the same entity for another period (inter-temporal) (IFRS Conceptual Framework.QC21). With regard to the management approach, the European Parliament was concerned that the introduction of IFRS 8 would decrease the comparability of segment reports (*European Parliament,* (2007*a*)). In fact, there is much more flexibility in the definition of segments under the management approach compared to the risk-and-reward approach. It is possible that firms in the same industry and with identical business activities report entirely different segments (*Maier* (2008), p. 256). Moreover, the management approach introduces a wider variability of segment items that are disclosed by different entities. Hence, there is less standardization (*Blase* (2011), pp. 36–37). In terms of inter-temporal comparability, there may also be more variability in the segment definition or the items reported as any time an entity changes its internal reporting, for instance due to chief executive officer (CEO) turnovers, it has to change its segment report as well. Yet, international comparability may increase due to the convergence of segment reporting requirements with US-GAAP. In sum, however, it is expected that the comparability of segment disclosures under the management approach will decrease compared to the risk-and-reward approach.

Verifiability means that different observers would reach the same conclusion that the depiction of a certain economic phenomenon is faithfully represented (IFRS Conceptual Framework.QC27). With regard to segment reporting under the management approach, the verifiability of segment information largely depends on the auditor because users of financial statements cannot check the consistency of internal and external information. If the auditors have access to internal reporting and protocols of management, they should be able to verify the consistency of internal and external information (*Böcking/Benecke*

(1999), p. 840; *Blase* (2011), p. 40). It is, however, questionable whether the auditors will c.p. be able to do so unless provided with more time for the audit.

Timeliness entails that decision-makers are provided with the information in time that it can still influence their decisions (IFRS Framwork.QC29). When preparing segment information for financial reporting, IFRS 8 should speed up the process as segment information is already at hand. A substantial impact on the timeliness of annual financial reporting information is questionable as it is just a fraction of financial disclosures. However, there may be the potential to decrease the reporting lag particularly of interim reports.

Understandability requires information to be presented in a way that it is understandable for users of financial statements (IFRS Conceptual Framework.QC30). To the extent that IFRS 8 leads to the disclosure of non-IFRS-conform measures, users may have difficulties in understanding them.

4.1.3 Theoretical framework of the capital market perspectives

Next, a theoretical framework for each of the three perspectives that delineates on the theoretical link between disclosures and economic consequences for investors, companies and financial analysts is introduced. "Disclosures" is a broad term which can be manifold. It comprises, for instance, annual reports, earnings announcements, financial analysts' reports, non-accounting information such as newspaper coverage. This study focuses on one specific aspect of information – financial disclosures. As elaborated before, this study defines the term "high quality financial disclosures" as financial information that is both relevant as well as faithfully represented and therefore decision useful (IFRS Conceptual Framework.QC5). In the following analyses, financial disclosures are assumed to be publicly available to every party concerned.[34]

4.1.3.1 Disclosure and information asymmetries

One of the most **fundamental links** in economic theory is the relationship between disclosure and information asymmetry. Information asymmetries arise when information is not equally distributed among all parties involved. In the secondary share market – that is investors trading with other investors – it means that there are uninformed or less informed investors and superiorly informed investors. When engaging in trade, the **uninformed investors** have to be concerned to trade with a **superiorly informed** counterparty (*Leuz/Wysocki* (2008)). Uninformed investors basically assume that informed investors only sell (buy) if the price is – relative to the private information – too high (low) (*Glosten/Milgrom* (1985)). Consequently, uninformed investors adjust the prices at which they are willing to trade to protect themselves against the potential losses when trading with superiorly informed counterparties. This kind of price adjustment is reflected in a **spread** between the price at which investors are willing to buy (bid) and at which they are willing to sell (ask).

---

[34] Note that this explicitly precludes private financial disclosures which are only available to particular individuals or groups (e.g., financial information such as internal budgets that are disclosed to potential buyers in a due diligence process).

Hence, information asymmetries introduce **adverse selection** into the secondary share market, which also impounds the number of stocks uninformed investors are willing to trade (*Leuz/Wysocki* (2008), p. 6). If it was certain to trade with informed investors, the share market would break down as illustrated by *Akerlof* (1970) and his example of the "market for lemons". The extent to which uninformed investors adjust prices depends on the **probability** to trade with superiorly informed investors and their respective **information advantage**. High quality disclosures can mitigate this problem in two ways and thus level the informational playing field (*Verrecchia* (2001)): First, more publicly available disclosures reduce the potential information advantage of informed investors. The level of information advantage simply decreases (c.p.). Second, more market-wide information increases the costs and makes it more difficult to obtain a private information advantage. Consequently, both, the probability to trade with superiorly informed investors as well as their potential information advantage attenuate and thus **less price protection** should occur and hence **share liquidity**[35] should improve (*Leuz/Wysocki* (2008), pp. 6–7).

Due to its strong theoretical foundation and proximity to the underlying concept as well as the common use in previous research (e.g., *Welker* (1995); *Healy et al.* (1999); *Leuz/Verrecchia* (2000)), this study uses the **bid-ask spread** to capture information asymmetry.

To comprehend how bid-ask spreads map into information asymmetry, one has to understand the **microstructure** of markets. The microstructure of a capital market determines how orders are placed, handled, and translated into trades and transaction prices (*Francioni et al.* (2008), p. 57). There are two fundamental **market concepts**: the dealer and the auction market.

In a **dealer market** market makers post prices at which they are willing to buy or sell a specific stock and thus provide liquidity to the market (*Huang/Stoll* (1996), p. 313). These market makers use their own capital to keep an inventory of stock that allows constant trading. To compensate for their services, they will buy stock at a lower price (bid price) compared to the price they sell stock (ask price) (*Madhavan* (2000), p. 212). Following *Demsetz* (1968), pp. 35–36:

"*The ask-bid spread is the markup that is paid for predictable immediacy.*"

A typical dealer market is the National Association of Securities Dealers Automated Quotation System (NASDAQ).

In contrast, market participants in an **auction market** directly transact with one another. They issue limit and market orders[36] and matching bids are paired and executed. It is the job of a different type of market maker, usually called "specialist", to match these orders and record unexecuted orders in an order book. A typical example of an auction market is the New York Stock Exchange (NYSE). There is usually just one specialist for each security, which is contrary to the multiple market makers for one security in a dealer market.

---

[35] Following *Lang/Maffett* (2010), liquidity is defined as "*the average ease, in terms of timeliness and cost, with which an investor can dispose of a position in a particular asset*" (*Lang/Maffett* (2010), p. 208).

[36] Limit orders are orders to buy (sell) if the price is below (above) a specific pre-set value. A market order is an order to buy or sell at current prices.

Today, many stock exchanges employ automated trading systems instead of specialists to match the orders (*Francioni et al.* (2008), p. 61). However, most markets are not only "pure" auction markets, but also allow for some market making: To maintain liquidity and trading at any time, specialists typically also place bids and offers (*Huang/Stoll* (1996), p. 314).

Following the analytical and empirical literature, the bid-ask spread comprises **three components** (e.g., *Copeland/Galai* (1983); *Glosten/Milgrom* (1985); *Glosten* (1987); *Glosten/Harris* (1988); *Grossman/Miller* (1988); *Hasbrouck* (1988)): First, **processing costs** for market makers who usually charge a fee for matching buy and sell orders or trading on their own accounts. Second, **inventory costs** are the costs of market makers for holding less than the optimal diversified portfolio. Third, there is an **information asymmetry component** for the risk of dealing with traders who are superiorly informed.

The relative magnitude of each component depends on market microstructure characteristics. There are empirical methods to **decompose** the spread and thus draw conclusions about the individual components (e.g., *Glosten/Harris* (1988); *Neal/Wheatley* (1998)). This study is only concerned with the spread arising from information asymmetry. All sample companies are traded via the electronic trading system XETRA of Deutsche Börse. The mircostructure of this system can be described as an **order-driven environment** (*Leuz/Verrecchia* (2000), p. 108).[37] There is continuous trading via an automated trading system as well as periodic call auctions in the beginning and end of each trading day (*Francioni et al.* (2008), p. 66). There are market makers – so-called designated sponsors – too. However, they quote prices mainly to ensure liquidity at any point in time and they are compensated by the issuing company for providing this service. Most of the trading occurs via the limit order book with other investors as actual counterparts. As a result, the spread under this system is represented as the highest bid and lowest ask prices among all limit orders in the automated trading system order book. Using this data is conceptually attractive as other components of the spreads such as inventory costs or monopoly gains of market makers are less relevant (*Leuz/Verrecchia* (2000), p. 109). Hence, the spreads used in this study largely reflect the information asymmetry component and there is no need for further decomposition.

In **summary**, if the introduction of the management approach to segment reporting improves financial disclosures (i.e., increased their decision usefulness), the informational playing field should be leveled. This in turn will mitigate information asymmetries and thus reduce bid-ask spreads.

4.1.3.2 Disclosure and cost of capital

The notion that more disclosure reduces the cost of capital is commonly acknowledged. For instance, Neel Foster, a former FASB member asserts:

---

[37] This is in contrast to the quote-driven dealer market which largely depends on the spreads quoted by market makers.

"More information always equates to less uncertainty, and it is clear that people pay more for certainty. [...] In the context of financial information, the end result is that better disclosure results in a lower cost of capital."

(*Foster* (2003), p. 1)

Although this idea might be intuitively appealing, the exact impact of disclosures via **various channels** on cost of capital is more complex and not as one-dimensional as outlined in the statement above. This section builds on some aspects of agency theory as detailed in the previous section to shed light upon the different features of this link.

Based on the link between disclosures and information asymmetry discussed in the previous section, the **information asymmetry component** in the cost of capital is **indirectly affected** by improved disclosures through stock liquidity. Limited tradability due to illiquid stocks and high bid-ask spreads imposes direct transaction costs on investors which they require compensation for in terms of higher security returns (*Amihud/Mendelson* (1986); *Constantinides* (1986)). Furthermore, the adverse selection problem goes back to the initial public offering (IPO) at the primary share market. Investors account for the potential future price protection they might face when trying to sell the shares on the secondary stock market and thus they pay less at the IPO (e.g., *Baiman/Verrecchia* (1996); *Verrecchia* (2001)). This in turn makes leads to less capital that firms can to raise.

A recent body of research has focused on the relationship between disclosures and **liquidity risk** instead of liquidity level. Investors are ultimately concerned about liquidity when they plan to trade and not about the current level. Accordingly, investors have a preference for high predictability of future liquidity. They associate highly fluctuating liquidity with increased uncertainty. In fact, *Acharya/Pedersen* (2005) demonstrate that the cost of capital is an increasing function of the covariance between firm-level liquidity and market liquidity. *Brunnermeier/Pedersen* (2009) show that liquidity can diminish due to a *"flight to quality"* (p. 2202) in times of financial distress. If there is uncertainty about the fundamental value, liquidity providers discard assets which show a high level of uncertainty about the fundamental value. If disclosures enhance transparency and facilitate better estimates of future cash flow, there is less uncertainty about the fundamental value of the firm and this potentially reduces the covariance of firm-level liquidity and market-wide liquidity (*Lang/Maffett* (2010), p. 216). Hence, high quality disclosures can reduce the risk induced by liquidity uncertainty and thus decrease the cost of capital.

Improved disclosures can also have a **direct impact** on the cost of capital of an entity. *Merton* (1987) introduces an intuitive model in which investors only know a fraction of all available securities and hence only trade securities that are known to them. Firms that are not widely known are not considered in a large number of potential investment choices and thus face a relatively low demand for their securities. This in turn results in a lower price and higher costs. Improved disclosures attract **investor attention** which potentially increases stock demand. This enlarges the investor base and improves risk sharing among investors which lowers cost of capital. However, this effect is negligible for the relatively large companies of this study which are widely known and a mere change in segment reporting should not affect the general level of investors' attention.

A different direct link between disclosure and the cost of capital is based on **estimation risk**. Estimation risk stems from the fact that underlying parameters are unknown and have to be estimated. Following the capital asset pricing model (CAPM), the beta factor helps investors to judge the associated systematic risk of a specific position. However, betas have to be estimated and increased disclosures help to attenuate parameter uncertainty and thus facilitate investors to increase the efficiency of their portfolios (*Lang/Maffett* (2010), p. 224).

To **sum up**, the different channels how disclosures potentially affect the cost of capital comprise the information asymmetry component, liquidity risk and uncertainty, investors' recognition and estimation risk. Although this theoretical framework provides a detailed description about the different links, the empirical analysis is not able to disentangle the various channels and thus gauges a joint impact. However, the general tenor in all channels is the same: an improvement in disclosures leads to a reduction in the cost of capital.

4.1.3.3 Disclosure and financial analysts' information environment

The **role of financial analysts** is largely regarded as information intermediaries of the capital market (*Chung/Jo* (1996), p. 493). They gather, process and distribute information (*Eberts* (1986), p. 98). Before laying out the theoretical framework, it is important to understand the **motivation** for studying financial analysts' information environment in the context of segment reporting. First, they are an important group of capital market participants and *Schipper* (1991) notes:

> "*Given their importance as intermediaries who receive and process financial information for investors, it makes sense to view analysts – sophisticated users – as representative of the group to whom financial reporting is and should be addressed.*"

> (*Schipper* (1991), p. 105)

Moreover, financial analysts are particularly **concerned with segment information**. The Association for Investment Management and Research (AIMR) points out that the need of financial analysts for disaggregated financial data

> "*... is vital, essential, fundamental, indispensable, and integral to the investment analysis process. Analysts need to know and understand how the various components of a multifaceted enterprise behave economically. [...] without disaggregation, there is no sensible way to predict the overall amounts, timing, or risks of a complete enterprise's future cash flows.*"

> (*AIMR* (1993), p. 59)

Furthermore, financial analysts have acknowledged the relevance of segment information prepared based on the **management approach** in the past:

"If we could obtain reports showing the details of how an individual business firm is organized and managed, we would assume more responsibility for making meaningful comparisons of those data to the unlike data of other firms that conduct their business differently."

(*AIMR* (1993), pp. 60–61)

This demand is directly addressed by the adoption of the management approach for segment reporting. Hence, analysts should be particularly affected by the introduction of IFRS 8 and thus it is reasonable to include an analysis from their perspective. There are two main types of financial analysts: buy side and sell side analysts:[38]

Buy side analysts are usually employed by money management firms such as funds or trusts (*Callsen-Bracker* (2007), p. 19). Based on their analyses, buy side analysts identify potential investment opportunities that are used by the funds or trusts to increase their portfolio's net worth (*Stubenrath* (2001), p. 22). The insights gained by these analysts, however, are not publicly available and hence academic research is seldom concerned with buy side analysts.

Sell side analysts are usually employed by broker or dealer firms and they issue forecasts and recommendations that are publicly available (*Groysberg et al.* (2008), p. 25). In general, single analysts cover 10-20 firms in a given industry sector (*Schipper* (1991), p. 112). They issue buy, hold, or sell recommendations based on an analysis of future earnings and cash flow potential. This study uses sell side analysts' forecasts due to their public availability.

The analysis of (sell side) financial analysts' information environment is based on the following **theoretical framework**: Each analyst receives two different signals about the future earnings of an entity (*Barron et al.* (1998), p. 422). One signal is publicly available and common to all analysts, for instance, financial statements or any press releases. The other signal is idiosyncratic to the individual analyst, for instance, through their own associations with the entity or distinctive information processing models (*Venkataraman* (2001), p. 3).[39] Subsequently, both signals are used to facilitate the earnings forecasts. Prior literature has shown that these signals can either be substitutes or complements.[40]

If signals are **substitutes**, an increase in the precision of public information will lead to less acquisition of private information. Put differently, if public information is sufficiently precise, financial analysts may cease to acquire more costly private information. Following

---

[38] There are also independent analysts who do not work for money management firms (*Weber* (2006), pp. 25–26). These analysts, however, usually do not play a role in empirical accounting research.

[39] For instance, a particular financial analyst may be a Certified Public Accountant who has a superior understanding when specific accruals will reverse and impact future earnings (*Barron et al.* (2002), p. 823). For a further discussion of this theoretical framework also refer to *Holthausen/Verrecchia* (1990); *Barry/Jennings* (1992) and *Abarbanell et al.* (1995).

[40] Some of the literature in the following discussion does not particularly focus on the behavior of financial analysts, but rather on investors. The arguments, however, apply for financial analysts in the same way as most of the results are based on analytical models which capture the behavior of homo oeconomicus.

Verrecchia (1982), public and idiosyncratic information signals can substitute each other when they are conditionally independent.[41]

If both signals are **complements**, an increase in the precision of the public signal will lead to more acquisition of private information. In an analytical analysis, *Kim/Verrecchia* (1991) demonstrate that a priori better informed investors acquire more private information upon an increase in the precision of the public signal. This in turn widens the gap between uninformed and informed investors.

Prior research has largely focused on the impact of changes in disclosures on the overall precision and dispersion of forecasts to draw conclusions whether public information increased in precision and is thus more informative (e.g., *Chen et al.* (1990); *Swaminathan* (1991); *Ayres/Rodgers* (1994); *Barron et al.* (1999); *Lang/Lundholm* (1996)). These studies usually infer from an increase in forecast accuracy (and a decrease in dispersion) that the quality of public information increased. However, this does not account for the **interplay** of a change in public information and the idiosyncratic information acquisition (*Venkataraman* (2001)). As elaborated above, the question whether public and private signals are **complements or substitutes** is not resolved and the answer largely depends on particular conditions. Hence, when assuming a substitutional relation it could well be the case that an increase in the precision of public information allows financial analysts to engage in less costly private information acquisition while keeping the precision of their forecasts constant due to better public information. In this case, an analysis of the forecast accuracy would indicate no impact of the change in disclosures, although the precision of public information increased. Hence, it is important to account for the relation between the impact of a change of public information on the idiosyncratic information component. This study explicitly distinguishes between both components by employing a model that is able to capture changes in the public and the private information signal (*Barron et al.* (1998)).

Finally, the overall information asymmetry between (potential) shareholders can also have an **indirect impact** on financial analysts' information environment since it may impact the demand for analysts' services. The incremental value of an analyst's coverage for investors is higher for more opaque firms with more information asymmetries. In contrast, analysts' may be opposed to follow non-transparent firms as there is less information available and hence there is more risk of making inaccurate forecasts. Since the exact impact is a priori uncertain, this indirect link between information asymmetry and financial analysts is not discussed further.[42]

In **summary**, the segment report is considered a public information signal. Hence, if the adoption of IFRS 8 changes the quality of publicly available information, a change in the financial analysts' information environment is expected. The direction of the change, however, depends on the exact interplay of the two information components.

---

[41] *Bushman* (1991), *Lundholm* (1991) and *Diamond* (1985) show other conditions which yield a substitutional relation between private and public information.

[42] In Figure 4-1 on the next page, this link is therefore depicted as a dotted line.

4.1.4 Summary

The principal agent theory and the efficient market hypothesis build the theoretical foundation of this study. The principal agent theory considers segment reporting as a reporting and signaling instrument and the efficient market hypothesis provides justification for analyzing capital market data.

The theoretical assessment of the impact introducing IFRS 8 on the quality of segmental disclosures shows that the relevance of segment information c.p. increases with the adoption of the management approach. On the other hand, the impact on the faithful representation is unclear. Moreover, there is less inter-company and inter-temporal comparability due to less uniform rules. There may also be a minor impact on the verifiability, timeliness and understandability of segments reports. Since all six qualitative characteristics **jointly determine** the decision usefulness of information according to the IFRS Conceptual Framework, it is unclear how the introduction of the management approach to segment information impacts the decision usefulness of segment reports.

However, if there is a change in the quality of disclosures, there will be an impact on each of the three capital market participants as elaborated above. This is summarized in Figure 4-1:

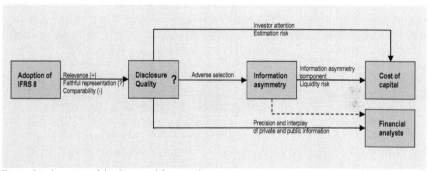

Figure 4-1: Summary of the theoretical framework

The three perspectives, in particular the information asymmetry component and the cost of capital, are neither independent nor mutually exclusive. Nevertheless, it is expected that all three perspectives indicate evidence in the same direction. The magnitude of the impact, however, may be different. Particularly the information asymmetry proxy is straightforward to measure and closely linked to the underlying concept. The other two proxies are based on sophisticated models that rest on several assumptions and thus may be more susceptible to measurement error and noise. The fact that the introduction of IFRS 8 directly addressed financial analysts' needs may also lead to a particularly pronounced effect from their perspective.

4.2   Hypotheses development

4.2.1   Changes in segment reporting practices

With the introduction of IFRS 8, the IASB hoped that entities would report segment information that is more consistent with other parts of the annual report and that some entities would report more segments (IFRS 8.BC9). Yet, the adoption of the management approach also introduced more flexibility to reporting and thus made it less predictable. The potential change in segment reporting practice largely depends on the proximity of segment reporting under IAS 14R to internal reporting. This is difficult to predict in a systematic manner. Hence, the following propositions[43] state in which areas a change is expected. However, they remain silent on the direction of the change. The propositions are derived on a broad level since there is no reasonable basis to derive expectations for several dimensions of segment reporting.[44] The following propositions can rather be regarded as guidance for **describing**[45] current accounting practice. The presentation of the empirical results will exceed the extent and detail of the questions raised in this section. Moreover, the results that are obtained – guided by these propositions – are necessary for the economic consequences analyses.

First, IFRS 8 requires more **narrative disclosures** than IAS 14R. For instance, factors used to identify segments, the basis of organization and types of products and services of each reportable segment have to be disclosed (IFRS 8.22).[46] Moreover, any potential differences of internally used measurements and general accounting principles have to be explained. These are two types of disclosure which were not required under IAS 14R. A different aspect that comes into play with the introduction of IFRS 8 is an enforcement issue: New standards are particularly often subject to enforcement scrutiny. In fact, the German Financial Reporting Enforcement Panel (FREP) declared in October 2009 that the implementation of IFRS 8 will be one of their main focus areas for 2010. Hence, the new requirements paired with increased scrutiny of auditors and enforcement institutions will likely have an impact on the extent of general narrative information:

> P_1:   *The extent of general (narrative) information changes after the adoption of IFRS 8.*

Second, as elaborated above, the IASB hoped that companies would **report more segments** under IFRS 8. Following *Botosan/Stanford* (2005), if given room for discretion,

---

[43]   Given the above argument, the term "hypothesis" is avoided and the expectations for the results of the content analysis in chapter five are labeled "propositions".

[44]   For instance, there may be a change in the basis of segmentation (business lines vs. geographical vs. matrix) for some companies, but there is neither a theoretical basis to predict a potential direction nor is there any reason to predict a change at all.

[45]   The description of accounting phenomena is in line with the positive nature of this study. The second part of the empirical analysis explains the impact of the particular accounting behavior.

[46]   Other narrative disclosures comprise the basis of inter-segment pricing, a discussion of any differences between the entity's and the segments' measures of profit or loss before tax, assets and liabilities, a discussion of any deviations from prior periods in the measurement basis of segment profits and a discussion of the nature and effect of any asymmetrical allocations (IFRS 8.27).

managers have proprietary cost motives to hide profitable segments in less competitive industries. *Berger/Hann* (2007) support this argument. They also find agency cost motives which prevent managers from disclosing segments that earn low abnormal profits which may lead to increased external monitoring. These **incentives** are similar under IFRS 8 and IAS 14R. However, under the management approach in IFRS 8, management may be less prone to manipulate the internal segmentation to avoid the disclosure of specific segments since management relies on this segmentation for resource allocation and performance evaluation purposes. Hence, manipulating the internal segmentation may impair management's own decision making.

Moreover, it is questionable whether IFRS 8 provides more **room for discretion**. In terms of segmentation, this study argues that the introduction of IFRS 8 increased reporting flexibility. For instance, firms can avoid the disclosure of a specific segmentation if another reporting level is introduced and deemed as the CODM-level. Other studies, however, maintain that there is **less discretion** under IFRS 8 compared to IAS 14R. *Trapp/Wolz* (2008) argue that managerial discretion was already given for segment reporting according to IAS 14R. Under IAS 14R, the segmentation is solely designed for external reporting purposes (*Trapp/Wolz* (2008), p. 87). Moreover, management only has to demonstrate the similarity of the risk-and-reward structures which is also subjective and discretionary (*Müller/Peskes* (2006), p. 819). It is easier for an auditor to compare the segmentation with internal documents (IFRS 8) than to judge the similarity of risk-and-reward structures (IAS 14R) (*Peskes* (2004), p. 354; *Trapp/Wolz* (2008), p. 88). Since it is a priori unclear how the incentives of management and the room for managerial discretion changed, it may or may not be that:

> P_2:   *The segmentation and in particular the number of reported segments change after the adoption of IFRS 8.*

Third, the basis of measurement under IAS 14R follows a "*full financial accounting approach*" (*Ulbrich* (2006), pp. 21–22). Financial information in the segment report is solely based on the **measurement principles** of the financial statements. In contrast, the management approach of IFRS 8 introduces more flexibility to the measurement of segment items. Thus, there should be a change in the measurement of segment items under IFRS 8. However, in case a firm already uses a fully harmonized management and financial accounting system (i.e., one-book system), the introduction of the management approach does not change much in terms of measurement. Hence, it is possible that:

> P_3:   *The measurement of segment items changes after the adoption of IFRS 8.*

A comparison of the reporting requirements for the **segments' line items** under IAS 14R and IFRS 8 shows substantial differences. While there are at least eight mandatory line items under IAS 14R for primary segments, IFRS 8 only requires the disclosure of a profit and loss measure for operating segments. Other line items such as revenues or assets[47] only

---

[47]   Refer to section 2.2.4.1 for a full list of the conditional disclosures.

have to be disclosed if reported to the CODM. Given management's **proprietary cost motives** and the conditional disclosure requirement, companies may try to avoid the disclosure of specific line items under IFRS 8. This is also in line with the circularity effect which states that management may manipulate internal reporting systems to avoid disclosure (e.g., *Himmel* (2004), p. 138). Hence, it is expected that:

> P_4:   *The extent of segment disclosures and in particular the number of reported segment line items change after the adoption of IFRS 8.*

The importance of reconciliations of segment to total amounts increases if items based on internal measurements are reported in the segment report. The IASB has addressed this issue by requiring firms to provide **reconciliations** of total segment revenue, total segment profit or loss or every other material item disclosed in accordance with IFRS 8.23 to the corresponding GAAP amounts (IFRS 8.28). Material reconciling items, for instance due to different accounting policies, must be described separately. Additionally, the increased enforcement pressure, as elaborated above, should also incentivize the provision of sound reconciliations under IFRS 8. Hence, it is expected that:

> P_5:   *The provision of reconciliation information changes after the adoption of IFRS 8.*

As described above, these five propositions form general pillars for the descriptive study of segment reporting practice in chapter five. The analysis will be more detailed by considering various additional aspects related to the propositions.

4.2.2   Economic consequences

In contrast to the previous section, there is a **sound theoretical foundation** for deriving hypotheses about the economic consequences of the adoption of IFRS 8. The general tenor of the theoretical framework for each perspective is that an improvement in disclosures will improve the situation of each major capital market participant. Hence, if one assumes that the introduction of IFRS 8 improved the quality of disclosures, information asymmetries and cost of capital should decrease and the reliance on the public information signal of financial analysts should increase.

However, it is not obvious whether disclosures have improved. The discussion of the theoretical impact of introducing IFRS 8 on disclosure quality draws an ambiguous picture: The relevance of segment reporting should increase. The effect on faithful representation is unclear since there is more flexibility and room for managerial discretion on the one hand, but fewer incentives for management to exploit this discretion on the other hand. Moreover, inter-company and inter-temporal comparisons should be more difficult. However, due to the convergence with US-GAAP, the potential for international comparability has increased. This ambiguity makes it difficult to derive the **direction of the change** in disclosure quality.

Additionally, empirical results of other studies in different settings indicate that there was not a **sizeable change** in segment reporting practice and thus in the quality of disclosures (in either direction) due to IFRS 8's adoption *on average*. Moreover, given the inherent measurement error and noise in empirical proxies, it is difficult to obtain significant results if the magnitude of the effect is small (*Kinney* (1986)).[48] To improve the power of the test, a researcher can either increase the sample size or improve the research design so that the magnitude of the effect increases. The former is not feasible at reasonable costs. The latter, however, is addressed in this study: The fact of having only a small effect of IFRS 8 on average is due to a substantial number of firms that already reported compliant to the management approach under IAS 14R. The research design in this study, however, focuses on the companies which changed their segment reporting practice. This naturally increases the magnitude of the effect and thus increases the power of the tests.

The ambiguity in the theoretical discussion whether IFRS 8 actually improved financial reporting quality does not allow for directional hypotheses. The research design, however, provides some confidence that if there is an effect in either direction, it is likely to be detected. Hence, the following non-directional **hypotheses** are posited:

H_1	*There will be a change in information asymmetries after the adoption of IFRS 8.*

H_2:	*There will be a change in the cost of capital after the adoption of IFRS 8.*

H_3	*There will be a change in the financial analysts' information environment after the adoption of IFRS 8.*

---

[48] It is difficult to obtain significant results, even if the fundamental relation is true.

5 Analysis of segment reporting practice

In the following, the descriptive analysis of segment reporting before and after the adoption of IFRS 8 is presented. Section 5.1 describes the methodological approach and the sample selection process. Section 5.2 presents the results organized along the five dimensions: general information, segmentation, measurement, disclosures and reconciliation.[49] The findings are discussed in section 5.3.

5.1 Methodological approach

5.1.1 Content analysis

5.1.1.1 Development of the catalogue

This study employs a **content analysis** to systematically capture the differences in segment reporting practice between IFRS 8 and IAS 14R. The content analysis is an empirical tool which is frequently used in accounting research.[50] It helps researchers to **describe** accounting practice in a structured way. *Berelson* (1971) defines it as follows:

> "*Content analysis is a research technique for the objective, systematic, and quantitative description of the manifest content of communication.*"

> (*Berelson* (1971), p. 18)

This definition entails three criteria that constitute desirable characteristics of a content analysis: objectivity, systematization and quantification.[51] **Objectivity** means that different researchers would generate the same findings based on the same content analysis catalogue (*Kassarjian* (1977), p. 9). Moreover, there should be **systematization** in the choice of items analyzed in the catalogue. This means that the inclusion or exclusion of items should be done according to a consistent set of rules (*Holsti* (1969), p. 4). Finally, the items should be **quantifiable** to allow statistical analysis and testing (*Kassarjian* (1977), pp. 9–10).

With regard to this study, the content analysis was conducted single-handedly by the author. This helps to avoid any bias that may result from cognitive differences among different analysts. Yet, to strengthen **objectivity** and to reduce the risk of inconsistencies which might result due to the collection over a three-month period, the author re-collected the first five companies for a second time after the initial data-collection was finished. However, there were not any differences in the observations that had been double-checked. Moreover, the content analysis catalogue was carefully designed and pre-tested with five randomly selected companies.

---

[49] In prior sections, reconciliation was subsumed under disclosures. However, due to the importance of reconciliations under IFRS 8, it is presented as a separate category in the following.

[50] For instance, most studies cited in section 3.1.1 and 3.1.2 use content analyses as primary research methods.

[51] See *Kassarjian* (1977), pp. 8–9, for an overview of other definitions commonly used in the literature. However, most of them agree that the distinctive features of a content analysis are objectivity, systematization and quantification.

In terms of **systematization**, the content analysis catalogue and thus the choice of relevant items was developed closely related to the actual standards IFRS 8 and IAS 14R. Most items yield a direct reference to standard requirements.[52] In addition, almost every item is a binary or category variable, which allows **quantification**.

General structure of the content analysis catalogue
A. General Information
▪ Year of IFRS 8's adoption ▪ Placement of the segment report ▪ Segment narratives ▪ Inter-segment pricing ▪ Role of the CODM
B. Segmentation
▪ Basis of segmentation ▪ Number of segments ▪ One segment companies ▪ Fineness of geographical segments ▪ Other separate positions ▪ Aggregation ▪ Consistency
C. Measurement
▪ Basis of measurement ▪ Non-IFRS line items
D. Disclosures
▪ Mandatory disclosures ▪ Voluntary disclosures ▪ Measures used to judge performance ▪ Second tier segment disclosures ▪ Information about major customers
E. Reconciliation
▪ Reconciliation information ▪ Magnitude of reconciliations

Figure 5-1: Content analysis catalogue

The content analysis catalogue has been **developed** based on five pillars: general information, segmentation, measurement, disclosures and reconciliation (see Figure 5-1). **General information** issues such as year of IFRS 8's adoption, placement of the segment report in the annual report, extent of segment narratives, inter-segment pricing and the role of the CODM. The category **segmentation** includes information about the basis of segmentation as well as number of segments, one segment companies, fineness of geographical segments, other separate positions, aggregation and consistency. **Measurement** deals with the basis of measurement for the segment line items and the usage of non-IFRS figures. **Disclosures** includes all mandatory and voluntary information such as line items, measures used to judge performance, second tier segment disclosures[53] and information about major customers. Finally, the **reconciliation** category provides information about all reconciled items, the corresponding positions and their magnitude. The five categories

---

[52] See Appendix for the references of specific items to the IFRS 8 and IAS 14R standards.
[53] In the following, secondary segments (under IAS 14R) and entity-wide disclosures (under IFRS 8) are labeled second tier segment information.

are chosen because they resemble the most important aspects of segment reporting in general. The items within the categories are selected for two reasons. First, these items are subject to **substantial changes** due to the adoption of IFRS 8 and thus reflect interesting areas for research. Second, some items are chosen since they substantially contribute to the **decision usefulness** of segment information. Although the latter reason is subjective and reflects the author's opinion, all items in this study cover at least all aspects that were analyzed by prior descriptive research on SFAS No. 131 and IFRS 8 in different settings.

The general structure of the content analysis catalogue is used for segment reports under IFRS 8 and IAS 14R. However, there are some adjustments necessary for the different standards. For instance, the classification of mandatory and voluntary items differs among IFRS 8 and IAS 14R. Moreover, there is also a "delta-sheet" in the content analysis catalogue that summarizes the **differences** between the two segments reports. For a detailed overview refer to the appendix, which contains all sub-sheets of the content analysis catalogue of this study.

5.1.1.2 Data collection process

Segment reports are part of the notes to financial statements. Annual reports including financial statements as well as segment reports were obtained from the **official website** of Deutsche Börse for each company of the sample. Retrieving annual reports from the individual investor relations websites was avoided because these websites may provide reports that were subsequently corrected or re-stated. It is, however, critical to analyze the very same information that investors and financial analysts had at the time they made their investment and forecast decisions. Otherwise, results of the economic consequences studies may be biased. After the collection of the annual reports, the date of IFRS 8's adoption was determined. This date varies from 2007 to 2009 due to early adopters. Subsequently, the content analysis was conducted based on the PDF versions of the annual reports. Most companies publish a German and an English annual report. However, there were a few companies that solely publish German reports. To ensure consistency, the analysis was run based on the German versions.[54]

The content analysis only considers disclosures with actual information content that is non-transitory. For instance, information about **non-recurring events** such as discontinued operations or reorganizations are disregarded when obtaining the word count of segment narratives. These disclosures are independent of the underlying standard. Additionally, any explanations of changes induced by the adoption of IFRS 8 were discarded. This allows a better comparability of segment disclosures under the two different standards.

5.1.2 Sample selection and distribution

The initial sample covers the 160 largest German public firms of the DAX, MDAX, TecDAX and SDAX stock indices as of January 1, 2010. These companies were chosen

---

[54] To check for the sensitivity of results, five companies were randomly chosen and the analysis was repeated based on the English versions. However, there were no differences except for the word count measures.

because they comprise the majority of the total German market capitalization. The **DAX** includes the 30 largest German companies according to market capitalization with a minimum free float of ten per cent.[55] The **MDAX** is a mid-cap stock index for the 50 largest German companies below the DAX constituents from classical industries. The **TecDAX** constitutes the 30 largest technology sector securities and the **SDAX** comprises the 50 largest companies (below the MDAX). To be part of any of these stock indices, companies have to fulfill the requirements of the **Prime Standard**. The Prime Standard is a market segment of the regulated market. Its transparency regulations exceed those of the General Standard. This includes quarterly reporting in German and English, ad-hoc disclosure also in German and English, publication of a financial calendar and staging a minimum of one analysts conference per year. Moreover, companies in any of these indices have to either have their legal or operational headquarters situated in Germany or their headquarters are situated in any EU or European Free Trade Association (EFTA) country and the majority of their securities' trading volume is generated at the Frankfurt Stock Exchange. Hence, the sample comprises highly transparent companies with a major interest in Germany.

For each company, the last year under IAS 14R and the first year under IFRS 8 are obtained. However, to ensure that any changes in segment disclosure practices are driven by the standard change and not by any concurrent developments, this study exploits that firms must provide prior year information in their current financial statements (based on the current accounting standards).[56] Therefore, in the first year of IFRS 8 (adoption year), the segment information for the prior year (historical year) had to be restated based on IFRS 8. This restated segment information is labeled **lag-adoption year**. Hence, comparing the lag-adoption year with the historical year yields segment reports for the same year and the same company, but under different standards. Figure 5-2 illustrates this approach and the general empirical timeline:

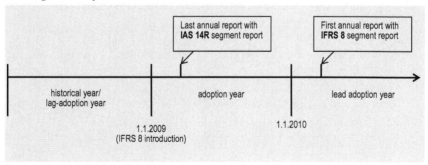

Figure 5-2: General empirical timeline
(Following *Berger/Hann* (2007), p. 9)

Two financial years for all DAX, MDAX, TecDAX and SDAX companies comprise 320 firm-year observations which provide a sufficient **number of observations** for the subse-

---

[55] Here and in the following cf. *Deutsche Börse AG* (2014), pp. 8–9.
[56] Refer to *Berger/Hann* (2007) for a similar approach used for an analysis of SFAS No. 131.

quent empirical analysis. However, to ensure comparability with other studies and due to data issues, certain sample selection criteria apply (Table 5-1):

Selection process of the final sample		
	Sample size	
	Firms	Firm years
Initial sample of DAX, MDAX, TecDAX and SDAX firms	160	320
less bank, insurance or financial sector firms	-20	-40
less no IAS 14R report/former US-GAAP reporters	-18	-36
less no segment report under either standard	-5	-10
less no annual report available	-3	-6
less entities with different currencies	-1	-2
less other reasons	-4	-8
Final sample	109	218

Table 5-1: Sample selection process

20 firms from the **financial sector** including banking, insurance or financial services are excluded from the sample as they differ substantially from other industries in terms of their business models and they are subject to different regulatory requirements.[57]

Moreover, with the mandatory introduction of IFRS in the EU in 2005, there was an exemption for former US-GAAP reporters to delay the adoption of IFRS until 2007. Since the introduction of the Kapitalaufnahmeerleichterungsgesetz in 1998, a substantial number of German firms started to voluntarily adopt US-GAAP or IFRS. Most former US-GAAP reporters in this sample took advantage of the exception rule and adopted IFRS in 2007. Being already used to the segment reporting requirements of SFAS No. 131, all of these firms adopted IFRS 8 early with the adoption of IFRS in 2007. Hence, 36 firm-years are eliminated since there is **no segment report under IAS 14R** available to allow for the comparison of the two standards.

Furthermore, there are five firms that **do not provide a segment report** under either standard. These firms claim to be operating in one segment only. For instance, the SKY Deutschland Group notes:

> "The application of this standard [IFRS 8] had no impact on the company's consolidated financial statements since the group operates in just one segment."

(*SKY Deutschland*, Annual Report 2009, p. 69)

These firms are **eliminated** from the sample since there is no segment information available.

Further, the annual reports of three firms could not be obtained due to a **delisting**. Therefore, these firms are removed from the sample as well.

---

[57] This is done in the majority of empirical accounting research studies (e.g., *Maury/Pajuste* (2005); *Faulkender/Petersen* (2006)) and also in studies related to segment reporting (e.g., *Blase/Müller* (2009); *Matova/Pelger* (2010)).

One firm does not report **in Euros** and is thus discarded. Four other firms are eliminated for other reasons including three firms that disclose segment information in a way that does not allow determining the IFRS 8's adoption date and one firm that still reports under US-GAAP. Hence, the final sample for the descriptive analysis includes 218 firm-year observations.

From the original 30 firms in the DAX, only 13 firms remain in the sample, which is the highest **drop-out rate** of all four indices. This is due to a substantial number of financial sector firms and former US-GAAP reporters in the DAX. For the other indices, the drop-out rate is far less than 50 per cent. Finally, there is one firm that changed from the SDAX to the MDAX in the first year of IFRS 8's adoption. For simplicity, this firm is treated as a MDAX firm in the following.

Industry distribution

Figure 5-3 presents the general **industry distribution** of the final sample. There is a wide spread among different industries. The largest industry group is Industrial with more than 31 per cent of firms. Chemicals & Energy and Personal Goods & Retail represent 26 per cent of all firms together. The category Other includes three firms from the Travel & Leisure sector and one firm from the utility sector. Overall, the industries are also well spread within the different indices except for the TecDAX, which has a natural focus on technology firms. In the empirical analyses of chapter six, industry fixed effects are introduced to control for any difference that may be driven by the sample's industry composition.

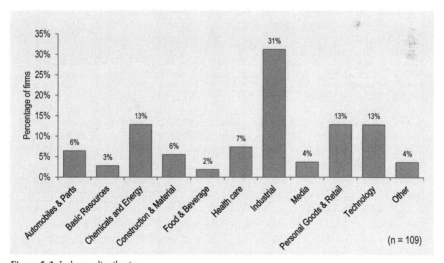

Figure 5-3: Industry distribution

Fundamental firm characteristics

Table 5-2 presents some fundamental characteristics for the final sample. The mean, median, standard deviation (std. dev.) as well as the 25 per cent (Q25) and 75 per cent quartiles (Q75) are reported separately for each index. Note that the number of observations (N) differs slightly for the different variables. This is due to limited data availability for some firms.

Fundamental firm characteristics for each index						
Variables[a]		mean	std. dev.	Q25	median	Q75	N
Market cap	DAX	19,707.62	17,391.99	6,595.04	12,867.12	26,192.80	26
	MDAX	2,633.97	3,161.21	981.60	1,569.84	2,843.25	78
	TecDAX	732.26	935.34	213.27	420.27	766.18	44
	SDAX	583.13	766.27	174.64	306.49	648.00	70
	Total	3,652.10	8,683.73	343.39	848.13	2,406.00	216
Total assets	DAX	56,626.92	64,584.63	15,018.00	32,710.50	88,277.00	26
	MDAX	6,229.84	12,638.77	1,494.10	2,374.33	4,876.28	78
	TecDAX	597.18	526.74	207.88	401.49	721.67	42
	SDAX	974.04	957.81	296.58	648.27	1,155.20	70
	Total	9,590.32	29,349.76	531.64	1,311.95	3,481.34	214
Total equity	DAX	13,716.36	12,959.65	5,079.00	8,001.00	18,897.00	26
	MDAX	1,482.61	2,166.60	443.45	792.48	1,432.00	78
	TecDAX	272.59	194.43	149.86	209.92	345.32	42
	SDAX	348.16	339.06	114.11	239.41	468.11	70
	Total	2,371.55	6,295.02	206.96	445.15	1,174.70	214
Equity ratio	DAX	34.07%	14.26%	23.12%	34.18%	40.40%	26
	MDAX	32.98%	12.20%	25.97%	31.30%	39.26%	78
	TecDAX	55.41%	20.56%	40.21%	58.26%	72.82%	42
	SDAX	40.74%	16.81%	30.37%	38.27%	51.37%	70
	Total	41.00%	17.88%	27.94%	36.29%	48.81%	214
Return on assets	DAX	3.97%	5.53%	1.17%	2.66%	3.56%	26
	MDAX	4.07%	6.72%	0.21%	3.59%	7.07%	78
	TecDAX	1.07%	21.28%	0.83%	6.21%	8.22%	42
	SDAX	3.54%	7.86%	1.30%	3.54%	7.00%	70
	Total	3.25%	11.29%	0.50%	3.51%	7.60%	214
Number of analysts following	DAX	35.20	4.56	33.00	34.00	35.00	24
	MDAX	21.42	6.24	17.00	21.50	26.00	62
	TecDAX	13.82	6.79	9.00	13.50	17.00	38
	SDAX	9.09	5.65	5.00	7.50	11.00	58
	Total	17.81	10.48	9.00	16.00	26.00	180

[a]Market cap, total assets and total equity are presented in million Euros. Equity ratio is the quotient of total equity to total assets. Return on assets is the quotient of net income to total assets.

Table 5-2: Fundamental firm characteristics

The first two variables **market capitalization** (market cap) and **total assets** are size indicators. The DAX includes by far the largest firms with a mean market capitalization of almost € 20 billion and total assets of more than € 56 billion. This is followed by the MDAX firms which are substantially smaller with a mean market capitalization of about € 2.5 billion and total assets of more than € 6 billion. The TecDAX and SDAX firms are rather similar in terms of size. Based on market capitalization, TecDAX firms are on average larger than SDAX firms. However, it is the other way round in terms of total assets. This may be due to fewer tangible assets that are recognized in the balance sheet of the more technology focused TecDAX firms. The differences between the means of the different indices as well as the standard deviation and interquartile range (Q75-Q25) signal substantial within- and between-variation in size for all indices.

The variables **total equity** and **equity ratio** indicate the financial structure of the sample firms. The total amount of equity is similarly distributed among the different indices as total assets (in relative amounts). DAX firms show a mean book value of equity of almost € 14 billion while TecDAX firms report on average € 270 million. The equity ratio –

which is the quotient of total equity to total assets – is a better indicator for the financial structure since it is a relative measure. For the full sample, on average 41 per cent of total capital is equity. This is lower for DAX and MDAX firms which show a mean equity ratio of 34 and 33 per cent and higher for TecDAX and SDAX firms with a mean equity ratio of 55 and 41 per cent, respectively. Again, the standard deviation and interquartile range show a substantial within- and between-variation for all indices.

The variable **return on assets** indicates the sample firms' profitability. The DAX and MDAX firms show a mean return on assets of about four per cent. The profitability of SDAX firms is slightly less. TecDAX firms have the lowest return on assets with about one per cent. This once more underlines the substantial variation of the firms in the final sample. Finally, the **number of analysts following** reflects the public coverage and scrutiny as well as the general richness of a firm's information environment. DAX firms are on average covered by 35 analysts. This is less for MDAX (TecDAX; SDAX) firms which are followed by 21 (14; 9) analysts.

In **summary**, Table 5-2 emphasizes the variability of the sample firms in terms of fundamental characteristics such as size, financial structure, profitability and information environment. Hence, where appropriate, the following results of the content analysis are presented separately for each index to see whether any size-related patterns exist in the segment reporting practice. Moreover, the economic consequences studies in chapter six mostly control for size, financial structure, profitability and information environment. Finally, further descriptive statistics such as bid-ask spreads, cost of capital or financial analysts' forecast properties as well as additional risk-related variables or other control variables are presented in the univariate analysis of each economic consequences sub-study.

5.2 Results

The following sections present the empirical findings of the content analysis. Results for segment reporting practice under the last year of IAS 14R and the first year of IFRS 8 are described and compared. The presentation of the results is organized along the five general pillars of the content analysis catalogue: general information, segmentation, measurement, disclosure and reconciliation. The objective of the following sections is purely descriptive.

5.2.1 General information

This section presents information that relates to **general and formal aspects** of segment reporting and its structure. First, the year of IFRS 8's adoption is determined, which is necessary to identify early adopters that require a different treatment in the economic consequences study in chapter six. Moreover, the placement of the segment report within the annual report is presented which may indicate the relative importance that firms put on the segment report. Furthermore, the word count of the segment report is compared between the two standards. This yields information about the mere extent of narrative segment information. Finally, the basis for inter-segment pricing and information about the CODM are presented.

Year of IFRS 8's adoption

The IASB supported **early adoption** of IFRS 8 and several firms followed this call. Table 5-3 shows the year of IFRS 8's adoption for all firms in the final sample. In total, 22 per cent (2 per cent in 2007; 20 per cent in 2008) voluntarily adopted IFRS 8 early. The early adoption rate is above (below) average for the TecDAX firms with 32 per cent and for the DAX firms with 25 per cent (MDAX firms with 17 per cent and SDAX firms with 19 per cent). Early adopters expect net benefits from the early adoption. Due to the voluntary nature of this choice, these firms are analyzed separately in chapter six to avoid any self-selection bias.

The number of firms adopting IFRS 8 early is slightly biased downwards due to the sample selection criteria in this study (see section 5.1.2). Most **former US-GAAP** reporters which adopted IFRS in 2007 started to report segment information under IFRS 8 right away due to its similarity to SFAS No. 131. These firms, however, never prepared a segment report under IAS 14R and are therefore not included in the final sample.

Year of IFRS 8's adoption			
Percentage of firms (n=109)	2007	2008	2009
DAX	1%	2%	9%
MDAX	0%	6%	29%
TecDAX	1%	6%	15%
SDAX	0%	6%	25%
∑	2%	20%	78%

Table 5-3: Year of IFRS 8's adoption

Placement of the segment report in the annual report

During the pre-test of the content analysis catalogue, it was noted that some firms disclosed the segment report right after the statement of financial position and statement of profit or loss. These firms may put a similar weight on the segment report as on other financial statements such as the statement of changes in equity or the cash flow statement. Table 5-4, however, shows that the majority of firms (about 63 per cent) report segment information in the notes to the financial statements. The rest of the firms report the segment table after the main financial statements and the segment narratives in the notes. There is one firm that also reports the segment narratives with the segment table right after the statement of financial position and statement of profit or loss. This is basically the same under both standards. Only one firm changes the **placement of the segment report** to the notes section upon adoption of IFRS 8. Hence, there is a similar pattern in the pre and post IFRS 8 period and the placement of the segment report is not affected by the introduction of the new standard.

Location of the segment report		
Percentage of firms (n=108)[58]	IAS 14R	IFRS 8
Placed after financial statements; before the notes	1%	1%
Placed in the notes	63%	64%
Table placed after financial statements; segment narratives in the notes	36%	35%

Table 5-4: Location of the segment report

Quantity of segment narratives

The quantity of segment narratives is proxied by the number of words.[59] Table 5-5 reports the word count for each index. As explained in section 5.1.1.2, only informative segment disclosures that are recurring are considered in the word count. Any one-time disclosures explaining the effects and changes of adopting IFRS 8 are not taken into account either. The **number of words** ranges from a minimum of 17 words in the segment report under IAS 14R of the Krones Group in 2008 to a maximum of 1,335 words for the United Internet Group under IFRS 8 in 2009. Among the different indices, the DAX and MDAX firms have a higher word count than the TecDAX and SDAX firms reflecting the size of these companies. Size is also statistically positively correlated with the word count indicating that word count is an increasing function of size.[60]

Quantity of segmental narratives										
Number of words (n=108)	DAX		MDAX		TecDAX		SDAX		Total	
	IAS 14R	IFRS 8	IAS 14R	IFRS 8	IAS 14R	IFRS 8	IAS 14R	IFRS 8	IAS 14R	IFRS 8
Mean	408	545	361	482	268	469	325	369	335	451
(std. dev.)	(272)	(258)	(221)	(214)	(106)	(265)	(164)	(198)	(194)	(231)
Min.	64	223	17	114	46	169	68	73	17	73
Q25	191	324	245	306	176	287	216	222	211	284
Median	257	475	305	445	279	402	293	380	297	428
Q75	640	724	431	601	333	507	399	460	410	537
Max.	900	1093	942	1006	484	1335	767	1016	923	1,335
Mean change in word count	+80		+127***		+180**		+53		+109***	
(p-value)	(0.247)		(0.000)		(0.010)		(0.119)		(0.000)	
Percentage change in word count	+20%		+35%		+67%		+16%		+33%	

*, **, and *** indicate statistical significance for a two-tailed t-test at the 10%, 5%, and 1% levels, respectively.

Table 5-5: Quantity of segmental narratives

---

[58] The numbers in Table 5-4 and several other tables only add up to 108 segment reports under each standard, although the final sample comprises 109 firms. This is due to two firms: The Jungheinrich Group did not (Evotec Group did) disclose segment information under IAS 14R, but started (stopped) to do so under IFRS 8.

[59] Some studies use page count or number of sentences as proxies for narrative disclosure quantity. However, since segment reports are usually less than five pages and word count is more detailed than number of sentences, word count is used in this study.

[60] This is consistent with the literature on the determinants of corporate disclosures (e.g., *Lang/Lundholm* (1993)).

Comparing the **change in word count** from the IAS 14R to the IFRS 8 period, there is an overall mean growth of 33 per cent or 109 words respectively. This is significant[61] at the one per cent level.[62] Moreover, each index separately shows an increase, which is significant for the MDAX and TecDAX.[63] The mean percentage growth in word count reaches from 16 per cent for the SDAX to 67 per cent for the TecDAX. Hence, there is an increase in qualitative information accompanying the segment report.

This increase is similar to the results of *Crawford et al.* (2012), who document a growth of 19 per cent on average for their sample of UK firms (*Crawford et al.* (2012), p. 24). The overall word count in the segmental notes, however, is substantially higher in their sample with a mean of 894 words pre IFRS 8 and 1,060 words post IFRS 8. This is more than double the extent of segmental narratives compared to the German firms of this sample. However, different to this study, *Crawford et al.* (2012) do not acknowledge the fact that there is a natural increase in the word count because one-time effects of the adoption of IFRS 8 may also be explained in the segmental notes. One of their explanations for the increase in word count is even that "*companies may have been explaining the details behind the new standard which was introduced*" (*Crawford et al.* (2012), p. 24). This study better isolates the effect of IFRS 8 on the segmental narratives by eliminating transitory or non-recurring disclosures.

The description of the **types of products and services** of each segment became mandatory under IFRS 8.22. This disclosure may help users of financial statements to get a better understanding of the business model of the entire company as well as each segment and thus increase overall decision usefulness of segment information. Hence, Table 5-6 presents the word count of the description of types of products and services. Under IAS 14R, 67 per cent provide this information. Upon adoption of IFRS 8, the number increases to 83 per cent. There is a similar pattern for the word count[64] of this sub-information compared to the overall word count: The mean word count increases by 37 words or 29 per cent, which is significant at the one per cent level. Furthermore, each index separately shows an increase of ten per cent (SDAX) to 74 per cent (TecDAX).

---

[61] In the following, the terms "significant" or "significance" always refer to statistically significant or statistical significance. For brevity, "statistical(ly)" is omitted.

[62] All tests in Table 5-5 and in the following are non-parametric ranksum tests that are not sensitive to the assumptions of the t-test (i.e., normal distribution and variance homogeneity). (Untabulated) results of t-tests, however, are the same if not indicated otherwise.

[63] The increase for the SDAX is marginally insignificant at the 12 per cent level. Although there is an increase of 34 per cent for the DAX, it is statistically insignificant which might be due to the low number of observations in the DAX index and thus low power for the test.

[64] The mean word count is only calculated for those firms that provide this information.

	Description of types of products and services									
(n=108)	DAX		MDAX		TecDAX		SDAX		Total	
	IAS 14R	IFRS 8	IAS 14R	IFRS 8	IAS 14R	IFRS 8	IAS 14R	IFRS 8	IAS 14R	IFRS 8
Percentage of firms providing a description of types of products and services	6%	9%	20%	28%	17%	19%	24%	28%	67%	83%
Mean number of words (std. dev.)	221 (165)	213 (138)	135 (114)	151 (97)	84 (49)	139 (189)	130 (80)	127 (98)	129 (101)	147 (129)
Min.	25	23	30	29	13	20	24	13	13	13
Q25	83	144	49	70	45	61	68	61	56	67
Median	217	178	98	143	87	94	110	103	106	125
Q75	351	206	197	187	123	139	160	169	160	174
Max.	503	459	508	442	174	926	353	394	508	926
Mean change in word count (p-value)	+45 (0.165)		+41*** (0.000)		+62 (0.149)		+13 (0.233)		+37*** (0.001)	
Percentage change in word count	+20%		+30%		+74%		+10%		+29%	

*, **, and *** indicate statistical significance for a two-tailed t-test at the 10%, 5%, and 1% levels, respectively.

Table 5-6: Description of types of products and services

In **summary**, the results of Table 5-5 and Table 5-6 suggest that users of financial statements receive more narrative information accompanying the quantitative disclosures. This finding, however, is not surprising given the requirements of IFRS 8.22 and the potential need to explain any deviations from GAAP resulting from the application of the management approach.

Basis of inter-segment pricing of transactions

IFRS 8.27 (a) and IAS 14R.75 require firms to disclose the **basis of inter-segment pricing**. Although it is mandatory, only 80 per cent explicitly report this information under IFRS 8 and only 72 per cent under IAS 14R. Hence, there is a compliance issue under both standards which improved slightly upon adoption of IFRS 8. However, it is questionable whether this improvement is due to IFRS 8 or rather due to the increased enforcement of segment reporting by the FREP. The 80 per cent of all firms that do disclose this information state that inter-segment pricing is based on market prices. This is identical under both standards. Only seven per cent report that inter-segment pricing is based on internal costs under either standard. For instance, the Axel Springer Group notes:

> "*The internal revenues consist of revenues from the exchange of goods and services between the various segments. The transfer pricing is based on cost coverage ...*"

(*Axel Springer*, Annual Report (2008), p. 157)

The Evotec Group bases segment prices on internal costs plus a profit margin:

> "*Net sales and operating expenses in the segments include both sales to customers and inter-segment transfers, which are priced to recover cost plus an appropriate profit margin according to the at arm's length principle.*"

(*Evotec*, Annual Report (2007), p. 65)

13 per cent report a **mixed approach**. This means that they use market prices for some internal services and products and cost-based prices for others. For instance, the Deutsche Post Group reports:

"If comparable external market prices exist for services or products offered internally within the Group, these market prices or market-oriented prices are used as transfer prices (arm's length principle). The transfer prices for services for which an external market exists are generally based on incremental costs."

(*Deutsche Post*, Annual Report (2009), p. 146)

Another example is the INDUS Group in 2008:

"Intersegment prices are based on arm's length prices to the extent that they can be established in a reliable manner and are determined using the cost-plus pricing method."

(*INDUS*, Annual Report (2008), p. 120)

Table 5-7 summarizes the basis of inter-segment pricing under both standards:

Basis of inter-segment pricing		
Percentage of firms (n=108)	IAS 14R	IFRS 8
No information	27%	20%
Information about pricing available:	73%	80%
- thereof market prices	(80%)	(80%)
- thereof cost-based approach	(7%)	(7%)
- thereof mixed approach	(13%)	(13%)

Table 5-7: Inter-segment pricing

In this study, market prices are the prevalent basis for inter-segment pricing. This is the same for IFRS 8 and IAS 14R. Hence, this area is **unaffected** by the adoption of the new standard. This may be due to the fact that inter-segment prices often have other important implications for taxation and intra-country or intra-entity profit distribution that go beyond the scope of segment reporting.

Role of the CODM

The **CODM** plays a major role in the identification of operating segments and the disclosure of items in the segment report under IFRS 8. The CODMs do not have to be a single person. Groups such as the executive board may also operate as CODM. Although it is not explicitly required to disclose the identity of the CODM, some users of financial statements may benefit from the information about the CODM because they get some insight about a firm's organizational structure and who is making operating decisions. Because the term CODM only became relevant after the introduction of IFRS 8, this study does not report how many firms disclosed its identity under IAS 14R.

In this study, only 43 per cent of all firms **disclose the identity** of the CODM (see Table 5-8). For 76 per cent of these firms, the executive board is deemed CODM. Surprisingly, another 7 per cent report that the executive board and the supervisory board jointly make operating decisions about resource allocation and performance evaluation. In 2 per cent of the firms that provide information about the CODM, the CEO alone acts as the CODM. Furthermore, 13 per cent use the vague term of "management" for their CODM, which does not reveal their identity. Finally, another 2 per cent explicitly designate the executive board members who are responsible for the specific divisions as CODMs.

Contrastingly, *Crawford et al.* (2012) report that almost 70 per cent of their UK sample firms reveal the identity of the CODM (*Crawford et al.* (2012), p. 22). This signals **international differences** in the segment reporting practices. UK firms seem to have a preference for more transparency in this regard. Moreover, given different corporate governance structures, the role of the CODM may differ substantially in a one tier board system compared to the traditional German two tier board system. This area, however, is unexplored thus far.

Role of the CODM	
Percentage of firms (n=108)	**Post IFRS 8**
Firms disclosing the identity of the CODM	43%
Thereof role of the CODM:	
- Executive board	(76%)
- Executive board and supervisory board	(7%)
- CEO	(2%)
- "Management"	(13%)
- "Board members for the respective divisions"	(2%)

Table 5-8: Role of the CODM

Summary

To **sum up**, there is no distinctive difference in the general and formal aspects of segment reporting and its structure between the two standards. Only two things are different to some extent: First, the overall quantity of segment narratives and description of types and products of each segment increase significantly upon adoption of IFRS 8. Second, about 43 per cent reveal the identity of the CODM under IFRS 8. These two changes may help investors and other users of financial disclosures to better understand segment data and the way the firm uses it internally.

5.2.2 Segmentation

This section presents descriptive information about all aspects that concern **segmentation**. First, the basis of segmentation is described for both standards. Second, there is a detailed analysis of the change in the number of reported segments upon adoption of the management approach. These two issues are core features of a company's segment report that may largely impact the usefulness of segment reports. Third, the number of firms that disclose only one segment under IAS 14R and that turn to disclose multiple segments under IFRS 8 (or vice versa) is presented. Fourth, the fineness of geographical segment information for both the primary/operating segments and the second tier segmentation are analyzed. Furthermore, the distribution of other columns in the segment report table such as "headquarters" or "other segments" and thus the fineness and structure of the segmentation are described. Finally, the aggregation of segments as well as the consistency of segment information with other parts of the annual report are analyzed. In particular the two latter aspects may also impact the decision usefulness of segment information.

Basis of segmentation

The management approach of IFRS 8 requires that **segments are identified** based on internal reporting. In fact, 87 per cent of the sample firms state that the segmentation of the segment report under IFRS 8 is the same as used for internal purposes. Under IAS 14R, however, the main criterion for identifying reportable segments is the risk-and-reward structure of business activities. Nonetheless, more than 63 per cent also report that segments are based on internal reporting under IAS 14R. This is in line with *McConnel/Pacter* (1995), who refer to IAS 14R's underlying concept as "*a management approach with a risks-and-rewards safety net*" (*McConnel/Pacter* (1995), p. 36; also see section 2.2.3.2). For instance, the Highlight Communications Group states under IAS 14R:

> "*The segmentation criteria applied by the Group for segment reporting are primarily based on the business segments and secondarily on geographic segments. The Group's income and risks are largely dependent on products manufactured by the Group and services it provides and less dependent on the geographical location of its entities. This is reflected in the management and organizational structure as well as the Group's internal reporting.*"

(*Highlight Communications*, Annual Report (2008), p. 82)

Another example is the KUKA Group in its segment report under IAS 14R in 2008:

> "*The structure follows internal reporting (management approach). The segmentation is intended to create transparency with regard to the earning power and the prospects, as well as the opportunities and threats for the various business fields within the Group.*"

(*KUKA*, Annual Report (2008), p. 72)

Interestingly, the KUKA Group uses exactly the same description of their basis for segmentation under IFRS 8 (see *KUKA*, Annual Report (2009), p. 74).

Table 5-9 shows the **basis of the primary/operating segmentation**: 84 per cent of the sample firms use business lines under IAS 14R. This is similar for the first time application of IFRS 8, where 82 per cent use business lines as the basis of segmentation. 15 per cent (11 per cent) use geographical regions as the primary segmentation criterion under IAS 14R (IFRS 8). Thereof, 56 per cent (50 per cent) explicitly state that geographical segments are either based on the location of customers or the location of assets (e.g., production facilities). For 44 per cent (50 per cent), it is unclear how the geographical segmentation was determined. Interestingly, one firm uses a mixed business lines and geographical segmentation under IAS 14R for the primary segmentation, although this category was not intended under IAS 14R. With the adoption of IFRS 8, there is an increase in 6 percentage points of firms that report a mixed segmentation.

The latter is the only major change in terms of segmentation caused by the adoption of IFRS 8. The firms that start to report a **mixed** business lines/geographical segmentation use the flexibility of the new standard to demonstrate their internal organizational structure, which they could not do under IAS 14R.

Basis of primary/operating segmentation		
Percentage of firms (n=108)	IAS 14R	IFRS 8
Business lines	84%	82%
Geographical:	15%	11%
- thereof location of customers	(31%)	(25%)
- thereof location of assets	(25%)	(25%)
- thereof undetermined	(44%)	(50%)
Mixed business lines and geographical	1%	7%

Table 5-9: Basis of primary/operating segmentation

The findings in this study are similar to previous literature which shows that the **predominant basis of segmentation** is business lines. This is independent of the underlying segment reporting standard: For instance, *Herrmann/Thomas* (2000) find that 71 per cent of U.S. blue chip firms define segments by business lines under SFAS No. 131 (*Herrmann/Thomas* (2000), p. 291). Similarly, *Street et al.* (2000) show that 66 per cent of their international sample use business lines as the predominant segmentation criterion in the first year of SFAS No. 131 adoption (*Street et al.* (2000), p. 267).

Similarly, *KPMG* (2010) finds that 66 per cent of their **international sample** report segment data according to products or services for the segmentation under IFRS 8 (*KPMG* (2010), pp. 19–20). This is supported by the findings of *Weißenberger/Franzen* (2011), who report 78 per cent of business line segmentation firms for their relatively small sample of **German firms** (*Weißenberger/Franzen* (2011), p. 343).

Number of reported segments

The IASB hoped that some firms would increase the **number of reported segments** with the issuance of IFRS 8 (IFRS 8.BC9). To analyze this, Table 5-10 reports the mean number of segments for the main segmentation, that is, the primary segmentation under IAS 14R and the operating segments under IFRS 8. Panel A shows the result for the full sample. The mean number of segments under IAS 14R is 3.02. Similar to the word count, the DAX and MDAX firms report more segments than the SDAX and TecDAX firms. This also indicates that size is an important determinant of segment reporting practice among different firms. Upon the adoption of IFRS 8, there is an increase in the mean number of segments to 3.37, which is significant at the ten per cent level. Furthermore, each index separately shows an increase in the number of segments. Due to the relatively low number of observations in each index, only the increase for the MDAX firms is significant at the ten per cent level. Another notable aspect is the increase in the standard deviation of the number of segments. After the adoption of IFRS 8, there is more variability which is consistent with the notion that IFRS 8 offers more flexibility.

The picture is very similar when **only considering business line** segmentation (see Panel B). There is an increase in the mean number of segments for each index, which is again significant for MDAX firms at the ten per cent level. Panel C shows the results for **geographical segmentation only.**[65] Findings, however, should be interpreted cautiously because there are only a few firms showing geographical segments as their predominant seg-

---

[65] The findings for a mixed business lines and geographical segmentation are not reported separately since there are even fewer firms.

ments. Therefore, statistical tests for significant differences in the means might suffer from low power in Panel C. Nonetheless, results are substantially similar for all three panels which corroborates the expectation of the IASB that the introduction of IFRS 8 would increase the number of reported segments.

Number of primary/operating segments					
Panel A. Full sample (n=108)	**DAX**	**MDAX**	**TecDAX**	**SDAX**	**Total**
- IAS 14R - mean (std. dev.)	4.08 (1.50)	3.19 (1.10)	2.39 (0.84)	2.88 (1.41)	3.02 (1.29)
- IFRS 8 - mean (std. dev.)	4.15 (1.46)	3.69 (1.49)	2.77 (1.07)	3.09 (1.66)	3.37 (1.52)
Difference in means (p-value)	+0.07 (0.91)	+0.50* (0.10)	+0.38 (0.20)	+0.21 (0.58)	+0.35* (0.07)
Panel B. Business line segmentation (IAS 14R: n=91; IFRS 8: n=89)					
- IAS 14R - mean (std. dev.)	4.07 (1.50)	3.16 (1.07)	2.30 (0.80)	3.03 (1.48)	3.07 (1.31)
- IFRS 8 - mean (std. dev.)	4.16 (1.53)	3.77 (1.59)	2.73 (1.15)	2.81 (1.44)	3.31 (1.54)
Difference in means (p-value)	+0.09 (0.88)	+0.61* (0.08)	+0.43 (0.18)	-0.22 (0.59)	+0.24 (0.26)
Panel C. Geographical segmentation (IAS 14R: n=16; IFRS 8: n=12)					
- IAS 14R - mean (std. dev.)	-	2.86 (0.69)	3.00 (1.00)	2.83 (0.75)	2.88 (0.72)
- IFRS 8 - mean (std. dev.)	4.00 (-)	3.00 (0.63)	3.00 (0)	4.00 (2.71)	3.38 (1.50)
Difference in means	-	+0.14 (0.59)	0	+1.17 (1.00)	+0.50 (0.25)
*, **, and *** indicate statistical significance for a two-tailed t-test at the 10%, 5%, and 1% levels, respectively.					

Table 5-10: Number of primary/operating segments

This is also supported by prior research. For instance, *Nichols et al.* (2012) find an increase in the mean number of segments for an international sample from 3.84 segments under IAS 14R to 4.19 segments on average under IFRS 8 (*Nichols et al.* (2012), p. 92). Moreover, *Meyer/Weiss* (2010) show that the percentage of Swiss blue chip firms reporting just one segment decreased from 24.4 per cent to 16.7 per cent (*Meyer/Weiss* (2010), p. 851). Finally, *Blase* (2011) reports an increase in the mean number of segments from 3.2 to 3.5 (*Blase* (2011), p. 177).

Table 5-11 sheds some more light on the **change in the number of reported segments**. By comparing the restated IFRS 8 segment report with the last year of IAS 14R, it is ascertained that only changes due to the adoption of the new standard are classified as such.[66] Overall, only 34 per cent of the firms change the number of reported segments. Thereof, 26 firms show an increase while 11 firms reduce the number of segments. Most firms show an increase or decrease of only one segment. This pattern is similar for all indices. There are a few exceptions with an increase of up to four or five segments upon adoption of IFRS 8. These results are in line with prior research on IFRS 8. For instance,

---

[66] Hence, changes due to mergers and acquisitions or discontinued operations were not considered.

Crawford et al. (2012) find that 60 per cent of their UK sample firms do not change the number of reported segments. Similarly, *Pisano/Landriana* (2012) report that 75 per cent of their Italian sample firms show the same number of reported segments under IAS 14R and IFRS 8.

Change in the number of primary/operating segments						
Number of firms (n=109)[67]	DAX	MDAX	TecDAX	SDAX	Total	
	n	n	n	n	n	%
- increase	4	10	6	6	26	24%
+1 segment	3	6	4	4	17	16%
+2 segments	1	2	0	1	4	4%
+3 segments	0	0	1	0	1	1%
+4 segments	0	0	1	0	1	1%
+5 segments	0	2	0	1	3	3%
- decrease	4	0	4	3	11	10%
-1 segment	4	0	3	2	9	8%
-2 segments	0	0	1	1	2	2%
- no change	5	29	13	25	72	66%

Table 5-11: Change in the number of primary/operating segments

Most increases in the number of segments are due to a finer segmentation of an existing segmentation structure. For instance, the Vossloh Group reports two more segments under IFRS 8 by **breaking down** operating divisions to business units:

> "*Since the application of IFRS 8, segment reporting has encompassed not only the identifiable two operating divisions (Rail Infrastructure and Motive Power&Components) but also separately presented their business units.*"

(*Vossloh*, Annual Report (2009), p. 142)

Similarly, the Nordex Group increased the number of segments upon IFRS 8's adoption from three to four by **disaggregating** the former "Rest of the world" segment into "Asia" and "America" (*Nordex*, Annual Report (2009), pp. 110–111).

In contrast, the Axel Springer Group lowered the number of segments from five to four. They argue, however, that this segmentation is more in line with the **strategic positioning** of the company:

> "*An important change in the segment reporting of Axel Springer involves the assignment of all the brand-related online activities of the newspapers and magazines (such as Bild.de, for example) in Germany and abroad to the Digital Media segment. As a result of this change, the principal elements of the company's business strategy [...] are presented without overlaps, in the most transparent way possible.*"

(*Axel Springer*, Annual Report (2008), p. 23)

---

[67] The two firms that started respectively stopped to provide segment reports with the adoption of IFRS 8 are included in this table. The year without a segment report is counted as one segment in the change calculations. However, the results do not change much if these firms are eliminated from the sample since one firm shows an increase of two segments and the other one a decrease of two segments from IAS 14R to IFRS 8.

As the firms' reactions differ, it is important that the classification of firms into the (positive/negative) change and no change groups for the economic consequences study in chapter six does not solely rely on the number of segments. In **summary**, this study largely confirms the findings of other studies that the introduction of IFRS 8 increased the number of reported segments to some extent.

One segment companies

With the adoption of SFAS No. 131, there was a substantial number of firms that claimed to **operate in only one segment** under SFAS No. 14, but started to disclose multiple segments afterwards (e.g., *Herrmann/Thomas* (2000); *Botosan/Stanford* (2005)). This was largely due to the vague requirements under SFAS No. 14 which improved with the introduction of SFAS No. 131. In contrast, the requirements of IAS 14R are well specified and thus there are only six firms in the initial sample that do not disclose segment information under IAS 14R. Five of these six firms still claim to be single-product companies under IFRS 8 and thus do not start to disclose segment reports. However, one firm that does not report segment information under IAS 14R starts to provide segment information with the adoption of IFRS 8.[68] The Jungheinrich Group notes in 2008 under IAS 14R:

> "*The Group defines itself as a single-product company since it classifies all its product ranges and services as a single business segment. None of the Group's business or geographical areas can be demarcated due to a difference in risks and returns, making Jungheinrich a single-segment group in its core business. Therefore, there is no need to present detailed information in the primary reporting format set forth in IAS 14.*"

(*Jungheinrich*, Annual Report (2008), p. 109)

One year later under IFRS 8, they report:

> "*Jungheinrich introduced segment reporting in line with its internal organizational and reporting structure effective January 1, 2009, when IFRS 8 "Business Segments" entered into force. The two reportable segments, i.e. 'Intralogistics' and 'Financial Services' are thus now presented within the scope of segment reporting.*"

(*Jungheinrich*, Annual Report (2009), p. 120)

In contrast, one firm **stopped** to provide segment information upon adoption of the new standard. The Evotec Group states:

> "*Pursuant to IFRS 8, reporting on the financial performance of the segments has to be prepared in accordance with the so-called management approach. The internal organisation as well as the management reporting does not identify several segments from 1 January 2008 onwards. The allocation of resources and the internal evaluation of Evotec's performance by the management are for the entire Evotec group. Following the adoption of IFRS 8 Evotec does not report segment information.*"

(*Evotec*, Annual Report (2008), p. 77)

---

[68] The two companies are the C.A.T. oil Group and the Jungheinrich Group.

These **results are similar** to *Nichols et al.* (2012) who find that four firms of their European sample (361 firms) moved from a single segment to multiple segments upon adoption of IFRS 8 (*Nichols et al.* (2012), p. 91). One firm, however, stopped to report multiple segments after the adoption of the new standard. Hence, they only find a marginal decrease of less than one per cent in the number of firms claiming to operate in only one segment.

In summary, the introduction of IFRS 8 **does not cause a significant shift** from firms showing no segment information at all to first time segment reporters. This is in contrast to U.S. studies analyzing the effect of the first time adoption of the management approach in segment reporting under US-GAAP. However, this is largely due to the relatively low level of segment reporting requirements under SFAS No. 14. The requirements under IAS 14R, however, are already strict so that the introduction of IFRS 8 does not lead to considerable changes in that regard. Moreover, this strengthens the notion that U.S. studies analyzing the effect of SFAS No. 131 cannot disentangle whether the main driver of potential economic consequences is the introduction of the management approach or the mere increase in segment information. This study, however, isolates the effect of the change in fundamental concepts.

Fineness of geographical segments

Geographical segmentation can be on different levels reaching from a very detailed segmentation based on individual countries to a broad classification of domestic and foreign activities. Following the fineness theorem (*Demski* (1973)), a finer segmentation should be more decision useful than a broader and more aggregated segmentation. Geographical segmentations provide a natural classification of the **degree of fineness** given that business activities can be broken down to the different levels. Segment disclosures on the individual country level provide useful information for users of financial statements since they can use supplementary data such as country specific expected growth or risk rates when estimating future cash flows. However, some firms operate in a large number of different countries and a country-specific segmentation may not be the most suitable approach for these firms given information processing costs of users. Yet, in general, a finer segmentation should provide more useful information.

A comparison of the fineness of geographical disclosures under IFRS 8 and IAS 14R needs to consider the **different classifications** of segment information under the two standards: IAS 14R distinguishes between primary and secondary segments. On the other hand, the main segmentation of IFRS 8 is based on operating (and reportable) segments, but further segment information is provided within the entity-wide disclosures which is comparable to the secondary reporting format under IAS 14R. Hence, primary segments are treated similar to operating segments and secondary segments are equal to entity-wide disclosures for the following comparison.

Table 5-12 presents the fineness of geographical segments under the two standards and for the primary/operating segment category and the secondary segment/entity-wide disclosures category. There are four **different levels of fineness**. Country level means that firms solely report segment information for individual countries. The mixed country and continental level category comprises firms reporting both individual countries and continental[69] geographical areas.[70] The continental level entails segments on the continental level and the category domestic/foreign solely differentiates between two segments: domestic and foreign.

The first row in Table 5-12 reports the fineness of geographical segments for the **first tier segmentation** (primary/operating segments). About 66 per cent provide geographical information on the continental level under IAS 14R. This number increases to 75 per cent under IFRS 8. Moreover, there is a shift to more country-specific segments and less domestic/foreign segmentations upon adoption of IFRS 8. This signals a finer segmentation for the primary/operating segments after the adoption of the management approach. However, the numbers are based on a rather small number of firms as most firms use business lines for their main segmentation (see Table 5-9). Therefore, results should be treated with caution.

The second row shows the same information for the **second tier** disclosures (secondary segments/entity-wide disclosures). The percentages for country level segments and domestic/foreign segmentations are basically the same under the two different standards. However, there is a shift of about ten percentage points from the continental level to the mixed country and continental level segmentation upon adoption of the management approach. These firms show additional country level segments which should increase decision usefulness of geographical segment disclosures. This change may be due to IFRS 8.33, which requires that material individual countries shall be disclosed separately. In **summary**, some critics of IFRS 8 were concerned that IFRS 8 would lead to the loss of second tier geographical information. However, the results show that this is not the case for the firms in this study. In contrast, there is rather an increased fineness which may help users of financial statements to facilitate better decisions.

Fineness of geographical segments							
Percentage of firms (n=108)	IAS 14R				IFRS 8			
	Country level	Mixed country level and continental level	Continental level	Domestic/ foreign	Country level	Mixed country level and continental level	Continental level	Domestic/ foreign
Primary segments/ operating segments	7%	7%	66%	20%	17%	0%	75%	8%
Secondary segments/ entity-wide disclosures	6%	11%	71%	12%	5%	21%	63%	11%

Table 5-12: Fineness of geographical segments

---

[69] This study defines continental as any geographical segmentation that comprises more than one individual country. This does not necessarily have to be a full continent. For instance, some firms report "Austria/Germany/Switzerland" as one segment and others use broader classifications such as "Emerging Markets". Any of these segments account for a continental level segmentation.

[70] If at least one segment is on the continental level, the segmentation is classified as a mixed country and continental level.

Other separate positions in the segment report

The main segment reporting table often includes **other columns** than the reportable segments. Most frequently, there is a reconciliation column which reconciles the sum of total segment items to the financial statements amounts by eliminating intra-segment transactions or other non-GAAP amounts. About 57 per cent of all firms show a reconciliation column under IAS 14R (see Table 5-13). This increases to 72 per cent under IFRS 8. Other positions are headquarters and other segments which are included in less than 30 per cent of all segment reports under either standard. Sometimes, firms disclose combined columns that show the aggregated values of, for instance, headquarters and other segments. In total, 20 per cent of all firms show combined columns under IAS 14R. This decreases to 12 per cent under IFRS 8.

In terms of other separate positions in the segment report, there is a tendency towards **more and finer information** after the adoption of IFRS 8. Under the new standard, more firms report reconciliations, headquarters and other segments positions in the segment report. Moreover, there are fewer firms that use combined columns which prevents an information loss through aggregation. This is largely due to firms that start to separately report the previously aggregated positions. Furthermore, the particular increase in firms providing a single reconciliation column could be due to the increased importance of such information because the management approach allows firms to disclose information that deviates from financial statements amounts.

Other separate positions in the segment report				
(n=108)	IAS 14R		IFRS 8	
	n	%	n	%
Reconciliation	62	57%	78	72%
Headquarters	24	22%	30	28%
Other segments	21	19%	31	29%
Combined – Reconciliation & Headquarters	12	11%	9	8%
Combined – Reconciliation & Other segments	7	6%	2	2%
Combined – Other segments & Headquarters	3	3%	2	2%

Table 5-13: Other separate positions

Aggregation of segments

IFRS 8.14 and IAS 14R.36 allow the **aggregation of similar operating segments** under certain conditions. This may be used by management to avoid the disclosure of specific segments. However, it is difficult to gauge the extent of aggregated segments among the sample firms as only three note that some segments were aggregated under IAS 14R and six do so under IFRS 8. The adidas Group provides the most detailed explanation of their aggregation under IFRS 8 in 2009. They identify six segments, but only report two:

> "*In accordance with the definition of IFRS 8, six operating segments have been identified: Wholesale, Retail, TaylorMade-adidas Golf, Rockport, Reebok-CCM Hockey and Other centrally managed brands. According to the criteria of IFRS 8 for reportable segments, the first two are reported separately while the other four are aggregated under 'Other Businesses' due to their only subordinate materiality.*"

(*adidas*, Annual Report (2009), p. 204)

Similarly, the Smartrac Group identifies four business units, however, due to aggregation they only report two segments:

> "*The Business Unit eID and the Business Unit Cards were aggregated as reportable segment 'Security' and the Business Unit Industry & Logistics and the Business Unit Tickets & Labels were aggregated as reportable segment 'Industry'. All other business activities are included in the 'All other' segment.*"

(*Smartrac*, Annual Report (2009), p. 108)

The **explanations** of the few other firms that make a reference to aggregation are rather vague. They just note that their business activities were aggregated to a certain number of reported segments.

The findings of this study with regard to aggregation are in line with *Meyer/Weiss* (2010). They show that only 15 firms of their Swiss sample make a reference to the aggregation of segments (*Meyer/Weiss* (2010), p. 850). Although the number of firms providing information about aggregation doubled, it is still very low. However, this may just be due to few firms using the aggregation allowed by IFRS 8.14 and IAS 14R.36. In **summary**, this area is not particularly affected by the adoption of IFRS 8. Yet, there is a minor increase in firms providing information about it.

Consistency

More consistency of segment information with other parts of the annual report or management disclosures was one of the major benefits associated with the introduction of IFRS 8 (IFRS 8.BC9). In this study, it is analyzed whether segment information is more consistent with the management report and the letter of the CEO. Under IAS 14R, about 78 per cent of all segment reports are consistent with these other financial disclosures. This increases to 95 per cent under IFRS 8. Hence, the adoption of IFRS 8 **increased the consistency** of segment information, which can be considered as an improvement of financial disclosures. This allows users of financial statements to get a more consistent picture of a firm's business activities because different financial disclosures better align. Moreover, as indicated by the results of the PIR, there may be a spill-over effect of credibility to other parts of consistent segment information since IFRS 8 information is audited.[71]

This is partly supported by prior research. *Street/Nichols* (2002) show that more than 80 per cent of their sample firms already report segment data that is **consistent** with the introductory annual report material under IAS 14R (*Street/Nichols* (2002), p. 108). Hence, it is questionable whether the adoption of IFRS 8 significantly increases consistency. Moreover, *Nichols et al.* (2012) only find that four per cent of their sample of European blue chips report inconsistencies under IAS 14R (*Nichols et al.* (2012), pp. 87–88). This number marginally decreases to three per cent under IFRS 8. *Weißenberger et al.* (2013)

---

[71] This does also include online disclosures on corporate websites that sometimes contain segmental information.

also document a comparable increase in the consistency of segment information for a similar German sample.[72]

Summary

Overall, more firms use a mixed business lines/geographical segmentation and there is an increase in the number of segments as well as in the consistency with other parts of the annual report. Moreover, there is also an increased fineness of geographical segment information. These features determine the structure and fineness as well as comparability of segment information with other disclosures of a firm which may largely impact the decision usefulness of segment information. However, neither the number of firms that report only one segment nor the information about aggregated segments are substantially affected by the adoption of IFRS 8. This shows once more the difference of U.S. studies which analyze the impact of introducing SFAS No. 131 and this study: While SFAS No. 14 allowed firms to circumvent segment reporting,[73] IAS 14R does not provide such a flexibility. Hence, this study analyzes the impact of a change in underlying concepts instead of the introduction of segment reporting or a mere increase in segment disclosures.

5.2.3 Measurement

This section presents the **basis of measurement** for the line items of the segment report. Specific non-IFRS line items are described as well. These are important factors that may impact the understandability of segment information which was a major concern voiced by opponents of IFRS 8.

Basis of measurement

Following IFRS 8.25-27, segment information does not necessarily have to comply with the IFRS measurement principles. Under IAS 14R, however, segment information is prepared based on the **same measurement principles** that are used for the financial statements. In fact, 31 per cent of the sample firms explicitly note under IAS 14R that segment information is in line with IFRS. Interestingly, 51 per cent of the firms report the same under IFRS 8. On the one hand, this indicates integrated financial and management accounting systems (one-book systems) for these firms. On the other hand, this also signals an increased awareness of firms that segment information could be different from IFRS (under IFRS 8) so that they want to show users of financial statements that their segment numbers are in line with GAAP – something they did not consider necessary under IAS 14R.

Non-IFRS line items

Only three firms state that the amounts reported in the segment report may (partly) **deviate** from the accounting principles used for the IFRS financial statements. For instance, the Aurubis Group notes in 2009 under IFRS 8:

---

[72] The analysis of *Weißenberger et al.* (2013) is more detailed than this study since it compares several dimensions of consistency. However, the key finding of an increased consistency is comparable.

[73] For instance, *Street et al.* (2000) report that almost 24 per cent of their sample firms claim to be operating in only one segment under the old standard.

"The segment information was determined applying the same accounting policies as for the remaining financial statements, but using the LIFO method for the valuation of inventories. This is because internal reporting to management for decision-making and group management control purposes is also based on the figures obtained by the application of the LIFO method. These figures are regarded as the most appropriate for the external presentation [...] since they are much less influenced by metal price fluctuations."

(*Aurubis*, Annual Report, (2009), p. 171)

Moreover, **imputed costs** such as imputed depreciation, interest or rent are rarely used for measuring segment performance. Although IFRS 8 allows the disclosure of imputed segment performance measures, only the Fraport Group uses imputed interest. They state in the notes to the financial statements in 2009:

*"Inter-segment income is generated essentially by Fraport AG's intercompany charge of rent for land, buildings, and space as well as of maintenance service and energy/associated services. The corresponding segment assets are allocated to the Retail & Real Estate segment. The relevant units are charged on the basis of the costs incurred, **including imputed interest** [emphasis added]."*

(*Fraport*, Annual Report (2009), p. 140)

Interestingly, the GESCO Group 2009/2010 uses figures based on the German Commercial Code for internal purposes and notes:

"Compared to the previous year, segment reporting policies were changed to comply with the new requirements of IFRS 8 and to include information used by management as performance indicators. As a result, the figures for the operating segments tool manufacture and mechanical engineering as well as plastics technology are reported in accordance with the German Commercial Code (HGB) [...] and reconciled with Group IFRS figures in the item other/consolidation."

(*GESCO*, Annual Report (2009/2010), p. 66)

The Gfk Group reports under IAS 14R that it uses an adjusted profitability measure to judge the performance of segments. However, they are not allowed to report it due to the requirements of IAS 14R:

"The Group measures the success of its divisions by reference to the adjusted operating income. The adjusted operating income of a division is determined on the basis of the operating income net of the following income and expenses: integration costs linked to company acquisitions, write-ups/write-downs on additional assets identified on acquisitions, personnel expenses from share-based payments and long-term incentives, other operating income and expenses. However, according to IAS 14, operating income must be presented by segment."

(*Gfk*, Annual Report (2007), p. 121)

Summary

In **summary**, the vast majority of firms report information in line with IFRS. Only a few firms use figures that (partly) deviate from the measurement principles for financial statements. These firms, however, all provide reconciliations to IFRS amounts so that users of financial statements can reconcile to these numbers. Although the theoretical change in segment reporting requirements was substantial with regard to the basis of measurement, the change in the actual segment reporting practice is far less extensive. Most German blue chip firms seem to have integrated accounting systems at least on the segment level so that they do not report non-IFRS measures. Hence, the fear that the introduction of the management approach to segment reporting might impair the understandability of segment information is unfounded – at least for the firms in this sample.

5.2.4 Disclosures

This section presents the disclosure of line items for the primary/operating segments as well as the second tier segments. These **disclosures** constitute the core information content of segment reports and are therefore important determinants of decision usefulness. The requirements to report specific items vary substantially between the two standards (see section 2.2.5). Therefore, this study differentiates between mandatory, conditional and voluntary items. Moreover, information about the measures which are used by management to judge segments' performance as well as information about major customers are described as well. These factors provide some additional insights for users of financial statements.

Segment line items – Overview

Similarly to the number of reported segments, the IASB also expected an increase in the number of **reported segment items** (IFRS 8.BC9). Prior research, however, indicates that the adoption of IFRS 8 led to a decrease in the number of line items.[74] For instance, *Crawford et al.* (2012) find on average 7.02 segment line items under IAS 14R and 6.43 under IFRS 8 (*Crawford et al.* (2012), p. 20).

Table 5-14 presents the mean number of segment line items for all indices categorized in mandatory, conditional and voluntary items. Under IAS 14R, there are in total ten **mandatory items**[75] while there is only one item (i.e., segment result) under IFRS 8. The mean number of reported mandatory items under IAS 14R, however, is only 8.32. This number even includes multiple segment result items that were counted more than once. Hence, there is a compliance issue. Under IFRS 8, the mean number of mandatory items is 2.88, which is due to the multiple segment result measures used by the firms.

---

[74] In this context, only line items of primary segments (IAS 14R) or operating segments (IFRS 8) are considered.

[75] These include internal and external segment revenue, segment result, segment assets, segment liabilities, segment capital expenditures, segment depreciation and amortization, significant non-cash expenses as well as amount and profit from investments accounted for under the equity method (see section 2.2.5.2 for a detailed description).

The category **conditional items**[76] is only relevant for segment reports according to IFRS 8. These items only have to be reported if they are regularly reviewed by the CODM. Although there may be some discretion or other ways for firms to prevent the disclosure of these items, they should not be regarded as voluntary and thus they are presented separately here. In total, the mean number of conditionally disclosed items is 5.10. Interestingly, the sum of the mean number of conditional and mandatory items under IFRS 8 is 7.98, which is very close to the mean number of mandatory items of 8.32 under IAS 14R. Moreover, there is also an overlap of the actual items because all former mandatory items except for segment result are classified as conditional under IFRS 8. Hence, there is not a substantial change in this regard.

Number of primary/operating segment items										
(n=108)	DAX		MDAX		TecDAX		SDAX		Total	
	IAS 14R	IFRS 8	IAS 14R	IFRS 8	IAS 14R	IFRS 8	IAS 14R	IFRS 8	IAS 14R	IFRS 8
Mean number of mandatory items (std. dev.)	8.31 (1.89)	3.08 (1.12)	8.92 (2.04)	3.05 (1.12)	7.52 (1.89)	2.68 (1.04)	8.13 (1.58)	2.74 (1.05)	**8.32** **(1.91)**	**2.88** **(1.08)**
Mean number of conditional items (IFRS 8 only) (std. dev.)	-	5.46 (2.11)	-	5.41 (1.71)	-	4.25 (1.29)	-	5.09 (1.99)	**-**	**5.10** **(1.81)**
Mean number of voluntary items (std. dev.)	6.46 (7.04)	11.23 (19.26)	3.97 (3.81)	4.27 (2.95)	4.93 (3.28)	3.79 (2.94)	3.62 (2.90)	3.21 (2.96)	**4.37** **(4.13)**	**4.87** **(8.06)**
Mean number of total items (std. dev.)	14.77 (8.23)	19.77 (21.32)	12.89 (5.14)	12.73 (12.08)	12.45 (4.82)	10.72 (4.60)	11.75 (3.36)	11.04 (4.63)	**12.69** **(5.17)**	**12.85** **(8.90)**
Difference in means of total items (p-value)	+5.00 (0.438)		-0.16 (0.940)		-1.73* (0.061)		-0.71 (0.472)		**+0.16** **(0.872)**	

*, **, and *** indicate statistical significance for a two-tailed t-test at the 10%, 5%, and 1% levels, respectively.

Table 5-14: Number of primary/operating segment items

This is also corroborated by the mean number of **voluntary items** which is very similar under both standards with 4.37 under IAS 14R and 4.87 under IFRS 8. The **total number of items** comprises the sum of all categories. There is only a marginal increase from 12.69 to 12.85 items after the adoption of the new standard. This is in contrast to most other studies which document a decrease in the number of reported line items upon adoption of IFRS 8. The data under IFRS 8, however, contains one influential outlier: The BMW Group reports a whole statement of financial position and statement of profit or loss on segment level under IFRS 8, which includes 88 segment line items in total. Eliminating this outlier leads to a mean number of line items of 11.08 with a standard deviation of 4.96. The decrease in the number of total line items is then statistically significant with a p-value of 0.021. This is consistent with findings of prior research.

---

[76] Conditional items comprise external and internal segment revenue, segment assets, segment liabilities, segment interest revenue and expense, segment depreciation and amortization, material items of income and expense, amount and profit from investments accounted for under the equity method, income taxes, material non-cash items and the amount of additions to non-current assets (see section 2.2.5.1 for a detailed description).

In general, the picture is similar for all **four indices**. The indices that include the larger firms show on average a higher number of reported line items. All indices except for the DAX experience a decrease, which is significant at the ten per cent level for the TecDAX. Eliminating the BMW Group from the DAX sample changes the direction from an increase to a decrease in the number of line items. Furthermore, it is notable that the variability of the number of line items increases substantially. This is, however, also driven by the outlier observation. If the BMW Group is removed, the variability is very similar under both standards.

Segment line items – Mandatory and conditional items

Table 5-15 analyzes the disclosure of **mandatory and conditional line items** in more detail. Segment result is the only item that is mandatory under both standards. There is a very high compliance rate that slightly decreases with the adoption of IFRS 8. 97 per cent of all firms report segment profit under IAS 14R and almost 94 per cent do so under IFRS 8.

The differentiation between **internal and external revenues** is important under IFRS 8 because the amount of external revenues for operating segments is used as a quantitative threshold in the process of determining reportable segments. However, IAS 14R.51 also requires to separately disclose internal and external revenues. In fact, external revenues are presented by every firm under either standard. Internal revenues, however, are disclosed by 73 per cent under IAS 14R with a small increase to 79 per cent under IFRS 8. This may be due to the increased importance of internal revenues under IFRS 8 because it is not required that the majority of revenues of an operating segment stems from external sales.

Segment assets and **segment liabilities** experience a decline of 14 respectively 26 percentage points. Notably, the percentage of firms reporting **capital expenditures** also decreased from 98 per cent to 85 per cent. Information about the extent of investments of the different segments may be particularly relevant for investors as it yields insights about future growth and prospects for different parts of an entity. The decline in the number of firms reporting this item is exemplary for all items in Panel B which are mandatory under IAS 14R and conditional under IFRS 8. Since these items are no longer mandatory, many firms cease to report them when they are not used for internal reporting. For instance, the Gfk Group notes:

> "*Segment reporting on the sectors includes no information about segment assets and investments, since these are not calculated for the individual sectors for the purposes of internal reporting and internal management and are not reported to the Management Board.*"

(*Gfk*, Annual Report 2008, p. 129)

In the future, even more firms may cease to report segment assets because the **amendments** to IFRS 8 in 2010 clarified that segment assets have to be disclosed only if they are reported internally to the CODM. This study uses segment data for the first year of IFRS 8 in 2009 and therefore the amendment is not yet reflected in the data.

Panel C presents the three items that are **voluntary** under IAS 14R, but **conditional** under IFRS 8. While only about six to seven percent disclose interest revenue and expense under IAS 14R, this number increases to 22 per cent under the new standard. This is similar for income tax expenses: only one per cent of firms report it voluntarily under IAS 14R, which increases to nine per cent under IFRS 8.

The results across Panel A to C are very similar when considering single indices. In **summary**, Table 5-15 underlines the decrease in the number of reported items. This decrease is largely driven by the reclassification of mandatory items to conditional items as the extent of voluntary disclosures remains very similar.

	Specific primary/operating segment disclosures									
Percentage of firms (n=108)	DAX		MDAX		TecDAX		SDAX		Total	
	IAS 14R	IFRS 8	IAS 14R	IFRS 8	IAS 14R	IFRS 8	IAS 14R	IFRS 8	**IAS 14R**	**IFRS 8**
Panel A. Mandatory items under IAS 14R and IFRS 8										
Segment result	92%	85%	97%	92%	100%	96%	97%	97%	**97%**	**94%**
Segment revenue with external customers[b]	100%	100%	100%	100%	100%	100%	100%	100%	**100%**	**100%**
Segment revenue with other segments[b]	77%	77%	64%	72%	67%	77%	78%	82%	**73%**	**79%**
Panel B. Further mandatory items under IAS 14R / Conditional items under IFRS 8										
Total assets[a]	100%	100%	100%	72%	95%	77%	100%	82%	**99%**	**85%**
Total liabilities[a]	92%	92%	100%	62%	95%	64%	100%	71%	**98%**	**72%**
Capital expenditures[a]	100%	92%	100%	95%	91%	73%	100%	79%	**98%**	**85%**
Depreciation and amortization[b]	92%	100%	97%	100%	100%	86%	100%	91%	**98%**	**94%**
Significant non-cash expenses[b]	31%	15%	51%	31%	24%	27%	47%	24%	**42%**	**26%**
Profit or loss from investment in associated entities[b]	62%	54%	64%	54%	33%	23%	50%	30%	**53%**	**40%**
Amount of investment in associated entities[a]	62%	46%	46%	41%	24%	22%	55%	27%	**46%**	**33%**
Panel C. Further conditional items under IFRS 8 that are voluntary under IAS 14R										
Interest revenue[b]	8%	15%	5%	26%	4%	5%	6%	32%	**6%**	**22%**
Interest expense[b]	8%	15%	5%	26%	9%	5%	6%	32%	**7%**	**22%**
Income tax expense[b]	0%	15%	3%	8%	0%	5%	0%	12%	**1%**	**9%**

[a]The information is required under IFRS 8 if it is included in segment assets or regularly reported to the CODM, even if it is not part of segment assets.
[b]The information is required under IFRS 8 if it is included in segment profit or loss or regularly reported to the CODM, even if it is not part of segment profit or loss.

Table 5-15: Specific primary/operating segment disclosures

Segment line items – Voluntary items

Table 5-14 indicates that firms report on average four **voluntary items**. However, there is substantial variety. Table 5-16 presents the most frequently disclosed items. Notably, 46 to 47 per cent of all firms report other impairments under either standard. This is followed by the number of employees, which is disclosed by 45 per cent under IAS 14R and 35 per cent under IFRS 8. Research and development expenditures are reported by about 12 (IFRS 8) and 13 (IAS 14R) per cent of the firms. Only one firm reports capitalized research and development under both standards. The remaining items shown in Table 5-16 are reported by less than ten per cent of all firms. Similar to previous findings, DAX and MDAX firms slightly disclose more voluntary items than TecDAX and SDAX firms. However, there is no distinctive difference between the two standards in the items and fraction of firms reporting these items. In terms of the nature of the voluntary items, there is no clear-cut change upon the adoption of IFRS 8.

Voluntary primary/operating segment disclosures										
Percentage of firms (n=108)	DAX		MDAX		TecDAX		SDAX		Total	
	IAS 14R	IFRS 8	IAS 14R	IFRS 8	IAS 14R	IFRS 8	IAS 14R	IFRS 8	IAS 14R	IFRS 8
Voluntary items										
Goodwill	0%	8%	0%	13%	0%	9%	0%	0%	0%	7%
Inventories	8%	8%	3%	5%	0%	0%	3%	3%	3%	4%
Trade receivables	8%	8%	0%	3%	0%	0%	3%	3%	2%	3%
Cash and cash equiva- lents	8%	8%	2%	3%	0%	5%	3%	3%	3%	4%
Goodwill impairment	0%	0%	13%	8%	14%	5%	6%	3%	10%	5%
Other impairments	54%	62%	49%	56%	38%	27%	47%	41%	47%	46%
Research and Develop- ment expenditures	31%	31%	13%	13%	24%	18%	0%	0%	13%	12%
Operating cash flow	54%	46%	5%	3%	10%	5%	6%	0%	12%	7%
Number of employees	69%	46%	51%	46%	29%	23%	38%	26%	45%	35%

Table 5-16: Voluntary primary/operating segment disclosures

Segment line items – Profitability measures

Table 5-17 presents the **profitability measures** that are used to report on the performance of each segment. On average, firms provide about two measures under either standard (Panel A). DAX and MDAX firms show a slightly higher mean number of profitability measures than TecDAX and SDAX firms, which is consistent with some of the results shown above. About 46 to 49 per cent of firms disclose only one measure while 26 to 29 per cent report two measures. Three measures are reported by 15 to 17 per cent and only 8 to 11 per cent report more than three measures. Again, this is very similar under either standard. Moreover, there is no significant change after the adoption of IFRS 8.

Panel B reports the disclosure rate[77] of specific **profitability measures**. The two most frequently reported items are EBIT and EBITDA. Under IFRS 8, more than 82 per cent report EBIT and 38 per cent report EBITDA. This is similar under IAS 14R: almost 91 per cent disclose EBIT and 31 per cent disclose EBITDA. 20 to 26 per cent of firms report EBT. The other profitability measures, however, are seldom disclosed. For instance, less than eight per cent of firms report net income. However, this is not surprising since a lot of firms do not break down income taxes to the segmental level. In **summary**, the disclosure of specific standardized profitability measures is similar under either standard and also substantially similar among the different indices.

Some firms **adjust** the profitability measures[78] for certain items or transactions. Panel C reports the percentage of firms that make adjustments. Most frequently, firms exclude special items, goodwill impairments or certain group expenses. Under IFRS 8, about 15

---

[77] Disclosure rate is defined as the percentage of firms reporting this specific item.
[78] If a firm reports a pre-goodwill impairment EBIT, EBIT is still counted as a profitability measure in Panel B. Additionally, Panel C shows the adjustment.

per cent exclude special items, 5 per cent use a pre-goodwill measure and 4 per cent exclude certain group expenses. There are less adjustments under IAS 14R. This reflects the full financial accounting approach which is part of the risk-and-reward approach under IAS 14R.

	Profitability measures									
(n=108)	DAX		MDAX		TecDAX		SDAX		Total	
	IAS 14R	IFRS 8	IAS 14R	IFRS 8	IAS 14R	IFRS 8	IAS 14R	IFRS 8	IAS 14R	IFRS 8
Panel A. Number of profit or loss measures										
Mean number of profitability measures (std. dev.)	1.92 (1.19)	2.08 (1.12)	2.33 (1.36)	2.05 (1.12)	1.90 (1.22)	1.68 (1.04)	1.63 (0.91)	1.74 (1.05)	**1.98 (1.21)**	**1.89 (1.08)**
Percentage of firms reporting:										
One measure	46%	38%	33%	41%	52%	59%	56%	56%	**46%**	**49%**
Two measures	31%	30%	28%	26%	24%	23%	31%	27%	**29%**	**26%**
Three measures	15%	15%	23%	26%	10%	14%	9%	9%	**15%**	**17%**
More than three	8%	16%	15%	8%	14%	5%	3%	9%	**11%**	**8%**
Panel B. Specific profitability measures										
Gross Profit	23%	8%	13%	10%	24%	18%	3%	3%	**13%**	**9%**
EBITDAR	0%	8%	3%	3%	0%	0%	0%	0%	**1%**	**2%**
EBITDA	23%	39%	44%	46%	24%	32%	25%	28%	**31%**	**38%**
EBITA	0%	0%	13%	13%	0%	0%	6%	9%	**7%**	**7%**
EBIT	85%	85%	92%	80%	91%	82%	91%	85%	**91%**	**82%**
EBT	15%	15%	33%	26%	14%	0%	28%	29%	**26%**	**20%**
Net income	0%	8%	13%	5%	10%	9%	3%	9%	**8%**	**7%**
Panel C. Adjustments of profitability measures										
Pre-special items	15%	23%	13%	46%	10%	0%	0%	12%	**9%**	**15%**
Pre-goodwill impairment	0%	0%	10%	10%	0%	0%	0%	3%	**4%**	**5%**
Pre-group expenses	0%	8%	0%	0%	0%	9%	5%	3%	**1%**	**4%**

Table 5-17: Profitability measures

Measures used to assess performance of segments

The definition of an operating segment under IFRS 8.5 (b) entails that the operating results are regularly reviewed by the CODM to decide about resource allocation and performance assessment. For users of financial statements, it may also be useful to know the KPIs which are used by the management to facilitate decisions. The disclosure of these **performance measures**, however, is voluntary under both IFRS 8 and IAS 14R.[79]

About seven per cent of all firms report at least one performance measure that is used by management under IAS 14R (Table 5-18, Panel A). This increases to almost 57 per cent of firms under IFRS 8. There are several firms that report multiple performance measures under the management approach. For instance, the Continental Group notes under IFRS 8:

---

[79] In contrast to the previous sub-section *Segment line items – Profitability measures*, this sub-section only presents the profitability measures that are primarily used by management to assess the performance of segments. This is the case if a company explicitly states that a particular measure is used for segment performance evaluation.

"The corporation measures the performance of segments on the basis of their operating result (EBIT). This is expressed as the return on sales (RoS), and as the return on capital employed (ROCE), which represents EBIT as a percentage of average operating assets."

(*Continental,* Annual Report (2009), p. 227)

A majority of 40 per cent, however, solely reports one **performance measure** under IFRS 8 followed by 11 per cent reporting two measures. Three or more measures are disclosed by 6 per cent of all firms based on IFRS 8. These percentages are much lower under the former standard: 5 per cent disclose one measure and only 2 per cent report more than one measure. In total, the mean number of reported performance measures increases from 0.13 under IAS 14R to 0.85 under IFRS 8. The DAX and MDAX firms report the most measures with a mean of 1.15 and 1.13 under IFRS 8 compared to 0.61 and 0.59 for the TecDAX and MDAX. Very few firms provide different performance measures for different segments. The BMW Group, for instance, uses EBIT and capital employed for the internal management of their operating automobile and motorbikes segments and they assess the performance of the financial services segment based on EBT and net assets (*BMW,* Annual Report (2009), p. 133).

Performance measures										
(n=108)	DAX		MDAX		TecDAX		SDAX		Total	
	IAS 14R	IFRS 8	IAS 14R	IFRS 8	IAS 14R	IFRS 8	IAS 14R	IFRS 8	IAS 14R	IFRS 8
Panel A. Number of performance measures										
Mean number of performance measures	0.08	1.15	0.26	1.13	0.04	0.61	0.06	0.59	0.13	0.85
Percentage of firms reporting:										
No measure	92%	39%	90%	33%	96%	57%	94%	47%	93%	43%
One measure	8%	39%	5%	41%	4%	30%	6%	47%	5%	40%
Two measures	0%	8%	3%	18%	0%	9%	0%	6%	1%	11%
Three measures	0%	8%	0%	3%	0%	4%	0%	0%	0%	3%
More than three	0%	8%	0%	5%	0%	0%	0%	0%	1%	3%
Panel B. Specific performance measures										
Revenues	0%	8%	0%	10%	0%	13%	0%	3%	0%	8%
EBITDA	0%	8%	3%	8%	0%	9%	3%	9%	2%	8%
EBIT	8%	46%	3%	28%	4%	39%	3%	27%	4%	34%
EBT	0%	0%	3%	7%	0%	0%	0%	3%	0%	4%
adj. EBITDA	0%	0%	0%	5%	0%	0%	0%	0%	0%	2%
adj. EBIT	0%	15%	5%	18%	0%	0%	0%	9%	2%	11%
adj. EBT	0%	0%	0%	0%	0%	0%	0%	3%	0%	0%
Cash flow measure	0%	23%	0%	3%	0%	0%	0%	0%	0%	4%

Table 5-18: Performance measures

Panel B of Table 5-18 presents those **items which are most frequently used** for internal performance measurement. Adj. EBT, adj. EBIT and adj. EBITDA reflect measures that exclude or include specific items such as goodwill impairments, reorganizational expenses etc. The cash flow measure comprises all cash flow-related items such as free cash flow, operating cash flow or "cash generation". There is a distinct difference between the two standards as only a few firms report which measures they use to assess segment performance under IAS 14R. Therefore, only the disclosures under IFRS 8 are discussed in detail. 34 per cent of all firms under IFRS 8 use EBIT for internal performance measurement of segments followed by adj. EBIT, which is used by 11 per cent. The other items are utilized by less than ten per cent. Notably, TecDAX and SDAX firms barely use any adjusted measures which is in contrast to the DAX and MDAX firms. This might be due to more sophisticated internal management control systems of larger firms.

Second tier segment disclosures

Similar to the category "Fineness of geographical segments" in the segmentation section, **second tier disclosures** are defined as either disclosures for the secondary segments under IAS 14R or the entity-wide disclosures under IFRS 8. There are far less disclosures mandated by IAS 14R and IFRS 8 compared to the first tier segmentation. Under IAS 14R, firms are only required to disclose segment revenues, assets and capital expenditures. This is even less under IFRS 8 as the requirement to disclose capital expenditures was removed upon the adoption of the management approach. Opponents of IFRS 8 voiced concerns about a loss of second tier information with the adoption of the new standard.

Table 5-19 provides an overview of the second tier disclosures for each index under both standards. The results in Panel A show that there is a substantial decrease in the **mean number of reported second tier items** from 4.23 under IAS 14R to 2.51 under IFRS 8. This decrease is similar for all four indices while it is the largest for the SDAX (4.06 to 1.75) and the smallest for the DAX (5.92 to 5.17). Consistent with the size of the firms in the different indices, DAX and MDAX firms generally disclose the most items.

Panel B provides an overview of the **distribution of firms** disclosing one, two, three or more items. Interestingly, the vast majority of firms report three or more than three items under IAS 14R. There is only one SDAX firm that solely reports revenues and one MDAX firm that reports revenues and gross profit margin. Other than that, firms generally comply with the requirement to disclose the three mandatory items. The picture is different for the disclosures under IFRS 8. Firms are only obliged to disclose revenues and assets. Moreover, IFRS 8.32 and IFRS 8.33 allow to refrain from the disclosure if the information is not available and costs to obtain it would be excessive. This is reflected in a relatively high proportion of firms (36 per cent) that only report one item under IFRS 8. Almost the same number of firms (37 per cent) report exactly the two required items under IFRS 8. Only a minority of less than 18 per cent voluntarily reports more than three items. In **summary**, there is a substantial decline in the number of second tier line items upon adoption of IFRS 8. This decline seems to be driven by both the reduction in the number of mandatory items as well as by fewer voluntary items.

Disclosures for the second tier segments									
(n=108)	DAX		MDAX		TecDAX		SDAX		Total	
	IAS 14R	IFRS 8	IAS 14R	IFRS 8	IAS 14R	IFRS 8	IAS 14R	IFRS 8	IAS 14R	IFRS 8
Panel A. Number of second tier items										
Mean number second tier items	5.92	5.17	3.57	2.35	4.16	2.18	4.06	1.75	4.23	2.51
Panel B. Distribution of second tier items										
Percentage of firms reporting:										
One measure	0%	25%	0%	24%	0%	35%	4%	57%	1%	36%
Two measures	0%	17%	3%	50%	0%	41%	0%	29%	1%	37%
Three measures	25%	8%	60%	12%	58%	12%	52%	4%	54%	9%
More than three	75%	50%	37%	15%	42%	12%	45%	11%	44%	18%
Panel C. Specific second tier items										
Revenues[a]	100%	100%	100%	100%	100%	100%	100%	90%	100%	97%
Assets[a]	100%	100%	97%	91%	100%	94%	93%	86%	97%	90%
Capital expenditures[b]	100%	58%	97%	56%	100%	41%	93%	28%	97%	45%
Number of employees[c]	50%	58%	14%	12%	11%	12%	17%	7%	19%	14%
Performance measures[c]	50%	33%	3%	0%	26%	6%	10%	7%	16%	8%
R&D expenses[c]	25%	17%	6%	9%	5%	0%	0%	0%	6%	5%
Liabilities[c]	8%	8%	3%	3%	11%	6%	4%	7%	5%	5%

[a] The information is required under IFRS 8 and IAS 14R.
[b] The information is required only under IAS 14R.
[c] The information is voluntary under both standards. The item is selected because it is disclosed most frequently.

Table 5-19: Disclosures for the second tier segments

Panel C provides an overview of the **disclosure of specific items**. As elaborated above, revenues and assets are mandatory items under both standards, while capital expenditures are only required under IAS 14R. The number of employees, performance measures, R&D expenses and liabilities are selected voluntary items that are reported most frequently. All firms disclose second tier **revenues** under IAS 14R while a few firms (three per cent) stop to do so upon adoption of IFRS 8. Segment **assets** are disclosed by almost 97 per cent under IAS 14R which declines to 90 per cent under IFRS 8. Both items are mandatory under either standard. The decline may also be due to IFRS 8.32 and IFRS 8.33, which allow firms to not report assets and revenues if they are not available or too costly to obtain. However, most firms that do not disclose second tier assets do not provide reasons why. For instance, Puma Group just notes in their first segment report under IFRS 8 in 2008:

> "*The operating result and most of the asset and liability items cannot be allocated in a reasonable manner.*"

> (*Puma*, Annual Report (2008), p. 112)

Most notably, 97 per cent of all firms report second tier **capital expenditures** under IAS 14R while this drops to less than 45 per cent upon adoption of IFRS 8. This is may be due to the fact that the disclosure turned from mandatory to voluntary. However, information about capital expenditures particularly helps users of financial statements to identify a firm's strategic direction and thus may help them to better estimate future developments. Hence, there may be a loss of important information about those firms that stop the disclosure.

With regard to the items that are voluntary under both standards, there is no such distinctive difference. However, there is in general a minor decline in the number of firms voluntarily providing second tier items after the adoption of the new standard: About 19 per cent report the **number of employees** under IAS 14R and only 14 per cent do so under IFRS 8. This is similar for **performance measures** (**R&D expenses**) which show a decline from about 16 to 8 per cent (six to five per cent). Only the disclosure of **liabilities** remains virtually unchanged as only five per cent of all firms report this item under either standard.

Second tier **performance measures** are not reported frequently under IAS 14R and IFRS 8. Given that the majority of second tier segments are geographical, firms may want to avoid the scrutiny of national tax authorities or other government regulations if they disclose their local profits. For instance, the STADA Group notes that:

> "*However, in the scope of this reporting of the secondary segments, STADA does not disclose financial results of the consolidated companies in this Group Annual Report. As STADA is mainly active in markets which are subject to distinct government regulation on a national level, the stressing of its local Group profit allocation could stimulate detrimental regulatory measures in individual national markets.*"

(*STADA*, Annual Report (2008), p. 174)

Among the **different indices**, there is a similar pattern for Panel B and Panel C as described above. However, DAX firms and to some extent TecDAX firms show on average more compliance and more voluntary disclosures compared to the other indices.

In **summary**, there is a particular loss of second tier segment information about capital expenditures after the adoption of IFRS 8. Moreover, there is a decline in the mean number of line items. Hence, the concerns of some opponents of IFRS 8 that the new standard would lead to a loss of second tier segment information are somewhat supported. However, it is questionable to which extent investors and financial analysts focus on the second tier information if they have more detailed primary and operating segment information at hand.

Information about major customers

One major amendment to segment disclosures introduced by IFRS 8 is the requirement to report the revenue with **major single external customers** if these exceed ten per cent of the firm's total revenue (IFRS 8.34). Under IAS 14R, only the Duerr Group reports this information. After the adoption of IFRS 8, however, almost 40 per cent of all firms in this study make a reference to revenues with major customers.

Most disclosures about revenues with single external customers are **rather vague**. For instance, the Constantin Medien Group reports:

> "*In total, the Constantin Medien Group generated with two customers more than 10 percent of total sales, respectively. These sales relate to both the Film Segment and the Sports- and Event-Marketing Segment.*"

(*Constantin Medien*, Annual Report (2009), p. 136)

One of the more **detailed** examples is Roth & Rau:

> *"Sales of € 25,751k were generated with a single customer in the photovoltaics segment equipment business. These sales therefore account for 13 % of the Group's total sales of € 197,903k."*

(*Roth & Rau*, Annual Report (2009), p. 127)

However, none of the firms disclosing information about single external customers reveals the **identity of the customers**. This may be due to potential disadvantages if this information is available to competitors. Moreover, some customers may not want the information about the business relationship to be publicly available. The proprietary nature of this disclosure is underlined by the case of the MEDION Group in 2009:

> *"Following a thorough examination, the Management Board has come to the conclusion that disclosing sales revenues per major external customer amounting to 10% or more of total Group sales revenues at MEDION, as stipulated in IFRS 8.34, could, from the perspective of a prudent businessman, lead to significant negative effects for MEDION. The Management Board has therefore decided, against the background of Section 131 (3) sentence 1 of the German Stock Corporation Act (AktG) and the protective clause against such a detailing provided under Section 286 (2) of the German Commercial Code (HGB), to refrain from disclosing sales per major customers in the consolidated financial statements prepared in accordance with IFRS despite the ensuing qualification of the audit certificate as regards the missing disclosure of sales per major customers as stipulated by IFRS 8.34."*

(*MEDION*, Annual Report (2009), p. 12)

Table 5-20 reports the percentage of **firms disclosing information about major customers** under IFRS 8 for each index and for the whole sample. About 15 per cent disclose the revenues of specific customers with particular segments. Another three per cent disclose total revenues with major customers – without allocation to particular segments. More than 20 per cent state that no single customer accounts for ten per cent of revenues. 61 per cent give no information at all. However, note that it is not mandatory to disclose that there are no major customers. Hence, it can be assumed that the 60 per cent of firms that make no statement at all may not have had single major customers. These findings are similar to *Crawford et al.* (2012), who report that about 21 per cent provide some information about major customers and 17 per cent make a negative statement (*Crawford et al.* (2012), p. 22).

Notably, the **larger DAX firms and MDAX firms** disclose less information about major customers compared to the smaller firms in the TecDAX and SDAX indices. This is in contrast to prior findings in this study which indicate that larger firms are usually more forthcoming in their segment reports and tend to disclose more information. However, the particular proprietary nature of this information or the fact that larger firms may not depend that often on single customers could be the reason for this finding.

In **summary**, disclosures about major customers can be an important source of information for users of financial statements that indicates potential dependencies of a firm.

This information was largely unavailable under IAS 14R. The adoption of IFRS 8 changed this to some extent, which should be helpful for users of segment information. Yet, there are still less than 20 per cent of firms that disclose revenues with major customers. However, since the introduction of IFRS 8, users of financial statements can assume that there are no major customers if a company does not provide any information. This was different under the former standard.

Information about major customers (IFRS 8 only)					
Percentage of firms (n=108)	DAX	MDAX	TecDAX	SDAX	Total
Revenues of major customers with specific segments	0%	8%	23%	24%	15%
Total revenues of major customers	0%	0%	9%	3%	3%
Statement that no revenues with external customers exceeded ten per cent	23%	28%	18%	15%	21%
Σ Total firms with references to major customers	23%	36%	50%	42%	39%
No statement	77%	64%	50%	58%	61%

Table 5-20: Information about major customers

Summary

To **sum up**, there is a decrease in the number of reported items if the influence of outliers is removed. This decrease is largely due to the reclassification of mandatory items under IAS 14R to conditional items under IFRS 8. In particular items such as segment assets, liabilities and capital expenditures are reported less frequently. Furthermore, there is also a decrease in the number of second tier segment items provided by firms. Particularly the disclosure of capital expenditures drops by more than 50 per cent.

However, the disclosures of the measures that are used by the firms to manage the segments increase substantially. This information may be **particularly useful** for users of financial statements since they receive the same information that is used by management. Moreover, the number of firms providing information about major customers increases as well.

It is unclear how the changes in disclosures impact **decision usefulness** of segment information. Firms may just have ceased to report items that are of no interest for sophisticated users such as investors or financial analysts and hence the decrease in the number of line items does not impair decision usefulness. However, in particular items such as segment assets, liabilities and capital expenditures help users of financial statements to gauge the financial position and future development of a firm's segments. Therefore, it is questionable whether users of financial statements can indeed forgo this information.

5.2.5   Reconciliation

This section provides descriptive statistics for the reconciliation of certain line items to the corresponding GAAP amounts under both standards. First, the availability of reconciliations and their form (i.e., column in the main table or as a separate table) are presented. Second, the magnitude of certain **reconciliation** positions for the line items segment revenues, segment result, segment assets and segment liabilities are described. Reconciliation information helps users of segment reports to better understand the segment items, in particular if they differ from GAAP amounts.

Reconciliation information

IFRS 8.28 and IAS 14R.67 both require firms to provide reconciliations for specific segment line items to the corresponding GAAP amounts. The level of detail, however, varies substantially among the sample firms. Table 5-21 shows **how often firms provide reconciliations** of segment revenue, profit or loss, assets and liabilities. The reconciliation can either be reported in the main table with a reconciliation column or in a separate reconciliation table. The latter is generally done when there are several reconciliation positions and usually yields more information.

Reconciliation information										
Percentage of firms (n=108)	DAX		MDAX		TecDAX		SDAX		Total	
	IAS 14R	IFRS 8	IAS 14R	IFRS 8	IAS 14R	IFRS 8	IAS 14R	IFRS 8	IAS 14R	IFRS 8
Firms providing reconciliations										
Reconciliation of segment revenues	77%	85%	77%	92%	65%	65%	79%	94%	75%	86%
- Thereof separate reconciliation table	10%	27%	0%	0%	0%	0%	0%	0%	1%	3%
Reconciliation of segment result	77%	77%	77%	87%	70%	74%	82%	94%	77%	85%
- Thereof separate reconciliation table	10%	31%	10%	15%	6%	12%	4%	13%	5%	16%
Reconciliation of segment assets	92%	92%	90%	80%	65%	57%	82%	74%	83%	74%
- Thereof separate reconciliation table	33%	50%	29%	29%	13%	15%	21%	16%	24%	26%
Reconciliation of segment liabilities	85%	77%	93%	64%	61%	39%	82%	64%	82%	61%
- Thereof separate reconciliation table	36%	40%	33%	24%	14%	22%	14%	14%	25%	23%

Table 5-21: Reconciliation information

In total, about 75 per cent of all firms reconcile total **segment revenues** to total revenue under IAS 14R. The remaining 25 per cent do not have reconciliation positions and the sum of segment revenues equals total revenues.[80] Out of the firms that provide a reconciliation of revenues, one per cent report a separate reconciliation column. This very low fraction is due to the fact that revenues usually entail only a few reconciliation positions like headquarters or consolidation. This is in contrast to other items such as assets or liabilities for which some positions like deferred taxes are not allocated on segmental level. After the adoption of IFRS 8, more than 86 per cent provide reconciliation information for segment revenues. This is largely due to the increased disclosure of internal segment revenues that requires the elimination of internal amounts for consolidation. Moreover, there is also a minor increase in separate reconciliation tables to three per cent. The avail-

---

[80] A missing reconciliation can be due to two reasons: either the item is not disclosed in the segment report or the sum of segment amounts adds up to the total amount. For segment revenues under IAS 14R, however, Table 5-14 shows that all sample firms report segment revenue and thus the latter holds.

ability of segment revenue reconciliation is largely similar among the different indices. Only TecDAX firms report on average a little less compared to firms in the other indices. Moreover, only DAX firms disclose separate reconciliation tables for this item.

Firms can either reconcile the total of the segments' measure of profit or loss to the firm's profit or loss before or after tax (IFRS 8.28b). The vast majority of firms, however, reconciles to profit or loss before taxes because taxes are usually not allocated on segmental level. In total, the reconciliation information about **segment result** is very similar to segment revenues. Under IAS 14R, about 77 per cent report this information and there is an increase to 85 per cent upon the adoption of IFRS 8. A separate reconciliation table is available for about five per cent under IAS 14R which increases to 16 per cent under IFRS 8. This increase is in line with the notion that the introduction of the management approach to segment reporting leads to the disclosure of non-IFRS profitability measures that require more reconciliation information. The pattern across the different indices is comparable to segment revenues: TecDAX firms reconcile segment results less often compared to the other three indices.

Reconciliation information about **segment assets** and **segment liabilities** is affected differently by the adoption of the management approach: While 83 per cent (82 per cent) reconcile segment assets (segment liabilities) under IAS 14R, only 74 per cent (61 per cent) do so under IFRS 8. This decrease, however, is largely due to the fact that less firms report segment assets and in particular segment liabilities under the new standard since it is no longer required unless used for internal purposes. The availability of separate reconciliation tables is generally higher for segment assets and liabilities compared to segment revenues and segment profitability. More than 20 per cent of firms that provide reconciliation information for segment assets or liabilities disclose a separate table under either standard. As elaborated above, assets and liabilities usually entail more positions that are reconciled separately because items such as deferred taxes or financial assets or liabilities are frequently not allocated on segmental level. Among the different indices, DAX firms provide reconciliations for segment assets and liabilities most often.

Magnitude of reconciliations

The next table provides information about the relative **magnitude of single reconciliation positions** for the items segment revenue, segment earnings, segment assets and segment liabilities. The columns "Inter-segment elimination/consolidation" represent the magnitude of the eliminated inter-segment amount to the GAAP amount. This reflects the degree of inter-segment entanglement. "Headquarters" comprises the ratio of the amounts allocated to the headquarters relative to the GAAP amounts. The "Headquarters" position may, for instance, include certain financial liabilities that are not allocated to segmental level because financing is done by a central unit. Moreover, some firms provide very detailed reconciliations with specific reconciliation positions. For instance, a few firms report adjusted profitability measures that exclude goodwill impairments or extraordinary expenses which need to be reconciled to total earnings. However, these positions vary substantially among the different items and therefore they are aggregated to the "Other" column. The last column "Mean number of reconciliation positions" represents the average number of such positions for all firms that provide reconciliation information for the respective item.

Note that 11 per cent of firms report an **aggregated** "Consolidation and headquarters" column under IAS 14R. This decreases to eight per cent because some firms start to report these positions separately upon adoption of the new standard. For simplicity, the aggregated positions are divided equally between the respective columns when determining the relative magnitude of the positions.

(n=108)	**Magnitude of reconciliation positions**							
	IAS 14R				**IFRS 8**			
	Inter-segment elimination/ consolidation	Head-quarters	Other	Mean number of reconciliation positions	Inter-segment elimination/ consolidation	Head-quarters	Other	Mean number of reconciliation positions
Revenues	-6%	3%	-	1.20	-7%	4%	-4%	1.28
Earnings	12%	6%	1%	1.27	-4%	-4%	-25%	1.44
Assets	-2%	15%	19%	1.93	-6%	25%	27%	2.23
Liabilities	4%	24%	47%	1.78	3%	27%	51%	1.94

Table 5-22: Magnitude of reconciliation positions

The first row of Table 5-22 reports the reconciliation information for **segment revenues**. The mean values of -6 per cent (IAS 14R) and -7 per cent (IFRS 8) for intersegment elimination and consolidation indicates that about 6 to 7 per cent of total revenues are internal transactions under both standards. This is a substantial amount in absolute terms given that total revenues of the sample firms reach up to two-digit billion Euros figures. Moreover, the headquarters account for three per cent of total revenues under IAS 14R and for four per cent under IFRS 8. Under IAS 14R, there are no firms that report other reconciliation positions. In contrast, there is one firm under IFRS 8 that shows another position labeled with the vague term "non-allocated revenues". Furthermore, under IAS 14R firms report on average 1.20 reconciliation positions which slightly increases to 1.28 under the management approach. In total, there is no substantial difference between the two standards in the extent of inter-segment entanglement and the amount of revenues allocated to the headquarters. However, there are slightly more reconciliation positions under IFRS 8. This may be due to the fact that more firms report separate consolidation and headquarters columns rather than aggregating them.

The results for the reconciliation of **segment earnings** are similar to segment revenues. However, the reconciliation ratios are more dispersed and noisier because profits can be positive and negative. Notably, the mean value in the consolidation column under IAS 14R is positive which signals that inter-segment transactions are unprofitable on average. This is, however, driven by one outlier with a ratio above 15 which stems from a profit that is close to zero inflating the proportion relative to total earnings. Removing this outlier yields a mean value of -35 per cent which is more consistent with the notion that inter-segment transactions based on the arm's length principle (or cost plus pricing) should be profitable. Under IFRS 8, intersegment earnings account for four per cent of total earnings. The headquarters show a small profit of about six per cent of total earnings on average under IAS 14R and a small loss under IFRS 8 of about minus four per cent. The magnitude of other reconciliation positions with less than one per cent is negligible in the IAS 14R period. However, they amount to almost 25 per cent in the IFRS 8 period. This supports prior findings which show more adjusted profitability measures under IFRS 8 that require reconciliations. But also note that this is only the mean value for five firms which report other positions. In total, the mean number of reconciliation positions increases from 1.27 to 1.44 upon adoption of the management approach.

The reconciliation of **segment assets** to total assets is different to revenues or earnings. Inter-segment eliminations or consolidations are less important. This is usually only relevant if assets are allocated to several segments. However, a relatively large amount of assets are held by the headquarters (15 per cent under IAS 14R and 25 per cent under IFRS 8). Moreover, other positions comprise about 19 per cent of total assets in the IAS 14R period and 27 per cent in the IFRS 8 period. The mean number of total reconciliation positions increases from 1.93 to 2.23 upon adoption of IFRS 8. Deferred tax assets, current and non-current financial assets, tax receivables, cash and cash equivalents and other investments are the most common reconciliation positions which are not allocated on segmental level. This is similar under both standards.

The reconciliation of **segment liabilities** is comparable to segment assets. Again, inter-segment eliminations or consolidations are less important: They only comprise four per cent of total liabilities under IAS 14R and three per cent under IFRS 8. Not surprisingly, the headquarters hold about 24 per cent (IAS 14R) and 27 per cent (IFRS 8) of all liabilities. This may be due to a centralized financing so that some liabilities are not allocated to segmental level. Moreover, the other reconciliation positions amount to 47 per cent (IAS 14R) and 51 per cent (IFRS 8) of total liabilities. This is very high in particular compared to the relative fraction of assets that are not allocated to segmental level. No firm provides any information about this asymmetrical allocation of assets and liabilities to segmental level. In this context, *Kajüter/Nienhaus* (2013) proxy for segment equity by the difference of segment assets and segment liabilities. They find that segment equity does not yield any value relevant information for investors. Their result may be due to the asymmetrical allocation of assets and liabilities that potentially overstates their segment equity proxy. In total, there is again an increase in the mean number of reconciliation positions from 1.78 under IAS 14R to 1.94 under IFRS 8.

Summary

Reconciliation information is an integral part of segment reporting which is **increasingly important** if segment items differ from total IFRS amounts. The latter is particularly the case for segment reports under the management approach. In fact, firms report more reconciliation information for segment revenues and segment earnings upon adoption of IFRS 8. The number of separate reconciliation tables increases as well. Furthermore, there is a slight increase in the number of reconciliation positions for the main line items upon adoption of IFRS 8. However, the amounts allocated to the headquarters or inter-segment eliminations do not change much.

5.3 Discussion

The **objective** of chapter five is to describe the change in segment reporting practice due to the adoption of the management approach. Segment disclosures of the last year under IAS 14R are compared to the disclosures of the first year under IFRS 8. By comparing the restated lag-adoption year to the historical year, this study isolates the effect of the standard change from any concurrent developments that may also impact segment disclosures. The analysis is structured in five categories:

In the **general information** category, this study documents a significant increase in the narrative information accompanying the segment report. This may be due to the increased need of explanatory notes if a company is depicted from the management's perspective. However, there is also a particular increase in description of the types of **products and services**. This may specifically contribute to a better understanding of a company's segmentation for users of financial statements. Moreover, with the adoption of IFRS 8 almost fifty per cent of the companies provide information about the **CODM**. This may also be particularly useful for users of financial statements to get a better understanding of the management structures of a company.

Yet, areas such as the **placement** of the segment report or **inter-segment pricing** are entirely unaffected by the adoption of IFRS 8. This is not surprising given that these aspects are either not covered by the rules (placement of the segment report) or IFRS 8 did not change the rules (inter-segment pricing). In addition, inter-segment pricing has implications for taxation and intra-country or intra-entity profit distribution that may go beyond the scope of segment reporting. In **summary**, the expected change in the general information category upon adoption of the management approach (P_1) is supported by the empirical findings:

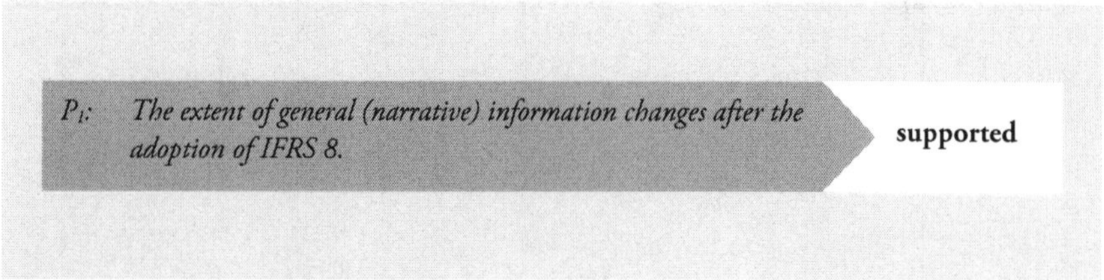

P_1: *The extent of general (narrative) information changes after the adoption of IFRS 8.* **supported**

Figure 5-4: Results for proposition one

With regard to the **segmentation** category, this study finds an increase in the number of reported segments and an increased **consistency** of segment information with other parts of financial disclosures upon adoption of the new standard. Following the fineness theorem (*Demski* (1973)), an increased fineness of segmentation should be at least as valuable as a broader segmentation. Hence, it is expected that the decision usefulness of segment information with a finer segmentation increases. Furthermore, more consistency of (audited) segment disclosures with other disclosures likely enhances the relevance and reliability of a firm's overall disclosures. In addition, some firms start to report a **mixed segmentation** upon adoption of IFRS 8. Under IAS 14R, they were not allowed to provide this information. Users of financial statements of these firms now receive a picture that is more in line with the managements' view. Moreover, there is a moderate increase in the **fineness of second tier** geographical information. Hence, the fear of some critics that the adoption of IFRS 8 would lead to a loss of geographical information is unfounded – at least in terms of its fineness.

In contrast, there are some areas within the category segmentation that are **unaffected** by the adoption of IFRS 8. For instance, neither the number of **one segment companies** nor the **aggregation** of similar segments change substantially upon the adoption of the management approach. However, overall the proposition that the adoption of IFRS 8 led to a change in the segmentation (P₂) is supported:

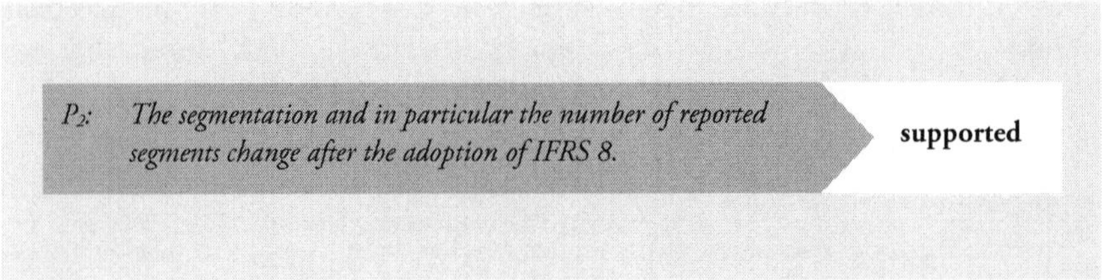

P_2: *The segmentation and in particular the number of reported segments change after the adoption of IFRS 8.* **supported**

Figure 5-5: Results for proposition two

The basis of **measurement** is the category that caused the most upset among opponents of IFRS 8. Critics voiced concerns about less understandability and too much flexibility if segment information deviates from the measurement principles used for the financial statements. The findings of this study, however, show that these concerns are largely unfounded. Almost all firms in the sample use numbers that are in line with **measurement principles of IFRS**. Those few firms that use non-GAAP measures provide sound reconciliation information that help to understand any differences. Therefore, the proposition that IFRS 8 caused a change in the basis of measurement (P₃) is not supported:

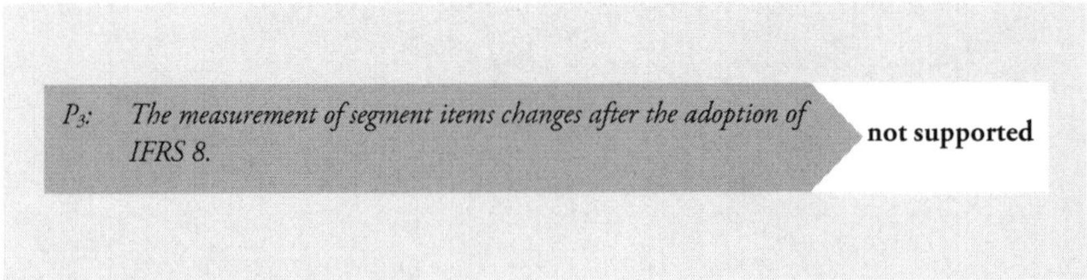

P_3: *The measurement of segment items changes after the adoption of IFRS 8.* **not supported**

Figure 5-6: Results for proposition three

The category **disclosures** comprises the actual content of the segment report and it is thus an essential determinant of the decision usefulness of segment reporting. Upon adoption of IFRS 8, the extent of **mandatory segment disclosures** decreased. Mandatory items were replaced by conditional items that only have to be disclosed if they are used internally as well. This leads to a general decrease in the number of reported line items for both the primary segmentation as well as the second tier segments. This decrease is particularly pronounced for the **second tier segment items** – which largely comprise geographical segment information. Hence, the fear of some opponents of IFRS 8 about the loss of geographical information is supported to some extent.

Furthermore, more firms report measures that are used by the firms to **manage the segments**. This may be an important piece of information for users of financial statements and it also represents the core feature of the management approach. Understanding how the management runs the company may also increase the users' overall understanding of the business. Finally, some firms start to report their revenues with **major single customers** which provides additional information about a firm's potential dependencies.

Hence, there is a substantial change in the extent and kind of segment disclosures after the adoption of IFRS 8 and thus P4 is supported:

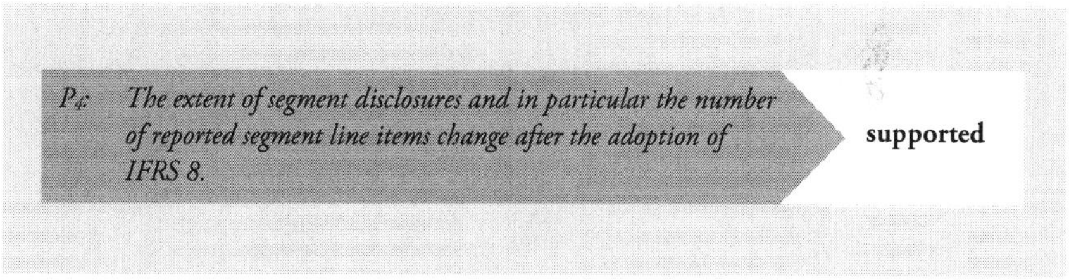

P4:   The extent of segment disclosures and in particular the number of reported segment line items change after the adoption of IFRS 8.   **supported**

Figure 5-7: Results for proposition four

The category **reconciliation** plays an important role if inter-segment transactions occur and non-IFRS numbers are used in the segment report. The former does not change much upon the adoption of IFRS 8 as the relative magnitudes of inter-segment elimination or headquarters positions in the reconciliations are substantially the same. However, there is a general increase in the number of **reconciled positions** and in the firms that provide **separate reconciliation tables**. This may help users of financial statements to better understand the segment data and thus increase decision usefulness. In total, the empirical findings support the proposition that IFRS 8 led to a change in the provision of reconciliation information (P5):

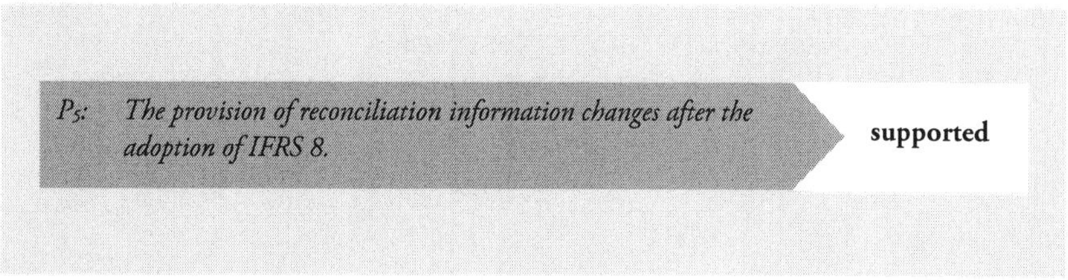

P5:   The provision of reconciliation information changes after the adoption of IFRS 8.   **supported**

Figure 5-8: Results for proposition five

Four of the five propositions are supported and indicate that there is a change in segment reporting practice. However, as noted earlier, some of the changes in segment reporting may not solely be due to the adoption of the new standard, but rather due to an **increased enforcement**. The FREP declared IFRS 8 as one of their main focus areas for the financial year 2009. Moreover, new standards are often particularly subject to auditor scrutiny.

This may especially be the case for IFRS 8 given the **contentious political debate** surrounding its introduction. An increased scrutiny of auditors and enforcement institutions likely impacted the segment reporting practice of firms. Therefore, the empirical findings may not be solely attributable to the introduction of the management approach.

The findings of chapter five indicate that the adoption of IFRS 8 influenced segment reporting practice in particular with regard to segmentation, disclosures and reconciliation. General information aspects are less affected and the basis of measurement is hardly affected at all. However, note that the descriptive findings in this chapter reflect the **average change** among all firms. Hence, results are diluted by a relatively high proportion of firms that already reported in line with the management approach under IAS 14R and thus did not change anything upon the adoption of IFRS 8. Some firms did not even decide to adjust the terms to the new standard. For instance, the Gerry Weber Group still uses the terms primary and secondary segments in the first year of IFRS 8:

> *"In accordance with IFRS 8, the business activities of the GERRY WEBER Group are divided into business segments as the primary reporting format and into geographical segments as the secondary reporting format."*

> (*Gerry Weber*, Annual Report (2009/2010), p. 96)

Firms that actually change their segment reporting generally show a substantial change in **multiple aspects**.[81] The following analysis on the capital market implications of the adoption of IFRS 8 on information asymmetry, cost of capital and the financial analysts' information environment in chapter six takes this aspect into account. The analysis builds on the descriptive findings of this chapter and focuses on the firms that changed segment reporting practice.

---

[81]   The Praktiker Group is an example for this: It substantially increases the general narrative disclosures that accompany the quantitative segment information. Moreover, it increases the number of segments and change from a geographical segmentation to a mixed business lines/geographical approach. Furthermore, it provides additional information about the CODM and major customers. Finally, the reconciliations include more positions.

6   Analysis of economic consequences

6.1   Methodological approach

This section presents the methodological approach used to gauge the capital market effects of IFRS 8's adoption. The analysis comprises three sub-analyses from the perspectives of investors, companies and financial analysts. After some preliminary considerations, the general research design as well as the main variables for each of the sub-analyses are introduced.

6.1.1   Preliminary considerations

Making causal claims about the impact of financial disclosures, in particular the adoption of a new accounting standard, on capital markets is very challenging. In general, researchers face three problems.

First, it is difficult to rule out any **confounding time effects** that may impact the measures used to gauge capital market implications. Usually, accounting standards come into effect for all firms in a jurisdiction at the same point in time. Any changes that happen concurrently, either accounting-related or general economic developments, may also impact the measures used to capture capital market effects. Hence, it is generally impossible to solely attribute potential reactions by the capital market to the adoption of the accounting standard itself.

Second and in a similar vein, it is difficult to **narrow down the channel** of financial disclosures that actually causes the capital market effects. This is particularly the case when discretion or voluntary disclosure decisions are involved. For instance, a company that decides to be more transparent and forthcoming in their segment report can simultaneously improve several other disclosures as part of a general transparency improvement strategy. Hence, potential capital market effects may be induced by the joint effect of several changes in disclosures.

Third, a concern that is inherent in most archival research designs is potential **endogeneity**.[82] Different factors such as reverse causality, self-selection or correlated omitted variables can cause endogeneity (*Antonakis et al.* (2010)). Reverse causality means that independent variables may not be driving the dependent variable, but vice versa: For instance, firms with extensive voluntary disclosures may not experience a lower cost of capital, it is rather the low cost of capital that allows firms to spend more money on voluntary financial disclosures in the first place. Self-selection occurs if companies choose to do something such as the voluntary early adoption of an accounting standard and this decision is driven by factors that also affect the capital market effect measure at hand: For instance, a firm with a lot of growth opportunities opts to voluntary adopt international accounting standards instead of local GAAP to attract more investors. One may find a subsequent decline in the cost of capital. However, this decline may not solely or even primarily be

---

[82]   The technical consequence of endogeneity is a correlation of independent variables with the error term in a regression model. This is a violation of the OLS regression which leads to biased estimates and thus invalid inferences.

driven by the adoption of international accounting as cost of capital is also very sensitive to growth opportunities. Hence, failure to account for this will lead to false causal claims.

Finally, any relevant omitted variables that are both correlated with an independent variable and the error term can cause endogeneity and thus problems with the causal interpretations of regression results.

The research design of this study attempts to address each of the concerns. In the following, the methodological features and characteristics of the design are introduced and it is discussed how the challenges described above are addressed to **approximate causality**.

6.1.2 Research design

The **optimal research design** to analyze the capital market effects of the adoption of IFRS 8 would be a randomized experiment: Some firms of an economy would be randomly chosen to adopt IFRS 8 while the other firms would have to stick with IAS 14R. The randomization process would address most issues raised in the previous section and in such a laboratory setting the firms would on average only differ in the treatment effect. This research design would allow strong causal claims about the capital market implications of IFRS 8. Unfortunately, this is not feasible.

Empirical research, however, has developed other techniques which can be used to approximate causality under certain assumptions in non-experimental settings. One method is the **difference-in-differences** design. The difference-in-differences research design uses a natural experiment in which one group is affected by a certain phenomenon at a certain point in time (treatment group) while the other group is not (control group). Under optimal conditions, the two groups only differ in the treatment effect and they are exposed to the same environmental conditions.

Figure 6-1 demonstrates the **general concept** of the difference-in-differences design. The difference in a particular outcome measure from the pre-treatment period to the post-treatment period of the treatment group (B-A) is compared to the difference in the control group (D-C). The difference in these differences ((B-A)-(D-C)) reflects the treatment effect adjusted for potential confounding effects that equally affect the two groups.

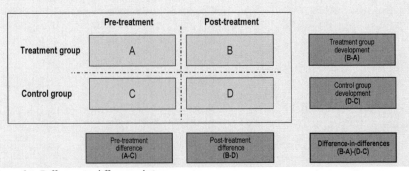

Figure 6-1: Difference-in-differences design

This study exploits a **unique setting** that allows for a difference-in-differences research design: A large fraction of companies already reported segment information in line with the management approach under IAS 14R. Hence, these companies did not have to change their segment reporting practices upon adoption of IFRS 8 and thus they serve as the control group. The companies that had to change their segmental disclosures to comply with IFRS 8 and the management approach form the treatment group. Boths groups should be exposed to the same environmental conditions and only differ in the aspect that the treatment group provides segment information *"through the management's eyes"* (*Martin* (1997), p. 29) for the first time upon adoption of IFRS 8.

The general regression model for the difference-in-differences setting in the subsequent analyses is as follows:

$$(6.1) \quad EconCons_{i;t} = \alpha + \beta_1\,Post_t + \beta_2 Change_i + \beta_3 Post_t \times Change_i + \sum_{k=1}^{K}\beta_{k+3}\,Control_{i;t}^k + \varepsilon_{i;t}$$

where,

$EconCons_{i;t}$ = measure used to gauge the economic consequences in each of the three sub-studies for firm i and period t;

$Post_t$ = dummy variable that is 1 for an observation from the post IFRS 8 adoption period and 0 otherwise;

$Change_i$ = dummy variable that is 1 for an observation from the treatment group and 0 otherwise; and

$Control_{i;t}^k$ = represents one of the K control variables, which differ in every sub-study.

The coefficient β_1 can be interpreted as the general change in the economic consequences measure from the pre IFRS 8 to the post IFRS 8 period, which all companies are subject to. β_2 is the average difference between the treatment and the control group before the treatment (i.e., adoption of IFRS 8). β_3 is the incremental change of the change firms and thus reflects the **treatment effect**. For instance, if one expected an incremental reduction in the cost of capital for the treatment group, the sign of β_3 would be negative. This model is estimtaed on a balanced firm-year panel covering two years for each firm – one year pre IFRS 8 adoption and the other year post IFRS 8 adoption.

Moreover, this study uses two ways to control for the **self-selection bias** of early adopters: First, all early adopters are eliminated and equation (6.1) is run on the reduced sample. Second, equation (6.1) is augmented by a dummy variable indicating whether a firm is an early adopter:

(6.2) $EconCons_{i;t} = \alpha + \beta_1 Post_t + \beta_2 Change_i + \beta_3 Early_i + \beta_4 Post_t \times$
$Change_i + \beta_5 Post_t \times Early_i + \beta_6 Change_i \times Early_i +$
$\beta_7 Post_t \times Change_i \times Early_i + \sum_{k=1}^{K} \beta_{k+7} Control_{i;t}^k + \varepsilon_{i;t}$

where,

$Early_i$ = dummy variable that is 1 for an observation from an early adopting
                firm and 0 otherwise; and

all other variables as defined above.

To capture differences for **early adopters**, $Post_t$ and $Change_i$ are fully interacted with
$Early_i$ in equation (6.2). The coefficient β_3 represents the average difference of early
adopting firms compared to non-early adopters. β_5 and β_6 reflect the incremental effect
for early adopters in the IFRS 8 period and in the change group. However, the most important coefficient with regard to early adopters is β_7 which represents the incremental
treatment effect of the early adopting firms. If β_7 turns out to be significant and β_4 ceases
to be significant, it would indicate that a potential treatment effect is only driven by early
adopters.

Moreover, to gain more confidence in the causality of the treatment effect, equation (6.1)
is further augmented. Given that some firms use the adoption of IFRS 8 to report less
segment information, $Change_i$ is split into a positive and a negative change group. This
allows to separately analyze the effect for firms that **increased respectively decreased
segment disclosures** upon adoption of IFRS 8:

(6.3) $EconCons_{i;t} = \alpha + \beta_1 Post_t + \beta_2 Change_{i;Positive}^g + \beta_3 Change_{i;Negative}^g +$
$\beta_4 Post_t \times Change_{i;Positive}^g + \beta_5 Post_t \times Change_{i;Negative}^g +$
$\sum_{k=1}^{K} \beta_{k+6} Control_{i;t}^k + \varepsilon_{i;t}$

where,

$Change_{i;Positive}^g$ = dummy variable that is 1 for an observation from the treatment
                    group of positive change firms (grouping g)[83] and 0 otherwise;

$Change_{i;Negative}^g$ = dummy variable that is 1 for an observation from the treatment
                    group of negative change firms (grouping g) and 0 otherwise; and

all other variables as defined above.

If the change in segment reporting is really causing an effect, there should be a difference
between positive and negative change firms. Hence, it is expected that β_4 shows the oppo-

---

[83] There will be different groupings for the treatment firms. Section 6.1.4 classifies different degrees of
     changes that are used in the empirical analyses.

site sign of β_5. Exploiting such a **cross-sectional variation** in the treatment group emphasizes the causality of the treatment effect.

This research design addresses many concerns raised in section 6.1.1. For instance, **confounding time effects** are not an issue since the treatment and the control group both encounter the same economic and legislative changes that may also have an effect on the empirical measures used in this study. For instance, if the global financial crisis fostered uncertainties and thus increased information asymmetries during the research period, it would equally affect both groups.

The issue of **narrowing down the channel** is less severe in this research design since the adoption of IFRS 8 is mandatory. Thus, any other voluntary changes in disclosures should be randomly spread among the treatment and the control group. Moreover, there were not any other major changes in disclosure requirements that coincide with the introduction of IFRS 8.

Furthermore, **endogeneity** induced by reverse causality is not a problem as the changes specification in the difference-in-differences design rules out most alternative explanations of a potentially inverted causation. However, endogeneity due to self-selection is more of a concern. This concern hinges on the assumption that is made about whether the decision to change segment reporting to comply with IFRS 8 is voluntary or mandatory. In case it is assumed that discretion and flexibility allow circumventing a change in segmental disclosures to comply with IFRS 8, it is possible that there are factors that jointly impact the decision to change segment reporting and the change in information asymmetries and cost of capital. For instance, firms that face an increase in growth opportunities decide to change segment information to comply with the management approach as they think that this yields certain benefits that help to exploit the higher growth opportunities. However, cost of capital is very respondent to a firm's growth opportunities and thus one would find a relationship between the adoption of IFRS 8 and cost of capital which is actually driven by increased growth opportunities. The problem disappears if the change is mandatory as firms would not self-select to change segment reporting to comply with the management approach and thus the change is independent of other factors that simultaneously impact information asymmetries or cost of capital. The mandatory character of adopting the new standard requirements seems reasonable as an auditor's involvement should ensure that entities comply with IFRS. However, particularly due to the concerns of discretion and managerial flexibility voiced by critics of IFRS 8, it is not possible to entirely rule out the possibility that some firms use their discretion to not comply with the new standard.

Finally, the challenge in this study is to **clearly distinguish** between change and no-change firms and to ensure that the change is actually due to the adoption of the new standard. Although the identification strategy already isolates the effect of the standard change to some extent by comparing lag-adoption and historical year, there is still a chance that the restated lag-adoption year data captures differences other than reporting changes. For instance, in case of discontinued operations in the adoption year, segment information for the lag-adoption year would be restated without the discontinued operation. If one fails to control for this, the respective observation would incorrectly be flagged as a change firm although the change is due to other reasons. However, all annual reports are carefully analyzed to detect observations that reflect changes other than reporting changes.

A further concern is the notion that a change in segment reporting practice is assumed to be a change from segment reporting under IAS 14R to IFRS 8 while non-change (control group) represents firms that were already compliant with the management approach and IFRS 8 under IAS 14R rules. However, there might be firms that change their segmentation to increase or decrease their segmental disclosures **for other reasons** although they were already compliant with IFRS 8 and the management approach in the pre-IFRS 8 period. Hence, the change simply coincides with the adoption of IFRS 8. It is unfeasible to entirely rule out this possibility. However, this simply imposes a caveat on the interpretation of the results. One should be cautious to attribute the findings to the adoption of IFRS 8 but rather to a change in segment reporting. Nonetheless, assuming that there is a high probability that the change in segment reporting is due to the new standard, however, is reasonable. Moreover, segment report narratives are screened for any signs of indication.[84]

Finally, it is important to determine the exact **timing** of the treatment effect. In the literature, the proxies of information asymmetries, cost of capital, and financial analysts' forecast properties are usually calculated over an estimation window beginning 90 days after fiscal year end if information from the annual report is analyzed. This ensures that the annual report is publicly available and information from the annual report is impounded in stock prices and financial analysts' data. For instance, the first annual report with segment information under IFRS 8 for the financial year 2009 is published in the beginning of 2010. Hence, information asymmetries, cost of capital and financial analysts' measures are calculated as of March 31, 2010.[85] This procedure is used if the information is only conveyed by the annual report. The first segmental information under IFRS 8, however, is already available in the first quarterly report of 2009. Following, IAS 34 "Interim Financial Reporting", firms need to disclose segment information in their interim report if they are required to provide a segment report in their annual financial statements (IAS 34.16A (g)). Yet, the requirements for these disclosures (IAS 34.16A (g).i-vi) are lower compared to the full segment report under IFRS 8.[86] Moreover, interim reports are not audited and only a few firms voluntarily purchase interim reviews from external auditors (*Kajüter et al.* (2014), pp. 18–19). Given the nature of the management approach, the involvement of an external auditor for the preparation of segment reporting is particularly important. Therefore, it is questionable in how far users of financial statements rely on segment information from quarterly reports. Yet, to address this, the treatment effect is analyzed at two dates: 90 days after fiscal year end in case users largely rely on the audited full segment report and 45 days after quarter one end if users also make use of reduced interim

---

[84] In fact, three firms are identified as having a merger or internal restructuring at the time of IFRS 8's adoption. These firms are eliminated from the sample (see section 6.1.4).

[85] The estimation windows vary among the different measures and usually cover 30 to 90 days. The exact window for each proxy is described in the following sections.

[86] For instance, firms do not need to provide second tier segment information, information about products and services or information about major customers.

segment information. This also provides some insights on the dissemination of segment information over time for the different types of users in this study.

Furthermore, note that the different proxies of the economic constructs used in this study also behave differently with regard to the timing of potential effects. The information asymmetry measure is less **anticipatory** compared to cost of capital or financial analysts' measures (e.g., *Daske et al.* (2008); *Christensen et al.* (2013)). Ultimately, investors are concerned about adverse selection and transparency when they trade.[87] In contrast, financial analysts adjust valuations or estimates the moment their prospects about future transparency change (*Christensen et al.* (2013), p. 152). Hence, the cost of capital and financial analysts' measures may already show an effect once a change in segment reporting can be expected. This is the case with segment information in the first quarterly report in 2009 under the new standard. Although the quarterly segment report is reduced and unaudited, it reveals to some extent how segment reporting is going to change in the annual financial statements. Hence, financial analysts may already adjust their expectations at that time. This aspect is addressed and discussed in the empirical analyses of section 6.2, section 6.3 and section 6.4.

6.1.3 Variables for the regression analyses

6.1.3.1 Information asymmetry

Information asymmetries introduce **adverse selection** into the secondary share market: Less informed investors adjust the prices at which they are willing to trade to protect themselves against potential losses when trading with superiorly informed investors (*Glosten/Milgrom* (1985)). This adjustment is reflected in the liquidity of a security. According to *Lang/Maffett* (2010):

> "*Perhaps the best developed liquidity measure is bid-ask spread, which attempts to directly capture a stock's trading costs.*"

Due to its strong theoretical foundation and proximity to the underlying concept as well as the common use in previous research (e.g., *Welker* (1995); *Healy et al.* (1999); *Leuz/Verrecchia* (2000)), this study uses the **bid-ask spread** to capture information asymmetries. Following extant literature (e.g., *Daske et al.* (2008)), the bid-ask spread is measured as the median of the difference between the daily closing bid and ask prices divided by the midpoint for the three-month period starting 90 days after fiscal year end or 45 days after the end of the first quarter:

$$(6.4) \qquad Spread_{i;t} = \frac{(P_{i;t}^{bid} - P_{i;t}^{ask}) * 2}{P_{i;t}^{bid} + P_{i;t}^{ask}}$$

---

[87] *Christensen et al.* (2013), p. 152, acknowledge that investors may also anticipate future improvements in transparency to reduce adverse selection when they sell. However, they argue that this effect is likely small.

where,

$Spread_{i;t}$ = bid-ask spread for trading day t and firm i;

$P_{i;t}^{bid}$ = bid closing price for trading day t and firm i; and

$P_{i;t}^{ask}$ = ask closing price for trading day t and firm i.

Control variables

Previous literature has found that bid-ask spreads systematically depend on trading volume, return volatility, and firm size (e.g., *Stoll* (1978a); *Glosten/Milgrom* (1985); *Chiang/Venkatesh* (1988); *Chordia et al.* (2000); *Leuz/Verrecchia* (2000)).

More frequent trading reduces the probability that a stock has to be kept in inventory for a long time and thus reduces spreads (*Chordia et al.* (2000), p. 24). **Trading volume** is the annual median of the daily turnover ratio, that is, trading volume in Euro divided by the market value of outstanding equity for the 12 months following the fiscal year end (*Leuz/Verrecchia* (2000), p. 105).

Return volatility increases the risk of holding a specific security (*Chordia et al.* (2000), p. 24). Thus, it is positively related to the spread. **Return volatility** is measured as the standard deviation of daily stock returns for the 12 months following the fiscal year end (*Leuz/Verrecchia* (2000), p. 105).

Moreover, larger firms usually have a richer information environment which mitigates the risk of adverse selection (*Gode/Mohanram* (2003), p. 405). The increased availability of public information makes it more difficult for insiders to gain an information advantage (*Leuz/Wysocki* (2008), pp. 6–7). **Size** is measured as the market value of a firm's equity at the beginning of the financial year (e.g., *Leuz/Verrecchia* (2000), p. 105; *Daske et al.* (2008), p. 1104).

Basic regression model

The regression model is based on equation (6.1) from section 6.1.2. Following extant literature, this study takes the natural logarithm[88] of all continuous variables (e.g., *Leuz/Verrecchia* (2000); *Daske et al.* (2008)). Hence, the main specification of the bid-ask spread analysis is:

---

[88] A log-linear specification allows for multiplicative relations between the control variables, which is suggested by prior literature (e.g., *Stoll* (1978b); *Glosten/Milgrom* (1985)).

(6.5) $\log(Spread_{i;t}) =$ $\alpha + \beta_1 Post_t + \beta_2 Change_i + \beta_3 Post_t \times Change_i +$
$\beta_4 \log(Trading\_volume_{i;t}) +$
$\beta_5 \log(Return\_volatility_{i;t}) + \beta_6 \log(Size_{i;t}) + \varepsilon_{i;t}$

where,

$Trading\_volume_{i;t}$ = annual median of the daily turnover divided by market value of outstanding equity for the 12 months following the fiscal year end of firm i in year t;

$Return\_volatility_{i;t}$ = annual standard deviation of monthly stock returns of firm i in year t;

$Size_{i;t}$ = market value of a firm's equity at the beginning of the financial year of firm i in year t; and

all other variables as defined above.

6.1.3.2   Cost of capital

Measuring the cost of capital of a firm is difficult. Prior research has primarily used stock returns or dividend yields (e.g., *Campbell/Shiller* (1988); *Foerster/Karolyi* (1999); *Errunza/Miller* (2000); *Foerster/Karolyi* (2000)). These measures, however, are also influenced by the market's expectations of future cash flows and thus it is difficult to disentangle the cost of capital (*Bekaert/Harvey* (2000); *Hail/Leuz* (2009)). In the last decade, empirical research has developed an approach that uses valuation models and analyst forecast data to gauge an **ex ante measure** of the cost of capital.[89] There are several different methodologies in the **implied** cost of equity models (e.g., *Claus/Thomas* (2001); *Gebhardt et al.* (2001); *Ohlson/Juettner-Nauroth* (2005); and *Easton* (2004)), which all yield certain advantages and shortcomings. These models are based on the discount dividend valuation model (*Hail/Leuz* (2009), p. 432) and equate current market value with a stream of discounted future earnings.[90] However, the models differ in the use of forecast periods, assumptions on long-term growth, and incorporation of inflation and industry effects (*Hail/Leuz* (2009), p. 432).

Yet, the general concept for the **empirical implementation** of the models is similar: Stock price, book value of equity, and expected earnings are substituted by stock data and financial data from DataStream and analyst forecast data from I/B/E/S. Subsequently, the internal rate of return that equates stock price and future expected earnings is backed out.

---

[89]   For an overview see *Lang/Maffett* (2010), p. 207.
[90]   The assumption about the future earnings sequence differs among the models. They are either based on residual income or abnormal earnings – both derived from the dividend discount model.

As there is an ongoing debate on which **measure** is optimal (e.g., *Botosan/Plumlee* (2005); *Lee et al.* (2009); *Hail/Leuz* (2009)), this study uses four models which are frequently used in the extant literature:

Claus and Thomas (2001)

$$(6.6) \quad Price_t = \quad BVE_t + \sum_{\tau=1}^{T} \frac{(\widehat{EPS}_{t+\tau} - r_{CT} * \widehat{BVE}_{t+\tau-1})}{(1+r_{CT})^\tau} + \frac{(\widehat{EPS}_{t+T} - r_{CT} * \widehat{BVE}_{t+T-1})(1+g)}{(1+r_{CT})^T (r_{CT}-g)}$$

where,

$Price_t$ = current market price of a company's security at date t;

BVE_t = book value of common equity per share at the beginning of the financial year t;

$\widehat{EPS}_{t+\tau}$ = expected earnings per share for fiscal year $t+\tau$ based on analyst consensus mean forecast;

$\widehat{BVE}_t$ = estimated book value of common equity per share at the end of the financial year t based on the relation: $\widehat{BVE}_t = BVE_{t-1} + \widehat{EPS}_t - \hat{d}_t$, where $\hat{d}_t$ equals the future expected net dividends per share;

g = expected future growth rate; and

r_{CT} = implied costs of equity according to the *Claus/Thomas* (2001) model.

This model is based on the residual income model which goes back to *Preinreich* (1938) and *Edwards/Bell* (1961). Residual income is defined as earnings per share minus a charge for cost of capital on the beginning of the period's book value of equity. The model uses explicit forecasts for t+5 periods in the future.[91] After that, it is assumed that abnormal earnings permanently grow with a growth rate of g. The last term represents the perpetuity value of the abnormal earnings stream beyond period t+5. The model is based on the clean surplus assumption and presumes that dividends are a constant fraction of future earnings (*Claus/Thomas* (2001), pp. 1635–1636).

Gebhardt, Lee, and Swaminathan (2001)

$$(6.7) \quad Price_t = \quad BVE_t + \sum_{\tau=1}^{T} \frac{(\widehat{EPS}_{t+\tau} - r_{GLS} * BVE_{t+\tau-1})}{(1+r_{GLS})^\tau} + \frac{(\widehat{EPS}_{t+T} - r_{GLS} * BVE_{t+T-1})}{(1+r_{GLS})^T r_{GLS}}$$

where,

r_{GLS} = implied costs of equity according to the *Gebhardt et al.* (2001) model; and

---

[91] I/B/E/S does not provide forecasts for periods beyond that.

all other variables as defined above.

This model is also based on the residual income model. Again, it is assumed that clean surplus holds and that dividends are a constant fraction of future earnings. Explicit earnings per share forecasts are used for period t+1 to t+3. After that, the return on equity of period t+3 is linearly faded to the industry specific median return of the last three years by linear interpolation to period t+12. This captures the long-term erosion of abnormal returns. Over time, firms tend to become more similar to their industry peers (*Gebhardt et al.* (2001), pp. 141–142). After t+12 it is assumed that the industry specific return is earned for infinity.

Ohlson and Juettner-Nauroth (2005)

$$(6.8) \quad Price_t = \left(\frac{EPS_{t+1}}{r_{OJ}}\right) * \frac{(g_{st} + r_{OJ} * \widehat{d_{t+1}} / \widehat{EPS_{t+\tau}} - g_{lt})}{(r_{OJ} - g_{lt})}$$

where,

g_{st} = short-term growth rate;

g_{lt} = long-term growth rate;

$\widehat{d_{t+1}}$ = estimated future net dividends per share for period t+1;

r_{OJ} = implied costs of equity according to the *Ohlson/Juettner-Nauroth* (2005) model; and

all other variables as defined above.

This equation is the abnormal earnings growth valuation model by *Ohlson/Juettner-Nauroth* (2005). Similar to the *Claus/Thomas* (2001) and the *Gebhardt et al.* (2001) model, this model assumes clean surplus accounting and presumes that dividends are a constant fraction of future earnings. It uses t+1 forecasts for earnings and dividends. The short-term growth rate g_{st} is approximated by the mean of the percentage change in the earnings forecast from t+1 to t+2 and the five year growth forecast on I/B/E/S (*Gode/Mohanram* (2003), p. 403; *Daske et al.* (2008), p. 1136). The change in earnings forecasts from t+1 to t+2 has to be positive to solve the equation. This may limit the sample to firms with better future prospects.[92] The long-term growth rate g_{lt} is estimated by the t+1 median of realized monthly inflation rates (*Daske et al.* (2008), p. 1137).

Easton (2004)

$$(6.9) \quad Price_t = \frac{(\widehat{EPS_{t+2}} + r_E * \widehat{d_{t+1}} - \widehat{EPS_{t+1}})}{r_E^2}$$

where,

---

[92] This study, however, performs robustness checks to gauge the sensitivity of results due to this assumption (see section 6.3.2).

r_E = implied costs of equity according to the *Easton* (2004) model; and
all other variables as defined above.

This model is also based on the abnormal earnings growth valuation model by *Ohlson/Juettner-Nauroth* (2005). Explicit earnings per share forecasts are necessary only for periods t+1 and t+2 as well as estimated dividends per share for period t+1. Note that the model also requires a positive growth in forecasted earnings from period t+1 to t+2. Furthermore, the model assumes that the growth in abnormal earnings persists infinitely.

Empirical implementation

Following *Daske et al.* (2008), it is **required** that there are forecasts available on I/B/E/S for either t+1, t+2 and t+3 or t+1, t+2 and an analyst estimate of the long-term earnings growth (*ltg*) to calculate the implied cost of capital for a given firm-year (*Daske et al.* (2008), pp. 1137–1138). In case of missing earnings forecasts for t+4 and t+5, the forecasts from period t+3 are projected either using the *ltg* (if available) or the growth rate from period t+2 to t+3. Only positive forecasts and growth rates are used in the models. Earnings forecasts are based on the mean analyst consensus forecast.

Security prices and earnings forecasts are measured as of 90 days after the fiscal year end or 45 days after the first quarter end. As elaborated before, this allows enough time for segment data to be publicly available and thus to be **impounded** in security prices and analysts' forecasts.[93]

Future net dividends ($\widehat{d_{t+1}}$) are estimated based on the dividend payout ratio (d_t/EPS_t) in t=0. A **constant payout fraction** is assumed for the following years. If $\widehat{d_{t+1}}$ cannot be determined or is out of the range between 0 and 1, it is replaced by the year median payout ratio of all other firms that have a valid estimate.

In some of the models r appears in both the numerators and denominators of the equation. Hence, there is no closed form solution of the polynomial (*Claus/Thomas* (2001), pp. 1640-1641)). Following *Hail/Leuz* (2006), p. 528, this study uses an **iterative process** to solve the equation that stops if the imputed price falls within a range of 0.001 to the actual price. Estimates that are negative or exceed 50 per cent are set to missing values and disregarded in the analyses.

Control variables

Following extant literature (e.g., *Hail/Leuz* (2006); *Daske et al.* (2008)), this study uses control variables for firm size, risk, financial leverage and a firm's growth opportunities.

Firm size is a proxy for the general information environment of a company. Larger firms tend to be more informative and forthcoming in terms of disclosures. Moreover, securities of larger firms are usually more liquid which mitigates liquidity risk. Similar to the information asymmetry study, firm size is approximated by the log of the market value of equity.

---

[93] This means that analysts' t+1 (t+2, t+3 ...) forecasts represent estimates for a nine (21, 33 ...) month period. Robustness tests, however, show the results are not sensitive to this assumption.

Investors require a higher return on their investment if there is more **risk**. Hence, there is a positive association between the risk of an investment and the cost of capital. This study uses one year beta factors based on weekly returns for financial year t=0 as a control variable for risk.[94]

Moreover, **financial leverage** also has a positive impact on the investment risk. Investors demand a higher compensation for increased risk and thus the cost of capital increases (*Modigliani/Miller* (1958)). The proxy for financial leverage is measured as the ratio of total liabilities to total assets at financial year end t=0 (*Hail/Leuz* (2009), p. 436).

Following extant literature (e.g., *Fama/French* (1992); *Fama/French* (1993)), a firm's book-to-market ratio captures its **growth opportunities**. A larger difference between the book value of equity and the market value of equity and thus a lower book-to-market ratio indicates that the market assumes that there are future benefits which are not yet reflected in the book value of equity. Hence, the book-to-market ratio is positively associated with the cost of capital.

Basic regression model

The regression model follows equation (6.1) from section 6.1.2. Following extant literature, the different proxies for the cost of capital are regressed on the test and control variables. Moreover, to mitigate noise related to the models this study also employs an aggregate cost of capital measure of all four models (for a similar approach see *Hail/Leuz* (2006); *Daske et al.* (2008)).

$$(6.10) \quad Cost\ of\ capital_{i;t} = \alpha + \beta_1 Post_t + \beta_2 Change_i + \beta_3 Post_t \times Change_i + \beta_4 \log(Size_{i;t}) + \beta_5 Beta_{i;t} + \beta_6 Leverage_{i;t} + \beta_7 BTM_{i;t} + \varepsilon_{i;t}$$

where,

$Cost\ of\ capital_{i;t}$ = one of the four cost of capital measures or an aggregated measure of all four models of firm i in year t;

$Beta_{i;t}$ = one year beta factor based on weekly returns of firm i in year t;

$Leverage_{i;t}$ = total liabilities divided by total assets of firm i in year t;

$BTM_{i;t}$ = book-to-market ratio calculated as book value of equity divided by market value of equity of firm i in year t; and

all other variables as defined above.

---

[94] The CDAX serves as the reference market index.

6.1.3.3   Financial analysts' information environment

Barron et al. (1998) have developed a **theoretical model** of financial analysts' information environment that incorporates both public and private information as well as their inter-play.[95] *Barron et al.* (1998) relate observable outcomes of analysts' forecasts to the properties of their information environment.[96]

Assume that a particular firm is covered by N analysts. Each analyst receives a common public signal and a private signal to facilitate their forecasts. h denotes the precision of the public signal and s denotes the precision of the private signal of analyst i. *Barron et al.* (1998) show that the analysts' **overall uncertainty** V results from the common uncertainty C that is due to the reliance on the public signal and the idiosyncratic uncertainty due to the reliance on their private signal:

$$(6.11) \qquad\qquad V = C + D$$

C is the common uncertainty that is shared by all analysts. **Common uncertainty** can be interpreted as the covariance of the belief of each analyst with all other analysts. Put differently, C is the covariance of errors in the individual forecasts.

The **idiosyncratic uncertainty** D can simply be interpreted as the dispersion in analysts' forecasts. If all analysts only relied on public information they would facilitate equal forecasts and there would be no dispersion. Hence, greater dispersion is an indicator for more reliance on idiosyncratic information. In summary, overall uncertainty is the sum of the average covariance and the dispersion of forecasts.

Barron et al. (1998) define analysts' **consensus** ρ as the relative reliance on public information compared to private information. They capture this by gauging the proportion of uncertainty that is common to all analysts to total uncertainty:

$$(6.12) \qquad\qquad \rho = C/V$$

Furthermore, they show that the **squared error** in the analysts' mean forecast SE is fully driven by common uncertainty, but only partially driven by idiosyncratic uncertainty. This holds due to the fact that averaging across N analysts does not affect the common uncertainty, but the idiosyncratic uncertainty is diversified away by this process:

$$(6.13) \qquad\qquad SE = C + D/N$$

---

[95] Refer to *Barron et al.* (1998) for the following description of the theoretical model (*Barron et al.* (1998), pp. 423–428).

[96] Their measure can also be interpreted as a metric of the consensus concept in *Holthausen/Verrecchia* (1990) and *Indjejikian* (1991).

In other words, the error in individual analysts' forecasts that is due to idiosyncratic information cancels out on average. In case of $N=1$, the squared forecast error fully represents overall uncertainty because there is no diversification.

Barron et al. (1998) relate the unobservable concepts of consensus and uncertainty to the following **observable features** of analysts' forecasts. First, the squared mean forecast error is the squared difference of the actual earning realization and the mean forecast:

(6.14)
$$SE = (E_{it} - \overline{FE}_{it})^2$$

where,

SE	= squared error in the analysts' mean forecast for company i and time t;
E_{jt}	= actual earnings realization for company i and time t; and
$\overline{FE}_{jt}$	= mean of the analysts' forecast for company i and time t.

The **observed dispersion** among individual analysts' forecasts can be expressed as their variance:

(6.15)
$$D = \frac{1}{N_{jt} - 1} \sum_{i=1}^{N} (FE_{jti} - \overline{FE}_{jt})^2$$

where,

FE_{jti}	= forecast of analyst j for company i and time t; and

all other variables as defined above.

Using equations (6.11) and (6.13), one can express the observable features of dispersion and squared error in the analysts' mean forecast as **functions** of consensus and overall uncertainty:

(6.16)
$$D = V - C = V(1 - \rho)$$

(6.17)
$$SE = \frac{V + (N - 1)C}{N} = V(\rho + \frac{1 - \rho}{N})$$

Equation (6.16) shows forecast dispersion as an increasing function of overall uncertainty and a decreasing function of consensus. The error in the mean forecast is increasing in both uncertainty and consensus.

By using simple algebra one can reverse equations (6.16) and (6.17) and express common uncertainty and consensus as functions of D, SE and N:

(6.18) $$V = \left(1 - \frac{1}{N}\right)D + SE$$

This allows the **empirical implementation** of the concepts of overall uncertainty and consensus since all right-hand-side variables are observable.

Under the assumption that the private information of each analyst is of equal precision, one can state V and ρ in terms of the **precision** of the public and private signal:[97]

(6.19) $$\rho = \frac{SE - \frac{D}{N}}{\left(1 - \frac{1}{N}\right)D + SE}$$

(6.20, 6.21) $$V = \frac{1}{h + s} \; ; \rho = \frac{h}{h + s}$$

Note that **consensus** can be expressed as the ratio of the precision of the common signal to total precision of both signals. Hence, the extent of consensus among different analysts is a function of the relative precision of the public information signal. Based on this, *Barron et al.* (1998) further derive metrics of the precision of the private (s) and public information signal (h):

(6.22) $$s = \frac{D}{\left[\left(1 - \frac{1}{N}\right)D + SE\right]^2}$$

(6.23) $$h = \frac{SE - \frac{D}{N}}{\left[\left(1 - \frac{1}{N}\right)D + SE\right]^2}$$

The analysis of the **changes in h and s** helps to characterize the nature of the impact of IFRS 8 on the information environment of financial analysts: An increase in h combined with a decrease in s can be interpreted as a case of *"leveling the playing field"* (*Venkataraman* (2001), p. 18).

Empirical implementation

For the empirical implementation, one-year-ahead forecasts of annual earnings are used to determine h, s and ρ. Following *Botosan/Stanford* (2005), only the most recent forecast of each analyst in the estimation periods are retained. To analyze the **changes in the infor-**

---

[97] The common and idiosyncratic uncertainty can be interpreted as the reciprocal of the public and individual information signal. A higher precision means lower uncertainty.

mation environment, the pre (IAS 14R) and post (IFRS 8) period have to be defined. Similar to the sub-studies on information asymmetry and the cost of capital, the estimation window covers 60 days beginning 90 days after the fiscal year end in 2009 or 45 days after the first quarter end for both years. This ensures that segment information is published and disseminated.

Changes in the metrics of h, s and p from the IAS 14R period to the IFRS period are compared. Following *Venkataraman* (2001) and *Botosan/Stanford* (2005), these metrics do not require further control variables since there are no other factors known that systematically impact the metrics. The empirical analysis focuses on differences in the **mean change** of these metrics for the treatment and the control group.

6.1.4 Classification of the treatment and the control group

Based on the content analysis in chapter five, the sample firms are sub-divided into the treatment and the control group. Firms that had to (did not have to) change their segmentation upon adoption of IFRS 8 are classified as change (no change) firms. A change firm has to meet at least one of the following criteria which are assumed to represent **major structural changes** to the way segment information is presented:[98]

- a change in the basis of segmentation,
- a change in the number of reported segments,
- a change in the consistency with other parts of the annual report,[99] or
- a change in the structure of segments with the same number of segments and the same basis of segmentation.[100]

For further sensitivity analyses, the following criteria are also considered for the change classification, which represent **content-related changes**:

- a change in the number of line items, or
- a change in the extent of segmental narratives.

This study distinguishes between major **structural changes** and **content-related changes** because the former is closely related to a change in underlying concepts of segment reporting, which is the focal point of this study. Moreover, a mere increase in content such as the number of line items or the extent of segmental narratives does not necessarily mean that there is more useful information available to users of financial statements. However, a change in the content of segment reports may also have an impact on the decision usefulness of segment information.

---

[98] *Venkataraman* (2001) uses a similar approach. However, he simply assigns a firm to the treatment group when it shows a change in the number of segments. Thereby, *Venkataraman* (2001) misclassifies firms that, for instance, show a change in the segmentation without a change in the number of segments. In contrast, the classification procedures in this study are more detailed and accurate.

[99] Analogous to section 5.2.2, consistency is defined as the equivalence of the segmentation in the segment report and the management report as well as the letter of the CEO.

[100] This entails firms that restructure their segments that they better reflect the internal organizational structure, although they report the same number of segments and stick with, for instance, business lines or geographical segmentation.

A change in some of the criteria does not necessarily have to be a change for the better. For instance, firms may use the discretion of IFRS 8 to report fewer segments or stop the disclosure of specific information. To control for this, the treatment group is further classified into a "**positive change**" and a "**negative change**" group. Positive generally means an increase in the fineness or quantity of disclosures, while negative means an aggregation or decrease of disclosures. This does not address potential "cheap talk" or "information overload" issues associated with a consideration of the quantity of disclosure. However, this is one way to ensure a certain degree of objectivity in the classification of "positive" or "negative" change firms.

Table 6-1 provides an overview of the change firm classification. Of the 109 firms in the final sample, 35 show a positive structural change. The predominant reason for the classification as a positive structural change firm is an increase in the number of segments (24 firms). This is followed by an increase in the consistency with other parts of the annual report (15 firms). A firm is classified as a change firm if it meets at least one criterion. However, several firms meet multiple criteria and therefore the numbers do not add up to 35. In the following analyses, structural changes are referred to as **group one changes** and the positive change group one ($Change^1_{positive}$) includes all 35 firms that show a positive structural change.

12 firms show an increase in the number of line items of at least three items and 28 firms increase their word count in the segmental narratives by more than 200 words.[101] These changes represent positive content-related changes. Again, there are several firms that show both an increase in the number of line items and in the segmental narratives. Therefore, the numbers do not add up to 34. **Group two changes** include structural and content-related changes. In total there are 35 structural and 34 content-related positive changes. However, there is an overlap for 18 firms that show both changes at the same time so that the total number of positive change group two firms is only 51.

The same classification is used for negative changes: Seven firms are **negative group one change** firms ($Change^1_{negative}$) since they show fewer segments after the adoption of IFRS 8. 33 firms are allocated to the **negative change group two** ($Change^2_{negative}$) because these firms either report fewer line items (29 firms) or report less segmental narrative information (3 firms).

Three firms that show a decrease in the number of segments simultaneously show positive structural changes. These firms are **reclassified** as positive change firms. This is in line with the example of the Axel Springer Group (see section 5.2.2) which reports a different segmentation with fewer segments that is more consistent with the strategic positioning of the company. Results, however, are unaffected whether these three firms are classified as either no change or negative change firms.

---

[101] Results and inferences of the following analyses remain qualitatively unchanged if a change of at least five line items or 100 words is used (in any combination).

Change firm classification	Firms	Observations
Positive change		
Structural changes	35	70
- thereof change in the basis of segmentation	(7)	(14)
- thereof increase in the number of segments	(24)	(48)
- thereof better consistency with other parts of the annual report	(15)	(30)
- thereof change in the structure	(7)	(14)
Change¹$_{positive}$ **(only structural changes):**	35	70
Content-related changes	34	68
- thereof increase in the number of line items	(12)	(24)
- thereof increase in the extent of segment narratives	(28)	(56)
Change²$_{positive}$ **(structural and content-related changes):**	51	102
Negative change		
Structural changes	7	14
- thereof decrease in the number of segments	(7)	(14)
Change¹$_{negative}$ **(only structural changes):**	7	14
Content-related changes:	30	60
- thereof decrease in the number of line items	(29)	(58)
- thereof decrease in the extent of segment disclosures	(3)	(6)
Change²$_{negative}$ **(structural and content-related changes):**	33	66

Table 6-1: Change firm classification

All firms that do not undergo any changes upon adoption of IFRS 8 are labeled **no change firms** and they represent the control group. The composition of the control group depends on whether the group one or group two classification is used. As elaborated above, this study uses the group one classification for most analyses because the structural changes are most closely related to a change in underlying concepts of segment reporting. Group two changes, however, are also considered for robustness and sensitivity analyses.

Moreover, it is important to distinguish between a change in the way segment information is presented induced by the change in standards or induced by a **change of internal structures** that coincides with the adoption of IFRS 8. Otherwise, economic effects that are driven by the incentives of firms to change the internal structure would falsely be attributed to the standard change. For instance, the QSC Group notes:

"In accordance with IFRS 8, the source of QSC's reportable segments is the internal organization used by management for making operating decisions and assessing performance. In the fourth quarter of 2007, QSC conducted an extensive reorganization, consolidating its major lines of business into three business units. This also resulted in a change in the segment reporting effective January 1, 2008."

(*QSC*, Annual Report (2008), p. 110)

QSC and two other firms are removed from the analysis to avoid any bias. These changes are labeled **coinciding structural changes**.

Table 6-2 shows the final treatment and control **group distribution** separately for the group one change classification and the group two change classification. Under the former, 42 firms constitute the treatment group and 64 firms the control group. Under the group two change classification, there are 84 firms in the treatment group of which 51 show a positive change and 33 a negative change upon adoption of IFRS 8. These classifications are used in all following analyses.

Treatment and control group classification		
	Firms	**Observations**
Final sample	**109**	**218**
Change group one classification:		
Treatment group	42	84
Change^{1}positive	35	70
Change^{1}negative	7	14
Control group	64	128
Coinciding structural change	3	6
Change group two classification:		
Treatment group	84	168
Change^{2}positive	51	102
Change^{2}negative	33	66
Control group	22	44
Coinciding structural change	3	6

Table 6-2: Treatment and control group classification

6.1.5 Sample selection adjustments

The sample selection process is based on the final sample for the content analysis in chapter five (see Table 5-1). This is necessary because the results of the content analysis are needed for the classification of firms into the treatment and the control group. The following three sub-studies have different data requirements for the dependent and independent variables. If any variable is missing for a firm in a given year, both firm observations need to be eliminated to retain a **balanced panel**. A balanced panel is necessary for the difference-in-differences research design that compares firms of different groups at two different points in time.

Table 6-3 presents the **final sample** for each of the three sub-studies. The analysis of the information asymmetries in form of bid-ask spreads includes the most valid observations. Bid-ask spreads are a very simple construct and they are readily available for most firms of the final sample. The other two studies comprise substantially less observations. For instance, the analyses of the cost of capital and the financial analysts' information environment rely on the availability of a sufficient number of earnings forecasts. Moreover, the iterative procedures to determine the cost of capital do not always yield numerical solutions. Finally, the studies use different control variables. In some cases, these variables are not available for certain firms and thus the final sample is reduced.

Sample selection process		
	Firms	Observations
Final sample content analysis chapter five	109	218
Bid-ask spread analysis:		
- less missing bid-ask spreads	(2)	(4)
- less missing control variables	(2)	(4)
- less coinciding change firms	(3)	(6)
Final sample (6.2):	102	204
Cost of capital analysis:		
- less missing data for Claus and Thomas (2001)	(11)	(22)
- less missing data for Gebhardt et al. (2001)	(9)	(18)
- less missing data for Ohlson and Juettner-Nauroth (2005)	(16)	(32)
- less missing data for Easton (2004)	(20)	(40)
- less missing data for average cost of capital	(23)	(46)
- less missing control variables	(2)	(4)
- less coinciding change firms	(3)	(6)
Final sample (6.3):	82	164
Financial analysts analysis:		
- less missing financial analysts data	(24)	(48)
- less coinciding change firms	(3)	(6)
Final sample (6.4):	82	164

Table 6-3: Sample selection process

6.2 Information asymmetry

The following sections present the sub-study of the economic consequences of introducing the management approach to segment reporting from the **perspective of investors**. Therefore, information asymmetries are analyzed: First, general descriptive statistics and a correlation matrix of the dependent and independent variables are provided. This allows to get a basic understanding of the data. Second, univariate comparisons of the bid-ask spreads are presented for the treatment and the control group around the IFRS 8 adoption date based on a difference-in-differences design. This allows to control for unobserved differences between the treatment and the control group as well as for concurrent changes that affect both groups. Finally, multivariate regressions are used to control for other influences on the dependent variables. These steps help to analyze whether the adoption of IFRS 8 led to a change in information asymmetries for those firms that reorganized their segment reports to comply with the management approach.

6.2.1 Univariate and bivariate analyses

Descriptive statistics

Table 6-4 presents the descriptive statistics for all continuous variables used in the bid-ask spread regression of equation (6.5). To facilitate a better understanding of the data, the mean, median, standard deviation (std. dev.) as well as the 25 per cent (Q25) and 75 per cent quartiles (Q75) are reported separately for each index. This allows to identify any size- or industry-related patterns and thus to plausibilize the empirical proxies.

The mean **bid-ask spread** for the full sample is 0.81 per cent. This is slightly lower compared to prior research: For instance, *Leuz/Verrecchia* (2000) report median spreads of 1.96 per cent for a German sample and *Daske et al.* (2008) of 1.50 per cent for a world sample (*Leuz/Verrecchia* (2000), p. 104; *Daske et al.* (2008), p. 1104). However, the firms in this study are on average larger compared to the sample firms of *Leuz/Verrecchia* (2000) and *Daske et al.* (2008) and therefore it is plausible that they have lower spreads. In this study, the DAX constituents show the lowest spreads which is also plausible because these firms are usually the most liquid and transparent firms in the German economy. In contrast, SDAX firms show a mean spread of 1.78 per cent. This is also in line with the notion that smaller firms are on average less liquid and transparent and thus investors tend to price protect themselves when trading these securities. The MDAX and TecDAX firms are somewhere in between with a mean spread of 0.32 per cent and 0.54 per cent. Finally, the standard deviation and the interquartile range indicate some variability within the indices.

Trading volume indicates the liquidity of a stock relative to its market capitalization. Higher values signal more frequently traded securities. The mean value of the full sample is 0.37 per cent. This is largely consistent with the German sample from 1998 and 1999 of *Leuz/Verrecchia* (2000), who report a mean trading volume of 0.74 per cent (*Leuz/Verrecchia* (2000), p. 104). Not surprisingly, the DAX and MDAX firms are the most frequently traded securities with a mean trading volume of 0.61 per cent and 0.54 per cent. They are followed by the TecDAX firms that show a mean trading volume of 0.46 per cent. As expected, the smaller firms in the SDAX are traded the least frequent with a mean of 0.02 per cent.

Return volatility reflects the risk of holding a security. A higher volatility indicates more risk. The mean value for all firms is 3.45 per cent which is similar to prior research (e.g., *Leuz/Verrecchia* (2000), p. 104, report a return volatility of 2.63 per cent). DAX firms are the least risky investments (mean value of 2.81 per cent) followed by the SDAX (3.18 per cent) and the MDAX (3.54 per cent). Stocks in the TecDAX show the most volatile returns with a mean of 4.11 per cent.

In **summary**, the bid-ask spreads and control variables[102] exhibit no unusual values or patterns. The different indices show amounts that are in line with theoretical expectations for relatively larger (DAX, MDAX) and smaller firms (TecDAX and SDAX). Moreover, the magnitude of the variables is also consistent with prior research.

Descriptive statistics of the bid-ask spreads and control variables for each index							
Variables[a]		mean	std. dev.	Q25	median	Q75	N
Bid-ask spread	DAX	0.10%	0.06%	0.06%	0.08%	0.12%	24
	MDAX	0.32%	0.16%	0.22%	0.27%	0.37%	78
	TecDAX	0.54%	0.40%	0.30%	0.41%	0.63%	42
	SDAX	1.78%	0.78%	1.38%	1.83%	1.97%	68
	Total	**0.81%**	**0.84%**	**0.24%**	**0.39%**	**1.36%**	**212**
Trading volume	DAX	0.61%	0.28%	0.43%	0.61%	0.78%	24
	MDAX	0.54%	0.35%	0.26%	0.47%	0.74%	78
	TecDAX	0.46%	0.30%	0.23%	0.39%	0.65%	42
	SDAX	0.02%	0.01%	0.00%	0.01%	0.02%	70
	Total	**0.37%**	**0.36%**	**0.02%**	**0.28%**	**0.63%**	**212**
Return volatiliy	DAX	2.81%	0.88%	2.31%	2.78%	3.30%	24
	MDAX	3.54%	0.93%	2.87%	3.57%	4.36%	78
	TecDAX	4.11%	1.56%	3.21%	3.78%	4.72%	42
	SDAX	3.18%	0.99%	2.43%	3.10%	3.61%	70
	Total	**3.45%**	**1.17%**	**2.66%**	**3.27%**	**4.06%**	**212**
Size	DAX	19,707.62	17,391.99	6,595.04	12,867.12	26,192.80	26
	MDAX	2,633.97	3,161.21	981.60	1,569.84	2,843.25	78
	TecDAX	732.26	935.34	213.27	420.27	766.18	44
	SDAX	583.13	766.27	174.64	306.49	648.00	70
	Total	**3,652.10**	**8,683.73**	**343.39**	**848.13**	**2,406.00**	**216**

[a]Bid-ask spread is the median of the difference between the daily closing bid and ask prices divided by the midpoint for the three-month period starting 90 days after fiscal year end. Trading volume is the annual median of the daily turnover divided by the market value of outstanding equity for the 12 months following the fiscal year end. Return volatility is the annual standard deviation of monthly stock returns. Size is the market capitalization presented in million Euros.

Table 6-4: Descriptive statistics of bid-ask spreads and controls

Table 6-5 presents the same descriptive statistics as the previous table for the **treatment and the control group** over the whole sample period. In the first row, the statistics of the positive change group one specification, that is positive structural changes, are presented. Second, descriptives of the no change control group are reported. The third row shows the difference in means between the two groups and whether this difference is statistically significant at the ten, five or one per cent level. Due to the low number of observations in the negative change groups, they are not analyzed separately in the univariate analysis.[103]

Along all variables, there is **no distinctive discrepancy** between the two groups. None of the differences in means is significant at conventional levels. This provides some confidence that the distribution of firms into treatment and control firms is not driven by a systematic influence – which supports the quasi-experimental research design of this study.

---

[102] Size is not discussed in detail because section 5.1.2 already provides a discussion for each index.

[103] For instance, the negative change group one only yields seven observations for each period. This reflects very low power for univariate statistical analyses. However, dummy variables allow to separately analyze their impact in the multivariate analyses without losing much power.

Descriptive statistics of the bid-ask spreads and control variables for the treatment and control group one						
Variables[a]		mean	std. dev.	Q25	median	Q75
Bid-ask spread	Change[1]positive	0.75%	0.67%	0.24%	0.39%	1.34%
	No change	0.88%	0.93%	0.26%	0.39%	1.75%
	(Difference)[b]	-0.13%				
Trading volume	Change[1]positive	0.36%	0.34%	0.03%	0.28%	0.65%
	No change	0.36%	0.37%	0.02%	0.27%	0.61%
	(Difference)[b]	-0.01%				
Return volatiliy	Change[1]positive	3.59%	1.44%	2.62%	3.52%	4.20%
	No change	3.46%	1.00%	2.82%	3.36%	4.00%
	(Difference)[b]	0.13%				
Size	Change[1]positive	3,755.96	10,230.73	410.21	935.39	2,949.44
	No change	3,067.26	6,772.67	295.88	732.24	2,123.17
	(Difference)[b]	688.49				

[a]Bid-ask spread is the median of the difference between the daily closing bid and ask prices divided by the midpoint for the three-month period starting 90 days after fiscal year end. Trading volume is the annual median of the daily turnover divided by the market value of outstanding equity for the 12 months following the fiscal year end. Return volatility is the annual standard deviation of monthly stock returns. Size is the market capitalization presented in million Euros. Change[1]positive represents positive structural changes in the way segment information is presented upon adoption of IFRS 8.
[b] *, **, and *** indicate statistical significance at the 10%, 5%, and 1% levels (two-tailed), respectively.

Table 6-5: Descriptive statistics of bid-ask spreads and controls for group one

Table 6-6 provides the same information as the table before just for the **change two specification**. The results are virtually identical for the change grouping that takes account of structural *and* content-related changes: None of the differences in means is significant. This once more supports the quasi-experimental research design of this study.

Descriptive statistics of the bid-ask spreads and control variables for the treatment and control group two						
Variables[a]		mean	std. dev.	Q25	median	Q75
Bid-ask spread	Change[2]positive	0.75%	0.73%	0.25%	0.34%	1.33%
	No change	0.88%	0.90%	0.27%	0.44%	1.71%
	(Difference)[b]	-0.12%				
Trading volume	Change[2]positive	0.33%	0.31%	0.04%	0.25%	0.47%
	No change	0.35%	0.37%	0.01%	0.28%	0.61%
	(Difference)[b]	-0.02%				
Return Volatiliy	Change[2]positive	3.52%	1.37%	2.64%	3.45%	4.20%
	No change	3.63%	1.00%	2.90%	3.52%	4.00%
	(Difference)[b]	-0.11%				
Size	Change[2]positive	2,874.05	5,152.82	404.21	1,003.94	2,949.44
	No change	2,539.11	4,991.69	339.92	699.16	2,123.17
	(Difference)[b]	334.94				

[a]Bid-ask spread is the median of the difference between the daily closing bid and ask prices divided by the midpoint for the three-month period starting 90 days after fiscal year end. Trading volume is the annual median of the daily turnover divided by the market value of outstanding equity for the 12 months following the fiscal year end. Return volatility is the annual standard deviation of monthly stock returns. Size is the market capitalization presented in million Euros. Change[2]positive represents positive structural and content-related changes in the way segment information is presented upon adoption of IFRS 8.
[b] *, **, and *** indicate statistical significance at the 10%, 5%, and 1% levels (two-tailed), respectively.

Table 6-6: Descriptive statistics of bid-ask spreads and controls for group two

Finally, Table 6-7 presents pairwise **Spearman correlation** coefficients for the relevant continuous variables.[104] The values above the diagonal are the correlation coefficients for the treatment group (positive change one) and the values below are based on the control group sample (no change). As expected, trading volume and size are significantly negative-

---

[104] The non-parametric Spearman correlation coefficients are based on ranks and do not assume normally distributed data. However, the correlations are virtually the same when Pearson correlation coefficients are used.

ly related to the bid-ask spreads: Larger firms with more liquid securities show smaller spreads. In contrast to theoretical expectations, return volatility is not correlated with the bid-ask spreads.[105] Expectedly, trading volume is positively correlated with size because larger firms are usually traded more frequently. Finally, return volatility and trading volume are also positively correlated. This could be mechanical because a higher return variation requires c.p. more trading activities. In total, the pairwise correlations are as expected. Furthermore, the correlations are virtually the same for the treatment and the control group, which also supports the quasi-experimental feature of this study.

Correlation matrix bid-ask spreads and control variables				
Variables[a]	Bid-ask spread	Trading volume	Return Volatiliy	Size
Bid-ask spread		-0.820*** (0.000)	-0.117*** (0.000)	-0.752*** (0.000)
Trading volume	-0.741*** (0.000)	-	0.385*** (0.000)	0.458*** (0.000)
Return Volatiliy	0.079 (0.520)	0.357*** (0.003)	-	-0.020 (0.822)
Size	0.710*** (0.000)	0.354*** (0.003)	-0.125 (0.310)	-

[a]Spearman correlation coefficients are presented for the pairwise correlations of the bid-ask spreads and control variables. P-values are below the correlation coefficients in parentheses. Correlations for the treatment group positive change one are reported above the diagonal and for the no change control group are presented below the diagonal.
*, **, and *** indicate statistical significance at the 10%, 5%, and 1% levels, respectively.

Table 6-7: Correlation matrix bid-ask spreads and controls

To **sum up**, the descriptive statistics show results as expected: The spreads and control variables display variation between the four indices that is in line with the different sizes of the firms. Moreover, the magnitude of the variables is consistent with prior research based on largely comparable samples. Furthermore, there are no distinct differences between the treatment and the control group. Finally, the correlation matrix largely shows correlation coefficients in the expected direction and magnitude. Hence, the empirical proxies of this study seem to be well-specified and the quasi-experimental feature of the research design is supported by the data. The following sections focus on the bid-ask spreads analysis based on the (univariate and multivariate) difference-in-differences research design. This allows to analyze whether the disclosure of segment information based on the management approach is useful information to mitigate information asymmetries from an investor's perspective.

Difference-in-differences

Table 6-8 reports the univariate difference-in-differences analysis of the mean of the **median absolute spread** of the 3-months-period beginning 90 days after fiscal year end. Bid-ask spreads of the treatment and the control group are compared before and after the adoption of the new standard to determine the treatment effect. The left column of Table 6-8 presents values for the IAS 14R period and the right column values for the IFRS 8 period. Next to it, the change between the two periods is reported. Furthermore, the first

---

[105] However, the coefficient for return volatility is significant in the expected direction in the following multivariate regressions. This may be due to the log-specification in the regression models which mitigates the influence of outliers. Therefore, the negative change group is analyzed separately in the multivariate analyses of section 6.2.2.

row shows the treatment group and the second row the control group. The bottom row shows the difference between the two groups.

Panel A uses the group one change specification, that is, **only structural changes**. Hence, the positive change group one (Change$^1_{positive}$) represents the treatment group. The width of the spreads is between 0.75 per cent and 1.01 per cent. In the pre-adoption period, the treatment and the control group are virtually the same. They only show a marginal difference of -0.01 per cent in the bid-ask spreads. In the adoption year, the no change group shows an increase to a mean spread of more than one per cent which is significant[106] at the five per cent level. The treatment group, however, displays a less steep increase of +0.06 per cent which is insignificant. The **difference-in-differences** of -0.19 per cent (marginally insignificant with a p-value of 0.118) signals that the treatment and the control group are affected differently by the adoption of IFRS 8.

Panel B reports the results for the group two change specification, that is, **structural and content-related changes**. The picture is very similar to Panel A. Under IAS 14R, the treatment and the control group are almost identical in terms of bid-ask spreads. Upon adoption of IFRS 8, however, the control group shows a much steeper increase than the treatment group. The **difference-in-differences** of -0.23 per cent is significant at the five per cent level.

Univariate difference-in-differences analyses of the bid-ask spreads for the full sample			
Panel A. Group one changes	IAS 14R (Pre-adoption Year) (a)	IFRS 8 (Adoption Year) (b)	(b) – (a)
Change$^1_{positive}$ (i)	0.75%	0.81%	+0.06%
No change (ii)	0.76%	1.01%	+0.25%**
(i) – (ii)	-0.01%	-0.20%	**-0.19%**
Panel B. Group two changes	IAS 14R (Pre-adoption Year) (a)	IFRS 8 (Adoption Year) (b)	(b) – (a)
Change$^2_{positive}$ (i)	0.72%	0.76%	+0.04%
No change (ii)	0.74%	1.01%	+0.27%*
(i) – (ii)	-0.02%	-0.25%	**-0.23%**

Change$^1_{positive}$ represents positive structural changes in the way segment information is presented upon adoption of IFRS 8. Change$^2_{positive}$ represents positive structural and content-related changes in the way segment information is presented upon adoption of IFRS 8.
*, **, and *** indicate statistical significance at the 10%, 5%, and 1% levels (two-tailed), respectively.

Table 6-8: Univariate difference-in-differences bid-ask spreads

First, these findings show that the treatment and thecontrol group are very similar in the pre-adoption period. This once more underlines the **quasi-experimental feature** of this study's unique research setting. Moreover, it provides some confidence that results are not driven by any endogeneity issues.[107] The findings also indicate that there is an increase in

---

[106] Again, normal t-tests as well as a non-parametric Wilcoxon ranksum tests show similar results. In the remainder of this study, significance levels reflect both tests and there will only be a further discussion of this issue in case the tests show different results.

[107] If there was a systematic difference between the two groups before the treatment effect, it would cast doubt on the quasi-randomized treatment and control group distribution that allows for causal interpretations.

information asymmetries and thus less transparency from the IAS 14R to the IFRS 8 period. This is consistent with the notion that the global financial crisis and its aftermath caused increasing uncertainties at the capital markets in 2008 and 2009. However, the increase is less steep for the firms that started to report segment information in line with the management approach at the same time. Assuming that the treatment effect (i.e., starting to disclose segment reports based on the management approach) is the only systematic difference between these two groups, one can infer that the disclosure of segmental information from the management's perspective provides investors with **useful information**. This information helps to mitigate the overall downward trend in transparency in the sample period.

Table 6-9 presents the same analysis for the sample **without early adopters**. These firms might induce endogeneity into the research design. Hence, if the results change upon eliminating early adopters, it would show that the findings in Table 6-8 are driven by the incentives to early adopt the new standard rather than by the standard itself. Yet, the elimination of more than 40 observations also leads to less power for statistical testing.

However, the results without the early adopters are **very similar** to the full sample. Under IAS 14R in 2008, the treatment and the control group are almost identical for both group one (Panel A) and group two (Panel B) change specification. All firms show an increase in bid-ask spreads from 2008 to 2009, which is again higher and significant for the control group. The difference-in-differences is negative and marginally insignificant for the change group one and negative and significant at the ten per cent level for the change group two.

Univariate difference-in-differences analyses of the bid-ask spreads without early adopters			
Panel A. Group one changes	IAS 14R (Pre-adoption Year) (a)	IFRS 8 (Adoption Year) (b)	(b) – (a)
Change[1]positive (i)	0.76%	0.84%	+0.08%
No change (ii)	0.80%	1.06%	+0.26%*
(i) – (ii)	-0.04%	-0.22%	-0.18%
Panel B. Group two changes	IAS 14R (Pre-adoption Year) (a)	IFRS 8 (Adoption Year) (b)	(b) – (a)
Change[2]positive (i)	0.78%	0.84%	+0.06%
No change (ii)	0.78%	1.03%	+0.25%
(i) – (ii)	0.00%	-0.19%	-0.19%*

Change[1]positive represents positive structural changes in the way segment information is presented upon adoption of IFRS 8. Change[2]positive represents positive structural and content-related changes in the way segment information is presented upon adoption of IFRS 8.
*, **, and *** indicate statistical significance at the 10%, 5%, and 1% levels (two-tailed), respectively.

Table 6-9: Univariate difference-in-differences bid-ask spreads – No early adopters

In **summary**, the findings in Table 6-9 **corroborate** the **initial results**. Hence, the improvement in transparency due to the adoption of the management approach to segment reporting is not driven by the early adopters and thus potential endogeneity is of limited concern. The univariate analysis, however, only provides preliminary evidence. Factors such as trading volume, return volatility or size systematically impact the width of the bid-ask spreads. Therefore, the following sections use multivariate regression models that control for other influences on the dependent variable.

6.2.2 Regression analysis

This section presents the multivariate bid-ask spread analysis. All following regressions are estimated with **ordinary least squares** (OLS). In the output tables, t-statistics are presented in parentheses below the coefficients. The asterisks indicate statistical significance at the ten, five or one per cent level. If a variable has a predicted sign (indicated by a plus or minus in parentheses next to the variable name), the significance levels are based on one-tailed tests. Two-tailed tests are used otherwise.

OLS regression models must satisfy certain assumptions to yield valid and un-biased results.[108] A potential violation of these assumptions is the **correlation** of **independent variables** with the **error term** induced by endogeneity. However, as discussed in section 6.1.1, this is addressed by the research design. Furthermore, due to the central limit theorem, the error term can be assumed to asymptotically follow a **normal distribution** once a certain number of observations is available (30-50), which is the case in every regression model of this study. Moreover, **multicollinearity** is not an issue since it causes an inflation of standard errors which makes it more difficult to find significant coefficients. This would work against the findings of this study.[109] Finally, **heteroscedasticity** and **autocorrelation** of standard errors are not an issue either: All regressions are rerun based on robust *White* (1980) and *Newey/West* (1987) standard errors. (Untabulated) results and inferences, however, remain the same.

In **panel data** sets, residuals can be correlated across firms or across time which also leads to biased estimates. There are different ways to address this issue. Most commonly, clustering standard errors or introducing fixed effects are used in the finance and accounting literature.[110] Following *Petersen* (2008), if there are unobserved firm or industry effects, standard errors should be clustered along this dimension in case a sufficient number of clusters is available. Moreover, *Petersen* (2008) suggests if both a firm and a time effect are present, one could address one issue parametrically by introducing dummies and cluster on the other dimensions. Clustering along multiple dimensions is an alternative treatment. However, too few clusters along either dimension can introduce biased standard

---

[108] For the following discussion about OLS assumptions refer to *Auer* (2011) or *Wooldridge* (2012).

[109] However, additional analyses of variance inflation factors (VIFs) are run. None of the VIFs of any of the regression models exceeds five which indicates that there is no harmful presence of multicollinearity. *Belsley et al.* (1980) argue that VIFs are not sufficient to detect multicollinearity. They suggest a different diagnostic procedure that analyzes the condition indices of the matrix of independent variables and their variance decomposition proportion. When applying their procedure to the data of this study, there are no regressions that show condition indices above 30 combined with variance decomposition proportions above 50 per cent for at least two coefficient variances of the respective eigenvalues. Hence, multicollinearity is not a problem in this study.

[110] Other ways are estimation of coefficients and standard errors based on the Fama-MacBeth procedure (*Fama/MacBeth* (1973)), generalized least squares (GLS) estimates of a random effects model, or the above mentioned robust standard errors following *White* (1980) and *Newey/West* (1987). For an overview, refer to *Petersen* (2008).

errors. To address the variety of potential treatments, this study employs different ways: The most conservative approach is to cluster standard errors on firm level, which yields a sufficient number of 102 clusters. Moreover, due to the short period of time (2008-2009), time dummies[111] are used instead of multiple clusters. Alternatively, standard errors can be clustered along industries or industry fixed effects can be used. For sensitivity, all alternatives are used in this study. However, for brevity, results are only reported for the basic specification in Table 6-10. After that, all results are reported based on firm level clustered standard errors only. Yet, none of the other specifications leads to different inferences.

Treatment effect timing – Financial year end

Table 6-10 presents the base model from equation (6.1) for the bid-ask spreads based on the full sample for the treatment effect measured 90 days after fiscal year end. Model A, Model B, and Model C show different specifications in terms of clustering and fixed effects. Following the discussion in section 6.1.3.1, it is expected that the control variables Log(Trading_Volume) and Log(Size) are negatively related to the spreads and that Log(Volatility) is positively related to the spreads. There are no predictions for Post and $Change^1_{positive}$. The main variable of interest in this regression model is the interaction term **Post x $Change^1_{positive}$**, which is presented in bold. Although there is no directional hypothesis derived in section 4.2.2, it is expected that the interaction term shows a negative sign. A directional hypothesis could not be derived because it was unclear whether the adoption of IFRS 8 actually improved segmental disclosures. However, in the empirical analysis it is further differentiated between positive and negative change groups, which allows for **predicted signs**.

All three models in Table 6-10 perform very well with an adjusted R^2 above 80 per cent, which is comparable to prior research.[112] Moreover, all three control variables are highly significant in each model, which confirms well-specified empirical proxies for the underlying economic variables. Neither Post nor $Change^1_{positive}$ are statistically significant. However, Post is positive in all three models and only marginally insignificant. This suggests an increase in information asymmetries in the post IFRS 8 era which corroborates the univariate findings. The insignificance of $Change^1_{positive}$ signals that the treatment and the control group do not differ substantially under IAS 14R. Most importantly, the interaction term **Post x $Change^1_{positive}$** is negative and significant at the five per cent level in all three models. Hence, the treatment group shows an incremental negative effect on the bid-ask spreads upon adoption of IFRS 8. This supports the univariate findings that the disclosure of segment information from the management's perspective mitigates the overall increase in information asymmetries from the IAS 14R period to the IFRS 8 period.

Finally, there are **only marginal differences** between firm level clustered standard errors (Model A), industry level clustered standard errors (Model B), and firm level clustered standard errors plus firm fixed effects (Model C). Hence, the following regression models

---

[111] The Post dummy variable is virtually a time dummy because it indicates two different time periods. Moreover, in the sample without early adopters it particularly differentiates between the years 2008 and 2009.

[112] For instance, *Leuz/Verrecchia* (2000) report an adjusted R^2 of 82 per cent for a German sample and *Daske et al.* (2008) report a R^2 over 90 per cent for a world sample.

use the more conservative specification of firm level clustered standard errors. Industry fixed effects are not reported in the results because they do not add much explanatory power and limit the degrees of freedom. However, all following regressions are also estimated including industry fixed effects, which neither changes results nor inferences.

Regression bid-ask spreads				
Variables	Predicted sign	Model A Firm level clustered standard errors	Model B Industry level clustered standard errors	Model C Firm level clustered standard errors plus industry fixed effects
Post		0.070	0.070	0.068
		(1.508)	(1.418)	(1.359)
Change$^1_{positive}$		0.092	0.092	0.148
		(1.054)	(1.207)	(1.596)
Post x Change$^1_{positive}$	(-)	-0.170**	-0.170**	-0.169**
		(-1.962)	(-2.207)	(-1.912)
Log(Trading_Volume)	(-)	-0.522***	-0.522***	-0.479***
		(-14.787)	(-14.908)	(-11.627)
Log(Volatiliy)	(+)	0.449***	0.449***	0.514***
		(3.312)	(3.005)	(3.907)
Log(Size)	(-)	-0.585***	-0.585***	-0.589***
		(-26.184)	(-29.742)	(-22.240)
Constant		-6.455***	-6.455***	-6.191***
		(-15.909)	(-19.213)	(-12.151)
Firm level clustered standard errors		YES	NO	YES
Industry level clustered standard errors		NO	YES	NO
Industry fixed effects		NO	NO	YES
N		204	204	204
adj. R²		0.843	0.843	0.861
F-stat		173.972	261.424	60.631

The table reports OLS coefficient estimates and t-statistics in parentheses below the coefficients. The predicted signs are presented next to the variables in parentheses. Change$^1_{positive}$ represents positive structural changes in the way segment information is presented upon adoption of IFRS 8.
*, **, and *** indicate statistical significance at the 10%, 5%, and 1% levels (one-tailed for coefficients with predicted signs and two-tailed otherwise), respectively.

Table 6-10: Regression bid-ask spreads

Table 6-11 addresses the potential self-selection issue due to 21 **early adopters** in the full sample. As elaborated above, these firms have incentives to opt for an early adoption of IFRS 8. These incentives may also be related to a firm's information environment and thus impact information asymmetries.

To control for this, Model A presents the regression based on equation (6.2). Model A includes an additional dummy variable (and further interactions) indicating whether an observation stems from an early adopting firm. The results are very similar to Table 6-10, albeit slightly weaker with regard to the treatment effect: **Post x Change$^1_{positive}$** is still significantly negative, but only at the ten per cent level. Moreover, Early and all interactions with Early are insignificant indicating that there is no systematic impact of early adopting firms. The control variables as well as the overall explanatory power are substantially the same compared to the base specification in Table 6-10. Hence, augmenting the regression model with an early adopter dummy variable does not add much to the overall explanatory power.

Model B is the same model as in equation (6.1). However, all early adopters are eliminated resulting in a reduced sample of 166 observations. Again, results are very similar to Table 6-10: **Post x Change$^1_{positive}$** is significant at the ten per cent level. Moreover, the control variables are all significantly different from zero in the expected directions. The adjusted R^2 of 86 per cent is marginally higher compared to the base model on the full sample in Table 6-10.[113]

Regression bid-ask spreads – Early adopters			
Variables	Predicted sign	Model A Full Sample	Model B No early adopters
Post		0.028	0.033
		(0.390)	(0.473)
Change$^1_{positive}$		0.030	0.023
		(0.344)	(0.270)
Early		-0.257	-
		(-1.370)	-
Post x Change$^1_{positive}$	(-)	**-0.157***	**-0.155***
		(-1.544)	**(-1.547)**
Post x Early		0.177	-
		(1.107)	-
Change$^1_{positive}$ x Early		0.347	-
		(1.191)	-
Post x Change$^1_{positive}$ x Early		-0.081	-
		(-0.394)	-
Log(Trading_Volume)	(-)	-0.517***	-0.504***
		(-13.992)	(-14.542)
Log(Volatiliy)	(+)	0.379**	0.456**
		(1.862)	(2.244)
Log(Size)	(-)	-0.591***	-0.604***
		(-25.700)	(-23.923)
Constant		-6.230***	-6.135***
		(-11.614)	(-12.415)
Firm level clustered standard errors		YES	YES
N		204	166
adj. R^2		0.843	0.858
F-stat		110.600	152.769

The table reports OLS coefficient estimates and t-statistics in parentheses below the coefficients. The predicted signs are presented next to the variables in parentheses. Change$^1_{positive}$ represents positive structural changes in the way segment information is presented upon adoption of IFRS 8.

*, **, and *** indicate statistical significance at the 10%, 5%, and 1% levels (one-tailed for coefficients with predicted signs and two-tailed otherwise), respectively.

Table 6-11: Regression bid-ask spreads – Early adopters

---

[113] This increase does not necessarily mean that the model performs better: *Cramer* (1987) shows that the adjusted R^2 is biased upwards in smaller samples.

In **summary**, the results in Table 6-11 show a slightly weaker, but still significant treatment effect[114] once the influence of early adopters is controlled for (Model A) or eliminated (Model B). This provides some confidence that the results are not driven by the endogenous nature of early adopting firms. The slight decrease in the magnitude as well as significance level of the treatment effect can be due to two reasons: On the one hand, adding more variables to the model (Model A) or reducing the sample size (Model B) decreases the power of the estimation. This makes it more difficult to detect an effect even though this effect is present in the population. On the other hand, the early adopters may in fact have a minor incremental effect that is eliminated once controlled for. However, the fact that the treatment effect remains significant provides evidence that the disclosure of segment information based on the management approach mitigates information asymmetries.

Next, a further **cross-sectional variation** in the treatment group is exploited: Some firms report fewer segments (structural negative change) or less segment information (content-related negative change) upon adoption of IFRS 8. These firms should show no impact or rather a negative effect on the bid-ask spreads if it is the segment report that is driving the results.

Table 6-12 reports the regression results for the bid-ask spreads based on equation (6.3): The base model is augmented with another dummy variable (and further interactions) indicating whether an observation stems from a firm that showed a **negative structural change** (negative change group one). Model A is based on the full sample and Model B eliminates all early adopting firms. Again, the results are very similar to all previous findings for both specifications: The treatment effect (**Post x Change$^1_{positive}$**) is significant at the five per cent level for the full sample (Model A) and at the ten per cent level without the early adopters. The slight decrease in the magnitude and significance of the treatment effect in Model B may be due to less power in the estimation or a minor incremental effect of early adopters as elaborated above. Furthermore, the firms that show a negative structural change upon adoption of IFRS 8 do not differ from the other firms in the pre IFRS 8 period either. Moreover, they are very similar to the control group since they do not show an incremental effect after the adoption of IFRS 8. The fact that **Post x Change$^1_{negative}$** is not significant strengthens the confidence in the results. Yet, a significantly positive coefficient would give even more support. However, there are two reasons why the coefficient may not be significantly positive: First, there are only seven firms in the negative structural change group, which represents very low statistical power to detect an effect even if it is present in the population. Second, some of the firms that show a negative structural change (i.e., decrease the number of reported segments) argue that a segmentation with fewer segments is more in line with the strategic positioning of the company.[115] Hence, the subjective classification as a negative change firm due to a decrease in the number of segments does not necessarily mean that investors have access to poorer information.

---

[114] The term treatment effect is used interchangeably with the effect of the interaction term Post x Change$^1_{positive}$ or Post x Change$^2_{positive}$.

[115] For instance, refer to the example of the Axel Springer Group in section 5.2.2.

In **summary**, the findings in Table 6-12 support the previous results that the disclosure of segment information based on the management approach provides users of financial statements with useful information.

Regression bid-ask spreads – Positive and negative change firms group one			
Variables	Predicted sign	Model A Full Sample	Model B No early adopters
Post		0.070	0.034
		(1.346)	(0.476)
Change^{1}positive		0.095	0.017
		(1.063)	(0.199)
Change^{1}negative		0.026	-0.105
		(0.155)	(-0.500)
Post x Change^{1}positive	(-)	-0.170**	-0.156*
		(-1.911)	(-1.518)
Post x Change^{1}negative	(+)	0.003	-0.007
		(0.028)	(-0.062)
Log(Trading_Volume)	(-)	-0.523***	-0.500***
		(-14.656)	(-14.389)
Log(Volatiliy)	(+)	0.452***	0.442**
		(3.275)	(2.093)
Log(Size)	(-)	-0.586***	-0.598***
		(-24.892)	(-21.168)
Constant		-6.466***	-6.112***
		(-15.776)	(-12.184)
Firm level clustered standard errors		YES	YES
N		204	166
adj. R^2		0.841	0.856
F-stat		130.046	114.180

The table reports OLS coefficient estimates and t-statistics in parentheses below the coefficients. The predicted signs are presented next to the variables in parentheses. Change^{1}positive represents positive structural changes in the way segment information is presented upon adoption of IFRS 8. Change^{1}negative represents negative structural changes in the way segment information is presented upon adoption of IFRS 8.
*, **, and *** indicate statistical significance at the 10%, 5%, and 1% levels (one-tailed for coefficients with predicted signs and two-tailed otherwise), respectively.

Table 6-12: Regression bid-ask spreads – Group one

As a further sensitivity check, this study uses an **alternative treatment group** and control group classification: While Change^{1}positive (Change^{1}negative) only considers positive (negative) structural changes, Change^{2}positive (Change^{2}negative) regard both structural and content-related changes.[116] Once more, the results are presented for the full sample (Model A) as well as the reduced sample without early adopters (Model B). The findings are very similar to the group one change specification in Table 6-12: The treatment effect is significant at the five per cent level for the full sample (Model A) and significant at the ten per cent level for the reduced sample (Model B). However, the magnitude of the effect is slightly lower. This may be due to the less strict treatment group change classification that classifies firms as treatment firms more easily. Nevertheless, the initial findings are once more supported.

[116] For a detailed overview of the classification criteria for structural and content-related changes refer to section 6.1.4.

Regression bid-ask spreads – Positive and negative change firms group two			
Variables	Predicted sign	Model A Full Sample	Model B No early adopters
Post		0.099	0.039
		(1.430)	(0.457)
Change²positive		0.028	0.005
		(0.354)	(0.061)
Change²negative		0.184**	0.113
		(2.032)	(1.207)
Post x Change²positive	(-)	-0.154**	-0.116*
		(-2.048)	(-1.293)
Post x Change²negative	(+)	-0.009	0.023
		(-0.116)	(0.281)
Log(Trading_Volume)	(-)	-0.541***	-0.521***
		(-16.057)	(-14.497)
Log(Volatiliy)	(+)	0.510***	0.497***
		(3.942)	(2.551)
Log(Size)	(-)	-0.585***	-0.605***
		(-25.741)	(-23.668)
Constant		-6.742***	-6.350***
		(-17.275)	(-12.951)
Firm level clustered standard errors		YES	YES
N		204	166
adj. R²		0.848	0.859
F-stat		136.456	127.309

The table reports OLS coefficient estimates and t-statistics in parentheses below the coefficients. The predicted signs are presented next to the variables in parentheses. Change²positive represents positive structural and content-related changes in the way segment information is presented upon adoption of IFRS 8. Change²negative represents negative structural and content-related changes in the way segment information is presented upon adoption of IFRS 8.
*, **, and *** indicate statistical significance at the 10%, 5%, and 1% levels (one-tailed for coefficients with predicted signs and two-tailed otherwise), respectively.

Table 6-13: Regression bid-ask spreads – Group two

Treatment effect timing – First quarter end

The first segment information under IFRS 8 already became available in May 2009 in the first quarterly report for the fiscal year 2009. However, these segmental disclosures are reduced in their extent and unaudited. Hence, it is questionable how relevant and reliable users of financial statements deem **quarterly segment information**. To analyze this, the bid-ask spreads are measured for a 90 days window beginning 45 days after the first quarter ends.

To get an understanding of the data, the **univariate difference-in-differences** for the quarter one end treatment timing are presented. Table 6-14 reports the group one change classification with (Panel A) and without (Panel B) early adopters.[117] The treatment and the control group are very similar to each other in the pre-IFRS 8 period in both Panel A and Panel B. While the control group shows an increase in information asymmetry in the post-treatment period, the treatment group retains a constant level of liquidity. This underlines the impact of introducing the management approach to segment reporting. How-

---

[117] The group two specifications are not reported for brevity. The results and inferences, however, are substantially similar.

ever, the magnitude of the effect is substantially lower compared to the fiscal year end treatment timing. Moreover, the difference-in-differences are insignificant in both panels. Hence, it seems that the main effect occurs when the full audited segment information is available. Yet, there is already some improvement in liquidity when the reduced quarterly segment information is released.

Univariate difference-in-differences analyses of the bid-ask spreads for group one at quarter one end			
Panel A. Full sample	IAS 14R (Pre-adoption Year) (a)	IFRS 8 (Adoption Year) (b)	(b) – (a)
Change$^1_{positive}$ (i)	0.76%	0.75%	-0.01%
No change (ii)	0.80%	0.96%	+0.16%
(i) – (ii)	-0.04%	-0.21%	**-0.17%**
Panel B. Without early adopters	IAS 14R (Pre-adoption Year) (a)	IFRS 8 (Adoption Year) (b)	(b) – (a)
Change$^1_{positive}$ (i)	0.75%	0.81%	+0.06%
No change (ii)	0.82%	1.00%	+0.18%
(i) – (ii)	-0.07%	-0.19%	**-0.12%**

Change$^1_{positive}$ represents positive structural changes in the way segment information is presented upon adoption of IFRS 8.
*, **, and *** indicate statistical significance at the 10%, 5%, and 1% levels (two-tailed), respectively.

Table 6-14: Difference-in-differences analyses of bid-ask spreads for group one at quarter one end

These findings are **corroborated** by multivariate regression models. For brevity, only the results for the group one change specification based on equation (6.3) are reported in Table 6-15. The results for the other specifications, however, are substantially similar. The overall explanatory power of the models is comparable to the fiscal year end treatment timing (see Table 6-12). Moreover, the control variables also perform similarly to the initial specification. Similar to the univariate analysis above, the treatment effect of the positive change group is insignificant. This indicates that quarterly segment information is not fully reflected in liquidity – which may be due to reliability issues of unaudited segmental disclosures. Another explanation is that some of the important aspects of IFRS 8 such as information about products and services or information about major customers are not required in interim segment reports and thus not available to the market at that time. Notably, the coefficient of **Post x Change$^1_{negative}$** is significantly negative indicating that firms which use the adoption of IFRS 8 to report more aggregated segment information already experience an increase in spreads upon release of the quarterly financial statements. Hence, negative prospects in terms of future transparency is penalized immediately while positive prospects are not fully recognized.

Regression bid-ask spreads – Positive and negative change firms group one at quarter one end			
Variables	Predicted sign	Model A Full Sample	Model B No early adopters
Post		-0.126**	-0.179**
		(-2.388)	(-2.490)
Change1positive		0.065	-0.010
		(0.754)	(-0.118)
Change1negative		-0.073	-0.134
		(-0.467)	(-0.688)
Post x Change1positive	(-)	-0.102	-0.054
		(-1.058)	(-0.486)
Post x Change1negative	(+)	0.286**	0.313***
		(2.511)	(2.763)
Log(Trading_Volume)	(-)	-0.513***	-0.501***
		(-15.131)	(-13.936)
Log(Volatiliy)	(+)	0.397***	0.426*
		(2.741)	(1.938)
Log(Size)	(-)	-0.575***	-0.588***
		(-21.974)	(-18.030)
Constant		-6.312***	-6.116***
		(-15.961)	(-12.006)
Firm level clustered standard errors		YES	YES
N		204	166
adj. R²		0.825	0.841
F-stat		98.966	87.906

The table reports OLS coefficient estimates and t-statistics in parentheses below the coefficients. The predicted signs are presented next to the variables in parentheses. Change1positive represents positive structural changes in the way segment information is presented upon adoption of IFRS 8. Change1negative represents negative structural changes in the way segment information is presented upon adoption of IFRS 8.
*, **, and *** indicate statistical significance at the 10%, 5%, and 1% levels (one-tailed for coefficients with predicted signs and two-tailed otherwise), respectively.

Table 6-15: Regression bid-ask spreads – Group one at quarter one end

6.2.3   Further robustness tests

The previous section has shown that the results are **robust** to the inclusion of firm and industry fixed effects, clustering at the firm or industry level or using *White* (1980) and *Newey/West* (1987) standard errors. Moreover, an analysis of VIFs and the analytical procedures following *Belsley et al.* (1980) show that multicollinearity is not an issue either. Furthermore, this study tests for the influence of early adopters by using additional dummy variables and eliminating early adopters from the sample. Finally, different treatment and control group specifications as well as treatment effect timings are used. None of these things substantially change results or inferences. This section provides a few more robustness tests to check for the sensitivity of the results.

Influence of outliers

An OLS regression is very **susceptible to the influence of outliers** because it minimizes the sum of squared residuals. Hence, extreme residuals have a relatively large impact on the sum of squares. Outliers may particularly change the outcome of an OLS regression based on small or medium samples sizes. Therefore, this study uses two procedures to check for the influence of outliers: First, all observations with studentized residuals greater than three are removed. Studentized residuals are calculated as the ratio of the estimated residual and the estimated standard deviation of all residuals (e.g., *Beckman/Trussell* (1974)). Second, Cook's Distance is another procedure to detect outliers. It tests how particular observations influence the parameter estimates of an OLS regression (*Cook* (1977)). Common cut-off values are 1/N or one, while the former is the more conservative approach.

Once outliers are identified, all firms that have at least one outlier in either the IAS 14R or IFRS 8 period **are removed from** the sample to retain a balanced panel. For brevity, Table 6-16 solely reports the results for the regression model with the positive and negative change group one specification.[118] Results for the other regressions, however, are basically the same.

Regression bid-ask spreads – Controlling for the influence of outliers full sample			
Variables	Predicted sign	Model A Studentized residuals Cut-off: 3 Full Sample	Model B Cook's Distance Cut-off: 1/N Full Sample
Post		0.064	-0.010
		(1.221)	(-0.212)
Change^1$_{positive}$		0.099	0.072
		(1.109)	(0.961)
Change^1$_{negative}$		0.020	0.128
		(0.118)	(1.516)
Post x Change^1$_{positive}$	(-)	-0.222***	-0.154**
		(-2.993)	(-2.138)
Post x Change^1$_{negative}$	(+)	0.009	-0.172
		(0.100)	(-1.880)
Log(Trading_Volume)	(-)	-0.530***	-0.498***
		(-14.860)	(-19.618)
Log(Volatiliy)	(+)	0.389***	0.325***
		(2.818)	(3.137)
Log(Size)	(-)	-0.587***	-0.608***
		(-25.065)	(-29.119)
Constant		-6.437***	-5.921***
		(-15.541)	(-19.009)
Firm level clustered standard errors		YES	YES
N		202	164
adj. R^2		0.850	0.906
F-stat		130.491	197.847

The table reports OLS coefficient estimates and t-statistics in parentheses below the coefficients. The predicted signs are presented next to the variables in parentheses. Change^1$_{positive}$ represents positive structural changes in the way segment information is presented upon adoption of IFRS 8. Change^1$_{negative}$ represents negative structural changes in the way segment information is presented upon adoption of IFRS 8.

*, **, and *** indicate statistical significance at the 10%, 5%, and 1% levels (one-tailed for coefficients with predicted signs and two-tailed otherwise), respectively.

Table 6-16: Regression bid-ask spreads – Without outliers

---

[118] This model is based on equation 6.3 and the initial results of the main specification are reported in Table 6-12.

Model A uses the common cut-off value of three for the **studentized residuals**. Only one observation is flagged as an outlier based on this procedure. Hence, the number of observations in Model A reduces to 202. The results, however, are basically the same. The significance level of the treatment effect even increases from five per cent to one per cent compared to the initial specification in Table 6-12.

Model B is based on **Cook's Distance**. As elaborated above, 1/N and one are common cut-off values. Because there is no observation that shows a Cook's Distance above one, only the more conservative cut-off value 1/N is used. In total, 40 potential outliers are removed from the sample. Although there is less power for statistical testing, the treatment effect remains significant at the five per cent level. Hence, results are not driven by an undue influence of extreme observations.

Regression bid-ask spreads – Controlling for the influence of outliers without early adopters			
Variables	Predicted sign	Model A Studentized residuals: Cut-off: 3 No early adopters	Model B Cook's Distance Cut-off: 1/N No early adopters
Post		0.013	-0.074
		(0.179)	(-1.184)
Change¹$_{positive}$		0.025	0.052
		(0.287)	(0.639)
Change¹$_{negative}$		-0.112	0.135
		(-0.529)	(1.417)
Post x Change¹$_{positive}$	(-)	**-0.226***	**-0.164**
		(-2.851)	**(-2.056)**
Post x Change¹$_{negative}$	(+)	**-0.019**	**-0.144**
		(-0.166)	**(-1.581)**
Log(Trading_Volume)	(-)	-0.504***	-0.491***
		(-14.210)	(-18.099)
Log(Volatiliy)	(+)	0.333	0.230
		(1.530)	(1.553)
Log(Size)	(-)	-0.600***	-0.622***
		(-21.443)	(-25.471)
Constant		-5.990***	-5.611***
		(-11.567)	(-15.101)
Firm level clustered standard errors		YES	YES
N		164	140
adj. R²		0.874	0.911
F-stat		115.315	167.509

The table reports OLS coefficient estimates and t-statistics in parentheses below the coefficients. The predicted signs are presented next to the variables in parentheses. Change¹$_{positive}$ represents positive structural changes in the way segment information is presented upon adoption of IFRS 8. Change¹$_{negative}$ represents negative structural changes in the way segment information is presented upon adoption of IFRS 8.
*, **, and *** indicate statistical significance at the 10%, 5%, and 1% levels (one-tailed for coefficients with predicted signs and two-tailed otherwise), respectively.

Table 6-17: Regression bid-ask spreads – Without outliers and early adopters

To jointly control for the influence of **early adopters and outliers**, the regressions of the previous table are rerun based on the sample without early adopters and without outliers. Table 6-17 reports the results. Model A once more uses studentized residuals greater than three to identify outliers, which leads to the elimination of one firm. This does not impact the initial results or inferences as the treatment effect remains highly significant at the one per cent level. Moreover, Model B removes 26 outliers with a Cook's Distance greater than $1/N$. Yet, this does neither change results nor inferences. The treatment effect is still highly significant at the five per cent level. The overall explanatory power of the model even increases to an adjusted R^2 of more than 91 per cent. In **summary**, the analysis of the influence of outliers suggests that the initial findings of this study are not driven by extreme observations.

Rank regressions

In addition to the OLS regression, this study uses non-parametric rank regressions. To perform a rank regression, all continuous variables are **transformed into ranks**. Subsequently, regressions are estimated based on the ranked variables. This procedure helps to remove the influence of highly skewed data and it provides some more confidence in the initial findings if the results hold for the rank regression.

Similar to the outlier robustness checks, Table 6-18 only presents the findings for the positive and negative change group one specification. Results for the other regressions, however, are virtually the same. **Model A** shows the results for the full sample. The magnitudes of the coefficients are entirely different which is natural due to the transformation in ranks. The signs and significance levels, however, are very similar. The treatment effect shows a coefficient of -13.5 which is significant at the five per cent level. This means that firms that start to disclose segment information based on the management approach experience a decline of about 13 ranks in the bid-ask spreads based on a sample of 204 observations. The other control variables show the expected signs and they remain highly significant. The explanatory power of the rank model with an adjusted R^2 of almost 79 per cent is slightly lower. This is not surprising because the transformation of continuous variables to ranks leads to a loss of information. However, an adjusted R^2 of 79 per cent is still very high.

Model B reports the results for the rank regression based on the sample without early adopters. The picture is very similar compared to the full sample and compared to the initial findings in Table 6-12. Firms adopting the management approach for their segment report experience a decrease of almost 13 ranks in the bid-ask spreads. This is significant at the five per cent level. Again, the other control variables except for Log(Volatility) show the signs as expected and they are highly significant. Moreover, the explanatory power is very high with an adjusted R^2 of 81 per cent.

In **total**, the findings are not sensitive to a different specification of the regression model. Rank regressions lead to similar results and inferences. Hence, highly skewed data does not unduly impact the findings of this study and the robustness tests provide confidence in the initial results.

Regression bid-ask spreads – Rank regressions			
Variables	Predicted sign	Model A Rank regression Full sample	Model B Rank regression No early adopters
Post		7.474**	2.729
		(2.171)	(0.595)
Change^{1}positive		7.137	1.365
		(1.069)	(0.219)
Change^{1}negative		1.548	-16.060
		(0.147)	(-1.639)
Post x Change^{1}positive	(-)	-13.488**	-12.649**
		(-2.373)	(-2.057)
Post x Change^{1}negative	(+)	-2.528	1.124
		(-0.551)	(0.250)
Log(Trading_Volume)	(-)	-0.504***	-0.451***
		(-11.747)	(-11.583)
Log(Volatiliy)	(+)	0.119***	0.070
		(2.837)	(1.112)
Log(Size)	(-)	-0.768***	-0.776***
		(-21.516)	(-18.891)
Constant		227.266***	234.892***
		(28.625)	(23.477)
Firm level clustered standard errors		YES	YES
N		204	166
adj. R^2		0.789	0.814
F-stat		96.018	91.313

The table reports OLS coefficient estimates and t-statistics in parentheses below the coefficients. The predicted signs are presented next to the variables in parentheses. Change^{1}positive represents positive structural changes in the way segment information is presented upon adoption of IFRS 8. Change^{1}negative represents negative structural changes in the way segment information is presented upon adoption of IFRS 8.
*, **, and *** indicate statistical significance at the 10%, 5%, and 1% levels (one-tailed for coefficients with predicted signs and two-tailed otherwise), respectively.

Table 6-18: Regression bid-ask spreads – Rank regressions

Summary

To **sum up**, the multivariate regression analyses and their robustness tests corroborate the univariate findings. Regression results show an incremental negative difference-in-differences in bid-ask spreads for the treatment group. This holds for several alternative specifications of clustering standard errors or introducing fixed effects. Moreover, findings indicate that the results are not driven by early adopters. Furthermore, differentiating between positive and negative change firms as well as differentiating between alternative change specifications (structural and content-related) confirms the initial findings. Moreover, the main liquidity effect is driven by the release of the full audited segment report. Yet, there is already a minor effect upon release of quarterly segment information. Hence, there is a sound empirical foundation that supports the notion that the disclosure of segment information based on the management approach is useful information and mitigates information asymmetries.

6.3   Cost of capital

The structure of the cost of capital analysis is very similar to the analysis of the bid-ask spreads in the previous section. The focus and potential implications, however, are very different because the **perspective of the firm** itself is assumed. Moreover, there is no consensus of a single measure that is accepted in the literature to gauge the cost of capital. Therefore, multiple measures are used which increases the extent of tables and discussions. The analysis starts with some descriptive statistics. In addition, correlation matrices are presented. Next, this section analyzes the economic consequences in terms of cost of capital based on a univariate and multivariate difference-in-differences analysis. Finally, the results are tested for robustness.

6.3.1   Univariate and bivariate analyses

Descriptive statistics

Table 6-19 shows the descriptive statistics of the **cost of capital** for each index. The mean, median, standard deviation (std. dev.) as well as the 25 per cent (Q25) and 75 per cent quartiles (Q75) for all four different models are presented separately. The average cost of capital shows the mean value of all models. However, the models are based on an iterative procedure and they have different assumptions so that some firm-years do not have a valid estimate. This is reflected in the varying numbers of observations. In particular, the *Ohlson/Juettner-Nauroth* (2005) model and the *Easton* (2004) model require a positive change from the t+1 earnings forecast to the t+2 earnings forecast. This restricts the sample to 186 respectively 178 observations compared to the 196 (*Claus/Thomas* (2001)) and 200 observations (*Gebhardt et al.* (2001)) of the other two models. The average cost of capital is only calculated if there is a valid estimate for all four models. Accordingly, only 172 observations are available for the aggregated measure.

The **magnitude** of the implied **cost of capital** varies between the four different models. The *Gebhardt et al.* (2001) model and the *Claus/Thomas* (2001) model show the lowest mean cost of capital of 9.25 per cent and 10.55 per cent. In contrast, the mean cost of capital following the approaches of *Ohlson/Juettner-Nauroth* (2005) and *Easton* (2004) is 12.77 per cent and 16.36 per cent respectively. This is consistent with prior research of *Hail/Leuz* (2006) who also report the lowest estimates for the *Gebhardt et al.* (2001) model with an average cost of capital of 9.25 per cent for a world sample.[119] Moreover, the estimates of all four models are within plausible ranges. The *Ohlson/Juettner-Nauroth* (2005) and *Easton* (2004) models are more **dispersed** with a standard deviation of 5.05 per cent and 8.42 compared to the other two models. This could be due to the longer and more detailed forecast horizon of the *Gebhardt et al.* (2001) and the *Claus/Thomas* (2001) model which may provide less noisy estimates.

---

[119] The mean estimate for the other models are: 12.17 per cent (*Claus/Thomas* (2001)), 14.59 per cent (*Ohlson/Juettner-Nauroth* (2005)) and 13.96 per cent (*Easton* (2004)). This is largely consistent with the estimates in this study.

Descriptive statistics of the cost of capital for each index							
Variables[a]		mean	std. dev.	Q25	median	Q75	N
Claus and Thomas (2001)	DAX	10.69%	1.77%	9.02%	11.16%	12.27%	24
	MDAX	10.03%	2.94%	8.26%	9.78%	11.65%	74
	TecDAX	10.51%	3.26%	8.94%	10.17%	11.91%	38
	SDAX	11.04%	3.98%	7.92%	10.62%	12.22%	60
	Total	10.55%	3.25%	8.46%	10.25%	12.18%	196
Gebhardt et al. (2001)	DAX	9.33%	2.23%	8.05%	8.66%	10.64%	24
	MDAX	8.87%	2.95%	6.94%	8.47%	10.27%	76
	TecDAX	8.97%	3.45%	6.43%	8.25%	10.33%	40
	SDAX	9.77%	3.19%	7.72%	9.82%	11.99%	60
	Total	9.25%	3.06%	7.03%	8.76%	10.82%	200
Ohlson and Juettner-Nauroth (2005)	DAX	11.95%	2.63%	9.87%	12.13%	13.38%	24
	MDAX	12.63%	5.77%	8.88%	12.63%	14.95%	70
	TecDAX	12.17%	3.85%	9.13%	12.25%	15.08%	38
	SDAX	13.58%	5.58%	9.72%	12.56%	16.19%	54
	Total	12.77%	5.05%	9.26%	11.99%	14.78%	186
Easton (2004)	DAX	15.60%	5.04%	12.95%	15.43%	17.36%	24
	MDAX	16.62%	10.34%	10.42%	12.23%	19.10%	64
	TecDAX	15.48%	6.46%	11.43%	13.66%	17.91%	38
	SDAX	15.26%	8.25%	11.51%	15.26%	20.65%	52
	Total	16.36%	8.41%	10.93%	14.02%	19.09%	178
Average cost of capital	DAX	11.89%	2.23%	10.39%	11.80%	14.12%	24
	MDAX	12.21%	4.48%	8.74%	10.79%	13.95%	62
	TecDAX	11.84%	3.43%	9.17%	11.78%	13.51%	38
	SDAX	12.58%	3.78%	9.88%	12.45%	14.37%	48
	Total	12.22%	3.78%	9.47%	11.50%	13.97%	172

[a]Claus and Thomas (2001), Gebhardt et al. (2001), Ohlson and Juettner-Nauroth (2005) and Easton (2004) represent the implied cost of capital based on the different models. The Average cost of capital is the mean value of all four models.

Table 6-19: Descriptive statistics of the cost of capital

Based on the **aggregated cost of capital** measure, DAX and TecDAX firms show the lowest cost of capital. The other firms have a higher cost of capital. This is consistent with the notion that larger firms (DAX) provide the least risky investments and thus investors require relatively less compensation for bearing risk. In contrast, SDAX and MDAX firms are in general smaller as well as younger and therefore it is not surprising that their cost of capital is substantially higher. Moreover, the technology sector firms of the TecDAX may have relatively high growth opportunities which are reflected in a low cost of capital.

In **summary**, all four models provide reasonable estimates which are in line with expectations and prior literature. To mitigate the measurement errors of the individual models, subsequent analyses largely rely on the average measure of the four proxies.[120] Although only the average cost of capital is reported in most subsequent models, this study also performs (but does not tabulate) estimations based on the individual proxies. Yet, results and inferences are substantially consistent across all specifications, albeit slightly weaker for some proxies.

Table 6-20 presents descriptive information of the **control variables** used in the cost of capital regressions.[121] **Beta** captures the risk of a security. Beta factors larger (smaller) than one represent riskier (less risky) stocks in comparison to the market index. The mean beta

---

[120] Most subsequent univariate analyses use the four different proxies while all regression analyses except for those in Table 6-31 are based on the average cost of capital measure.

[121] Again, size is not discussed in detail because section 5.1.2 already provides a discussion for each index

across all indices is 0.90. This is a reasonable number considering the fact that the CDAX is used as the market index to determine the betas: The CDAX comprises all securities listed in the Prime Standard and General Standard. Hence, the sample firms are on average larger and less risky compared to the smaller and less transparent firms in the General Standard. Therefore, a mean beta below one is a plausible estimate.[122]

Descriptive statistics of the cost of capital control variables for each index							
Variables[a]		mean	std. dev.	Q25	median	Q75	N
Size	DAX	19,707.62	17,391.99	6,595.04	12,867.12	26,192.80	26
	MDAX	2,633.97	3,161.21	981.60	1,569.84	2,843.25	78
	TecDAX	732.26	935.34	213.27	420.27	766.18	44
	SDAX	583.13	766.27	174.64	306.49	648.00	70
	Total	3,652.10	8,683.73	343.39	848.13	2,406	218
Beta	DAX	0.75	0.29	0.55	0.66	0.88	26
	MDAX	1.01	0.39	0.79	1.01	1.28	78
	TecDAX	1.10	0.46	0.78	1.05	1.38	42
	SDAX	0.72	0.41	0.52	0.71	0.93	70
	Total	0.90	0.43	0.64	0.85	1.14	216
Leverage	DAX	0.65	0.14	0.59	0.65	0.77	26
	MDAX	0.66	0.12	0.59	0.66	0.73	78
	TecDAX	0.43	0.21	0.25	0.42	0.57	42
	SDAX	0.58	0.16	0.48	0.60	0.69	70
	Total	0.59	0.18	0.51	0.62	0.71	216
BTM	DAX	1.08	1.73	0.32	0.65	0.83	26
	MDAX	0.63	0.43	0.36	0.55	0.76	78
	TecDAX	0.65	0.63	0.27	0.51	0.77	42
	SDAX	0.91	0.76	0.38	0.56	1.31	70
	Total	0.78	0.84	0.34	0.55	0.88	216

[a]Size is the market capitalization presented in million Euros. Beta represents one year beta factors based on weekly returns. Leverage is total liabilities divided by total assets. BTM is the book-to-market ratio calculated as book value of equity divided by market value of equity.

Table 6-20: Descriptive statistics of the cost of capital controls

Leverage represents the financial structure of a firm and to some extent a potential default risk. Higher leverage increases the risk for equity investors as debt contracts usually have a superior claim which means they are pursued first in times of financial distress. The mean leverage ratio over all four indices is about 59 per cent. DAX and MDAX firms are the most leveraged with a mean leverage of about 65 and 66 per cent. TecDAX and SDAX firms have more equity resulting in a mean leverage ratio of 43 and 58 per cent. These numbers are all within reasonable ranges.

The **book-to-market** ratio reflects differences in growth opportunities. Smaller values indicate more potential growth opportunities (as perceived by the market). The mean value across the full sample is 0.78 which is consistent with prior research (e.g., *Hail/Leuz* (2006), p. 499, report a mean BTM of 0.60 for a world sample). DAX firms have the least potential for future growth (mean value of 1.08) followed by the SDAX (0.91) as well as the TecDAX (0.65) and the MDAX (0.63). This is consistent with the notion that larger firms such as the DAX constituents are more saturated and have fewer opportunities for further growth compared to smaller and technology driven firms.

---

[122] If the sample of this study would contain all CDAX firms, the theoretical (value-weighted) mean beta would be exactly one.

In **total**, all control variables are within reasonable ranges that are largely in line with prior research. Moreover, differences between the stock indices are also consistent with theoretical expectations.

Similar to the information asymmetry study, Table 6-21 and Table 6-22 present descriptive information separately for the **treatment and the control** group (based on the group one classification). This helps to determine whether the distribution of treatment and control firms is quasi-randomized as suggested by the research design of this study. Except for the *Gebhardt et al.* (2001) model, there are significant differences in the cost of capital for the treatment and the control group. In particular, there is a substantial difference of 1.57 percentage points for the average cost of capital measure. This is very different for the differences in the control variables in Table 6-20. Size, beta and BTM are virtually similar for the two groups (Table 6-22). Only the difference in leverage is marginally significant at the ten per cent level. Hence, the descriptive statistics of the control variables for the treatment and the control group corroborate the quasi-experimental feature of the cost of capital study.

Descriptive statistics of cost of capital for the treatment and control group one						
Variables[a]		mean	std. dev.	Q25	median	Q75
Claus and Thomas (2001)	Change[1]positive	9.81%	3.30%	7.74%	9.41%	11.44%
	No change	10.83%	3.35%	8.88%	10.29%	12.47%
	(Difference)[b]	-1.02%**				
Gebhardt et al. (2001)	Change[1]positive	9.21%	3.28%	7.03%	8.72%	10.34%
	No change	9.18%	2.86%	7.02%	8.75%	10.97%
	(Difference)[b]	+0.03%				
Ohlson and Juettner-Nauroth (2005)	Change[1]positive	11.41%	4.86%	8.20%	9.98%	13.44%
	No change	13.33%	5.34%	9.60%	12.46%	15.77%
	(Difference)[b]	-1.92%**				
Easton (2004)	Change[1]positive	14.81%	6.48%	10.65%	12.90%	16.87%
	No change	17.22%	9.74%	10.77%	14.38%	19.65%
	(Difference)[b]	-2.41%*				
Average cost of capital	Change[1]positive	11.13%	3.35%	8.99%	10.22%	13.14%
	No change	12.70%	4.08%	10.04%	12.08%	14.12%
	(Difference)[b]	-1.57%**				

[a]Claus and Thomas (2001), Gebhardt at al. (2001), Ohlson and Juettner-Nauroth (2005) and Easton (2004) represent the implied cost of capital based on the different models. The Average cost of capital is the mean value of all four models. Change[1]positive represents positive structural changes in the way segment information is presented upon adoption of IFRS 8.
[b] *, **, and *** indicate statistical significance at the 10%, 5%, and 1% levels (two-tailed), respectively.

Table 6-21: Descriptive statistics of the cost of capital for group one

Descriptive statistics of cost of capital control variables for the treatment and control group one					
Variables[a]		mean	std. dev.	Q25	median	Q75
Size	Change[1]positive	3,755.96	10,230.73	410.21	935.39	2,949.44
	No change	3,067.26	6,772.67	295.88	732.24	2,123.17
	(Difference)[b]	+688.49				
Beta	Change[1]positive	0.92	0.45	0.58	0.86	1.14
	No change	0.92	0.40	0.65	0.86	1.14
	(Difference)[b]	0.00				
Leverage	Change[1]positive	0.56	0.18	0.49	0.60	0.69
	No change	0.61	0.17	0.50	0.64	0.75
	(Difference)[b]	-0.05*				
BTM	Change[1]positive	0.92	1.20	0.33	0.57	0.96
	No change	0.73	0.60	0.34	0.54	0.88
	(Difference)[b]	+0.19				

[a]Size is the market capitalization presented in million Euros. Beta represents one year beta factors based on weekly returns. Leverage is total liabilities divided by total assets. BTM is the book-to-market ratio calculated as book value of equity divided by market value of equity. Change[1]positive represents positive structural changes in the way segment information is presented upon adoption of IFRS 8.
[b] *, **, and *** indicate statistical significance at the 10%, 5%, and 1% levels (two-tailed), respectively.

Table 6-22: Descriptive statistics of the cost of capital controls for group one

Table 6-23 and Table 6-24 present the same descriptive statistics for the change group two specification. The findings are somewhat different to the group one specification in the previous two tables: The significant differences in the cost of capital models disappear. However, the differences between the control variables remain statistically insignificant. Hence, this once more supports the quasi-experimental research design.

Descriptive statistics of cost of capital for the treatment and control group two					
Variables[a]		mean	std. dev.	Q25	median	Q75
Claus and Thomas (2001)	Change[2]positive	10.51%	3.40%	8.05%	9.99%	12.56%
	No change	10.65%	4.45%	8.23%	10.28%	11.46%
	(Difference)[b]	-0.14%				
Gebhardt et al. (2001)	Change[2]positive	8.85%	3.11%	6.73%	8.18%	10.48%
	No change	8.81%	3.31%	6.37%	8.18%	10.99%
	(Difference)[b]	+0.04%				
Ohlson and Juettner-Nauroth (2005)	Change[2]positive	13.26%	5.20%	9.87%	11.84%	15.41%
	No change	13.11%	4.36%	10.12%	11.93%	15.55%
	(Difference)[b]	+0.15%				
Easton (2004)	Change[2]positive	14.40%	7.17%	10.26%	12.55%	16.27%
	No change	14.93%	8.82%	9.70%	11.81%	17.66%
	(Difference)[b]	-0.53%				
Average cost of capital	Change[2]positive	11.77%	4.11%	9.44%	10.82%	13.14%
	No change	11.66%	3.67%	8.97%	10.82%	13.75%
	(Difference)[b]	+0.11%				

[a]Claus and Thomas (2001), Gebhardt et al. (2001), Ohlson and Juettner-Nauroth (2005) and Easton (2004) represent the implied cost of capital based on the different models. The Average cost of capital is the mean value of all four models. Change[2]positive represents positive structural and content-related changes in the way segment information is presented upon adoption of IFRS 8.
[b] *, **, and *** indicate statistical significance at the 10%, 5%, and 1% levels (two-tailed), respectively.

Table 6-23: Descriptive statistics of the cost of capital for group two

Descriptive statistics of cost of capital control variables for the treatment and control group two					
Variables[a]		mean	std. dev.	Q25	median	Q75
Size	Change^{2}positive	2,874.05	5,152.82	404.21	1,003.94	2,949.44
	No change	2,539.11	4,991.69	339.92	699.16	2,123.17
	(Difference)[b]	+334.94				
Beta	Change^{2}positive	0.85	0.39	0.642	0.81	1.04
	No change	0.96	0.44	0.651	0.87	1.26
	(Difference)[b]	-0.11				
Leverage	Change^{2}positive	0.58	0.18	0.480	0.61	0.71
	No change	0.59	0.20	0.451	0.63	0.75
	(Difference)[b]	-0.01				
BTM	Change^{2}positive	0.89	1.19	0.325	0.57	0.83
	No change	0.82	0.68	0.354	0.51	1.00
	(Difference)[b]	+0.07				

[a]Size is the market capitalization presented in million Euros. Beta represents one year beta factors based on weekly returns. Leverage is total liabilities divided by total assets. BTM is the book-to-market ratio calculated as book value of equity divided by market value of equity. Change^{2}positive represents positive structural and content-related changes in the way segment information is presented upon adoption of IFRS 8.
[b] *, **, and *** indicate statistical significance at the 10%, 5%, and 1% levels (two-tailed), respectively.

Table 6-24: Descriptive statistics of the cost of capital controls for group two

Table 6-25 presents the **correlation matrix** of the four cost of capital proxies and the average measure. Correlation coefficients for the treatment group (positive change one specification) are shown above the diagonal and coefficients for the control group are reported below. Independent of the grouping, all four proxies are highly correlated indicating that they all capture the same underlying construct. Similar to *Hail/Leuz* (2006), the *Gebhardt et al.* (2001) model shows slightly lower correlations. This may be due to the fact that this model exhibits the longest explicit forecast horizon of 12 years and also incorporates industry information (*Hail/Leuz* (2006), p. 493). Not surprisingly, the average cost of capital measure shows the highest correlations.

Correlation matrix cost of capital					
Variables[a]	Claus and Thomas (2001)	Gebhardt et al. (2001)	Ohlson and Juettner-Nauroth (2005)	Easton (2004)	Average cost of capital
Claus and Thomas (2001)	-	0.737*** (0.000)	0.332** (0.014)	0.649*** (0.000)	0.808*** (0.000)
Gebhardt et al. (2001)	0.483*** (0.000)	-	0.372*** (0.006)	0.661*** (0.000)	0.830*** (0.000)
Ohlson and Juett-ner-Nauroth (2005)	0.262*** (0.009)	0.323*** (0.001)	-	0.452*** (0.001)	0.668*** (0.000)
Easton (2004)	0.162 (0.110)	0.434*** (0.000)	0.625*** (0.000)	-	0.902*** (0.000)
Average cost of capital	0.455*** (0.000)	0.635*** (0.000)	0.802*** (0.000)	0.908*** (0.000)	-

[a]Spearman correlation coefficients are presented for the pairwise correlations of the different cost of capital measures. P-values are below the correlation coefficients in parentheses. Correlations for the treatment group positive change one are reported above the diagonal and for the no change control group are presented below the diagonal.
*, **, and *** indicate statistical significance at the 10%, 5%, and 1% levels, respectively.

Table 6-25: Correlation matrix cost of capital

Table 6-26 presents the **correlation** coefficients of the average cost of capital measure and the control variables of the multivariate regressions for the **treatment and the control group**. Consistent with expectations, the average cost of capital is negatively related to size. This is plausible as larger firms are usually more transparent and represent less risky investments. Moreover, there is a positive correlation between cost of capital and beta. Naturally, investors require higher compensation for riskier investments. Furthermore, there is a positive relationship between cost of capital and BTM which means that firms with more growth opportunities show a lower cost of capital. The correlation coefficient of cost of capital and leverage is positive as expected. This is consistent with the notion that more leveraged firms have a greater default risk.

There are also some significant correlations between the **control variables**. For instance, size is positively correlated with leverage and negatively correlated with BTM. This means that larger firms are on average more leveraged and show less growth opportunities.

The correlations for the treatment group are in essence similar, albeit weaker for some variable pairs. In total, the correlation matrices largely show pairwise correlations that are as expected.

Correlation matrix cost of capital and control variables				
Variables[a]	Average cost of capital	Size	Beta	Leverage	BTM
Average cost of capital	-	-0.250* (0.069)	0.074 (0.593)	0.132 (0.343)	0.170 (0.219)
Size	-0.212** (0.036)	-	-0.170 (0.216)	0.573*** (0.000)	-0.367*** (0.006)
Beta	0.241** (0.017)	-0.109 (0.286)	-	-0.113 (0.417)	-0.057 (0.682)
Leverage	0.332*** (0.000)	0.106 (0.298)	0.035 (0.732)	-	-0.030 (0.827)
BTM	0.346*** (0.001)	-0.248** (0.014)	0.154 (0.130)	0.030 (0.769)	-

[a]Spearman correlation coefficients are presented for the pairwise correlations of the average cost of capital measure and control variables. P-values are below the correlation coefficients in parentheses. Correlations for the treatment group positive change one are reported above the diagonal and for the no change control group are presented below the diagonal.
*, **, and *** indicate statistical significance at the 10%, 5%, and 1% levels, respectively.

Table 6-26: Correlation matrix cost of capital and controls

To **sum up,** the descriptive statistics show plausible results. All empirical proxies used in the cost of capital study are within reasonable ranges and they exhibit variation between the different stock indices that is consistent with theoretical expectations. Moreover, all four proxies for the cost of capital are highly correlated indicating that they capture the same underlying construct. The control variables do not show substantial differences between the treatment and the control group which supports the quasi-experimental feature of the cost of capital study. In the following, univariate and multivariate results for the difference-in-differences analyses are presented. This helps to analyze whether the disclosure of segment information based on the management approach has an impact on the cost of capital.

Difference-in-differences

Similar to the bid-ask spread analysis, Table 6-27 shows the cost of capital pre and post IFRS 8 adoption for the treatment and the control group. Again, the left column presents values for IAS 14R and the right column for IFRS 8. The change between the two periods is reported next to it. Furthermore, the first row shows the treatment group and the second row the control group. The bottom row reports the difference between the two groups.

Table 6-27 uses the positive **change group one** specification that only considers major structural changes. In the pre IFRS 8 period, there are significant differences between the treatment and the control group for two out of the five cost of capital models. Across all models, the treatment group shows on average a lower cost of capital. The change in the cost of capital from the IAS 14R period to IFRS 8 period is inconsistent for the control and the treatment group based on the five models. In most cases and for both groups, however, there is a decrease in the cost of capital from the IAS 14R to the IFRS 8 period. This is in line with the notion that the impact of the global financial crisis already alleviated in the beginning of 2010 compared to 2009.

Univariate difference-in-differences analyses of the cost of capital for the full sample based on group one			
Claus and Thomas (2001)	IAS 14R (Pre-adoption Year) (a)	IFRS 8 (Adoption Year) (b)	(b) – (a)
Change[1]positive (i)	10.29%	9.32%	-0.97%**
No change (ii)	11.50%	10.16%	-1.34%
(i) – (ii)	-1.21%*	-0.84%*	+0.37%
Gebhardt et al. (2001)	IAS 14R (Pre-adoption Year) (a)	IFRS 8 (Adoption Year) (b)	(b) – (a)
Change[1]positive (i)	9.87%	8.55%	-1.32%**
No change (ii)	9.90%	8.45%	-1.45%***
(i) – (ii)	-0.03%	+0.10%	+0.13%
Ohlson and Juettner-Nauroth (2005)	IAS 14R (Pre-adoption Year) (a)	IFRS 8 (Adoption Year) (b)	(b) – (a)
Change[1]positive (i)	11.75%	11.06%	-0.69%
No change (ii)	14.05%	12.61%	-1.44%*
(i) – (ii)	-2.30%***	-1.55%	+0.75%
Easton (2004)	IAS 14R (Pre-adoption Year) (a)	IFRS 8 (Adoption Year) (b)	(b) – (a)
Change[1]positive (i)	14.94%	14.68%	-0.26%
No change (ii)	17.10%	17.34%	0.24%
(i) – (ii)	-2.16%	-2.66%	-0.50%
Average cost of capital	IAS 14R (Pre-adoption Year) (a)	IFRS 8 (Adoption Year) (b)	(b) – (a)
Change[1]positive (i)	11.54%	10.90%	-0.64%
No change (ii)	12.77%	12.00%	-0.77%
(i) – (ii)	-1.23%	-1.10%	+0.13%

Change[1]positive represents positive structural changes in the way segment information is presented upon adoption of IFRS 8.
*, **, and *** indicate statistical significance at the 10%, 5%, and 1% levels (two-tailed), respectively.

Table 6-27: Univariate difference-in-differences cost of capital – Group one

The difference-in-differences – which is indicative of a potential treatment effect – is insignificant and shows different signs for the five models. This signals that there is **no effect of IFRS 8** in any direction. However, note that this effect is measured at the time the first annual report was published. As discussed earlier, the cost of capital measure is largely anticipatory since financial analysts already adjust their estimates when future changes in transparency are expected (*Christensen et al.* (2013), p. 152). Moreover, the treatment group shows a lower cost of capital in the pre period which may indicate that there has already been a change in the cost of capital. Given the quasi-experimental feature of this study, one would not expect any differences between the treatment and the control group in the pre period as it is the case for the bid-ask spreads. Therefore, the analysis of a **different treatment effect timing** (i.e., first quarter end) at the end of this section is particularly important and sheds further light on this issue.

Table 6-28 presents the same analysis based on the **change group two** specification that takes structural and content-related changes into account. The findings are substantially similar to the previous table. The difference-in-differences are insignificant for all five models and also show different signs. Hence, there is no effect on the cost of capital for the group two specification either.

Univariate difference-in-differences analyses of the cost of capital for the full sample based on group two			
Claus and Thomas (2001)	IAS 14R (Pre-adoption Year) (a)	IFRS 8 (Adoption Year) (b)	(b) – (a)
Change$^2_{positive}$ (i)	10.87%	9.66%	-1.21%
No change (ii)	10.48%	9.45%	-1.03%
(i) – (ii)	+0.39%	+0.21%	**-0.18%**
Gebhardt et al. (2001)	IAS 14R (Pre-adoption Year) (a)	IFRS 8 (Adoption Year) (b)	(b) – (a)
Change$^2_{positive}$ (i)	9.83%	8.59%	-1.24%
No change (ii)	9.59%	8.45%	-1.14%
(i) – (ii)	+0.24%	+0.14%	**-0.10%**
Ohlson and Juettner-Nauroth (2005)	IAS 14R (Pre-adoption Year) (a)	IFRS 8 (Adoption Year) (b)	(b) – (a)
Change$^2_{positive}$ (i)	12.39%	11.71%	-0.68%
No change (ii)	13.80%	12.04%	-1.76%
(i) – (ii)	-1.41%	-0.33%	**+1.08%**
Easton (2004)	IAS 14R (Pre-adoption Year) (a)	IFRS 8 (Adoption Year) (b)	(b) – (a)
Change$^2_{positive}$ (i)	14.68%	15.05%	+0.37%
No change (ii)	18.75%	17.94%	-0.81%
(i) – (ii)	-4.07%	-2.89%	**+1.18%**
Average cost of capital	IAS 14R (Pre-adoption Year) (a)	IFRS 8 (Adoption Year) (b)	(b) – (a)
Change$^2_{positive}$ (i)	11.86%	11.30%	-0.56%
No change (ii)	12.84%	12.11%	-0.73%
(i) – (ii)	-0.98%	-0.81%	**+0.17%**

Change$^2_{positive}$ represents positive structural and content-related changes in the way segment information is presented upon adoption of IFRS 8.
*, **, and *** indicate statistical significance at the 10%, 5%, and 1% levels (two-tailed), respectively.

Table 6-28: Univariate difference-in-differences cost of capital – Group two

To address the **self-selection** issue of firms that adopt IFRS 8 early, Table 6-29 and Table 6-30 present the same analyses as in the previous two tables without **early adopters**. This helps to avoid an undue influence of firms that may have incentives (e.g., future growth opportunities or need of additional external capital) to early adopt IFRS 8 which may also impact the cost of capital. Again, the results are comparable to the initial findings from Table 6-29. There is a general decline in the cost of capital for all five models in the treatment and the control group. As elaborated before, the impact of the global financial crisis may already have attenuated in the beginning of 2010. Once more, the difference-in-differences is insignificant and shows inconsistent signs for all five models. Hence, there is no effect of IFRS 8's adoption at the time the annual report is published – even if the impact of early adopters is removed.

Univariate difference-in-differences analyses of the cost of capital without early adopters based on group one			
Claus and Thomas (2001)		IAS 14R (Pre-adoption Year) (a)	IFRS 8 (Adoption Year) (b)	(b) – (a)
Change[1]positive	(i)	10.68%	9.39%	-1.29%
No change	(ii)	11.66%	10.28%	-1.38%
	(i) – (ii)	-0.98%	-0.89%	**+0.09%**
Gebhardt et al. (2001)		IAS 14R (Pre-adoption Year) (a)	IFRS 8 (Adoption Year) (b)	(b) – (a)
Change[1]positive	(i)	10.27%	8.16%	-2.11%**
No change	(ii)	10.30%	8.23%	-2.07%***
	(i) – (ii)	-0.03%	-0.07%	**-0.04%**
Ohlson and Juettner-Nauroth (2005)		IAS 14R (Pre-adoption Year) (a)	IFRS 8 (Adoption Year) (b)	(b) – (a)
Change[1]positive	(i)	12.10%	10.96%	-1.14%
No change	(ii)	14.58%	12.72%	-1.86%**
	(i) – (ii)	-2.48%***	-1.76%	**+0.72%**
Easton (2004)		IAS 14R (Pre-adoption Year) (a)	IFRS 8 (Adoption Year) (b)	(b) – (a)
Change[1]positive	(i)	15.16%	14.89%	-0.27%
No change	(ii)	18.12%	17.47%	-0.65%
	(i) – (ii)	-2.96%	-2.58%	**+0.38%**
Average cost of capital		IAS 14R (Pre-adoption Year) (a)	IFRS 8 (Adoption Year) (b)	(b) – (a)
Change[1]positive	(i)	11.72%	10.89%	-0.83%
No change	(ii)	13.35%	11.90%	-1.45%*
	(i) – (ii)	-1.63%*	-1.01%	**+0.62%**

Change[1]positive represents positive structural changes in the way segment information is presented upon adoption of IFRS 8.
*, **, and *** indicate statistical significance at the 10%, 5%, and 1% levels (two-tailed), respectively.

Table 6-29: Univariate difference-in-differences cost of capital – Group one without early adopters

Univariate difference-in-differences analyses of the cost of capital without early adopters based on group two			
Claus and Thomas (2001)	IAS 14R (Pre-adoption Year) (a)	IFRS 8 (Adoption Year) (b)	(b) – (a)
Change²positive (i)	11.22%	9.63%	-1.59%
No change (ii)	10.52%	9.81%	-0.71%
(i) – (ii)	+0.70%	-0.18%	-0.88%
Gebhardt et al. (2001)	IAS 14R (Pre-adoption Year) (a)	IFRS 8 (Adoption Year) (b)	(b) – (a)
Change²positive (i)	10.08%	7.91%	-2.17%***
No change (ii)	10.32%	8.64%	-1.68%*
(i) – (ii)	-0.24%	-0.73%	-0.49%
Ohlson and Juettner-Nauroth (2005)	IAS 14R (Pre-adoption Year) (a)	IFRS 8 (Adoption Year) (b)	(b) – (a)
Change²positive (i)	12.90%	11.39%	-1.51%
No change (ii)	14.21%	12.58%	-1.63%
(i) – (ii)	-1.31%	-1.19%	+0.12%
Easton (2004)	IAS 14R (Pre-adoption Year) (a)	IFRS 8 (Adoption Year) (b)	(b) – (a)
Change²positive (i)	15.18%	14.52%	-0.66%
No change (ii)	19.91%	19.06%	-0.85%
(i) – (ii)	-4.73%	-4.54%*	+0.19%
Average cost of capital	IAS 14R (Pre-adoption Year) (a)	IFRS 8 (Adoption Year) (b)	(b) – (a)
Change²positive (i)	11.48%	10.78%	-0.70%
No change (ii)	13.14%	12.26%	-0.88%
(i) – (ii)	-1.66%*	-1.48%	+0.18%

Change²positive represents positive structural and content-related changes in the way segment information is presented upon adoption of IFRS 8.
*, **, and *** indicate statistical significance at the 10%, 5%, and 1% levels (two-tailed), respectively.

Table 6-30: Univariate difference-in-differences cost of capital – Group two without early adopters

In **summary**, the findings of the univariate difference-in-differences analyses signal that the disclosure of segment information based on the management approach does not have an effect on the cost of capital at the time it becomes available in the annual report. This is robust to different treatment group specifications and the exclusion of early adopters. However, to control for further influences on the cost of capital, the following section introduces multivariate regression models. This allows a more sophisticated analysis of the cost of capital effects.

6.3.2 Regression analysis

Similar to the bid-ask spread analyses, all regressions are **estimated** with OLS. In the output tables, t-statistics are presented in parentheses below the coefficients. The asterisks indicate statistical significance at the ten, five and one per cent level. If a variable has a predicted sign (indicated by a plus or minus in parentheses next to the variable name), the significance levels are based on one-tailed tests. Two-tailed tests are used otherwise. More-over, all models use standard errors clustered at the firm level.[123]

Table 6-31 presents the **basic regression model** following equation (6.1). Each of the four cost of capital proxies as well as the aggregated measure are presented in separate columns. Following the discussion in section 6.1.3.2, it is expected that size is negatively related to the cost of capital. The other control variables (beta, leverage and BTM) are expected to be positively related to the cost of capital.

All five models **perform decently** with an adjusted R^2 between 13 and 27 per cent. This is consistent with prior literature. *Hail* (2002) reports an adjusted R^2 of about 25 per cent for a Swiss sample and *Hail/Leuz* (2006) show one of 36 per cent for a world sample. Moreover, all control variables show signs in the expected directions and are largely significant among the different models. Post is negative and significant at the one per cent level for four of the five models. This indicates a general downward trend in the cost of capital from the beginning of 2009 to the beginning of 2010 period, which the univariate analysis has already shown. Furthermore, Change^1$_{positive}$ is negative and significantly different from zero for three out of the five specifications. Hence, the treatment firms already show a systematically lower cost of capital compared to the control group in the pre IFRS 8 period. Given the quasi-experimental feature of the research design, differences between the treatment and the control group in the pre period are not expected. However, taking the anticipatory nature of the cost of capital into account, it is possible that the actual effect on the cost of capital took place earlier. Therefore, the two groups are already statistically different in the pre-treatment period. This aspect is addressed at the end of this section.

The coefficient Post x Change^1$_{positive}$ is insignificant for all different proxies. This **corroborates** the univariate findings that the provision of segment information based on the management approach does not impact cost of capital – at least at the time the annual report is published.

Since the results for the different proxies for the cost of capital are very similar, the following regressions are solely run on the **average measure** for brevity. Still, all analyses are rerun using the other four proxies (but not tabulated). This does not change the results. Yet, the magnitude and significance level of the treatment effect is slightly weaker for some models. The general tenor of results, however, remains unchanged.

---

[123] Industry fixed effects are not reported in the following regressions because they do not add much explanatory power and limit the degrees of freedom. However, all models are also estimated including industry fixed effects, which does not change results or inferences.

Variables	Predicted sign	Model A Claus and Thomas (2001)	Model B Gebhardt et al. (2001)	Model C Ohlson and Juettner-Nauroth (2005)	Model D Easton (2004)	Model E Average cost of capital
Regression cost of capital – Base model						
Post		-0.016***	-0.018***	-0.021***	-0.011	-0.015***
		(-3.080)	(-5.138)	(-2.644)	(-0.779)	(-2.499)
Change^{1}positive		-0.012*	-0.001	-0.024**	-0.022	-0.017**
		(-1.654)	(-0.128)	(-2.159)	(-1.211)	(-2.204)
Post x Change^{1}positive	(-)	0.001	-0.004	0.004	-0.014	-0.004
		(0.183)	(-0.439)	(0.285)	(-0.809)	(-0.429)
Log(Size)	(-)	-0.004***	-0.003*	-0.013***	-0.014***	-0.007***
		(-2.393)	(-1.480)	(-4.957)	(-3.062)	(-3.764)
Beta	(+)	0.009*	0.010**	0.003	0.043***	0.021***
		(1.626)	(1.681)	(0.419)	(2.521)	(3.194)
Leverage	(+)	0.053***	0.040***	0.072***	0.145***	0.075***
		(3.635)	(3.077)	(3.366)	(3.738)	(5.163)
BTM	(+)	0.003*	0.010***	0.004*	0.019***	0.009***
		(1.480)	(3.886)	(1.422)	(3.100)	(3.824)
Constant		0.108***	0.081***	0.185***	0.136***	0.118***
		(6.892)	(5.317)	(10.475)	(3.466)	(6.338)
Firm level clustered standard errors		YES	YES	YES	YES	YES
N		188	192	178	170	164
adj. R^2		0.132	0.159	0.158	0.177	0.268
F-stat		5.857	7.294	6.375	4.912	9.386

The table reports OLS coefficient estimates and t-statistics in parentheses below the coefficients. The predicted signs are presented next to the variables in parentheses. Change^{1}positive represents positive structural changes in the way segment information is presented upon adoption of IFRS 8.
*, **, and *** indicate statistical significance at the 10%, 5%, and 1% levels (one-tailed for coefficients with predicted signs and two-tailed otherwise), respectively.

Table 6-31: Regression cost of capital

Table 6-32 reports the results when controlling for the influence of **early adopters**: Model A introduces an additional dummy (and further interactions) indicating whether an observation stems from an early adopting firm. Model B is based on a reduced sample without early adopters. The dependent variable for both models is the average cost of capital. Both models show an adjusted R^2 of approximately 29 per cent. Moreover, the control variables are all significant in the expected directions. Again, Post is significantly negative signaling a downward trend in the cost of capital from 2009 to 2010 for or all firms. Change^{1}positive is negative and significantly different from zero demonstrating that the treatment group already shows a lower cost of capital in the pre adoption period. In Model A, Early is negative and significant at the five per cent level. Hence, early adopters show on average a lower cost of capital in the pre adoption period. Moreover, Post x Change^{1}positive x Early is significantly positive which means that early adopters show an incremental treatment effect. This may be driven by self-selection and the effect cannot be attributed to the adoption of IFRS 8. Yet, the main treatment effect (**Post x Change^{1}positive**) remains insignificant. This is similar for the regression based on the reduced sample: the treatment effect Post x Change^{1}positive is still insignificant.

In **summary**, the lack of an effect on the cost of capital does not depend on a potential self-selection issue caused by early adopters. However, for consistency with the other two sub-studies, all results are also reported based on the reduced sample without early adopters.

Regression cost of capital – Early adopters			
Variables	Predicted sign	**Model A** Full Sample – Average cost of capital	**Model B** No early adopters – Average cost of capital
Post		-0.024***	-0.024***
		(-3.829)	(-3.783)
Change¹positive		-0.019**	-0.019**
		(-2.142)	(-2.188)
Early		-0.023***	-
		(-2.518)	-
Post x Change¹positive	(-)	**-0.000**	**-0.001**
		(-0.018)	**(-0.058)**
Post x Early		0.051***	-
		(4.468)	-
Change¹positive x Early		0.009	-
		(0.529)	-
Post x Change¹positive x Early		-0.022*	-
		(-1.476)	-
Log(Size) (-)	(-)	-0.008***	-0.007***
		(-3.851)	(-3.290)
Beta (+)	(+)	0.019***	0.023***
		(2.619)	(2.977)
Leverage (+)	(+)	0.076***	0.077***
		(4.971)	(4.832)
BTM (+)	(+)	0.010***	0.011***
		(3.616)	(3.519)
Constant		0.126***	0.117***
		(6.446)	(5.437)
Firm level clustered standard errors		YES	YES
N		164	138
adj. R²		0.297	0.292
F-stat		7.313	8.902

The table reports OLS coefficient estimates and t-statistics in parentheses below the coefficients. The predicted signs are presented next to the variables in parentheses. Change¹positive represents positive structural changes in the way segment information is presented upon adoption of IFRS 8.
*, **, and *** indicate statistical significance at the 10%, 5%, and 1% levels (one-tailed for coefficients with predicted signs and two-tailed otherwise), respectively.

Table 6-32: Regression cost of capital – Early adopters

Table 6-33 reports the regression results based on equation (6.3): The empirical model further distinguishes between **positive and negative change firms**. IFRS 8 allows for some flexibility and some firms use this discretion to report less information. Hence, firms that use IFRS 8 to conceal segmental disclosures should be affected negatively. This exploitation of the cross-sectional variation in the treatment group is supposed to analyze whether a potential effect depends on the direction of the change in segment reporting.

Regression cost of capital – Positive and negative change firms group one			
Variables	Predicted sign	Model A – Full Sample – Average cost of capital	Model B – No early adopters – Average cost of capital
Post		-0.017***	-0.025***
		(-2.666)	(-3.750)
Change^1$_{positive}$		-0.016**	-0.018**
		(-1.969)	(-1.891)
Change^1$_{negative}$		0.013	0.020**
		(1.094)	(2.253)
Post x Change^1$_{positive}$	(-)	-0.002	-0.000
		(-0.228)	(-0.024)
Post x Change^1$_{negative}$	(+)	0.017	0.005
		(1.129)	(0.428)
Log(Size)	(-)	-0.008***	-0.009***
		(-4.172)	(-3.514)
Beta	(+)	0.022***	0.022***
		(3.393)	(2.971)
Leverage	(+)	0.076***	0.080***
		(5.248)	(5.108)
BTM	(+)	0.009***	0.011***
		(3.897)	(3.640)
Constant		0.121***	0.126***
		(6.665)	(5.609)
Firm level clustered standard errors		YES	YES
N		164	138
adj. R^2		0.282	0.298
F-stat		8.522	13.001

The table reports OLS coefficient estimates and t-statistics in parentheses below the coefficients. The predicted signs are presented next to the variables in parentheses. Change^1$_{positive}$ represents positive structural changes in the way segment information is presented upon adoption of IFRS 8. Change^1$_{negative}$ represents negative structural changes in the way segment information is presented upon adoption of IFRS 8.
*, **, and *** indicate statistical significance at the 10%, 5%, and 1% levels (one-tailed for coefficients with predicted signs and two-tailed otherwise), respectively.

Table 6-33: Regression cost of capital – Group one

Model A reports the regression results based on the **full sample** and Model B uses the reduced sample **without early adopters**. Both models incorporate the average cost of capital as the dependent variable. Once more, the explanatory power of is moderate with an adjusted R^2 of 28 per cent and 30 per cent. All control variables are significant at least at the five per cent level with signs in the expected direction. Again, Post is significantly negative indicating a general decrease in the cost of capital for all firms. Change^1$_{positive}$ is also significantly negative which means that the treatment group already shows a lower cost of capital under IAS 14R. In contrast, the positive and significant coefficient of Change^1$_{negative}$ in Model B shows that the negative change firms have on average a higher cost of capital compared to the other firms. This also indicates that the actual treatment may have occurred earlier upon release of the first quarterly segment information.

Again, **Post x Change^1$_{positive}$** is insignificant. Post x Change^1$_{negative}$ is positive, however, also insignificant. Hence, similar to the positive change group, firms that change their segmental disclosures in a negative way upon adoption of IFRS 8 do not experience an effect on the cost of capital either. This supports the initial findings that IFRS 8 does not impact the cost of capital.

Table 6-34 shows the same analysis as in Table 6-33 for the **change two specification**. Without going into detail, the results corroborate the prior findings. Explanatory power as well as the control variables are consistent with expectations. The treatment effect remains insignificant. However, the magnitude of the coefficients is slightly higher. In total, the general tenor of the results is not sensitive to particular groupings of the treatment and the control firms.

Regression cost of capital – Positive and negative change firms group two			
Variables	Predicted sign	**Model A** Full Sample – Average cost of capital	**Model B** No early adopters – Average cost of capital
Post		-0.021***	-0.024***
		(-3.107)	(-3.132)
Change$^2_{positive}$		-0.016**	-0.015*
		(-2.042)	(-1.630)
Change$^2_{negative}$		-0.009	-0.007
		(-1.139)	(-0.725)
Post x Change$^2_{positive}$	(-)	**0.001**	**-0.003**
		(0.109)	**(-0.339)**
Post x Change$^2_{negative}$	(+)	**0.016***	**0.009**
		(1.572)	**(0.775)**
Log(Size)	(-)	-0.007***	-0.007***
		(-3.178)	(-2.748)
Beta	(+)	0.020***	0.020***
		(3.079)	(2.618)
Leverage	(+)	0.080***	0.080***
		(5.133)	(4.708)
BTM	(+)	0.008***	0.010***
		(3.100)	(2.966)
Constant		0.117***	0.117***
		(5.746)	(4.832)
Firm level clustered standard errors		YES	YES
N		164	138
adj. R^2		0.254	0.272
F-stat		8.923	33.624

The table reports OLS coefficient estimates and t-statistics in parentheses below the coefficients. The predicted signs are presented next to the variables in parentheses. Change$^2_{positive}$ represents positive structural and content-related changes in the way segment information is presented upon adoption of IFRS 8. Change$^2_{negative}$ represents negative structural and content-related changes in the way segment information is presented upon adoption of IFRS 8.
*, **, and *** indicate statistical significance at the 10%, 5%, and 1% levels (one-tailed for coefficients with predicted signs and two-tailed otherwise), respectively.

Table 6-34: Regression cost of capital – Group two

Treatment effect timing – First quarter end

All previous analyses in this section use the publication of the annual report, which includes the segment report, as the treatment effect. However, users of financial statements already receive an indication if and in how far segment reporting is going to change by observing the segment disclosures under IAS 34 in the **first quarterly financial statement** of 2009. Given the anticipatory nature of the cost of capital, it may well be that users already adjust valuations and estimates once their prospects about future transparency change (*Christensen et al.* (2013), p. 152). Furthermore, in contrast to the information asymmetry study, the treatment and the control group already show a different cost of capital in the pre-treatment period. This indicates that there may have been an effect on the cost of capital before.

Therefore, a **different timing** of the treatment effect is used: the cost of capital is measured 45 days after the first quarter end. To grasp an understanding for the data, the univariate difference-in-differences analysis is presented for each of the four models in Table 6-35.[124] In the pre IFRS 8 period, there are no significant differences between the treatment and the control group for any model. This is in line with the quasi-experimental feature of this study. The increase in the cost of capital from the IAS 14R period to the IFRS 8 period is significant (at least) at the five per cent level for the no change control group based on any of the four models. This is consistent with a general increase in the cost of capital from the beginning of 2008 to the beginning of 2009 – which coincides with the increasing heat and aftermath of the global financial crisis. However, this increase is less steep for the treatment group as the average cost of capital shows an insignificant difference for the positive change group one.

The difference-in-differences – which is indicative of a potential treatment effect – is negative for all four models and significant for four of the five proxies. In particular the average cost of capital shows a difference-in-differences of -1.83 percentage points which is significant at the five per cent level. This signals that providing segment information from the management's perspective has an **effect on the cost of capital** – if the right timing is considered.

---

[124] Table 6-35 only reports the difference-in-differences for the group one change specification based on the full sample. For brevity, the other specifications in terms of early adopters and group two change classifications are not tabulated. The results are, however, very similar to Table 6-35.

Univariate difference-in-differences analyses of the cost of capital for the full sample based on the group one change specification at quarter one end			
Claus and Thomas (2001)	IAS 14R (Pre-adoption Year) (a)	IFRS 8 (Adoption Year) (b)	(b) – (a)
Change¹positive (i)	9.23%	10.17%	+0.94%
No change (ii)	9.73%	11.79%	+2.06%***
(i) – (ii)	-0.50%	-1.63%*	-1.13%**
Gebhardt et al. (2001)	IAS 14R (Pre-adoption Year) (a)	IFRS 8 (Adoption Year) (b)	(b) – (a)
Change¹positive (i)	7.81%	9.66%	+1.85%**
No change (ii)	7.52%	9.91%	+2.39%***
(i) – (ii)	+0.28%	-0.25%	-0.53%
Ohlson and Juettner-Nauroth (2005)	IAS 14R (Pre-adoption Year) (a)	IFRS 8 (Adoption Year) (b)	(b) – (a)
Change¹positive (i)	12.74%	13.36%	+0.62%
No change (ii)	11.62%	14.03%	+2.42%**
(i) – (ii)	+1.12%	-0.67%	-1.80%*
Easton (2004)	IAS 14R (Pre-adoption Year) (a)	IFRS 8 (Adoption Year) (b)	(b) – (a)
Change¹positive (i)	13.37%	15.48%	+2.12%
No change (ii)	11.21%	16.79%	+5.58%***
(i) – (ii)	+2.15%	-1.31%	-3.46%*
Average cost of capital	IAS 14R (Pre-adoption Year) (a)	IFRS 8 (Adoption Year) (b)	(b) – (a)
Change¹positive (i)	10.89%	11.96%	1.07%
No change (ii)	10.01%	12.91%	2.90%***
(i) – (ii)	+0.88%	-0.95%	-1.83%**

Change¹positive represents positive structural changes in the way segment information is presented upon adoption of IFRS 8.
*, **, and *** indicate statistical significance at the 10%, 5%, and 1% levels (two-tailed), respectively.

Table 6-35: Univariate difference-in-differences cost of capital – Group one at quarter one end

The multivariate regression in Table 6-36 **supports the univariate findings**. For brevity, only the results for the group one change specification based on equation (6.3) are reported in Table 6-36. The results for the other specifications, however, are substantially similar. Equation (6.3) distinguishes between positive and negative change firms. Exploiting the cross-sectional variation in the treatment group helps to ascertain whether it is indeed the effect of the segment report that is driving the results.

Model A is run on the **full sample** and Model B uses the reduced sample **without early adopters**. Both models employ the average cost of capital 45 days after quarter one end as the dependent variable.[125] The explanatory power is moderate with an adjusted R^2 of 30 per cent and 29 per cent. All control variables are significant at least at the five per cent

---

[125] Note that the number of observations is reduced in both models because the cost of capital needs to be estimated for a different period of time. As elaborated before, there is no closed form solution of the polynomial and therefore an iterative procedure is used to solve the cost of capital equations. This iterative process, however, does not always yield valid estimates and these are excluded from the sample.

level with signs in the expected direction. Post is significantly positive indicating the general increase in the cost of capital for all firms. Change$^1_{positive}$ is insignificant which means that the control group is not different from the positive change group under IAS 14R. However, the positive and significant coefficient of Change$^1_{negative}$ shows that the negative change firms have on average a higher cost of capital compared to the other firms.

Most importantly, Post x Change$^1_{positive}$ shows a negative sign which is highly significant at the one per cent level in both models. This shows that the treatment group of firms that improve their segment reporting upon adoption of IFRS 8 experience a **reduction in the cost of capital**. Moreover, Post x Change$^1_{negative}$ is positive and significant at the ten per cent level for the reduced sample (Model B). Hence, firms that change their segmental disclosures in a negative way upon adoption of IFRS 8 do not experience an improvement in the cost of capital as the positive change firms do. In contrast, they marginally show an incremental increase in the cost of capital. This supports the notion that it is the effect of the segment report that is driving the results and thus it gives confidence in the general credibility of the findings of this study.

Regression cost of capital – Positive and negative change firms group one at quarter one end			
Variables	Predicted sign	**Model A** Full Sample – Average cost of capital	**Model B** No early adopters – Average cost of capital
Post		0.020***	0.021***
		(3.711)	(2.973)
Change$^1_{positive}$		0.007	0.006
		(0.850)	(0.694)
Change$^1_{negative}$		0.016**	0.022***
		(1.849)	(2.494)
Post x Change$^1_{positive}$	(-)	**-0.024***	**-0.028***
		(-3.277)	**(-3.179)**
Post x Change$^1_{negative}$	(+)	**0.001**	**0.011***
		(0.097)	**(1.421)**
Log(Size)	(-)	-0.007***	-0.008***
		(-3.402)	(-2.555)
Beta	(+)	0.015**	0.018**
		(1.949)	(1.868)
Leverage	(+)	0.039**	0.041**
		(1.982)	(1.807)
BTM	(+)	0.014***	0.014***
		(3.233)	(3.277)
Constant		0.112***	0.112***
		(5.105)	(3.584)
Firm level clustered standard errors		YES	YES
N		160	132
adj. R^2		0.297	0.286
F-stat		8.923	33.624

The table reports OLS coefficient estimates and t-statistics in parentheses below the coefficients. The predicted signs are presented next to the variables in parentheses. Change$^1_{positive}$ represents positive structural changes in the way segment information is presented upon adoption of IFRS 8. Change$^1_{negative}$ represents negative structural changes in the way segment information is presented upon adoption of IFRS 8.

*, **, and *** indicate statistical significance at the 10%, 5%, and 1% levels (one-tailed for coefficients with predicted signs and two-tailed otherwise), respectively.

Table 6-36: Regression cost of capital – Group one at quarter one end

6.3.3   Further robustness tests

Similar to the information asymmetry study, this section provides some additional sensitivity checks including the influence of outliers and rank regressions. These tests help to gain additional confidence in the initial results. Moreover, given that there is no effect on the cost of capital at the time the annual report is released, the robustness tests focus on the quarter one end treatment timing, which show significant results in the initial specification.

Influence of outliers

Similar to section 6.2.3, the following analyses use studentized residuals and Cook's Distance to **detect outliers**. Table 6-37 presents the results for equation (6.3), which employs the positive and negative change group one specification. For brevity, only the findings for this specification are reported. Untabulated results for equation (6.1) and (6.2), however, are substantially similar.

Model A eliminates all firm-year observations that show studentized residuals greater than three. In total, four firms are flagged as outliers.[126] Hence, the regression model uses 152 firm-year observations. However, the results are very similar when the influence of outliers is controlled for: The treatment effect remains highly significant at the one per cent level with a coefficient of -0.015. Moreover, all control variables show the expected signs at least at the five per cent significance level. The explanatory power of the model increases to an adjusted R^2 of 37 per cent.

Model B reports the results for the outlier treatment based on Cook's Distance. Recall that one and 1/N are common cut-off values. No observation, however, shows a Cook's Distance greater than one. Hence, Model B only reports the results for the more conservative threshold of 1/N. In total, 14 firms are flagged as outliers. This leaves 132 firm-year observations for the regression. The treatment effect is still existent, albeit weaker in terms of magnitude and only at a significance level of ten per cent. The other control variables are also comparable to the initial specification. However, Beta is only significant at the ten per cent level. The explanatory power of the model is still relatively high with an adjusted R^2 of almost 39 per cent.

---

[126] Again, both observations of one firm are eliminated if one firm-year is flagged as an outlier to retain a balanced panel.

Regression cost of capital – Controlling for the influence of outliers full sample at quarter one end			
Variables	Predicted sign	Model A Studentized Residuals Cut-off: 3 Full Sample	Model B Cook's Distance Cut-off: 1/N Full Sample
Post		0.017***	0.010***
		(4.174)	(2.687)
Change[1]positive		-0.003	-0.003
		(-0.587)	(-0.666)
Change[1]negative		0.011	0.020***
		(1.635)	(3.498)
Post x Change[1]positive	(-)	-0.015***	-0.008*
		(-2.583)	(-1.431)
Post x Change[1]negative	(+)	0.007	0.014***
		(1.008)	(4.414)
Log(Size)	(-)	-0.006***	-0.006***
		(-4.055)	(-3.864)
Beta	(+)	0.007**	0.006*
		(1.718)	(1.500)
Leverage	(+)	0.036***	0.039***
		(2.921)	(3.256)
BTM	(+)	0.012***	0.022***
		(4.311)	(5.454)
Constant		0.109***	0.105***
		(10.287)	(8.497)
Firm level clustered standard errors		YES	YES
N		152	132
adj. R^2		0.365	0.387
F-stat		10.653	10.183

The table reports OLS coefficient estimates and t-statistics in parentheses below the coefficients. The predicted signs are presented next to the variables in parentheses. Change[1]positive represents positive structural changes in the way segment information is presented upon adoption of IFRS 8. Change[1]negative represents negative structural changes in the way segment information is presented upon adoption of IFRS 8.
*, **, and *** indicate statistical significance at the 10%, 5%, and 1% levels (one-tailed for coefficients with predicted signs and two-tailed otherwise), respectively.

Table 6-37: Regression cost of capital – Without outliers at quarter one end

The regression models in Table 6-38 jointly control for the influence of **outliers and early adopters**. They use the same outlier detection procedures and thresholds as used in the previous table. Model A eliminates eight firm-year observations based on studentized residuals and Model B drops 24 observations based on Cook's Distance. The treatment effect remains highly significant for Model A. In Model B, however, it is marginally insignificant. However, note that the number of observations in Model B is reduced to 108. Hence, there is substantially less power in the estimation which may cause the treatment effect to disappear.

In **summary**, Table 6-37 and Table 6-38 signal that the results of the cost of capital study are substantially robust to the elimination of outliers. Hence, the initial findings are not driven by an undue impact of extreme observations.

Variables	Predicted sign	Model A Studentized residuals: Cut-off: 3 No early adopters	Model B Cook's Distance Cut-off: 1/N No early adopters
Regression cost of capital – Controlling for the influence of outliers without early adopters at quarter one end			
Post		0.017***	0.009**
		(3.334)	(1.759)
Change^1$_{positive}$		-0.005	-0.006
		(-0.878)	(-0.974)
Change^1$_{negative}$		0.017***	0.016**
		(3.256)	(2.291)
Post x Change^1$_{positive}$	(-)	**-0.017***	**-0.008**
		(-2.433)	**(-1.204)**
Post x Change^1$_{negative}$	(+)	**0.017***	**0.016***
		(2.779)	**(3.836)**
Log(Size)	(-)	-0.006***	-0.005***
		(-3.218)	(-2.892)
Beta	(+)	0.008**	0.009**
		(1.799)	(1.892)
Leverage	(+)	0.037***	0.041***
		(2.759)	(3.049)
BTM	(+)	0.012***	0.022***
		(4.407)	(4.886)
Constant		0.110***	0.100***
		(8.026)	(6.738)
Firm level clustered standard errors		YES	YES
N		124	108
adj. R^2		0.364	0.359
F-stat		8.808	7.665

The table reports OLS coefficient estimates and t-statistics in parentheses below the coefficients. The predicted signs are presented next to the variables in parentheses. Change^1$_{positive}$ represents positive structural changes in the way segment information is presented upon adoption of IFRS 8. Change^1$_{negative}$ represents negative structural changes in the way segment information is presented upon adoption of IFRS 8.

*, **, and *** indicate statistical significance at the 10%, 5%, and 1% levels (one-tailed for coefficients with predicted signs and two-tailed otherwise), respectively.

Table 6-38: Regression cost of capital – Without outliers and early adopters at quarter one end

Rank regression

As a final robustness test, all continuous variables are **transformed into ranks** and regressions are estimated based on these ranks. This helps to mitigate the influence of highly skewed data. Again, only the results for equation (6.3) are reported.[127] Due to the transformation into ranks, the magnitude of the coefficients changes substantially. The signs and significance levels, however, are consistent with the initial findings. Model A uses the full sample. The treatment effect shows a coefficient of about -28 which is significant at the one per cent level. This means that firms experience a mean decrease of 28 ranks in the cost of capital if they start to provide segment information under IFRS 8. The other control variables are all significant with the expected signs except for Beta.

---

[127] The findings for equation (6.1) and (6.2), however, are virtually the same.

The findings **without early adopters** in Model B are very similar. The treatment effect is significant at the five per cent level with a coefficient of -27. Moreover, the coefficient of Post x Change$^1_{negative}$ is positive and highly significant at one per cent level. This means that firms which use the adoption of IFRS 8 to decrease the extent of segment disclosures experience an increase in the cost of capital. This supports the notion that it is the effect of the segment report that is driving the results.

Regression cost of capital – Rank regression at quarter one end			
Variables	Predicted sign	**Model A** Rank regression Full sample	**Model B** Rank regression No early adopters
Post		22.154***	15.855**
		(2.997)	(1.679)
Change$^1_{positive}$		5.260	0.540
		(0.480)	(0.044)
Change$^1_{negative}$		21.142*	31.534***
		(1.481)	(2.842)
Post x Change$^1_{positive}$	(-)	-28.456***	-27.227**
		(-2.737)	(-2.328)
Post x Change$^1_{negative}$	(+)	9.950	28.956***
		(0.951)	(3.398)
Log(Size)	(-)	-0.219***	-0.226***
		(-3.483)	(-2.969)
Beta	(+)	0.074	0.066
		(1.242)	(0.958)
Leverage	(+)	0.149**	0.170***
		(2.360)	(2.425)
BTM	(+)	0.275***	0.291***
		(4.378)	(4.098)
Constant		47.697***	53.301***
		(3.498)	(3.222)
Firm level clustered standard errors		YES	YES
N		160	132
adj. R^2		0.324	0.310
F-stat		22.792	73.028

The table reports OLS coefficient estimates and t-statistics in parentheses below the coefficients. The predicted signs are presented next to the variables in parentheses. Change$^1_{positive}$ represents positive structural changes in the way segment information is presented upon adoption of IFRS 8. Change$^1_{negative}$ represents negative structural changes in the way segment information is presented upon adoption of IFRS 8.
*, **, and *** indicate statistical significance at the 10%, 5%, and 1% levels (one-tailed for coefficients with predicted signs and two-tailed otherwise), respectively.

Table 6-39: Regression cost of capital – Rank regression at quarter one end

Summary

The multivariate regressions **corroborate** the univariate findings. Results generally show no effect on the cost of capital for the treatment group. This is robust to a number of alternative specifications. For instance, findings are not influenced by early adopters. Furthermore, distinguishing between positive and negative change firms as well as between alternative change specifications (structural and content-related) confirms the initial findings. However, all these analyses use the publication of the annual report as the timing of the treatment effect. If one takes into account that users of financial statements already received the information whether a firm changes its segment reporting in the first quarter of 2009, one can find a substantial effect on the cost of capital at that time. This is in line with the notion that the cost of capital is a more anticipatory construct than liquidity proxied by bid-ask spreads. Hence, the disclosure of segment information based on the management approach is **useful information** and has a negative effect on the cost of capital.

6.4   Financial analysts' information environment

The analysis of the impact of introducing the management approach to segment reporting on **financial analysts' information environment** is slightly different compared to the previous two sub-studies. Based on the correlation in forecast errors, empirical measures for analysts' consensus as well as the precision of the common and idiosyncratic[128] information components of analysts are used. Following *Venkataraman* (2001) and *Botosan/Stanford* (2005), these metrics do not require further control variables. There are no firm fundamentals that systematically affect the metrics. A comparison of means for the different groups is sufficient and therefore the following sections do not use multivariate regression models.[129]

The analysis begins with some preliminary considerations about the interplay of the common and idiosyncratic information components in the context of segment reporting under the management approach. After that, descriptive statistics of the relevant variables are presented. Finally, the univariate difference-in-differences analyses and robustness checks are reported.

6.4.1   Univariate and bivariate analyses

The *Barron et al.* (1998) model allows to draw inferences whether the disclosure of segment information from the management's perspective changes financial analysts' information usage. On the one hand, financial analysts may rely more on common relative to idiosyncratic information since the availability of more useful segment information allows them to acquire less costly private information (**substitutional relation**). On the other hand, the adoption of IFRS 8 may stimulate the generation of additional private information (**complementary relation**). Supporting the latter notion, financial analysts have incentives to generate additional private information so that their clients can benefit given that trading on the analysts' idiosyncratic information yields higher profits (e.g., *Fischer/Verrecchia* (1998); *Barron et al.* (2002)). Segment information based on the management approach is particularly suited to stimulate the creation of additional private information: Most financial analysts already have a detailed knowledge of the company since they only cover a limited number of firms. Segment information from the management's perspective is more consistent with other disclosures and therefore allows them to improve their overall understanding of the firm and how it is governed. This can influence the structure and content of their estimation models. Adjustments or amendments of their

---

[128] Common and idiosyncratic are used synonymously with public and private in the following.

[129] For similar studies that use univariate comparisons of the *Barron et al.* (1998) measures refer to *Barron et al.* (2002) or *Botosan/Stanford* (2005).

private models likely increase the idiosyncratic information component of their estimates. Yet, it is unclear whether the substitutional or complementary effect dominates.

Descriptive statistics

Table 6-40 presents **descriptive information** of the financial analysts' information environment variables separately for each index. To get a better understanding of the data, the observable features squared forecast error (SE) and dispersion (D) are also reported. The main variables of interest, however, are consensus (ρ), common information precision (h) and private information precision (s). Recall that ρ reflects the commonality among different analysts and hence their consensus. h and s are the precision of the common and idiosyncratic information component. An increase in ρ after the adoption of IFRS 8 means that analysts rely more on common information that was released under IFRS 8. A decrease in ρ supports the notion that segment information based on the management approach stimulates the generation of additional idiosyncratic information. Changes in h or s reflect changes in the precision of the public or private information signal.

The derivation of the *Barron et al.* (1998) model is based on expected analysts' mean forecast error and expected dispersion. The substitution of realized ex post values for the expected values causes **measurement errors** in the estimates of consensus and the precision of common and idiosyncratic information. In large samples, this measurement error is ameliorated (e.g., *Barron et al.* (2002), p. 828). This study, however, has a relatively small sample compared to most of prior research that uses the *Barron et al.* (1998) model. In fact, the distributions of all five variables are highly skewed. A Shapiro-Wilk test rejects the null of normality for all variables at the one per cent level.[130] Hence, non-parametric ranksum tests are used to test for differences in the variables between the treatment and the control group since these tests are less susceptible to outliers. Nonetheless, results should be interpreted carefully due to the **noisy** nature of the empirical proxies and the relatively low number of observations in some of the sub-groups.

SE is the **squared error in the mean forecast** scaled by the absolute value of the earnings. The literature often uses SE as a measure for forecast accuracy. It fully captures common uncertainty, but it only partially captures idiosyncratic uncertainty as the idiosyncratic error is diversified away. It is unclear how the adoption of IFRS 8 affects SE: If analysts rely more on public information and avoid costly private information after the adoption of IFRS 8, the diversification effect vanishes. However, in case the precision of the public information based on IFRS 8 is sufficiently high, it may compensate for the lost diversification effect and thus SE may decrease (*Botosan/Stanford* (2005), p. 757).

The **median value** across the full sample is 0.12. This means that analysts' mean forecast is within a close range of the actual earnings realization. There is a substantial difference between the means and medians which underlines the highly skewed distribution for each index. Based on the medians, DAX and SDAX firms show the lowest forecast errors followed by the TecDAX and MDAX. There is no distinctive pattern between the indices. Finally, note that the maximum number of observations is 170, which is due to the availability of sufficient analysts' data.

---

[130] Refer to *Shapiro/Wilk* (1965) for a thorough description of the test.

D is the **dispersion** of individual analysts' forecasts expressed as their variance deflated by the absolute value of the actual earnings. Prior literature has generally perceived a decrease in dispersion as a signal for more precise public information (e.g., *Lang/Lundholm* (1996), pp. 468–469; *Healy et al.* (1999), p. 497). This view, however, neglects the interplay of public information and private information as elaborated above (*Venkataraman* (2001), pp. 11–12). Hence, even when assuming that IFRS 8 improved the informativeness of the public information component, it is unclear how the adoption of the management approach would affect dispersion. This depends on the extent to what analysts use the information under IFRS 8 to generate new idiosyncratic information.[131] The median dispersion across all indices is 0.02. This is comparable to prior research (e.g., *Barron et al.* (2002), p. 830). The DAX firms show the highest dispersion by far compared to the other three indices. This may be due the higher analysts' following of these firms and thus the more competitive environment that encourages analysts' to outperform other analysts which may lead to more dispersed forecasts.

Descriptive statistics of the financial analysts' information environment variables for each index							
Variables[a]		mean	std. dev.	Q25	median	Q75	N
Squared mean fore-cast error (SE)	DAX	2.04	6.18	0.23	0.12	0.58	24
	MDAX	1.72	6.30	0.01	0.16	0.77	60
	TecDAX	0.87	2.39	0.01	0.11	0.50	36
	SDAX	1.27	3.04	0.12	0.09	0.84	50
	Total	**1.46**	**4.83**	**0.15**	**0.12**	**0.64**	**170**
Dispersion (D)	DAX	0.55	1.75	0.02	0.12	0.17	24
	MDAX	0.20	0.65	0.01	0.02	0.13	60
	TecDAX	0.10	0.19	0.01	0.02	0.08	36
	SDAX	0.07	0.20	0.00	0.01	0.04	46
	Total	**0.19**	**0.79**	**0.01**	**0.02**	**0.11**	**166**
Consensus (ρ)	DAX	0.55	0.35	0.19	0.63	0.91	24
	MDAX	0.66	0.33	0.44	0.75	0.93	60
	TecDAX	0.60	0.40	0.33	0.80	0.91	36
	SDAX	0.69	0.41	0.53	0.89	0.98	44
	Total	**0.64**	**0.37**	**0.41**	**0.79**	**0.94**	**164**
Precision of common information (h)	DAX	2.79	6.95	0.14	0.55	1.75	24
	MDAX	6.33	15.51	0.30	1.21	5.44	60
	TecDAX	37.95	112.84	0.19	4.59	19.36	36
	SDAX	25.05	63.06	0.49	3.16	19.74	44
	Total	**17.86**	**64.12**	**0.30**	**1.80**	**7.62**	**164**
Precision of private in-formation (s)	DAX	14.04	58.40	0.09	0.48	2.20	24
	MDAX	7.41	16.91	0.04	0.41	7.24	60
	TecDAX	89.56	267.35	0.26	1.63	56.52	36
	SDAX	34.67	77.28	0.02	1.21	10.94	44
	Total	**34.12**	**136.84**	**0.06**	**0.74**	**8.89**	**164**

[a]SE is the squared mean forecast error calculated as the squared difference of the actual earnings realization and the mean forecast scaled by the absolute value of the actual earnings. D is the observed dispersion among individual analysts' forecasts expressed as their variance deflated by the absolute value of the actual earnings. Analysts' consensus ρ is the relative reliance on public information compared to private information. h denotes the precision of the public signal and s denotes the precision of the private signal.

Table 6-40: Descriptive statistics of the financial analysts' information environment variables

The **consensus** ρ is usually within the range from zero to one. Zero indicates that analysts solely rely on idiosyncratic information and a value of one signals that all analysts agree and their forecasts only reflect common information. The median consensus across all

---

[131] This emphasizes once more the importance of using the *Barron et al.* (1998) model instead of the classical approach in the analyst literature that is concerned with forecast accuracy and dispersion. The approach of *Barron et al.* (1998) allows disentangling these two possibly countervailing effects.

four indices is 0.79. This is similar to the median consensus of 0.83 reported by *Barron et al.* (2002) for a large sample of U.S. firms (*Barron et al.* (2002), p. 830). Moreover, there is a higher consensus for smaller firms of the TecDAX and SDAX indices compared to DAX and MDAX. This may also be due to the higher number of analysts for these firms and thus the more competitive environment as elaborated above.

The magnitude of the **precision of the common** (h) and **idiosyncratic** (s) **information** component is not readily interpretable. The distributions of both variables are highly dispersed. This is, however, due to the noisy nature of the empirical measures and not due to a particularity of this study's data. For instance, *Barron et al.* (2002) also report a highly skewed h (s) with a median of 6.79 (2.69) and a mean of 118.28 (207.84) (*Barron et al.* (2002), p. 830). h and s only yield useful interpretations when they are compared across different groups or time, which is done in the following difference-in-differences analyses.

In **summary**, the variables are within reasonable ranges. The distributions of all variables are substantially skewed. However, this is consistent with other studies that use the same empirical proxies. Yet, given the relatively low number of observations, the noise in the measures makes it considerably difficult to find an effect (even if it is present in the data). Hence, results in the following should be interpreted with caution.

Difference-in-differences analysis

Similar to the other two sub-studies, this section presents the mean values of the relevant variables separately for the treatment and the control group before and after the adoption of IFRS 8. Like the cost of capital, the financial analysts' information environment is also an anticipatory construct (*Christensen et al.* (2013), p. 152).[132] Therefore, the treatment effect is expected to take place at the time a change in transparency is anticipated. Hence, the empirical constructs are measured upon release of the **first quarterly segment information** in the initial specification. However, results for the annual report publication are also presented at the end of this section for consistency.

Table 6-41 displays the **univariate difference-in-differences** analyses of the **squared mean forecast error** (SE) for the full sample. Panel A shows the group one change specification which classifies firms that undergo structural changes as the treatment group.[133] Interestingly, there is a decrease in SE and thus an increase in the forecast accuracy from the IAS 14R period to the IFRS 8 period for both groups. This is in contrast to the increase in information asymmetry and cost of capital of the other two studies during the same time period. Seemingly, financial analysts – as sophisticated users of financial information – are less effected by the increasing uncertainties at that time. The decline in forecast error, however, is substantially smaller for the control group with a difference-in-differences of -0.53 that is significant at the five per cent level. This signals that forecast accuracy improved relatively more for the firms that had a structural change to their segmentation upon adoption of IFRS 8.

---

[132] Both measures basically rely on the same data (i.e., financial analysts' earnings forecasts).

[133] In the following, only the positive change treatment groups and the no change control group are reported in the univariate difference-in-difference analyses. The negative change group includes too few observations to yield reliable estimates.

The group two changes in Panel B are different. Recall that group two changes entail both **structural and content-related changes**. Again, the control group experiences a significant decline in forecast error. The treatment group, however, shows a small increase in forecast error. The difference-in-differences is positive, although insignificant. This finding may be due to the less strict treatment group classification of group two: Firms that have an increase of 200 words in the segmental narratives are classified as change firms even though the increase in words may solely be due to uninformative boilerplate language. Additionally, an increase of three line items per segment also leads to the classification as a change two firm – regardless which items are disclosed in particular and whether they are useful or not. Financial analysts may be specifically unaffected by these changes. They generally use sophisticated models that require certain quantitative input so that a mere change in word count or the disclosure of additional line items does not change much for them.

Univariate difference-in-differences analyses of the squared mean forecast error for the full sample			
Panel A. Group one changes (SE)	IAS 14R (Pre-adoption Year) (a)	IFRS 8 (Adoption Year) (b)	(b) – (a)
Change$^1_{positive}$ (i)	1.47	0.35	-1.12
No change (ii)	2.20	1.61	-0.59*
(i) – (ii)	-0.73	-1.26***	-0.53**
Panel B. Group two changes (SE)	IAS 14R (Pre-adoption Year) (a)	IFRS 8 (Adoption Year) (b)	(b) – (a)
Change$^2_{positive}$ (i)	1.17	1.33	+0.17
No change (ii)	2.75	1.10	-1.65*
(i) – (ii)	-1.59	+0.23**	+1.82

Change$^1_{positive}$ represents positive structural changes in the way segment information is presented upon adoption of IFRS 8. Change$^2_{positive}$ represents positive structural and content-related changes in the way segment information is presented upon adoption of IFRS 8.
*, **, and *** indicate statistical significance at the 10%, 5%, and 1% levels (two-tailed), respectively.

Table 6-41: Univariate difference-in-differences analyses of SE

Table 6-42 presents the same analysis as Table 6-41 **excluding early adopters**. Similar to the cost of capital analysis, 14 early adopters are eliminated from the sample. The noisy nature of the empirical constructs becomes evident as the results change slightly once more. For both specifications in Panel A and B, there is a decrease in the forecast error from pre-adoption year to the adoption year. This decrease, however, is steeper for the control firms indicating that forecast accuracy improved more for firms that did not adopt the management approach. It may be that analysts acquire less costly private information and the improved public disclosure is not able to fully compensate this. Nevertheless, the exact interplay of the common and idiosyncratic information component is analyzed below based on consensus, h and s.

Univariate difference-in-differences analyses of the squared mean forecast error without early adopters			
Panel A. Group one changes (SE)	IAS 14R (Pre-adoption Year) (a)	IFRS 8 (Adoption Year) (b)	(b) – (a)
Change¹ₚₒₛᵢₜᵢᵥₑ (i)	1.57	0.32	-1.25
No change (ii)	2.64	1.18	-1.46
(i) – (ii)	-1.07	-0.86***	+0.21**
Panel B. Group two changes (SE)	IAS 14R (Pre-adoption Year) (a)	IFRS 8 (Adoption Year) (b)	(b) – (a)
Change²ₚₒₛᵢₜᵢᵥₑ (i)	1.35	0.62	-0.73
No change (ii)	3.25	1.30	-1.96
(i) – (ii)	-1.90	-0.68**	+1.22

Change¹ₚₒₛᵢₜᵢᵥₑ represents positive structural changes in the way segment information is presented upon adoption of IFRS 8. Change²ₚₒₛᵢₜᵢᵥₑ represents positive structural and content-related changes in the way segment information is presented upon adoption of IFRS 8.
*, **, and *** indicate statistical significance at the 10%, 5%, and 1% levels (two-tailed), respectively.

Table 6-42: Univariate difference-in-differences analyses of SE without early adopters

Table 6-43 presents the univariate difference-in-differences analyses of **dispersion** for the full sample. Both groups experience an increase in dispersion which is significant for the control group at the five per cent level. The magnitude of the increase is higher for the treatment group, albeit insignificant. This is similar for Panel B which shows a positive, yet insignificant difference-in-differences of 0.01.

Univariate difference-in-differences analyses of dispersion for the full sample			
Panel A. Group one changes (D)	IAS 14R (Pre-adoption Year) (a)	IFRS 8 (Adoption Year) (b)	(b) – (a)
Change¹ₚₒₛᵢₜᵢᵥₑ (i)	0.04	0.25	+0.21
No change (ii)	0.12	0.24	+0.12**
(i) – (ii)	-0.08	+0.01	+0.09
Panel B. Group two changes (D)	IAS 14R (Pre-adoption Year) (a)	IFRS 8 (Adoption Year) (b)	(b) – (a)
Change²ₚₒₛᵢₜᵢᵥₑ (i)	0.04	0.20	+0.16
No change (ii)	0.18	0.33	+0.15
(i) – (ii)	-0.13	-0.13	+0.01

Change¹ₚₒₛᵢₜᵢᵥₑ represents positive structural changes in the way segment information is presented upon adoption of IFRS 8. Change²ₚₒₛᵢₜᵢᵥₑ represents positive structural and content-related changes in the way segment information is presented upon adoption of IFRS 8.
*, **, and *** indicate statistical significance at the 10%, 5%, and 1% levels (two-tailed), respectively.

Table 6-43: Univariate difference-in-differences D

The results **without early adopters** (Table 6-44) also display a general increase in dispersion from the pre-adoption year to the adoption year for both panels. The difference-in-differences is marginally negative this time. However, it is insignificant and signals that there is no distinctive incremental effect for either the treatment or the control group. In summary, the increasing dispersion supports the notion of increasing uncertainties during the financial crisis. Unlike the other two sub-studies, there is an impact of firms that early adopt IFRS 8 as results slightly change upon their elimination. Yet, the prior analyses of forecast error and dispersion are only supplementary. This study focuses on the financial analysts' information environment in terms of consensus and (common and idiosyncratic) information precision which is presented in the following.

Univariate difference-in-differences analyses of dispersion without early adopters			
Panel A. Group one changes (D)	IAS 14R (Pre-adoption Year) (a)	IFRS 8 (Adoption Year) (b)	(b) – (a)
Change^1$_{positive}$ (i)	0.03	0.15	+0.12
No change (ii)	0.14	0.28	+0.14*
(i) – (ii)	-0.11	-0.13	-0.02
Panel B. Group two changes (D)	IAS 14R (Pre-adoption Year) (a)	IFRS 8 (Adoption Year) (b)	(b) – (a)
Change^2$_{positive}$ (i)	0.05	0.16	+0.11
No change (ii)	0.21	0.39	+0.18
(i) – (ii)	-0.16	-0.24	-0.07

Change^1$_{positive}$ represents positive structural changes in the way segment information is presented upon adoption of IFRS 8. Change^2$_{positive}$ represents positive structural and content-related changes in the way segment information is presented upon adoption of IFRS 8.
*, **, and *** indicate statistical significance at the 10%, 5%, and 1% levels (two-tailed), respectively.

Table 6-44: Univariate difference-in-differences D without early adopters

The findings for **consensus** – which reflect the relative reliance on public and private information – are more robust. Table 6-45 presents the univariate difference-in-differences for the full sample. In the pre-adoption period, the treatment and the control group show a very similar consensus of 0.67 (Panel A). Upon adoption of IFRS 8, however, there is a significant decrease to 0.48 for the treatment group and an (insignificant) increase to 0.72 for the control group. The difference-in-differences of -0.25 is significant at the five per cent level. Hence, the relative reliance on idiosyncratic information for firms that change their segmentation upon adopting the management approach increases substantially while the control firms show the opposite. This means that the disclosure of information from the management's perspective stimulates **the generation of idiosyncratic information**. Financial analysts potentially use the new information based on the management approach to refine their estimation processes or estimation models. Moreover, the analysts may improve their overall understanding of the company once they are able to view it from the management's perspective. Finally, as noted by the IASB in the PIR, there may be a spill-over effect to the credibility of other sources of consistent segment information because IFRS 8 information is audited. This may open avenues for additional analyses.

Panel B reports very similar results for **the change group two specification**: The treatment and the control group are not significantly different under the former standard. After the adoption of IFRS 8, however, the treatment firms experience a decrease in consensus and the control firms show an increase. The difference-in-differences is once more significantly negative with a value of -0.27. This corroborates the initial findings that the adoption of IFRS 8 stimulated the generation of additional private information.

Univariate difference-in-differences analyses of consensus for the full sample			
Panel A. Group one changes (ρ)	IAS 14R (Pre-adoption Year) (a)	IFRS 8 (Adoption Year) (b)	(b) – (a)
Change[1]positive (i)	0.67	0.48	-0.20*
No change (ii)	0.67	0.72	+0.06
(i) – (ii)	+0.01	-0.25**	-0.25*
Panel B. Group two changes (ρ)	IAS 14R (Pre-adoption Year) (a)	IFRS 8 (Adoption Year) (b)	(b) – (a)
Change[2]positive (i)	0.69	0.54	-0.15
No change (ii)	0.63	0.74	+0.12
(i) – (ii)	+0.07	-0.20*	-0.27**

Change[1]positive represents positive structural changes in the way segment information is presented upon adoption of IFRS 8. Change[2]positive represents positive structural and content-related changes in the way segment information is presented upon adoption of IFRS 8.
*, **, and *** indicate statistical significance at the 10%, 5%, and 1% levels (two-tailed), respectively.

Table 6-45: Univariate difference-in-differences ρ

The findings for consensus are more robust to the exclusion of 14 **early adopters** compared to the findings for forecast error and dispersion. Table 6-46 presents the results without early adopters which are substantially the same as in the previous table: Under IAS 14R, there is no difference between the two groups. The treatment firms, however, experience a decrease in consensus and the control group displays an increase. The difference-in-differences of -0.22 is marginally significant at the ten per cent level. This is the same for the change group two specification in Panel B which reports a difference-in-differences of -0.22 (significant at the five per cent level). Hence, consensus decreases after the adoption of IFRS 8.

Univariate difference-in-differences analyses of consensus without early adopters			
Panel A. Group one changes (ρ)	IAS 14R (Pre-adoption Year) (a)	IFRS 8 (Adoption Year) (b)	(b) – (a)
Change[1]positive (i)	0.67	0.48	-0.20
No change (ii)	0.69	0.72	+0.03
(i) – (ii)	-0.02	-0.24**	-0.22*
Panel B. Group two changes (ρ)	IAS 14R (Pre-adoption Year) (a)	IFRS 8 (Adoption Year) (b)	(b) – (a)
Change[2]positive (i)	0.68	0.52	-0.16
No change (ii)	0.69	0.75	+0.06
(i) – (ii)	-0.00	-0.23**	-0.22**

Change[1]positive represents positive structural changes in the way segment information is presented upon adoption of IFRS 8. Change[2]positive represents positive structural and content-related changes in the way segment information is presented upon adoption of IFRS 8.
*, **, and *** indicate statistical significance at the 10%, 5%, and 1% levels (two-tailed), respectively.

Table 6-46: Univariate difference-in-differences ρ without early adopters

The impact of introducing IFRS 8 on the **precision of common information** (h) is presented in Table 6-47. Panel A reports the results for the change group one specification of the full sample. The treatment group shows an increase in h while there is a decline for the control group. Hence, the adoption of IFRS 8 helped to improve the informativeness of publicly available information. Similar to SE and dispersion, the results for the change group two specification in Panel B are different: The treatment group shows a decrease in h while the control group experiences an increase. Again, this may be due to the more permissive change group two specification criteria or the noisy nature of the empirical proxies. Particularly, h and s are noisier compared to consensus as they require some additional assumptions for the empirical implementation.[134] This notion is supported by the fact that none of the differences in means is significant although they are quite high in terms of magnitude.

Univariate difference-in-differences analyses of public information precision for the full sample			
Panel A. Group one changes (h)	IAS 14R (Pre-adoption Year) (a)	IFRS 8 (Adoption Year) (b)	(b) – (a)
Change$^1_{positive}$ (i)	10.54	13.06	+2.52
No change (ii)	27.07	22.36	-4.72
(i) – (ii)	-16.54	-9.30	**+7.24**
Panel B. Group two changes (h)	IAS 14R (Pre-adoption Year) (a)	IFRS 8 (Adoption Year) (b)	(b) – (a)
Change$^2_{positive}$ (i)	35.98	10.02	-25.96
No change (ii)	17.71	19.67	+1.96
(i) – (ii)	+18.27	-9.66	**-27.93**

Change$^1_{positive}$ represents positive structural changes in the way segment information is presented upon adoption of IFRS 8.
Change$^2_{positive}$ represents positive structural and content-related changes in the way segment information is presented upon adoption of IFRS 8.
*, **, and *** indicate statistical significance at the 10%, 5%, and 1% levels (two-tailed), respectively.

Table 6-47: Univariate difference-in-differences h

Table 6-48 reports basically the same results as in the previous table for the sample **without early adopters**. Based on the group one change specification, there is a positive difference-in-differences indicating the relatively steeper decrease in h for the control group. However, the group two change specification in Panel B shows the exact opposite with a negative difference-in-differences. The magnitudes of the difference-in-differences in both panels are also very similar to those for the full sample in Table 6-47. Hence, there is no undue influence of early adopters on the results for the precision of public information.

---

[134] For a detailed description of the assumptions see *Barron et al.* (1998), pp. 427–428.

Univariate difference-in-differences analyses of public information precision without early adopters			
Panel A. Group one changes (h)	IAS 14R (Pre-adoption Year) (a)	IFRS 8 (Adoption Year) (b)	(b) – (a)
Change¹$_{positive}$ (i)	11.64	7.67	-3.97
No change (ii)	26.01	13.95	-12.06
(i) – (ii)	-14.37	-6.28	**+8.09**
Panel B. Group two changes (h)	IAS 14R (Pre-adoption Year) (a)	IFRS 8 (Adoption Year) (b)	(b) – (a)
Change²$_{positive}$ (i)	43.20	6.60	-36.60
No change (ii)	10.06	0.91	-9.15
(i) – (ii)	+33.13	+5.69	**-27.44**

Change¹$_{positive}$ represents positive structural changes in the way segment information is presented upon adoption of IFRS 8. Change²$_{positive}$ represents positive structural and content-related changes in the way segment information is presented upon adoption of IFRS 8.
*, **, and *** indicate statistical significance at the 10%, 5%, and 1% levels (two-tailed), respectively.

Table 6-48: Univariate difference-in-differences h without early adopters

The **precision of the idiosyncratic information component** (s) reflects any changes in the quality of information that is exclusive to individual analysts and which may be due to the generation of additional private information based on superior estimation models or techniques. Interestingly, Table 6-49 reports an increase in the precision for the treatment group and a steep decrease for the control group in Panel A. The difference-in-differences is highly positive and significant at the one per cent level. This supports the notion that the availability of segment information from the management's perspective helps analysts to better understand the firm and thus to incorporate additional or refined analyses. Moreover, the steep decrease for the control group possibly reflects the increasing uncertainties during that time which made it in general more difficult for analysts to obtain precise private information. Panel B shows the same results for the change specification that takes account of structural and content-related changes (group two). The difference-in-differences is also highly positive and significant at the one per cent level.

Univariate difference-in-differences analyses of private information precision for the full sample			
Panel A. Group one changes (s)	IAS 14R (Pre-adoption Year) (a)	IFRS 8 (Adoption Year) (b)	(b) – (a)
Change¹$_{positive}$ (i)	24.18	27.34	+3.16
No change (ii)	85.17	27.99	-57.18
(i) – (ii)	-60.99***	-0.65	**+60.34***
Panel B. Group two changes (s)	IAS 14R (Pre-adoption Year) (a)	IFRS 8 (Adoption Year) (b)	(b) – (a)
Change²$_{positive}$ (i)	25.06	30.70	+5.64
No change (ii)	97.63	26.38	-71.25
(i) – (ii)	-72.58**	+4.31	**+76.89***

Change¹$_{positive}$ represents positive structural changes in the way segment information is presented upon adoption of IFRS 8. Change²$_{positive}$ represents positive structural and content-related changes in the way segment information is presented upon adoption of IFRS 8.
*, **, and *** indicate statistical significance at the 10%, 5%, and 1% levels (two-tailed), respectively.

Table 6-49: Univariate difference-in-differences s

The results are also robust to the treatment of **early adopters**: Panel A and B of Table 6-50 show similar difference-in-differences. They are slightly lower but still significant. Hence, the disclosure of segment information under the management approach provides financial analysts with information that they can use to generate additional, more precise private information.

Univariate difference-in-differences analyses of private information precision without early adopters			
Panel A. Group one changes (s)	IAS 14R (Pre-adoption Year) (a)	IFRS 8 (Adoption Year) (b)	(b) – (a)
Change$^1_{positive}$ (i)	27.45	28.92	+1.47
No change (ii)	42.70	16.40	-26.30
(i) – (ii)	-15.25	+12.53***	+27.78**
Panel B. Group two changes (s)	IAS 14R (Pre-adoption Year) (a)	IFRS 8 (Adoption Year) (b)	(b) – (a)
Change$^2_{positive}$ (i)	30.35	33.60	+3.26
No change (ii)	7.39	3.45	-3.94
(i) – (ii)	+22.96	+30.15**	+7.19*

Change$^1_{positive}$ represents positive structural changes in the way segment information is presented upon adoption of IFRS 8. Change$^2_{positive}$ represents positive structural and content-related changes in the way segment information is presented upon adoption of IFRS 8.
*, **, and *** indicate statistical significance at the 10%, 5%, and 1% levels (two-tailed), respectively.

Table 6-50: Univariate difference-in-differences s without early adopters

Treatment effect timing – Fiscal year end

For consistency, this section also presents the treatment effect timing 90 days after the fiscal year end when the **annual report** is released. Table 6-51 reports the univariate difference-in-differences for the full sample and the **group one change specification** of the variables squared mean forecast error, dispersion, consensus, public information precision and private information precision. Unlike to the prior specification, the treatment and the control group already show substantial differences in the pre-treatment period. This indicates that the treatment effect already took place. Moreover, the results are different from the initial findings: There is a marginally significant positive difference-in-differences for **forecast error** indicating that the control group experiences an incremental improvement in forecast accuracy. This is, however, very sensitive to the exclusion of early adopters and different treatment effect groupings (untabulated). The results substantially change to a negative difference-in-differences in the different specifications and should thus be interpreted with caution.

The variable **dispersion** shows a negative, yet insignificant difference-in-differences. This is in contrast to the initial positive difference-in-differences. However, once outliers are eliminated or the group two change classification is used, the results substantially change again. This is similar for **consensus** and the **precision** of the public information component and the idiosyncratic information component. Hence, unlike to the quarter one end treatment timing, there is no systematic effect on the financial analysts' information environment after the annual report is released. However, due to the noisy nature of the empirical constructs, this finding is very sensitive to alternative specifications and should thus not be taken as evidential.

Univariate difference-in-differences analyses of financial analysts' information environment at fiscal year end			
Panel A. Squared mean forecast error (SE)	IAS 14R (Pre-adoption Year) (a)	IFRS 8 (Adoption Year) (b)	(b) – (a)
Change[1]$_{positive}$ (i)	0.36	0.89	+0.53**
No change (ii)	1.62	0.33	-1.29
(i) – (ii)	-1.26**	+0.56	+1.82*
Panel B. Dispersion (D)	IAS 14R (Pre-adoption Year) (a)	IFRS 8 (Adoption Year) (b)	(b) – (a)
Change[1]$_{positive}$ (i)	0.24	0.04	-0.20*
No change (ii)	0.23	0.18	-0.05
(i) – (ii)	+0.01	-0.14**	-0.15
Panel C. Consensus (ρ)	IAS 14R (Pre-adoption Year) (a)	IFRS 8 (Adoption Year) (b)	(b) – (a)
Change[1]$_{positive}$ (i)	0.49	0.66	+0.17*
No change (ii)	0.73	0.53	-0.21**
(i) – (ii)	-0.25***	+0.13*	+0.38***
Panel D. Public information precision (h)	IAS 14R (Pre-adoption Year) (a)	IFRS 8 (Adoption Year) (b)	(b) – (a)
Change[1]$_{positive}$ (i)	12.68	44.75	+32.07
No change (ii)	23.25	-12.59	-35.84
(i) – (ii)	-10.57	+57.34	+67.91
Panel E. Private information precision (s)	IAS 14R (Pre-adoption Year) (a)	IFRS 8 (Adoption Year) (b)	(b) – (a)
Change[1]$_{positive}$ (i)	26.15	15.78	-10.37
No change (ii)	27.84	109.30	+81.47*
(i) – (ii)	-1.69	-93.52***	-91.83***

Change[1]$_{positive}$ represents positive structural changes in the way segment information is presented upon adoption of IFRS 8.
*, **, and *** indicate statistical significance at the 10%, 5%, and 1% levels (two-tailed), respectively.

Table 6-51: Univariate difference-in-differences financial analysts' information environment at fiscal year end

6.4.2   Further robustness tests

The previous section has shown that results on the first quarterly segment information are not sensitive to excluding early adopters or different change group specifications. This section makes **additional sensitivity checks** with regard to the influence of outliers and data skewness. Again, given that there is no effect at the time the annual report is released, the robustness tests focus on the quarter one end treatment timing.

Influence of outliers

The **outlier detection** procedures for the variables of the financial analysts' information environment are different. The other two studies use approaches that rely on OLS regression estimates. This is not possible for the univariate analyses of the financial analysts' study. Therefore, a simplified approach is used: Firm-year observations of consensus (ρ), public information precision (h) and private information precision (s) are designated as outliers if they deviate more than three standard deviations from their estimated means.[135]

For **consensus**, no observations are flagged as outliers. This is not surprising given that consensus is usually within the range from zero to one and that its standard deviation is about 0.37. Hence, consensus is not affected by outliers.

The precision of the public and private information component, however, is more dispersed. Four firms are classified as outliers for the **public information component** h. Table 6-52 reports the results for the difference-in-differences analysis of h using the group one change specification.[136] Panel A uses the initial sample and eliminates the four firms that have extreme values (n=156). Similar to the initial findings, the treatment firms experience an increase in the precision of public information while the control group shows a decline. Panel B further eliminates 14 early adopters from the sample (n=128). Although the treatment firms now also display a decline in precision, the decline is much steeper for the control group. Hence, outliers do not substantially affect h.

Univariate difference-in-differences analyses of public information precision without outliers			
Panel A. Full sample (h)	IAS 14R (Pre-adoption Year) (a)	IFRS 8 (Adoption Year) (b)	(b) – (a)
Change^1$_{positive}$ (i)	10.54	13.06	+2.52
No change (ii)	11.68	3.84	-7.84
(i) – (ii)	-1.14	+9.22	+10.36
Panel B. No early adopters (h)	IAS 14R (Pre-adoption Year) (a)	IFRS 8 (Adoption Year) (b)	(b) – (a)
Change^1$_{positive}$ (i)	11.64	7.67	-3.97
No change (ii)	9.30	1.90	-7.34
(i) – (ii)	+2.34	-9.66	+3.43

Change^1$_{positive}$ represents positive structural changes in the way segment information is presented upon adoption of IFRS 8.
*, **, and *** indicate statistical significance at the 10%, 5%, and 1% levels (two-tailed), respectively.

Table 6-52: Univariate difference-in-differences h without outliers

The picture is slightly different for the precision of the **private information components**. Only two firms have extreme values. Again, just the group one change specification is reported in Table 6-53 for brevity: While the treatment groups shows an increase in s, the control group experiences a decline. The highly significant difference-in-differences of 4.99 is consistent with the initial findings that the adoption of IFRS 8 stimulates the generation of additional private information. Panel B reports the same information excluding early adopters. The results, however, change substantially compared to the initial specification and Panel A: Both groups display an increase in the precision of private infor-

---

[135] The squared forecast error (SE) and dispersion (D) are not analyzed in the robustness test section since they are not the main variables of interest. However, untabulated results show extreme values for only two firms for SE and for three firms for D. Eliminating these observations does not change results or inferences.

[136] For brevity, the results for the group two change specification are not reported. Inferences, however, are the same.

mation. However, this increase is steeper for the control group with a negative difference-in-differences of -1.53.

Univariate difference-in-differences analyses of private information precision without outliers			
Panel A. Full sample (s)	IAS 14R (Pre-adoption Year) (a)	IFRS 8 (Adoption Year) (b)	(b) – (a)
Change[1]$_{positive}$ (i)	24.18	27.35	+3.16
No change (ii)	16.56	14.73	-1.83
(i) – (ii)	+7.62	+12.61**	**+4.99***
Panel B. No early adopters (s)	IAS 14R (Pre-adoption Year) (a)	IFRS 8 (Adoption Year) (b)	(b) – (a)
Change[1]$_{positive}$ (i)	27.45	28.92	+1.46
No change (ii)	11.44	14.44	+23.00
(i) – (ii)	+16.01	+14.49***	**-1.53***
Change[1]$_{positive}$ represents positive structural changes in the way segment information is presented upon adoption of IFRS 8. *, **, and *** indicate statistical significance at the 10%, 5%, and 1% levels (two-tailed), respectively.			

Table 6-53: Univariate difference-in-differences s without outliers

The main results have already shown that h and s are noisy proxies. Moreover, the bin size is reduced when eliminating further observations which reduces statistical power. Therefore, results in this robustness test section should be interpreted with caution. In **summary**, however, the overall tenor of results remains unchanged, in particular because consensus and h are unaffected by extreme observations.

Rank transformation

To retain consistency with the other two sub-studies, the financial analysts' variables are also **transformed into ranks**. This helps to control for the influence of highly skewed data. However, all prior analyses are based on Wilcoxon ranksum tests. This procedure implicitly transforms continuous values into ranks. Therefore, the results for tests of significant differences in means are identical. Hence, inferences remain unchanged and tables are not reported for brevity.

Summary

The analysis of the financial analysts' information environment signals that the adoption of IFRS 8 had an impact on the use of information by financial analysts. Most importantly, firms that adopt IFRS 8 experience a **decrease in consensus**. Moreover, these firms also show an increase in the precision of the idiosyncratic information component. These findings support the notion that the availability of segment information from the management's perspective **stimulates** the generation of additional private information. This may be due an increased overall understanding of the company or a more decision useful segmentation that allows financial analysts to understand the company the same way management does. Particularly the latter aspect may help analysts to better anticipate future actions of firms since analysts have access to relatively comparable information. This would be in line with the decrease in consensus and the increase in the private information precision. Similar to the cost of capital study, the main treatment effect happens at the time the change in segmentation is indicated by the **first quarterly segment infor-**

mation under the new standard. This is consistent with the anticipatory nature of the empirical constructs of financial analysts' information environment.

Overall, the findings are not as strong as in the other two sub-studies. This may be due to the noisy nature of the empirical proxies for the characteristics of financial analysts' information environment. However, the most important feature consensus shows results that are robust to different changes specifications and to the influence of early adopters.

6.5 Discussion

The objective of chapter six is to analyze the economic consequences of adopting IFRS 8 and thereby the introduction of the management approach to segment reporting. The empirical results provide evidence that investors, companies and financial analysts are affected by the adoption of IFRS 8: While **information asymmetries** generally increase for all firms during the sample period, firms that change their segment reporting to comply with IFRS 8 show a countervailing decrease in information asymmetries. This is similar for the **cost of capital** where these firms show an incremental decrease in the cost of capital. It is not surprising that the results of the information asymmetry study and cost of capital study are consistent because the two concepts are partly linked. Interestingly, however, the effect for the cost of capital is slightly stronger. This suggests that not only the information asymmetry component of the cost of capital is affected, but also one of the other potential channels how disclosure may impact cost of capital. In particular liquidity risk and estimation risk may be affected by the change in segment reporting.[137] These channels largely depend on the uncertainty of firms' fundamental values and, as elaborated before, segment information under IFRS 8 may be particularly helpful to provide decision useful information in that regard.

The results for the impact of IFRS 8 on **financial analysts' information environment** are slightly different. There is no clear effect on forecast accuracy or forecast dispersion per se. In contrast to the other two sub-studies, the results for accuracy and dispersion change substantially depending on whether only structural changes (group one) or structural and content-related changes (group two) are considered. Financial analysts are sophisticated users of financial statements (*Schipper* (1991), p. 105) and therefore they may be affected differently by particular changes in segment disclosures. A mere increase in segment narratives or more segment line items may not necessarily help financial analysts who generally use quantitative estimation models. This study documents an unambiguous change in the consensus for firms that adopt IFRS 8. The disclosure of segment information under IFRS 8 leads to increased reliance on private information for financial analysts. Hence, it stimulates the generation of additional private information for this group of sophisticated users of financial statements and the precision of the private information component increases upon IFRS 8's adoption. This is also indicative of the decision usefulness of segment information based on the management approach.

A benefit of this complementary analysis from three different perspectives is that the **timing** of the treatment effect can be investigated in more detail. The bid-ask spreads are less

---

[137] Refer to section 4.1.3.2 for a thorough discussion of the different channels.

anticipatory compared to the other two measures that rely on financial analysts' data (e.g., *Daske et al.* (2008); *Christensen et al.* (2013)). While investors are largely concerned about transparency when they trade, financial analysts adjust valuations at the time when their expectations about future transparency change (*Christensen et al.* (2013), p. 152). This is also reflected in the timing of the treatment effect in this study. The liquidity effect is most pronounced after the annual report including the full and audited segment report is released. The cost of capital and the financial analysts' information environment are already affected when the (reduced) quarterly segment information points at a change in segmental disclosures.

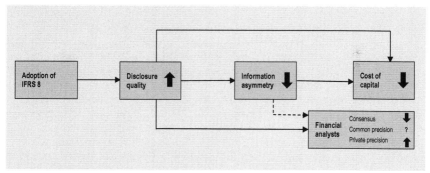

Figure 6-2: Empirical results presented within the theoretical framework

In summary, the empirical findings support that there is an effect of IFRS 8's adoption on information asymmetries, cost of capital and financial analysts. Figure 6-2 summarizes the findings within the theoretical framework that was developed in chapter four. The adoption of IFRS 8 largely reflects an improvement in disclosure quality which in turn leads to less information asymmetry. Similarly, the cost of capital decreases and there is also a decrease in financial analysts' consensus and an increase in the precision of financial analysts' private information precision. These findings are **consistent with the theoretical expectations** laid out in the underlying theoretical framework. Moreover, the definition of high quality disclosures and their operationalization in this study are supported by the subsequent economic changes upon adoption of IFRS 8. Otherwise, the empirical measures would have been unaffected since the tests used in this study are joint tests of the definition of quality and the effect of IFRS 8's adoption. Finally, the increase in the private information precision suggests a complementary relation between private and public information signals of financial analysts as discussed in section 4.1.3.3.

Prior research that is most closely related to this study are *Venkataraman* (2001) and *Botosan/Stanford* (2005). Both use a comparable difference-in-differences research design with a treatment group of firms that change the number of reported segments (*Venkataraman* (2001)) or a treatment group of single-segment firms that start to report multiple segments (*Botosan/Stanford* (2005)) upon adoption of SFAS No. 131. *Venkataraman* (2001) and *Botosan/Stanford* (2005) find a significant improvement in forecast accuracy for the treatment firms. This study, in contrast, does not provide evidence for a change in forecast accuracy. However, a mere change in the number of segments or an initiation of segment reporting as in *Venkataraman* (2001) and *Botosan/Stanford* (2005) is a different treatment effect than a change in fundamental principles of segment reporting. Moreover, this study focuses on different features of financial analysts' information environment. Therefore, the findings of prior research on forecast accuracy do not necessarily contradict the results of this study. Unfortunately, there is no prior research that is related to information asymmetry or cost of capital effects.

Finally, note that the impact is strongest for liquidity and the cost of capital. The link is slightly **weaker for the financial analysts'** information environment. This is in line with the findings of the IASB's staff paper from 2013 (*IASB* (2013b)): A survey of the CFA UK Institute reveals that about 50 per cent of financial analysts would agree that IFRS 8 helped them to get a better understanding of the firms (*IASB* (2013b), p. 8). Some noted, however, that the view through management's eyes is interesting, but "*it does not necessarily align with what analysts want to know*" (*IASB* (2013b), p. 8). Other analysts said "*that the numbers make sense to management but are often 'impossible' to forecast for an analyst*" (*IASB* (2013b), p. 8). In addition, some analysts hold the opinion that management is not really providing a view through the eyes of management. They consider that there are significant differences between what is communicated to management and what is communicated to the shareholders. Hence, not all analysts seem to benefit from the adoption of IFRS 8. On average, however, an impact of IFRS 8's adoption on financial analysts is supported by this study. Figure 6-3 recapitulates the results for hypotheses one to three:

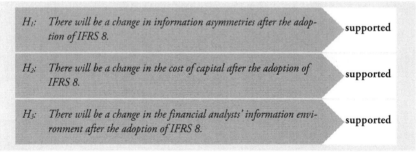

Figure 6-3: Results for hypotheses one to three

7 Conclusions

This study investigates the impact of introducing IFRS 8 for segment reporting practice and the respective economic consequences for capital market participants. Based on the previous empirical analyses, this chapter summarizes the main findings and discusses implications and the contribution of the results. Finally, limitations are considered and avenues for potential future research are presented.

7.1 Main findings and implications

Segment reporting has been a contentious and important topic in accounting practice and research ever since its first introduction in 1969. The latest major change in segment reporting regulation was the introduction of IFRS 8 and thereby the adoption of the **management approach**. On the one hand, this brought about convergence between IFRS and US-GAAP. On the other hand, it was heavily criticized and discussed due to turning away from a "*full financial accounting approach*" (*Ulbrich* (2006), pp. 21–22) to a system that allows internally used non-GAAP numbers to be disclosed in the segment report, although they may not comply with IFRS. Concerns were voiced by two members of the IASB and by the European Union. The latter feared that IFRS 8 would "*import into EU law an alien standard [SFAS No. 131] without having conducted any impact assessment*" (*European Parliament* (2007a), Section B5). Furthermore, companies were also concerned about the disclosure of proprietary information due to the adoption of IFRS 8. Some investors and in particular financial analysts, however, regarded the opportunity to the see the companies "*through the management's eyes*" (*Martin* (1997), p. 29) as a helpful tool to better understand the business of a company and to better assess management's decisions.

To address this ambiguity, the IASB initiated a PIR of IFRS 8 in 2012. The review of academic literature in the PIR report and the review of empirical literature in this study (see chapter three) identified a **significant research gap**. To this point, there has been barely any evidence on the economic consequences of the adoption of IFRS 8. Therefore, this study pursued the following objectives:

- a descriptive analysis of the changes in segment reporting practice;
- an analysis of the implications of introducing IFRS 8 for investors in terms of stock liquidity and information asymmetries;
- the consequences for firms with regard to the cost of capital; and of
- the impact on financial analysts' information environment.

The nature of the research questions required two different empirical approaches: First, the changes in segment reporting practices were documented based on a **content analysis**. This laid the foundation for the second step: the analysis of the economic consequences in a **difference-in-differences** design.

The analyses required a sound outline of the conceptual basis which was presented in chapter two. The **concept of segment reporting** and in particular of the management approach was discussed in detail. The second chapter also presented the **segment reporting requirements** under IFRS and their development. In the third chapter, the **related**

empirical literature was reviewed. The review was organized along the dimensions descriptive vs. consequences studies and SFAS No. 131 vs. IFRS 8 studies. It helped to identify the research gap and to further specify the research questions and the research design. The fourth chapter presented the **theoretical foundation** of the study and developed hypotheses. Chapter five dealt with the **content analysis** of 109 firms in two periods (i.e., the final IAS 14R and the first IFRS 8 period). Significant changes in the areas of general information, segmentation, measurement, disclosures and reconciliation were analyzed. Based on the content analysis, firms were sub-divided into a change group (i.e., firms that changed their segmentation upon adoption of IFRS 8) and a no-change group (i.e., firms that did not change their segmentation upon adoption of IFRS 8). Chapter six **empirically analyzed** whether these two groups were affected differently by the introduction of IFRS 8. Three different perspectives were assumed: investors, the reporting firm, and financial analysts.

With regard to the sub-objectives outlined above, the analyses found the following:

First, the **content analysis revealed** that segmentation, disclosures and reconciliation are affected the most by the adoption of IFRS 8. On average, there is an increase in the content and disclosures of segment reports. In particular, the extent of narrative information accompanying the segment report increases substantially. Moreover, the number of segments increases and more firms show a mixed segmentation. Furthermore, in contrast to the expectation of opponents of IFRS 8, there is no general loss in geographical second tier information as more firms use finer geographical segmentations. However, firms report less second tier items. In terms of measurement, there is no substantial change. Most firms report segment items that are measured in line with IFRS. Hence, the fear of some critics that the introduction of the management approach would impair understandability and comparability due to the use of non-GAAP measurement is unfounded. Another notable aspect is that the majority of firms is not affected at all by the adoption of IFRS 8 as they had already reported segment information in line with the management approach under IAS 14R. Yet, those firms that are affected generally show a substantial change in different areas of segment reporting.

The second study exploited this unique setting to analyze the **economic consequences** of IFRS 8 with a quasi-experimental research design. The results provide evidence that the disclosure of segment information from the management's perspective is decision useful for investors and helps to mitigate information asymmetries. Moreover, this study finds that firms can reduce their cost of capital through more transparent segment reporting. Finally, the precision of the common and private information sets used by financial analysts increases. The analysts also use the newly available segment information to generate additional private information which leads to less consensus. This provides evidence that the adoption of IFRS 8 had positive economic consequences for investors, firms and financial analysts – at least for those firms that changed their segment reports upon adoption of the new standard.

Notably, all of these effects only prevail if firms are considered that change their segment report in a **positive** and more transparent way. There are a few firms that use the adoption of IFRS 8 to report less than under IAS 14R arguing that this is more in line with internal reporting. These firms do not experience the positive effects in terms of reduced information asymmetry or lower cost of capital. In contrast, in some specifications they rather show a **negative** effect. Hence, the adoption of the management approach does not yield positive economic consequences per se. Nevertheless, most of the firms that change their segment reporting upon adoption of IFRS 8 increase the general level of disclosures.

The findings of this study have several **implications** for the IASB (and potentially the FASB and other standard setters), users of financial statements such as investors and financial analysts, preparers as well as auditors and enforcement institutions.

In general, the results of the content analysis show that the extent and fineness of segment disclosures increased. Moreover, there is increased consistency of segment information with other disclosures. Hence, the **IASB** can be affirmed in its expectations that some companies actually report more segments and that firms report segment information that is more consistent with other parts of the annual report (IFRS 8.BC9). Furthermore, the economic benefits in terms of reduced information asymmetries, reduced cost of capital and improved financial analysts' information environment support the IASB in its decision to adopt IFRS 8. However, it is questionable why not all firms would have voluntarily provided this information before if such benefits are available.[138] On the individual firm's level, the proprietary costs of disclosing this information may outweigh these benefits and therefore some firms chose not do so. Mandating to disclose this information may force some firms to miss their equilibrium and thus yield negative net benefits. These negative effects, however, are difficult to observe. Typically, it takes some time before this potentially proprietary information is exploited by competitors, customers or other parties and finally affects firm value. An alternative explanation why not all firms voluntarily provided this information before are the constraints of IAS 14R: For instance, firms that internally use a mixed business lines/geographical segmentation were not allowed to disclose this under IAS 14R. Similarly, the full financial accounting approach prevented the disclosure of non-GAAP measures. Hence, some firms may have wanted to provide this information, but they were not able to do so under IAS 14R. In this case, mandating IFRS 8 may be social welfare optimal. However, this aspect needs to be analyzed further by future research (see section 7.2).

In general, **users of financial statements** such as investors and financial analysts largely seem to benefit from the adoption of IFRS 8. The introduction of the management approach to segmental reporting reduces information asymmetries and improves the precision of analysts' public and private information. This may be driven by the finer segmentation of some firms or by other changes in segment reporting practice such as more detailed narrative information or the disclosure of measures used by management to assess segment performance. These findings are in line with the general support for IFRS 8 of users during its implementation. Nonetheless, some users feared that comparability of segment information might be impaired. However, this does not appear to decrease the overall decision usefulness of segment information from the management's perspective. Yet, there are a few firms that use the adoption of IFRS 8 to report less segment infor-

---

[138] The majority of firms, however, already did so by providing segment information in line with the management approach under IAS 14R.

mation. The inherent flexibility of the standard may help these firms to be more opaque and less transparent in terms of segmental disclosures. For these firms, users of financial statements do not experience the benefits as elaborated above.

The results of this study also have implications for **preparers**. When making disclosure decisions, preparers usually weigh benefits and costs of disclosing specific information. It was argued that IFRS 8 provides them with flexibility in terms of their segment reporting decisions.[139] Hence, preparers face a disclosure decision with regard to segmental reporting. The results of this study provide insights for the potential benefits of transparent segment reporting. Firms may lower their cost of capital by providing investors and other users of financial statements with a fair view of their company through the perspective of management. However, note that this study remains silent on the potential costs of segment reporting under the management approach.

Finally, the importance of **auditors and enforcement institutions** with regard to segment reporting has increased with the adoption of IFRS 8: In contrast to ordinary users of financial statements, auditors and the FREP have access to internal documents. Thus, they are the only ones that can verify that external segment information is in line with internal reporting. The fact that the FREP declared IFRS 8 as one of their main focus areas for the financial year 2009 underlines the increased importance. The results of the content analysis do not indicate any compliance issues. However, other than comparing segment reporting with other parts of a firm's financial disclosures, it is difficult to detect any inconsistencies with internal reporting from an external perspective. Nonetheless, the results of the FREP examinations in 2010 also indicate that firms largely comply with IFRS 8. In total, there are only three error statements with regard to IFRS 8 in the first year of its adoption (*FREP* (2011), p. 10). The adidas Group, for instance, defined cash generating units for impairment testing under IAS 36 ("Impairment of Assets") that exceeded the segments under IFRS 8. Subsequently, they had to refine their cash generating units to comply with the segmentation under IFRS 8. In total, auditors and enforcement institutions seem to acknowledge that their role is critical to ensure reliable segment reporting based on the management approach.

Given the results and implications discussed above, this study **contributes** to the existing literature in several ways. First, it adds to the body of research that analyzes the link between financial disclosures, investor information and the cost of capital (e.g., *Leuz/Schrand* (2009)). Investors are primary users of financial reporting. One objective of standard setters such as the IASB or FASB is to establish a reporting system that caters to investors' information needs and thus reduces information asymmetries. Hence, standard setters should have a particular interest in research that addresses the link between disclosures, investor information and the cost of capital (*Levitt* (1998), pp. 79–82). The findings of this study provide evidence that investors and in particular financial analysts are affected by a change in (the quality of) specific financial disclosures and thus corroborates findings of prior research (e.g., *Leuz/Verrecchia* (2000)). Additionally, this study also underlines cost of capital effects of financial disclosures.

---

[139] For instance, firms may define the role of the CODM differently or use additional IFRS-conform numbers to their pro-forma measures to adjust or avoid disclosures (see section 4.1.2.2).

This thesis also adds to the general segment reporting research. Although there is already a fair amount of research in this area, this study goes beyond the existing literature by documenting the change in segment reporting practice and its economic consequences for a change in specific segment reporting standards. Furthermore, the research design isolates the effect of the change in the underlying approach to segment reporting. Therefore, the results are also useful for the literature that is concerned with understanding the consequences of the **management approach** in financial reporting (for an overview refer to *Merschdorf* (2012)).

This thesis further helps to comprehend the role of segment reporting for **financial analysts**. Understanding how financial analysts process and make use of specific pieces of information is in particular a fruitful area of research that is far from conclusive.

Finally, the results of this study directly add to the literature on **IFRS 8.** Particularly the economic consequences of its adoption are barely known. The literature review in this study as well as the review of academic literature during the PIR revealed an extensive gap in this regard. Only *Kajüter/Nienhaus* (2013) have thus far investigated economic consequences of the adoption of IFRS 8. They, however, only focus on an investor perspective based on a value relevance approach.[140] This study, on the other hand, provides a broad view that facilitates an understanding of the economic consequences from the perspective of investors, firms and financial analysts.

7.2   Limitations and outlook

There are several limitations and drawbacks that go in hand with an empirical archival study of this type. First, **generalizability** may be impaired: This study focuses on the largest listed companies in Germany. It is debatable whether the results would hold in different settings and research designs. Although the study has made many efforts to check for the sensitivity of the results regarding different approaches to the research design, it is questionable whether the results would be the same for different countries or even different groups of firms in the same country. There is some variation in size of the sample firms given that this study uses four different stock indices. However, these firms are still relatively large and have a rich information environment. The impact of IFRS 8 on substantially **smaller firms** may be very different. For instance, disclosures about revenues with major customers are more likely to play an important role for smaller firms. The proprietary nature of these disclosures may even be more pronounced for small companies. Therefore, segment reporting practices as well as capital market effects can be very different for small public firms.

Furthermore, the perception of segment information based on the management approach may be particularly sensitive to **cultural influences**. For instance, companies from countries with a tendency to uncertainty avoidance may be very reluctant to disclose internal

---

[140] Moreover, the use of a value relevance approach yields several disadvantages (for an overview of the critique refer to *Holthausen/Watts* (2001)). Analyzing bid-ask spreads is a more direct approach to gauge consequences from an investor's perspective.

information and thus use the discretion of IFRS 8 to avoid such disclosure.[141] Hence, entirely different segment reporting patterns may emerge internationally. In a similar vein, the interpretation of segment information based on the management approach may also vary substantially in an international context. In countries with relatively high uncertainty avoidance and high power distance (such as Germany), investors and financial analysts may have a preference for uniformity (*Gray* (1988), p. 9) and therefore use and value segment information based on the management approach differently. The management approach – with its inherent flexibility and the deviation from the measurement principles for financial statements – is particularly prone to all these different cultural perceptions and interpretations.

A further particularity of the German sample is that these firms have to publish a **Management Commentary** (Lagebericht) according to the German Commercial Code (HGB).[142] These management commentaries often include information on the segmental level. For the content analysis, however, only information from the IFRS financial statements and notes were used. On the one hand, this allows comparability with other non-German studies. On the other hand, it may well be that investors and financial analysts also used information from the management commentary. To control for this potential bias, segment information in the management commentaries were analyzed as well during the data collection process. No significant changes in these disclosures from the IAS 14R to the IFRS 8 period were found. There was just an increase in the consistency of segment level information in the management commentaries with segment reports for a few firms.

Moreover, IFRS 8 has been analyzed at its **first year** of application. Some of the results may be driven by the fact that it is the first time application of a new standard and reporting companies, auditors, investors and financial analysts may not have been used to it yet. Hence, findings may well change once the standard is in force for a longer period of time. However, the focus of this study is the analysis of the consequences of IFRS 8's adoption compared to the preceding standard IAS 14R. This effect can only be analyzed around the change in the segment reporting rules.

Furthermore, the first time application of IFRS 8 coincides with a period where the aftermath of the **global financial crisis** still had an impact on firms and capital markets. There is the chance that this may have influenced the results. It is unclear, however, in which direction the global financial crisis would bias the results. Moreover, the difference-in-differences research design controls for any confounding time effects that all firms are exposed to in a similar way.

This study uses **empirical proxies** to capture the underlying concepts of information asymmetries, cost of capital, and financial analysts' information environment. These proxies rely on simplified empirical models that try to capture real life information dynamics. In particular, the use of capital market measures such as security data or analysts' forecasts

---

[141] This line of argument is based on the hypotheses of *Gray* (1988), who links the cultural dimensions by *Hofstede* (2001) to accounting values. For instance, *Gray* (1988) posits that uncertainty avoidance is positively related to the accounting value secrecy, which reflects a preference for confidentially and restrictive disclosure (*Gray* (1988), p. 11).

[142] For an overview refer to *Fink et al.* (2013).

involves a lot of noise. Hence, it is unclear whether this may impact the results in a certain way. However, unless shown that there is a systematic bias in a specific direction, the noise just impairs the power of statistical tests. Hence, the fact that this study finds statistically significant results in all the three economic consequences sub-studies just emphasizes the strength of the effect of IFRS 8 on information asymmetries, cost of capital and financial analysts' information environment.

Moreover, it is possible that the disclosure of segment information under the management approach of the treatment firms influences the control firms via **information spillover effects** (*Botosan/Stanford* (2005)). This may unduly impact the results in any of the three sub-studies of the economic consequences. However, potential information spillovers rather help users of financial statements of the control firms and, thus, it weakens the treatment effect and therefore works against the findings.

Although this study has implications for standard setting, it has to be noted that it only provides information about the decision usefulness for certain groups such as investors and financial analysts and the cost of capital consequences for reporting companies. However, it remains silent on any direct or indirect **cost considerations** for all other parties. Moreover, although investors (and financial analysts) represent an important group of users of financial statements, standard setters must also take **other aspects** into account such as social welfare implications or other objectives of financial reporting such as contracting, regulation or litigation (*Holthausen/Watts* (2001)).

Based on these limitations, there are a lot of fruitful avenues for **future research**. For instance, to address the generalizability issue described above, a similar research design could be used in **many countries**. It would be particularly interesting to analyze whether the results are similar in other countries such as Australia or Hong Kong, which have adopted IFRS but differ substantially from Germany in terms of culture and in the role of capital markets. As elaborated above, this study investigates the largest German blue chip firms. Usually, larger firms have a much richer information environment and the incremental effect of segment disclosures may be different compared to small firms with less public disclosures. Therefore, future research could focus on **SMEs**. This would also provide the IASB with some feedback for its decision to exclude mandatory segment reporting from IFRS for SMEs.

Furthermore, to address the potential issue with noisy measures used in this study, **an experimental research design** could be used. Experiments provide laboratory settings in which researchers can control for most issues that empirical archival studies suffer from. Although the difference-in-differences design is considered a quasi-experimental approach, the randomization process in a laboratory experiment would allow causal claims without restrictions. Moreover, researchers could obtain insights on the perception of segment information and also further understand how it is processed and used by investors and financial analysts.

Moreover, **the cost side** of segment reporting disclosure decisions is largely unknown to this point. Future studies could attempt to analyze the proprietary nature of segmental disclosures under the management approach. Furthermore, based on a case study, researchers could try to observe and analyze the process of preparing segment information.

This would shed some light on the direct costs and whether these costs are negligible under the management approach as some supporters of IFRS 8 argue. In total, more insights
on the cost side of segment reporting would help to better understand the disclosure decision of firms, which weigh costs and benefits.

The introduction of IFRS 8 led to uniform segment reporting regulation for more than
100 countries – including the U.S. This study has shown that the adoption of the management approach yields certain benefits for investors, firms and financial analysts. However, there are a lot of areas unexplored to this point which provide numerous future research opportunities. Given the prevalence and geographical extension of **segment reporting under the management approach**, this topic will continue to be of high relevance for
standard setters, investors and financial analysts, preparers as well as auditors and enforcement institutions.

Appendix
Content analysis catalogue for IFRS 8

A. General Information		
Criterion		Basis
1	Name	
2	Stock index	
2.1	DAX *(1/0)*	
2.2	MDAX *(1/0)*	
2.3	TecDAX *(1/0)*	
2.4	SDAX *(1/0)*	
3	Location of segment report *(1 = before the notes; 2 = in the notes; 3 = table before the notes, narratives in the notes)*	
4	Year of IFRS 8's adoption *(year)*	
B. Segmentation		
Criterion		Basis
1	Number of operating segments *(number)*	
2	Corporate/holding *(1/0)*	
3	Other segments *(1/0)*	8.16
4	Reconciliation column *(1/0)*	
5	Aggregation of segments *(1/0)*	8.12
6	Number of aggregated segments *(number)*	
7	Basis of segmentation	
7.1	Business lines *(1/0)*	
7.2	Geographical (location of customers) *(1/0)*	
7.3	Geographical (location of assets) *(1/0)*	
7.4	Geographical (undetermined) *(1/0)*	
7.5	Mixture of business lines/geographical *(1/0)*	
7.6	Matrix *(1/0)*	
8	General information about the segments	
8.1	Factors used to identify reportable segments *(1/0)*	8.22a (mandatory)
8.2	Factors used to identify reportable segments *(word count)*	
8.3	Types of products and services *(1/0)*	8.22b (mandatory)
8.4	Types of products and services *(word count)*	
8.5	Explanation of the basis of accounting for transactions between reportable segments *(1/0)*	8.27a (mandatory)
8.6	Basis *(market/cost)*	
8.7	Explanation of the basis of accounting for transactions between reportable segments *(word count)*	
8.8	Explanation of any changes of measurement methods used to determine segment profit or loss *(1/0)*	8.27e (mandatory if occurred)
8.9	Total number of words in the segment information narratives *(word count)*	
9	Other	
9.1	Definition of CODM *(1/0)*	8.7
9.2	CODM *(name)*	
9.3	Measure which is used to assess performance and allocate resources *(1/0)*	
9.4	Name of measure *(name)*	
9.5	Statement that segments are identified based on internal reporting *(1/0)*	
9.6	Statement that measurement and disclosure of segment data are consistent with the accounting policies used for the financial statements *(1/0)*	
9.7	Statement that measurement and disclosure of segment data may deviate from the accounting policies used for the financial statements *(1/0)*	
9.8	Consistency of segmentation with MD&A and other parts of the annual report *(1/0)*	

C. Disclosures		
Criterion		Basis
1	**Revenues**	
1.1	Total revenues *(1/0)*	voluntary
1.2	Revenues from external customers *(1/0)*	8.23a (CODM conditional)
1.3	Revenues with other segments *(1/0)*	8.23b (CODM conditional)
1.4	Reconciliation column *(1/0)*	-
2	**Profit or loss**	8.23 (mandatory)
2.1	Gross Profit *(1/0)*	
2.2	EBITDAR *(1/0)*	
2.3	EBITDA *(1/0)*	
2.4	EBITA *(1/0)*	
2.5	EBIT *(1/0)*	
2.6	EBT *(1/0)*	
2.7	Profit after tax *(1/0)*	
2.8	Other *(number)*	
2.9	Other *(specify)*	
2.10	Most similar aggregated measure *(name)*	
2.11	Adjustments	
2.11.1	- Only continued operations *(1/0)*	
2.11.2	- Pre-special items *(1/0)*	
2.11.3	- Pre-goodwill impairment *(1/0)*	
2.11.4	- Pre-group expenses *(1/0)*	
3	**Conditional disclosures**	
3.1	Assets *(1/0)*	8.23 (CODM conditional)
3.2	Liabilities *(1/0)*	8.23 (CODM conditional)
3.3	Interest revenue *(1/0)*	8.23c (CODM conditional)
3.4	Interest expense *(1/0)*	8.23d (CODM conditional)
3.5	Depreciation and amortization *(1/0)*	8.23e (CODM conditional)
3.6	Interest from associated entities accounted for under the equity method *(1/0)*	8.23g (CODM conditional)
3.7	Investments in associated entities accounted for under the equity method *(1/0)*	8.24a (CODM conditional)
3.8	Investments in non-current assets *(1/0)*	8.24b (CODM conditional)
3.9	Income tax expense or income *(1/0)*	8.23h (CODM conditional)
3.10	Material non-cash items *(1/0)*	8.23i (CODM conditional)
4	**Voluntary disclosures**	
4.1	Non-current assets	
4.1.1	- Intangible assets *(1/0)*	voluntary
4.1.2	- Property, plant, and equipment *(1/0)*	voluntary
4.1.3	- Equipment on operating leases *(1/0)*	voluntary
4.1.4	- Assets leased out *(1/0)*	voluntary
4.1.5	- Investment property *(1/0)*	voluntary
4.1.6	- Financial investments *(1/0)*	voluntary
4.1.7	- Receivables from financial services *(1/0)*	voluntary
4.1.8	- Other financial assets *(1/0)*	voluntary
4.1.9	- Non-current securities *(1/0)*	voluntary

4.1.10	- Loans and receivables *(1/0)*	voluntary
4.1.11	- Derivative financial instruments *(1/0)*	voluntary
4.1.12	- Deferred tax assets *(1/0)*	voluntary
4.1.13	- Other non-current assets *(1/0)*	voluntary
4.1.14	- Total non-current assets *(1/0)*	voluntary
4.2	**Current assets**	
4.2.1	- Inventories *(1/0)*	voluntary
4.2.2	- Trade receivables *(1/0)*	voluntary
4.2.3	- Derivative financial instruments *(1/0)*	voluntary
4.2.4	- Income tax receivables *(1/0)*	voluntary
4.2.5	- Accrued income and advance payments *(1/0)*	voluntary
4.2.6	- Receivables from financial services *(1/0)*	voluntary
4.2.7	- Securities *(1/0)*	voluntary
4.2.8	- Cash and cash equivalents *(1/0)*	voluntary
4.2.9	- Assets held for sale *(1/0)*	voluntary
4.2.10	- Total current assets *(1/0)*	voluntary
4.3	**Equity and liabilities**	
4.3.1	- Equity *(1/0)*	voluntary
4.3.2	- Non-current financial liabilities *(1/0)*	voluntary
4.3.3	- Pension obligations *(1/0)*	voluntary
4.3.4	- Deferred tax liabilities *(1/0)*	voluntary
4.3.5	- Other non-current provisions *(1/0)*	voluntary
4.3.6	- Other non-current liabilities *(1/0)*	voluntary
4.3.7	- Total non-current liabilities and provisions *(1/0)*	voluntary
4.3.8	- Current financial liabilities *(1/0)*	voluntary
4.3.9	- Trade payables *(1/0)*	voluntary
4.3.10	- Prepayments received *(1/0)*	voluntary
4.3.11	- Current income tax payables *(1/0)*	voluntary
4.3.12	- Liabilities associated with assets held for sale *(1/0)*	voluntary
4.3.13	- Other current provisions *(1/0)*	voluntary
4.3.14	- Other current liabilities *(1/0)*	voluntary
4.3.15	- Total current liabilities and provisions *(1/0)*	voluntary
4.4	**Other items**	
4.4.1	- Costs of goods sold *(1/0)*	voluntary
4.4.2	- Net interest *(1/0)*	voluntary
4.4.3	- Income tax expense or income *(1/0)*	voluntary
4.4.4	- KPI ratios *(number)*	voluntary
4.4.4.1	- KPI ratio #1 *(name)*	voluntary
4.4.4.2	- KPI ratio #2 *(name)*	voluntary
4.4.4.3	- KPI ratio #3 *(name)*	voluntary
4.4.5	- Added-value KPI *(number)*	voluntary
4.4.5.1	- Added value KPI #1 *(name)*	voluntary
4.4.5.2	- Added value KPI #2 *(name)*	voluntary
4.4.5.3	- Added value KPI #3 *(name)*	voluntary
4.4.6	- Other KPI *(number)*	voluntary
4.4.6.1	- Other KPI #1 *(name)*	voluntary
4.4.6.2	- Other KPI #2 *(name)*	voluntary
4.4.6.3	- Other KPI #3 *(name)*	voluntary
4.4.7	- Cash flow (operating) *(1/0)*	voluntary
4.4.8	- Cash flow (investing) *(1/0)*	voluntary
4.4.9	- Cash flow (finance) *(1/0)*	voluntary

4.4.10	- Goodwill *(1/0)*	voluntary
4.4.11	- Goodwill impairment *(1/0)*	voluntary
4.4.12	- Other impairments *(1/0)*	voluntary
4.4.13	- Research and development (expenditures) *(1/0)*	voluntary
4.4.14	- Capitalized development costs *(1/0)*	voluntary
4.4.15	- Number of employees (year-end) *(1/0)*	voluntary
4.4.16	- Number of employees (average) *(1/0)*	voluntary
4.4.17	- Number of employees adjusted for leased laborer *(1/0)*	voluntary
4.4.18	- Number of employees adjusted for apprentices *(1/0)*	voluntary
4.4.19	- Number of business units *(1/0)*	voluntary
4.4.20	- Sales area in sqm *(1/0)*	voluntary
4.4.21	- Other items *(number)*	voluntary
4.4.21.1	- Other item #1 *(name)*	voluntary
4.4.21.2	- Other item #2 *(name)*	voluntary
4.4.21.3	- Other item #3 *(name)*	voluntary
4.4.21.4	- Other item #4 *(name)*	voluntary
4.4.21.5	- Other item #5 *(name)*	voluntary
5	**Entity-wide disclosures**	
5.1	Revenues with external customers for each group of products/services *(1 = statement that costs to develop information too excessive; 2 = part of reportable segment information; 3 = separately available)*	8.32 (mandatory)
5.2	Geographical revenues with external customers *(1 = statement that costs to develop information too excessive; 2 = part of reportable segment information; 3 = separately available)*	8.33a (mandatory)
5.3	Geographical non-current assets *(1 = statement that costs to develop information too excessive; 2 = part of reportable segment information; 3 = separately available)*	8.33b (mandatory)
5.4	Further entity wide disclosures *(number)*:	voluntary
5.4.1	- Name of item #1 *(name)*	voluntary
5.4.2	- Name of item #2 *(name)*	voluntary
5.4.3	- Name of item #3 *(name)*	voluntary
5.4.4	- Name of item #4 *(name)*	voluntary
5.4.5	- Name of item #5 *(name)*	voluntary
5.5	Fineness of geographical segmentation *(1 = domestic/foreign level; 2 = continental level; 3 = country-level)*	8.33a
5.6	Revenues with major customers *(0 = no statement; 1 = statement that no revenues with single customers exceeded ten per cent of total revenues; 2 = just total revenues with major customers; 3 = total revenues of major customers with specific segments)*	8.34
6	**Reconciliation**	
6.1	Reconciliation of **total revenues** *(1/0)*	8.28a (mandatory)
6.1.1	- Reconciliation column in the main table *(1/0)*	
6.1.1.1	- Inter-segment/consolidation elimination *(1/0)*	
6.1.1.2	- Ratio inter-segment/consolidation elimination to total amount *(ratio)*	
6.1.1.3	- Headquarters/Group *(1/0)*	
6.1.1.4	- Ratio Headquarters/Group to total amount *(ratio)*	
6.1.2	- Separate reconciliation table *(1/0)*	
6.1.3	- Ratio of reconciled positions to total results measure *(ratio)*	
6.1.4	- Number of reconciliation positions *(number)*	
6.1.4.1	- Inter-segment elimination *(1/0)*	
6.1.4.2	- Ratio inter-segment elimination to total reconciled amount *(ratio)*	
6.1.4.3	- Headquarters/Group *(1/0)*	
6.1.4.4	- Ratio Headquarters/Group to total reconciled amount *(ratio)*	
6.1.4.4	- Ratio Headquarters/Group to total reconciled amount *(ratio)*	
6.1.4.5	- Non-IFRS measurement component *(1/0)*	
6.1.4.6	- Non-IFRS measurement component *(ratio)*	

6.1.4.7	- Other #1 *(name)*	
6.1.4.8	- Other #2 *(name)*	
6.1.4.9	- Other #3 *(name)*	
6.1.4.10	- Other #4 *(name)*	
6.1.4.11	- Other #5 *(name)*	
6.1.4.12	- Ratio all other items to total reconciled amount *(ratio)*	
6.2	Reconciliation of **earnings before taxes** measure *(1/0)*	8.28b (mandatory: either a before or after tax earnings measure has to be reconciled)
6.2.1	- Measure *(name)*	
6.2.2	- Reconciliation column in the main table *(1/0)*	
6.2.2.1	- Inter-segment/consolidation elimination *(1/0)*	
6.2.2.2	- Ratio inter-segment/consolidation elimination to total amount *(ratio)*	
6.2.2.3	- Headquarters/Group *(1/0)*	
6.2.2.4	- Ratio Headquarters/Group to total amount *(ratio)*	
6.2.3	- Separate reconciliation table *(1/0)*	
6.2.4	- Ratio of reconciled positions to total results measure *(ratio)*	
6.2.5	- Number of reconciliation positions *(number)*	
6.2.5.1	- Inter-segment elimination *(1/0)*	
6.2.5.2	- Ratio inter-segment elimination to total reconciled amount *(ratio)*	
6.2.5.3	- Headquarters/Group *(1/0)*	
6.2.5.4	- Ratio Headquarters/Group to total reconciled amount *(ratio)*	
6.2.5.5	- Non-IFRS measurement component *(1/0)*	
6.2.5.6	- Non-IFRS measurement component *(ratio)*	
6.2.5.7	- Other #1 *(name)*	
6.2.5.8	- Other #2 *(name)*	
6.2.5.9	- Other #3 *(name)*	
6.2.5.10	- Other #4 *(name)*	
6.2.5.11	- Other #5 *(name)*	
6.2.5.12	- Ratio all other items to total reconciled amount *(ratio)*	
6.3	Reconciliation of **earnings after taxes** measure *(1/0)*	8.28b (mandatory: either a before or after tax earnings measure has to be reconciled)
6.3.1	- Measure *(name)*	
6.3.2	- Reconciliation column in the main table *(1/0)*	
6.3.2.1	- Inter-segment/consolidation elimination *(1/0)*	
6.3.2.2	- Ratio inter-segment/consolidation elimination to total amount *(ratio)*	
6.3.2.3	- Headquarters/Group *(1/0)*	
6.3.2.4	- Ratio Headquarters/Group to total amount *(ratio)*	
6.3.3	- Separate reconciliation table *(1/0)*	
6.3.4	- Ratio of reconciled positions to total results measure *(ratio)*	
6.3.5	- Number of reconciliation positions *(number)*	
6.3.5.1	- Inter-segment elimination *(1/0)*	
6.3.5.2	- Ratio inter-segment elimination to total reconciled amount *(ratio)*	
6.3.5.3	- Headquarters/Group *(1/0)*	
6.3.5.4	- Ratio Headquarters/Group to total reconciled amount *(ratio)*	
6.3.5.5	- Non-IFRS measurement component *(1/0)*	
6.3.5.6	- Non-IFRS measurement component *(ratio)*	
6.3.5.7	- Other #1 *(name)*	
6.3.5.8	- Other #2 *(name)*	

6.3.5.9	- Other #3 *(name)*	
6.3.5.10	- Other #4 *(name)*	
6.3.5.11	- Other #5 *(name)*	
6.3.5.12	- Ratio all other items to total reconciled amount *(ratio)*	
6.4	Reconciliation of total **assets** *(1/0)*	8.28c (mandatory: However, this is an inconsistency that should have been removed together with the amendment in 2009)
6.4.1	- Reconciliation column in the main table *(1/0)*	
6.4.1.1	- Inter-segment/consolidation elimination *(1/0)*	
6.4.1.2	- Ratio inter-segment/consolidation elimination to total amount *(ratio)*	
6.4.1.3	- Headquarters/Group *(1/0)*	
6.4.1.4	- Ratio Headquarters/Group to total amount *(ratio)*	
6.4.2	- Separate reconciliation table *(1/0)*	
6.4.3	- Ratio of reconciled positions to total results measure *(ratio)*	
6.4.4	- Number of reconciliation positions *(number)*	
6.4.4.1	- Inter-segment elimination *(1/0)*	
6.4.4.2	- Ratio inter-segment elimination to total reconciled amount *(ratio)*	
6.4.4.3	- Headquarters/Group *(1/0)*	
6.4.4.4	- Ratio Headquarters/Group to total reconciled amount *(ratio)*	
6.4.4.5	- Non-IFRS measurement component *(1/0)*	
6.4.4.6	- Non-IFRS measurement component *(ratio)*	
6.4.4.7	- Other #1 *(name)*	
6.4.4.8	- Other #2 *(name)*	
6.4.4.9	- Other #3 *(name)*	
6.4.4.10	- Other #4 *(name)*	
6.4.4.11	- Other #5 *(name)*	
6.4.4.12	- Ratio all other items to total reconciled amount *(ratio)*	
6.5	Reconciliation of total **liabilities** *(1/0)*	8.28d (mandatory if reported in accordance with 8.23)
6.5.1	- Reconciliation column in the main table *(1/0)*	
6.5.1.1	- Inter-segment/consolidation elimination *(1/0)*	
6.5.1.2	- Ratio inter-segment/consolidation elimination to total amount *(ratio)*	
6.5.1.3	- Headquarters/Group *(1/0)*	
6.5.1.4	- Ratio Headquarters/Group to total amount *(ratio)*	
6.5.2	- Separate reconciliation table *(1/0)*	
6.5.3	- Ratio of reconciled positions to total results measure *(ratio)*	
6.5.4	- Number of reconciliation positions *(number)*	
6.5.4.1	- Inter-segment elimination *(1/0)*	
6.5.4.2	- Ratio inter-segment elimination to total reconciled amount *(ratio)*	
6.5.4.3	- Headquarters/Group *(1/0)*	
6.5.4.4	- Ratio Headquarters/Group to total reconciled amount *(ratio)*	
6.5.4.5	- Non-IFRS measurement component *(1/0)*	
6.5.4.6	- Non-IFRS measurement component *(ratio)*	
6.5.4.7	- Other #1 *(name)*	
6.5.4.8	- Other #2 *(name)*	
6.5.4.9	- Other #3 *(name)*	
6.5.4.10	- Other #4 *(name)*	
6.5.4.11	- Other #5 *(name)*	
6.5.4.12	- Ratio all other items to total reconciled amount *(ratio)*	

6.6	Reconciliation of other **items** (*number*)	8.28e (mandatory if reported in accordance with 8.23)
6.6.1	- Name of item #1 (*name*)	
6.6.2	- Name of item #2 (*name*)	
6.6.3	- Name of item #3 (*name*)	
6.6.4	- Name of item #4 (*name*)	
6.6.5	- Name of item #5 (*name*)	

Table A-1: Content analysis catalogue for segment reports under IFRS 8

Content analysis catalogue for IAS 14R

A. General information		
Criterion		**Basis**
1	Name	
2	**Stock index**	
2.1	DAX *(1/0)*	
2.2	MDAX *(1/0)*	
2.3	TecDAX *(1/0)*	
2.4	SDAX *(1/0)*	
3	Location of segment report *(1 = before the notes; 2 = in the notes; 3 = table before the notes, narratives in the notes)*	
4	Year of IFRS 8's adoption *(year)*	
B. Segmentation		
Criterion		**Basis**
1	**Number of primary segments** *(number)*	14R.50
2	**Number of secondary segments** *(number)*	14R.68
3	**Corporate/holding** *(1/0)*	
4	**Other segments** *(1/0)*	
5	**Reconciliation column** *(1/0)*	
6	**Aggregation of segments** *(1/0)*	
7	**Number of aggregated segments** *(number)*	
8	**Basis of primary segmentation**	
8.1	Business lines *(1/0)*	
8.2	Geographical (location of customers) *(1/0)*	
8.3	Geographical (location of assets) *(1/0)*	
8.4	Geographical (undetermined) *(1/0)*	
8.5	Mixture of business lines/geographical *(1/0)*	
8.6	Matrix *(1/0)*	
9	**Basis of secondary segmentation**	
9.1	Business lines *(1/0)*	
9.2	Geographical (location of customers) *(1/0)*	
9.3	Geographical (location of assets) *(1/0)*	
9.4	Geographical (undetermined) *(1/0)*	
9.5	Mixture of business lines/geographical *(1/0)*	
9.6	Matrix *(1/0)*	
10	**General information about the segments**	
10.1	Factors used to identify reportable segments *(1/0)*	voluntary
10.2	Factors used to identify reportable segments *(word count)*	
10.3	Types of products and services *(1/0)*	14R.81 (mandatory)
10.4	Types of products and services *(word count)*	
10.5	Explanation of the basis of accounting for transactions between reportable segments *(1/0)*	14R.75 (mandatory)
10.6	Basis *(market/cost)*	
10.7	Explanation of the basis of accounting for transactions between reportable segments *(word count)*	
10.8	Explanation of any changes of measurement methods used to determine segment profit or loss *(1/0)*	14R.74 (mandatory if occurred)
10.9	Total number of words in the segment information narratives *(word count)*	
11	**Other**	
11.1	Measure which is used to assess performance and allocate resources *(1/0)*	
11.2	Name of measure *(name)*	
11.3	Statement that segments are identified based on internal reporting *(1/0)*	

11.4	Statement that measurement and disclosure of segment data are consistent with the measurement principles used for financial statements *(1/0)*	
11.5	Consistency of segmentation with MD&A and other parts of the annual report *(1/0)*	
11.6	Fineness of geographical segmentation *(1 = domestic/foreign level; 2 = continental level; 3 = country-level)*	
11.7	Revenues with major customers *(0 = no statement; 1 = statement that no revenues with single customers exceeded 10 per cent of total revenues; 2 = just total revenues with major customers; 3 = total revenues of major customers with specific segments)*	
C. Disclosures		
Criterion		**Basis**
1	**Revenues**	
1.1	Total revenues *(1/0)*	14R.51 (mandatory)
1.2	Revenues from external customers *(1/0)*	14R.51 (mandatory)
1.3	Revenues with other segments *(1/0)*	14R.51 (mandatory)
1.4	Reconciliation column *(1/0)*	
2	**Profit or loss**	14R.52 (mandatory)
2.a	From continued operations *(1/0)*	14R.52 (mandatory)
2.b	From discontinued operations *(1/0)*	14R.52 (mandatory)
2.c	No information whether from continued or discontinued operations *(1/0)*	
2.1	Gross Profit *(1/0)*	
2.2	EBITDAR *(1/0)*	
2.3	EBITDA *(1/0)*	
2.4	EBITA *(1/0)*	
2.5	EBIT *(1/0)*	
2.6	EBT *(1/0)*	
2.7	Profit after tax *(1/0)*	
2.8	Other *(number)*	
2.9	Other *(specify)*	
2.10	Most similar GAAP measure *(name)*	
2.11	**Adjustments**	
2.11.1	- Only continued operations *(1/0)*	
2.11.2	- Pre-special items *(1/0)*	
2.11.3	- Pre-goodwill impairment *(1/0)*	
2.11.4	- Pre-group expenses *(1/0)*	
3	**Other mandatory primary line items**	
3.1	Assets *(1/0)*	14R.55 (mandatory)
3.2	Liabilities *(1/0)*	14R.56 (mandatory)
3.3	Capital expenditures *(1/0)*	14R.57 (mandatory)
3.4	Depreciation and amortization *(1/0)*	14R.58 (mandatory)
3.5	Significant non-cash expenses (other than depreciation and amortization) *(1/0)*	14R.61 (mandatory)
3.6	Profit or loss from investment in associated entities accounted for under the equity method *(1/0)*	14R.64 (mandatory)
3.7	Investments in associated entities accounted for under the equity method *(1/0)*	14R.66 (mandatory)
4	**Other voluntary disclosures primary segments**	
4.1	Non-current assets	
4.1.1	- Intangible assets *(1/0)*	voluntary
4.1.2	- Property, plant, and equipment *(1/0)*	voluntary
4.1.3	- Equipment on operating leases *(1/0)*	voluntary
4.1.4	- Assets leased out *(1/0)*	voluntary
4.1.5	- Investment property *(1/0)*	voluntary
4.1.6	- Financial investments *(1/0)*	voluntary
4.1.7	- Receivables from financial services *(1/0)*	voluntary
4.1.8	- Other financial assets *(1/0)*	voluntary

4.1.9	- Non-current securities *(1/0)*	voluntary
4.1.10	- Loans and receivables *(1/0)*	voluntary
4.1.11	- Derivative financial instruments *(1/0)*	voluntary
4.1.12	- Deferred tax assets *(1/0)*	voluntary
4.1.13	- Other non-current assets *(1/0)*	voluntary
4.1.14	- Total non-current assets *(1/0)*	voluntary
4.2	Current assets	
4.2.1	- Inventories *(1/0)*	voluntary
4.2.2	- Trade receivables *(1/0)*	voluntary
4.2.3	- Derivative financial instruments *(1/0)*	voluntary
4.2.4	- Income tax receivables *(1/0)*	voluntary
4.2.5	- Accrued income and advance payments *(1/0)*	voluntary
4.2.6	- Receivables from financial services *(1/0)*	voluntary
4.2.7	- Securities *(1/0)*	voluntary
4.2.8	- Cash and cash equivalents *(1/0)*	voluntary
4.2.9	- Assets held for sale *(1/0)*	voluntary
4.2.10	- Total current assets *(1/0)*	voluntary
4.3	Equity and liabilities	
4.3.1	- Equity *(1/0)*	voluntary
4.3.2	- Non-current financial liabilities *(1/0)*	voluntary
4.3.3	- Pension obligations *(1/0)*	voluntary
4.3.4	- Deferred tax liabilities *(1/0)*	voluntary
4.3.5	- Other non-current provisions *(1/0)*	voluntary
4.3.6	- Other non-current liabilities *(1/0)*	voluntary
4.3.7	- Total non-current liabilities and provisions *(1/0)*	voluntary
4.3.8	- Current financial liabilities *(1/0)*	voluntary
4.3.9	- Trade payables *(1/0)*	voluntary
4.3.10	- Prepayments received *(1/0)*	voluntary
4.3.11	- Current income tax payables *(1/0)*	voluntary
4.3.12	- Liabilities associated with assets held for sale *(1/0)*	voluntary
4.3.13	- Other current provisions *(1/0)*	voluntary
4.3.14	- Other current liabilities *(1/0)*	voluntary
4.3.15	- Total current liabilities and provisions *(1/0)*	voluntary
4.4	Other items	
4.4.1	- Costs of goods sold *(1/0)*	voluntary
4.4.2	- Interest revenue *(1/0)*	voluntary
4.4.3	- Interest expense *(1/0)*	voluntary
4.4.4	- Net interest *(1/0)*	voluntary
4.4.5	- Income tax expense or income *(1/0)*	voluntary
4.4.6	- KPI ratios *(number)*	voluntary
4.4.6.1	- KPI ratio #1 *(name)*	voluntary
4.4.6.2	- KPI ratio #2 *(name)*	voluntary
4.4.6.3	- KPI ratio #3 *(name)*	voluntary
4.4.7	- Added-value KPI *(number)*	voluntary
4.4.7.1	- Added value KPI #1 *(name)*	voluntary
4.4.7.2	- Added value KPI #2 *(name)*	voluntary
4.4.7.3	- Added value KPI #3 *(name)*	voluntary
4.4.8	- Other KPI *(number)*	voluntary
4.4.8.1	- Other KPI #1 *(name)*	voluntary
4.4.8.2	- Other KPI #2 *(name)*	voluntary
4.4.8.3	- Other KPI #3 *(name)*	voluntary

4.4.9	- Cash flow (operating) *(1/0)*	voluntary
4.4.10	- Cash flow (investing) *(1/0)*	voluntary
4.4.11	- Cash flow (finance) *(1/0)*	voluntary
4.4.12	- Goodwill *(1/0)*	voluntary
4.4.13	- Goodwill impairment *(1/0)*	voluntary
4.4.14	- Other impairments *(1/0)*	voluntary
4.4.15	- Research and development (expenditures) *(1/0)*	voluntary
4.4.16	- Capitalized development costs *(1/0)*	voluntary
4.4.17	- Number of employees (year-end) *(1/0)*	voluntary
4.4.18	- Number of employees (average) *(1/0)*	voluntary
4.4.19	- Number of employees adjusted for leased laborer *(1/0)*	voluntary
4.4.20	- Number of employees adjusted for apprentices *(1/0)*	voluntary
4.4.21	- Number of business units *(1/0)*	voluntary
4.4.22	- Sales area in sqm *(1/0)*	voluntary
4.4.23	- Other items *(number)*	voluntary
4.4.23.1	- Other item #1 *(name)*	voluntary
4.4.23.2	- Other item #2 *(name)*	voluntary
4.4.23.3	- Other item #3 *(name)*	voluntary
4.4.23.4	- Other item #4 *(name)*	voluntary
4.4.23.5	- Other item #5 *(name)*	voluntary
	Line items for secondary segments	
5	**Secondary main line items**	
5.1	Secondary segmentation$_{1/sec}$ *(0 = no secondary segmentation; 1 = secondary segmentation available)*	
5.2	Segment revenue from external customers *(1/0)*	14R.69a/70a (mandatory)
5.3	Segment assets *(1/0)*	14R.69b/70b (mandatory)
5.4	Segment capital expenditures *(1/0)*	14R.69c/70c (mandatory)
5.5	Segment result *(1/0)*	voluntary
6	**Other voluntary disclosures for secondary segments**	
6.1	Non-current assets	
6.1.1	- Intangible assets *(1/0)*	voluntary
6.1.2	- Property, plant, and equipment *(1/0)*	voluntary
6.1.3	- Equipment on operating leases *(1/0)*	voluntary
6.1.4	- Assets leased out *(1/0)*	voluntary
6.1.5	- Investment property *(1/0)*	voluntary
6.1.6	- Investments in associated entities accounted for under the equity method *(1/0)*	voluntary
6.1.7	- Investments in non-current assets *(1/0)*	voluntary
6.1.8	- Financial investments *(1/0)*	voluntary
6.1.9	- Receivables from financial services *(1/0)*	voluntary
6.1.10	- Other financial assets *(1/0)*	voluntary
6.1.11	- Non-current securities *(1/0)*	voluntary
6.1.12	- Loans and receivables *(1/0)*	voluntary
6.1.13	- Derivative financial instruments *(1/0)*	voluntary
6.1.14	- Deferred tax assets *(1/0)*	voluntary
6.1.15	- Other non-current assets *(1/0)*	voluntary
6.1.16	- Total non-current assets *(1/0)*	voluntary
6.2	Current assets	
6.2.1	- Inventories *(1/0)*	voluntary
6.2.2	- Trade receivables *(1/0)*	voluntary
6.2.3	- Derivative financial instruments *(1/0)*	voluntary
6.2.4	- Income tax receivables *(1/0)*	voluntary

6.2.5	- Accrued income and advance payments *(1/0)*	voluntary
6.2.6	- Receivables from financial services *(1/0)*	voluntary
6.2.7	- Securities *(1/0)*	voluntary
6.2.8	- Cash and cash equivalents *(1/0)*	voluntary
6.2.9	- Assets held for sale *(1/0)*	voluntary
6.2.10	- Total current assets *(1/0)*	voluntary
6.3	Equity and liabilities	
6.3.1	- Equity *(1/0)*	voluntary
6.3.2	- Non-current financial liabilities *(1/0)*	voluntary
6.3.3	- Pension obligations *(1/0)*	voluntary
6.3.4	- Deferred tax liabilities *(1/0)*	voluntary
6.3.5	- Other non-current provisions *(1/0)*	voluntary
6.3.6	- Other non-current liabilities *(1/0)*	voluntary
6.3.7	- Total non-current liabilities and provisions *(1/0)*	voluntary
6.3.8	- Current financial liabilities *(1/0)*	voluntary
6.3.9	- Trade payables *(1/0)*	voluntary
6.3.10	- Prepayments received *(1/0)*	voluntary
6.3.11	- Current income tax payables *(1/0)*	voluntary
6.3.12	- Liabilities associated with assets held for sale *(1/0)*	voluntary
6.3.13	- Other current provisions *(1/0)*	voluntary
6.3.14	- Other current liabilities *(1/0)*	voluntary
6.3.15	- Total current liabilities and provisions *(1/0)*	voluntary
6.4	Other items	
6.4.1	- Costs of goods sold *(1/0)*	voluntary
6.4.2	- Depreciation and amortization *(1/0)*	voluntary
6.4.3	- Interest from associated entities accounted for under the equity method *(1/0)*	voluntary
6.4.4	- Interest revenue *(1/0)*	voluntary
6.4.5	- Interest expense *(1/0)*	voluntary
6.4.6	- Net interest *(1/0)*	voluntary
6.4.7	- Income tax expense or income *(1/0)*	voluntary
6.4.8	- KPI ratios *(number)*	voluntary
6.4.8.1	- KPI ratio #1 *(name)*	voluntary
6.4.8.2	- KPI ratio #2 *(name)*	voluntary
6.4.8.3	- KPI ratio #3 *(name)*	voluntary
6.4.9	- Added-value KPI *(number)*	voluntary
6.4.9.1	- Added value KPI #1 *(name)*	voluntary
6.4.9.2	- Added value KPI #2 *(name)*	voluntary
6.4.9.3	- Added value KPI #3 *(name)*	voluntary
6.4.10	- Other KPI *(number)*	voluntary
6.4.10.1	- Other KPI #1 *(name)*	voluntary
6.4.10.2	- Other KPI #2 *(name)*	voluntary
6.4.10.3	- Other KPI #3 *(name)*	voluntary
6.4.11	- Cash flow (operating) *(1/0)*	voluntary
6.4.12	- Cash flow (investing) *(1/0)*	voluntary
6.4.13	- Cash flow (finance) *(1/0)*	voluntary
6.4.14	- Goodwill *(1/0)*	voluntary
6.4.15	- Goodwill impairment *(1/0)*	voluntary
6.4.16	- Other impairments *(1/0)*	voluntary
6.4.17	- Research and development (expenditures) *(1/0)*	voluntary
6.4.18	- Capitalized development costs *(1/0)*	voluntary
6.4.19	- Number of employees (year-end) *(1/0)*	voluntary

6.4.20	- Number of employees (average) *(1/0)*	voluntary
6.4.21	- Number of employees adjusted for leased laborer *(1/0)*	voluntary
6.4.22	- Number of employees adjusted for apprentices *(1/0)*	voluntary
6.4.23	- Number of business units *(1/0)*	voluntary
6.4.24	- Sales area in sqm *(1/0)*	voluntary
6.4.25	- Other items *(number)*	voluntary
6.4.25.1	- Other item #1 *(name)*	voluntary
6.4.25.2	- Other item #2 *(name)*	voluntary
6.4.25.3	- Other item #3 *(name)*	voluntary
6.4.25.4	- Other item #4 *(name)*	voluntary
6.4.25.5	- Other item #5 *(name)*	voluntary
6.4.26	- Total number of voluntary items *(number)*	
7	**Reconciliation**	
7.1	Reconciliation of **total revenues** *(1/0)*	14R.67 (mandatory)
7.1.1	- Reconciliation column in the main table *(1/0)*	
7.1.1.1	- Inter-segment/consolidation elimination *(1/0)*	
7.1.1.2	- Ratio inter-segment/consolidation elimination to total amount *(ratio)*	
7.1.1.3	- Headquarters/Group *(1/0)*	
7.1.1.4	- Ratio Headquarters/Group to total amount *(ratio)*	
7.1.2	- Separate reconciliation table *(1/0)*	
7.1.3	- Ratio of reconciled positions to total results measure *(ratio)*	
7.1.4	- Number of reconciliation positions *(number)*	
7.1.4.1	- Inter-segment elimination *(1/0)*	
7.1.4.2	- Ratio inter-segment elimination to total reconciled amount *(ratio)*	
7.1.4.3	- Headquarters/Group *(1/0)*	
7.1.4.4	- Ratio Headquarters/Group to total reconciled amount *(ratio)*	
7.1.4.4	- Ratio Headquarters/Group to total reconciled amount *(ratio)*	
7.1.4.5	- Non-IFRS measurement component *(1/0)*	
7.1.4.6	- Non-IFRS measurement component *(ratio)*	
7.1.4.7	- Other #1 *(name)*	
7.1.4.8	- Other #2 *(name)*	
7.1.4.9	- Other #3 *(name)*	
7.1.4.10	- Other #4 *(name)*	
7.1.4.11	- Other #5 *(name)*	
7.1.4.12	- Ratio all other items to total reconciled amount *(ratio)*	
7.2	Reconciliation of **segment results from continuing operations** measure *(1/0)*	14R.67 (mandatory)
7.2.1	- Measure *(name)*	
7.2.2	- Reconciliation column in the main table *(1/0)*	
7.2.2.1	- Inter-segment/consolidation elimination *(1/0)*	
7.2.2.2	- Ratio inter-segment/consolidation elimination to total amount *(ratio)*	
7.2.2.3	- Headquarters/Group *(1/0)*	
7.2.2.4	- Ratio Headquarters/Group to total amount *(ratio)*	
7.2.3	- Separate reconciliation table *(1/0)*	
7.2.4	- Ratio of reconciled positions to total results measure *(ratio)*	
7.2.5	- Number of reconciliation positions *(number)*	
7.2.5.1	- Inter-segment elimination *(1/0)*	
7.2.5.2	- Ratio inter-segment elimination to total reconciled amount *(ratio)*	
7.2.5.3	- Headquarters/Group *(1/0)*	
7.2.5.4	- Ratio Headquarters/Group to total reconciled amount *(ratio)*	
7.2.5.5	- Non-IFRS measurement component *(1/0)*	
7.2.5.6	- Non-IFRS measurement component *(ratio)*	

7.2.5.7	- Other #1 *(name)*	
7.2.5.8	- Other #2 *(name)*	
7.2.5.9	- Other #3 *(name)*	
7.2.5.10	- Other #4 *(name)*	
7.2.5.11	- Other #5 *(name)*	
7.2.5.12	- Ratio all other items to total reconciled amount *(ratio)*	
7.3	Reconciliation of **segment results from discontinued operations** measure *(1/0)*	14R.67 (mandatory)
7.3.1	- Measure *(name)*	
7.3.2	- Reconciliation column in the main table *(1/0)*	
7.3.2.1	- Inter-segment/consolidation elimination *(1/0)*	
7.3.2.2	- Ratio inter-segment/consolidation elimination to total amount *(ratio)*	
7.3.2.3	- Headquarters/Group *(1/0)*	
7.3.2.4	- Ratio Headquarters/Group to total amount *(ratio)*	
7.3.3	- Separate reconciliation table *(1/0)*	
7.3.4	- Ratio of reconciled positions to total results measure *(ratio)*	
7.3.5	- Number of reconciliation positions *(number)*	
7.3.5.1	- Inter-segment elimination *(1/0)*	
7.3.5.2	- Ratio inter-segment elimination to total reconciled amount *(ratio)*	
7.3.5.3	- Headquarters/Group *(1/0)*	
7.3.5.4	- Ratio Headquarters/Group to total reconciled amount *(ratio)*	
7.3.5.5	- Non-IFRS measurement component *(1/0)*	
7.3.5.6	- Non-IFRS measurement component *(ratio)*	
7.3.5.7	- Other #1 *(name)*	
7.3.5.8	- Other #2 *(name)*	
7.3.5.9	- Other #3 *(name)*	
7.3.5.10	- Other #4 *(name)*	
7.3.5.11	- Other #5 *(name)*	
7.3.5.12	- Ratio all other items to total reconciled amount *(ratio)*	
7.4	Reconciliation of total **assets** *(1/0)*	14R.67 (mandatory)
7.4.1	- Reconciliation column in the main table *(1/0)*	
7.4.1.1	- Inter-segment/consolidation elimination *(1/0)*	
7.4.1.2	- Ratio inter-segment/consolidation elimination to total amount *(ratio)*	
7.4.1.3	- Headquarters/Group *(1/0)*	
7.4.1.4	- Ratio Headquarters/Group to total amount *(ratio)*	
7.4.2	- Separate reconciliation table *(1/0)*	
7.4.3	- Ratio of reconciled positions to total results measure *(ratio)*	
7.4.4	- Number of reconciliation positions *(number)*	
7.4.4.1	- Inter-segment elimination *(1/0)*	
7.4.4.2	- Ratio inter-segment elimination to total reconciled amount *(ratio)*	
7.4.4.3	- Headquarters/Group *(1/0)*	
7.4.4.4	- Ratio Headquarters/Group to total reconciled amount *(ratio)*	
7.4.4.5	- Non-IFRS measurement component *(1/0)*	
7.4.4.6	- Non-IFRS measurement component *(ratio)*	
7.4.4.7	- Other #1 *(name)*	
7.4.4.8	- Other #2 *(name)*	
7.4.4.9	- Other #3 *(name)*	
7.4.4.10	- Other #4 *(name)*	
7.4.4.11	- Other #5 *(name)*	
7.4.4.12	- Ratio all other items to total reconciled amount *(ratio)*	
7.5	Reconciliation of total **liabilities** *(1/0)*	14R.67 (mandatory)
7.5.1	- Reconciliation column in the main table *(1/0)*	

7.5.1.1	- Inter-segment/consolidation elimination (1/0)	
7.5.1.2	- Ratio inter-segment/consolidation elimination to total amount (ratio)	
7.5.1.3	- Headquarters/Group (1/0)	
7.5.1.4	- Ratio Headquarters/Group to total amount (ratio)	
7.5.2	- Separate reconciliation table (1/0)	
7.5.3	- Ratio of reconciled positions to total results measure (ratio)	
7.5.4	- Number of reconciliation positions (number)	
7.5.4.1	- Inter-segment elimination (1/0)	
7.5.4.2	- Ratio inter-segment elimination to total reconciled amount (ratio)	
7.5.4.3	- Headquarters/Group (1/0)	
7.5.4.4	- Ratio Headquarters/Group to total reconciled amount (ratio)	
7.5.4.5	- Non-IFRS measurement component (1/0)	
7.5.4.6	- Non-IFRS measurement component (ratio)	
7.5.4.7	- Other #1 (name)	
7.5.4.8	- Other #2 (name)	
7.5.4.9	- Other #3 (name)	
7.5.4.10	- Other #4 (name)	
7.5.4.11	- Other #5 (name)	
7.5.4.12	- Ratio all other items to total reconciled amount (ratio)	
7.6	Reconciliation of other **items** (number)	voluntary
7.6.1	- Name of item #1 (name)	
7.6.2	- Name of item #2 (name)	
7.6.3	- Name of item #3 (name)	
7.6.4	- Name of item #4 (name)	
7.6.5	- Name of item #5 (name)	

Table A-2: Content analysis catalogue for segment reports under IAS 14R

Delta sheet content analysis catalogue

A. General information	
Criterion	Basis
1	**Name**	
2	**Stock index**	
2.1	DAX *(1/0)*	
2.2	MDAX *(1/0)*	
2.3	TecDAX *(1/0)*	
2.4	SDAX *(1/0)*	
3	**Year of IFRS 8's adoption** *(year)*	

B. Segmentation delta	
Criterion	Basis
1	**Change in the number of operating segments** *(number)*	Other segments/headquarters not included
2	**Change in the basis of segmentation** *(0 = none; 1 = geographic to business lines; 2 = business lines to geographic; 3 = geographic to mix; 4 = business lines to mix)*	
3	**Change in names of segments** *(0 = none; 1 = minor name change; 2 = major name change; 3 = name change induced by a change of segmentation)*	*Minor* name changes comprise simple extensions/cutbacks of prior names as well as German or English translations. *Major* name changes indicate that business activities could potentially be allocated differently among the segments. 3 indicates a change in segment names due to a change in the basis of segmentation as indicated above.
4	**Narrative information about the segments**	
4.1	Change in the word count: Factors used to identify reportable segments *(delta number of words)*	
4.2	Change in the word count: Types of products and services *(delta number of words)*	
4.3	Change in the word count: Explanation of the basis of accounting for transactions between reportable segments *(delta number of words)*	
4.4	Change in the total number of words in the segment report narratives *(delta number of words)*	
5	**Other**	
5.1	Change in consistency of segmentation with management report and other parts of the annual report *(0 = no change; 1 = from inconsistent to consistent; 2 = from consistent to inconsistent)*	
5.2	Statement by the company on the effect of the introduction of IFRS 8 on segment reporting *(0 = no statement; 1 = no change in segment reporting; 2 = no substantial change in segment reporting; 3 = change in segment reporting)*	

C. Disclosures delta	
Criterion	Basis
Line items for each reportable segment	
1	**Profit or loss**	
1.1	Change in the profit or loss measure *(1/0)*	
1.2	Change in the number of profit or loss measures *(delta)*	
2	**Other disclosures**	
2.1	Change in the total number of line items (both voluntary and mandatory) *(delta)*	This change comprises all line items. Under IAS 14R, only the number of line items of the primary segment.
2.2	Change in the number of voluntarily and conditionally disclosed line items *(delta)*	This change comprises all voluntarily reported items for the primary segment under IAS 14R and all voluntarily and conditionally disclosed items under IFRS 8.

| 2.3 | Change in the number of voluntarily disclosed line items *(delta)* | This change comprises all voluntarily reported items for the primary segment under IAS 14R and all voluntarily disclosed items under IFRS 8. |

Table A-3: Delta sheet content analysis catalogue

Bibliography

A

Abarbanell, J. S./Lanen, W. N./Verrecchia, R. E. (1995): Analysts' Forecasts as Proxies for Investor Beliefs in Empirical Research, in: Journal of Accounting and Economics, 20 (1), pp. 31–60.

Acharya, V. V./Pedersen, L. H. (2005): Asset Pricing with Liquidity Risk, in: Journal of Financial Economics, 77 (2), pp. 375–410.

AICPA (1994): Improving Business Reporting – A Customer Focus: Meeting the Information Needs of Investors and Creditors: A Comprehensive Report (Jenkins Report), New York 1994.

AIMR (1993): Financial Reporting in the 1990s and Beyond, Charlottesville 1993.

Ajinkya, B. B. (1980): An Empirical Evaluation of Line-of-Business Reporting, in: Journal of Accounting Research, 18 (2), pp. 343–361.

Akerlof, G. A. (1970): The Market for "Lemons": Quality Uncertainty and the Market Mechanism, in: The Quarterly Journal of Economics, 84 (3), pp. 488–500.

Albrecht, W. D./Chipalkatii, N. (1998): Looking for Better Answers? New Segment Reporting, in: The CPA Journal, 68 (5), pp. 46–52.

Alexander, D./Nobes, C. (2007): Financial Accounting – An International Introduction, 3rd ed., Harlow 2007.

Alvarez, M. (2003): Segmentberichterstattung und Segmentanalyse, Dissertation Universität Augsburg, Wiesbaden 2003.

Amihud, Y./Mendelson, H. (1986): Asset Pricing and the Bid-Ask Spread, in: Journal of Financial Economics, 17 (2), pp. 223–249.

Anderson, R./Epstein, M. (1995): The Usefulness of Annual Reports, in: Australian Accountant, 65 (1), pp. 25–28.

Antonakis, J./Bendahan, S./Jacquart, P./Lalive, R. (2010): On Making Causal Claims: A Review and Recommendations, in: Leadership Quarterly Yearly Review, 21 (6), pp. 1086–1120.

Arrow, K. J. (1985): The Economics of Agency, in: Pratt, J. W./Zeckhauser, R. J. (eds.), Principals and Agents: The Structure of Business, Boston 1985, pp. 37–51.

Auer, L. von (2011): Ökonometrie, 5th ed., Berlin 2011.

Ayres, F. L./Rodgers, J. L. (1994): Further Evidence on the Impact of SFAS 52 on Analysts' Earnings Forecasts, in: Journal of International Financial Management & Accounting, 5 (2), pp. 120–141.

B

Baetge, J./Haenelt, T. (2008): Kritische Würdigung der neu konzipierten Segmentberichterstattung nach IFRS 8 unter Berücksichtigung prüfungsrelevanter Aspekte, in: Zeitschrift für Internationale Rechnungslegung, 3 (1), pp. 43–50.

Baiman, S./Verrecchia, R. E. (1996): The Relation Among Capital Markets, Financial Disclosure, Production Efficiency, and Insider Trading, in: Journal of Accounting Research, 34 (1), pp. 1–22.

Balakrishnan, R./Harris, T. S./Sen, P. K. (1990): The Predictive Ability of Geographic Segment Disclosures, in: Journal of Accounting Research, 28 (2), pp. 305–325.

Baldwin, B. A. (1984): Segment Earnings Disclosure and the Ability of Security Analysts to Forecast Earnings Per Share, in: The Accounting Review, 59 (3), pp. 376–389.

Barron, O. E./Byard, D./Kim, O. (2002): Changes in Analysts' Information around Earnings Announcements, in: The Accounting Review, 77 (4), pp. 821–846.

Barron, O. E./Kile, C. O./Okeefe, T. B. (1999): MD&A Quality as Measured by the SEC and Analysts' Earnings Forecasts, in: Contemporary Accounting Research, 16 (1), pp. 75–109.

Barron, O. E./Kim, O./Lim, S. C./Stevens, D. E. (1998): Using Analysts' Forecasts to Measure Properties of Analysts' Information Environment, in: The Accounting Review, 73 (4), pp. 421–433.

Barry, C. B./Brown, S. J. (1985): Differential Information and Security Market Equilibrium, in: The Journal of Financial and Quantitative Analysis, 20 (4), pp. 407–422.

Barry, C. B./Jennings, R. H. (1992): Information and Diversity of Analyst Opinion, in: The Journal of Financial and Quantitative Analysis, 27 (2), pp. 169–183.

Bartel, R. (1990): Charakteristik, Methodik und wissenschaftsmethodische Probleme der Wirtschaftswissenschaften, in: Wirtschaftswissenschaftliches Studium, 19 (2), pp. 54–59.

Baumann, K.-H. (1987): Die Segment-Berichterstattung im Rahmen der externen Finanzpublizität, in: Havermann, H. (ed.), Bilanz- und Konzernrecht, Festschrift für Reinhard Goerdeler, Düsseldorf 1987, pp. 1–23.

Beaver, W. (1972): The Behavior of Security Prices and its Implications for Accounting Research (Methods), in: The Accounting Review, 47 (5) (Suppl.), pp. 407–437.

Beckman, R. J./Trussell, H. J. (1974): The Distribution of an Arbitrary Studentized Residual and the Effects of Updating in Multiple Regression, in: Journal of the American Statistical Association, 69 (345), pp. 199–201.

Behn, B. K./Nichols, N. B./Street, D. L. (2002): The Predictive Ability of Geographic Segment Disclosures by U.S. Companies: SFAS No. 131 vs. SFAS No. 14, in: Journal of International Accounting Research, 1 (1), pp. 31–44.

Bekaert, G./Harvey, C. R. (2000): Foreign Speculators and Emerging Equity Markets, in: The Journal of Finance, 55 (2), pp. 565–613.

Belsley, D. A./Kuh, E./Welsch, R. R. (1980): Regression Diagnostics: Identifying Influential Data and Sources of Collinearity, New York 1980.

Benston, G. J. (1984): The Costs of Complying with a Government Data Collection Program: The FTC's Line of Business Report, in: Journal of Accounting and Public Policy, 3 (2), pp. 123–137.

Berelson, B. (1971): Content Analysis in Communication Research, New York 1971.

Berger, P. G./Hann, R. (2003): The Impact of SFAS No. 131 on Information and Monitoring, in: Journal of Accounting Research, 41 (2), pp. 163–223.

Berger, P. G./Hann, R. (2007): Segment Profitability and the Proprietary and Agency Costs of Disclosure, Working Paper, University of Chicago.

Berger, P. G./Ofek, E. (1995): Diversification's Effect on Firm Value, in: Journal of Financial Economics, 37 (1), pp. 39–65.

Bernards, O. (1994): Segmentberichterstattung diversifizierter Unternehmen – Theoretische und empirische Analyse, Bergisch Gladbach 1994.

Blase, S. (2011): Segmentberichterstattung vor dem Hintergrund des Management Approach - Theoretische, regulatorische und empirische Erkenntnisse zur Harmonisierung der Segmentberichterstattung nach IFRS 8, Dissertation Helmut-Schmidt-Universität Hamburg, Edewecht 2011.

Blase, S./Müller, S. (2009): Empirische Analyse der vorzeitigen IFRS-8-Erstanwendung – Eine Analyse der Harmonisierung von interner und externer Segmentberichterstattung im Rahmen der vorzeitigen Umstellung auf IFRS 8 bei DAX-, MDAX- und SDAX-Unternehmen, in: Die Wirtschaftsprüfung, 62 (10), pp. 537–544.

Böckem, H./Pritzer, M. (2010): Anwendungsfragen der Segmentberichterstattung nach IFRS 8, in: Zeitschrift für internationale und kapitalmarktorientierte Rechnungslegung, 10 (12), pp. 614–620.

Böcking, H. J./Benecke, B. (1998): Neue Vorschriften zur Segmentberichterstattung nach IAS und US-GAAP unter dem Aspekt des Business Reporting, in: Die Wirtschaftsprüfung, 51 (3), pp. 92–107.

Böcking, H. J./Benecke, B. (1999): Der Entwurf des DRSC zur Segmentberichterstattung "E-DRS 3" – eine Orientierung an dem Standard SFAS 131 des FASB und/oder an dem Standard IAS 14 revised des IASC?, in: Die Wirtschaftsprüfung, 52 (21), pp. 839–844.

Boersema, J. M./van Weelden, S. J. (1992): A Segmented Picture, Toronto 1992.

Botosan, C. A./Plumlee, M. A. (2005): Assessing Alternative Proxies for the Expected Risk Premium, in: The Accounting Review, 80 (1), pp. 21–53.

Botosan, C. A./Stanford, M. (2005): Managers' Motives to Withhold Segment Disclosures and the Effect of SFAS no. 131 on Analysts' Information Environment, in: The Accounting Review, 80 (3), pp. 751–771.

Breid, V. (1995): Aussagefähigkeit agencytheoretischer Ansätze im Hinblick auf die Verhaltenssteuerung von Entscheidungsträgern, in: Zeitschrift für betriebswirtschaftliche Forschung, 47 (9), pp. 821–854.

Brown, P. R. (1997): Financial Data and Decision-Making by Sell-Side Analysts, in: The Journal of Financial Statement Analysis, 2 (2), pp. 43–48.

Brunnermeier, M. K./Pedersen, L. H. (2009): Market Liquidity and Funding Liquidity, in: Review of Financial Studies, 22 (6), pp. 2201–2238.

Bushman, R. M. (1991): Public Disclosure and the Structure of Private Information Markets, in: Journal of Accounting Research, 29 (2), pp. 261–276.

C

Callsen-Bracker, H.-M. (2007): Finanzanalysten und Preiseffizienz, Dissertation TU Berlin, Baden-Baden 2007.

Campbell, J. Y./Shiller, R. J. (1988): The Dividend-Price Ratio and Expectations of Future Dividends and Discount Factors, in: The Review of Financial Studies, 1 (3), pp. 195–228.

Chen, A. Y./Comiskey, E. E./Mulford, C. W. (1990): Foreign Currency Translation and Analyst Forecast Dispersion: Examining the Effects of Statement of Financial Accounting Standards No. 52, in: Journal of Accounting and Public Policy, 9 (4), pp. 239–256.

Cheung, S. N. S. (1970): The Structure of a Contract and the Theory of a Non-Exclusive Resource, in: Journal of Law and Economics, 13 (1), pp. 49–70.

Cheung, S. N. S. (1973): The Fable of the Bees: An Economic Investigation, in: Journal of Law and Economics, 16 (1), pp. 11–33.

Chiang, R./Venkatesh, P. C. (1988): Insider Holdings and Perceptions of Information Asymmetry: A Note, in: The Journal of Finance, 43 (4), pp. 1041–1048.

Chordia, T./Roll, R./Subrahmanyam, A. (2000): Co-Movements in Bid-Ask Spreads and Market Depth, in: Financial Analysts Journal, 56 (5), pp. 23–27.

Christensen, H. B./Hail, L./Leuz, C. (2013): Mandatory IFRS Reporting and Changes in Enforcement, in: Conference Issue on Accounting Research on Classic and Contemporary Issues University of Rochester, Simon Business School, 56 (2–3, Suppl.), pp. 147–177.

Chung, K. H./Jo, H. (1996): The Impact of Security Analysts' Monitoring and Marketing Functions on the Market Value of Firms, in: The Journal of Financial and Quantitative Analysis, 31 (4), pp. 493–512.

Claus, J./Thomas, J. (2001): Equity Premia as Low as Three Percent? Evidence from Analysts' Earnings Forecasts for Domestic and International Stock Markets, in: The Journal of Finance, 56 (5), pp. 1629–1666.

Coase, R. H. (1937): The Nature of the Firm, in: Economica, 4 (16), pp. 386–405.

Coase, R. H. (1960): The Problem of Social Cost, in: Journal of Law and Economics, 3 (1), pp. 1–44.

Coles, J. L./Loewenstein, U./Suay, J. (1995): On Equilibrium Pricing under Parameter Uncertainty, in: The Journal of Financial and Quantitative Analysis, 30 (3), pp. 347–364.

Collins, D. W. (1975): SEC Product-Line Reporting and Market Efficiency, in: Journal of Financial Economics, 2 (2), pp. 125–164.

Collins, D. W./Kothari, S. P./Shanken, J./Sloan, R. G. (1994): Lack of Timeliness and Noise as Explanations for the Low Contemporaneuos Return-Earnings association, in: Journal of Accounting and Economics, 18 (3), pp. 289–324.

Collins, D. W./Simonds, R. R. (1979): SEC Line-of-Business Disclosure and Market Risk Adjustments, in: Journal of Accounting Research, 17 (2), pp. 352–383.

Constantinides, G. M. (1986): Capital Market Equilibrium with Transaction Costs, in: Journal of Political Economy, 94 (4), pp. 842–862.

Cook, R. D. (1977): Detection of Influential Observation in Linear Regression, in: Technometrics, 19 (1), pp. 15–18.

Copeland, T. E./Galai, D. (1983): Information Effects on the Bid-Ask Spread, in: The Journal of Finance, 38 (5), pp. 1457–1469.

Cramer, J. S. (1987): Mean and Variance of $R2$ in Small and Moderate Samples, in: Journal of Econometrics, 35 (2–3), pp. 253–266.

Crawford, L./Extance, H./Helliar, C. V./Power, D. M. (2012): Operating Segments: The Usefulness of IFRS 8, Edinburgh 2012.

Crawford, L./Ferguson, J./Helliar, C. V./Power, D. M. (2013): Control Over Accounting Standards Within the European Union: The Political Controversy surrounding the adoption of IFRS 8, in: Critical Perspectives on Accounting, 25 (4–5), pp. 304–318.

D

Daske, H./Hail, L./Leuz, C./Verdi, R. (2008): Mandatory IFRS Reporting around the World: Early Evidence on the Economic Consequences, in: Journal of Accounting Research, 46 (5), pp. 1085–1142.

Decker, R. O. (1994): Eine Prinzipal-Agenten-theoretische Betrachtung von Eigner-Manager-Konflikten in der Kommanditgesellschaft auf Aktien und in der Aktiengesellschaft, Dissertation Freie Universität Berlin, Bergisch Gladbach 1994.

Demsetz, H. (1967): Toward a Theory of Property Rights, in: The American Economic Review, 57 (2), pp. 347–359.

Demsetz, H. (1968): The Cost of Transacting, in: The Quarterly Journal of Economics, 82 (1), pp. 33–53.

Demsetz, H. (1969): Information and Efficiency: Another Viewpoint, in: Journal of Law and Economics, 12 (1), pp. 1–22.

Demski, J. S. (1973): The General Impossibility of Normative Accounting Standards, in: The Accounting Review, 48 (4), pp. 718–723.

Denis, D. J./Denis, D. K./Sarin, A. (1997): Agency Problems, Equity Ownership, and Corporate Diversification, in: The Journal of Finance, 52 (1), pp. 135–160.

Deutsche Börse AG (2014): Leitfaden zu den Aktienindizes der Deutschen Börse, Frankfurt am Main 2014, available online: http://www.dax-indices.com/DE/-MediaLibrary/Document/Leitfaden_Aktienindizes.pdf, (last accessed: 11.11.2014).

Dhaliwal, D. S. (1978): The Impact of Disclosure Regulations on the Cost of Capital, in: FASB (ed.), Research Report: Economic Consequences of Financial Accounting Standards - Selected Papers, Stanford 1978, pp. 71–101.

Diamond, D. W. (1985): Optimal Release of Information by Firms, in: The Journal of Finance, 40 (4), pp. 1071–1094.

Dupnik, T. S./Rolfe, R. J. (1990): Geographic Area Disclosures and the Assessment of Foreign Investment Risk for Disclosure in Accounting Statement Notes, in: International Journal of Accounting, 25 (3), pp. 265–285.

E

Easton, P. D. (2004): PE Ratios, PEG Ratios, and Estimating the Implied Expected Rate of Return on Equity Capital, in: The Accounting Review, 79 (1), pp. 73–95.

Eberts, M. (1986): Das Berufsbild des Finanzanalysten in der Bundesrepublik Deutschland, Darmstadt 1986.

Edwards, E. O./Bell, P. W. (1961): The Theory and Measurement of Business Income, Berkeley 1961.

Eisenhardt, K. M. (1989): Agency Theory: An Assessment and Review, in: The Academy of Management Review, 14 (1), pp. 57–74.

Elliott, R. K./Jacobson, P. D. (1994): Costs and Benefits of Business Information Disclosure, in: Accounting Horizons, 8 (4), pp. 80–96.

Emmanuel, C. R./Garrod, N. (1992): Segment Reporting: International Issues and Evidence, London 1992.

Emmanuel, C. R./Pick, R. H. (1980): The Predictive Ability of UK Segment Reports, in: Journal of Business Finance & Accounting, 7 (2), pp. 201–218.

Ernst & Young (1998): Disclosures about Segments of an Enterprise and Related Information, London 1998.

Errunza, V. R./Miller, D. P. (2000): Market Segmentation and the Cost of Capital in International Equity Markets, in: The Journal of Financial and Quantitative Analysis, 35 (4), pp. 577–600.

Ettredge, M. L./Kwon, S. Y./Smith, D. B./Zarowin, P. A. (2005): The Impact of SFAS no. 131 Business Segment Data on the Market's Ability to Anticipate Future Earnings, in: The Accounting Review, 80 (3), pp. 773–804.

European Parliament (2007a): Motion for a Resolution by the Committee on Economic and Monetary Affairs, B6-0157/2007, 18.04.2007.

European Parliament (2007b): Motion for a Resolution by the Committee on Economic and Monetary Affairs, B6-0437/2007, 07.11.2007.

F

Fama, E. F. (1965): The Behavior of Stock-Market Prices, in: The Journal of Business, 38 (1), pp. 34–105.

Fama, E. F. (1970): Efficient Capital Markets: A Review of Theory and Empirical Work, in: The Journal of Finance, 25 (2), pp. 383–417.

Fama, E. F. (1991): Efficient Capital Markets: II, in: The Journal of Finance, 46 (5), pp. 1575–1617.

Fama, E. F./French, K. R. (1992): The Cross-Section of Expected Stock Returns, in: The Journal of Finance, 47 (2), pp. 427–465.

Fama, E. F./French, K. R. (1993): Common Risk Factors in the Returns on Stocks and Bonds, in: Journal of Financial Economics, 33 (1), pp. 3–56.

Fama, E. F./MacBeth, J. D. (1973): Risk, Return, and Equilibrium: Empirical Tests, in: Journal of Political Economy, 81 (3), pp. 607–636.

Faulkender, M./Petersen, M. A. (2006): Does the Source of Capital Affect Capital Structure?, in: The Review of Financial Studies, 19 (1), pp. 45–79.

Fey, G./Mujkanovic, R. (1999): Segmentberichterstattung im internationalen Umfeld, in: Die Betriebswirtschaft, 59 (2), pp. 261–275.

Fink, C./Kajüter, P./Winkeljohann, N. (2013): Lageberichterstattung - HGB, DRS und IFRS Practice Statement Management Commentary, Stuttgart 2013.

Fink, C./Ulbrich, P. R. (2006): Segmentberichterstattung nach ED 8 - Operating Segments, in: Zeitschrift für internationale und kapitalmarktorientierte Rechnungslegung, 6 (4), pp. 233–243.

Fischer, P. E./Verrecchia, R. E. (1998): Correlated Forecast Errors, in: Journal of Accounting Research, 36 (1), pp. 91–110.

Foerster, S. R./Karolyi, G. A. (1999): The Effects of Market Segmentation and Investor Recognition on Asset Prices: Evidence from Foreign Stocks Listing in the United States, in: The Journal of Finance, 54 (3), pp. 981–1013.

Foerster, S. R./Karolyi, G. A. (2000): The Long-Run Performance of Global Equity Offerings, in: The Journal of Financial and Quantitative Analysis, 35 (4), pp. 499–528.

Foster, N. (2003): The FASB and the Capital Markets, Norwalk 2003.

Francioni, R./Hazarika, S./Reck, M./Schwartz, R. A. (2008): Equity Market Microstructure: Taking Stock of What We Know, in: Journal of Portfolio Management, 35 (1), pp. 57–71.

Frank, U. (2003): Einige Gründe für eine Wiederbelebung der Wissenschaftstheorie, in: Die Betriebswirtschaft, 63 (3), pp. 278–292.

FREP (2011): Tätigkeitsbericht 2010, Berlin 2011.

Fröhling, O. (2000): KonTraG und Controlling - Eckpfeiler eines entscheidungsrelevanten und transparenten Segmentcontrolling und -reporting, München 2000.

Fülbier, U. (2004): Wissenschaftstheorie und Betriebswirtschaftslehre, in: Wirtschaftswissenschaftliches Studium, 31 (5), pp. 266–271.

G

Gebhardt, W. R./Lee, Charles M. C./Swaminathan, B. (2001): Toward an Implied Cost of Capital, in: Journal of Accounting Research, 39 (1), pp. 135–176.

Glaum, M./Street, D. L. (2003): Compliance with the Disclosure Requirements of Germany's New Market: IAS Versus US GAAP, in: Journal of International Financial Management & Accounting, 14 (1), pp. 64–100.

Glosten, L. R. (1987): Components of the Bid-Ask Spread and the Statistical Properties of Transaction Prices, in: The Journal of Finance, 42 (5), pp. 1293–1307.

Glosten, L. R./Harris, L. E. (1988): Estimating the Components of the Bid/Ask Spread, in: Journal of Financial Economics, 21 (1), pp. 123–142.

Glosten, L. R./Milgrom, P. R. (1985): Bid, Ask and Transaction Prices in a Specialist Market with Heterogeneously Informed Traders, in: Journal of Financial Economics, 14 (1).

Göbel, E. (2002): Neue Institutionenökonomik: Konzeptionen und betriebswirtschaftliche Anwendungen, Stuttgart 2002.

Gode, D./Mohanram, P. (2003): Inferring the Cost of Capital Using the Ohlson-Juettner Model, in: Review of Accounting Studies, 8 (4), pp. 399–431.

Gray, S. J. (1988): Towards a Theory of Cultural Influence on the Development of Accounting Systems Internationally, in: Abacus, 24 (1), pp. 1–15.

Gray, S. J./Radebaugh, L. H./Roberts, C. B. (1990): International Perceptions of Cost Constraints on Voluntary Information Disclosures: A Comparative Study of U.K. and U.S. Multinationals, in: Journal of International Business Studies, 21 (4), pp. 597–622.

Grochla, E. (1978): Einführung in die Organisationstheorie, Stuttgart 1978.

Grossman, S. J./Miller, M. H. (1988): Liquidity and Market Structure, in: The Journal of Finance, 43 (3), pp. 617–633.

Groysberg, B./Healy, P./Chapman, C. (2008): Buy-Side vs. Sell-Side Analysts' Earnings Forecasts, in: Financial Analysts Journal, 64 (4), pp. 25–39.

H

Haase, K. D. (1974): Segment-Bilanzen. Rechnungslegung diversifizierter Industrieunternehmen, Wiesbaden 1974.

Hacker, B. (2002): Segmentberichterstattung: Eine ökonomische Analyse, Frankfurt/Main 2002.

Hail, L. (2002): The Impact of Voluntary Corporate Disclosures on the Ex-Ante Cost of Capital for Swiss Firms, in: European Accounting Review, 11 (4), pp. 741–773.

Hail, L./Leuz, C. (2006): International Differences in the Cost of Equity Capital: Do Legal Institutions and Securities Regulation Matter?, in: Journal of Accounting Research, 44 (3), pp. 485–531.

Hail, L./Leuz, C. (2009): Cost of capital effects and changes in growth expectations around U.S. cross-listings, in: Journal of Financial Economics, 93 (3), pp. 428–454.

Haller, A. (2000): Segmentberichterstattung, in: Haller, A./Raffournier, B./Walton, P. (eds.), Unternehmenspublizität im internationalen Wettbewerb, Stuttgart 2000, pp. 755–805.

Haller, A./Park, P. (1994): Grundsätze ordnungsgemäßer Segmentberichterstattung, in: Zeitschrift für betriebswirtschaftliche Forschung, 46 (6), pp. 499–525.

Haller, A./Park, P. (1999): Segmentberichterstattung auf Basis des "Management Approach" – Inhalt und Konsequenzen, in: kostenrechnungspraxis (3), pp. 59–66.

Hart, O./Holmström, B. (1987): The Theory of Contracts, in: Bewley, T. F. (ed.), Advances in economic theory. Fifth World Congress (Economic Society Monographs No. 12) 1987, pp. 71–155.

Hartle, J. (1984): Möglichkeiten der Entobjektivierung der Bilanz - Eine ökonomische Analyse, Frankfurt 1984.

Hartmann-Wendels, T. (1989): Principal-Agent-Theorie und asymmetrische Informationsverteilung, in: Zeitschrift für Betriebswirtschaft, 59 (7), pp. 714–734.

Hasbrouck, J. (1988): Trades, Quotes, Inventories, and Information, in: Journal of Financial Economics, 22 (2), pp. 229–252.

Healy, P. M./Hutton, A. P./Palepu, K. G. (1999): Stock Performance and Intermediation Changes Surrounding Sustained Increases in Disclosure, in: Contemporary Accounting Research, 16 (3), pp. 485–520.

Heintges, S./Urbanczik, P./Wulbrand, H. (2008): Regelungen, Fallstricke und Überraschungen der Segmentberichterstattung nach IFRS 8, in: Der Betrieb, 61 (52), pp. 2773–2781.

Henze, J. (2004): Was leisten Finanzanalysten? – Eine empirische Analyse des deutschen Aktienmarktes, Dissertation Westfälische Wilhelms-Universität Münster, Lohmar 2004.

Herrmann, D./Thomas, W. B. (2000): An Analysis of Segment Disclosures under SFAS No. 131 and SFAS No. 14, in: Accounting Horizons, 14 (3), pp. 287–302.

Himmel, H. (2004): Konvergenz von interner und externer Unternehmensrechnung am Beispiel der Segmentberichterstattung, Dissertation Universität Bayreuth, Aachen 2004.

Hofstede, G. (2001): Culture's Consequences: Comparing Values, Behaviors, Institutions, and Organizations Across Nations, 2nd ed., Thousand Oaks 2001.

Holsti, O. R. (1969): Content Analysis for the Social Sciences and Humanities, Reading, Mass. 1969.

Holthausen, R. W./Verrecchia, R. E. (1990): The Effect of Informedness and Consensus on Price and Volume Behavior, in: The Accounting Review, 65 (1), pp. 191–208.

Holthausen, R. W./Watts, R. L. (2001): The Relevance of the Value-Relevance Literature for Financial Accounting Standard Setting, in: Journal of Accounting and Economics, 31 (1–3), pp. 3–75.

Hope, O.-K./Kang, T./Thomas, W. B./Vasvari, F. (2008): Pricing and Mispricing Effects of SFAS 131, in: Journal of Business Finance & Accounting, 35 (3-4), pp. 281–306.

Hope, O.-K./Kang, T./Thomas, W. B./Vasvari, F. (2009): The Effects of SFAS 131 Geographic Segment Disclosures by US Multinational Companies on the Valuation of Foreign Earnings, in: Journal of International Business Studies, 40 (3), pp. 421–433.

Hope, O.-K./Thomas, W. B. (2008): Managerial Empire Building and Firm Disclosure, in: Journal of Accounting Research, 46 (3), pp. 591–626.

Hope, O.-K./Thomas, W. B./Winterbotham, G. (2006): The Impact of Nondisclosure of Geographic Segment Earnings on Earnings Predictability, in: Journal of Accounting, Auditing & Finance, 21 (3), pp. 323–346.

Horsch, A. (2005): Agency und Versicherungsintermediation, in: Horsch, A./Meinhövel, H./Paul, S. (eds.), Institutionenökonomie und Betriebswirtschaftslehre, München 2005, pp. 81–99.

Hossain, M. (2008): Change in Value Relevance of Quarterly Foreign Sales Data of U.S. Multinational Corporations after Adopting SFAS 131, in: Review of Quantitative Finance and Accounting, 30 (1), pp. 1–23.

Hossain, M./Marks, B. R. (2005): Information Content of Mandatory Quarterly Foreign Sales Data of U.S. Multinational Companies under SFAS 131, in: Journal of International Accounting, Auditing and Taxation, 14 (2), pp. 105–120.

House, R. J./Hanges, P. J./Javidan, M./Dorfman, P./Gupta, V. (2004): Culture, Leadership, and Organizations: The Globe Study of 62 Societies, Thousand Oaks 2004.

Huang, R. D./Stoll, H. R. (1996): Dealer Versus Auction Markets: A Paired Comparison of Execution Costs on NASDAQ and the NYSE, in: Journal of Financial Economics, 41 (3), pp. 313–357.

Husmann, R. (1997): Segmentierung des Konzernabschlusses zur bilanzanalytischen Untersuchung der wirtschaftlichen Lage des Konzerns, in: Die Wirtschaftsprüfung, 50 (11), pp. 349–359.

I

IASB (2012): Post-implementation review: IFRS 8 Operating Segments – Request for Information, London 2012, available online: http://www.ifrs.org/Current-Projects/IASB-Projects/PIR/IFRS-8/Documents/IFRS8OperatingSegments.pdf, (last accessed: 11.11.2014).

IASB (2013a): Post-implementation review: IFRS 8 Operating Segments – Report and feedback statement, London 2013, available online: http://www.ifrs.org/IFRS-Research/Get-started/Documents/PIR-IFRS-8-Operatihg-Segments-July-2013.pdf, (last accessed: 11.11.2014).

IASB (2013b): Post-implementation review of IFRS 8: Review of academic literature to December 2012, available online: http://www.ifrs.org/IFRS-Research/Get-started/Documents/6B%20-%20Post-implementation%20review.pdf, (last accessed: 11.11.2014).

IASC (1994): Reporting financial information by segment: Draft Statement of Principles.

Indjejikian, R. J. (1991): The Impact of Costly Information Interpretation on Firm Disclosure Decisions, in: Journal of Accounting Research, 29 (2), pp. 277–301.

J

Jaffe, J. P. (1974): Special Information and Insider Trading, in: Journal of Business, 47 (3), pp. 410–428.

Jensen, M. C./Meckling, W. H. (1976): Theory of the firm: Managerial behavior, agency costs and ownership structure, in: Journal of Financial Economics, 3 (4), pp. 305–360.

Jones, C./Luther, R. G. (2005): Anticipating the Impact of IFRS on the Management of German Manufacturing Companies: Some Observations from a British Perspective, in: Accounting in Europe, 2 (1), pp. 165–193.

K

Kajüter, P. (2013): IFRS und Controlling, in: Baetge, J./Wollmert, P./Kirsch, H.-J./Oser, P./Bischof, S. (eds.), Rechnungslegung nach IFRS – Kommentar auf der Grundlage des deutschen Bilanzrechts, 2nd ed., Stuttgart 2013.

Kajüter, P./Barth, D. (2007): Segmentberichterstattung nach IFRS 8 – Übernahme des Management Approach, in: BetriebsBerater, 62 (8), pp. 428–434.

Kajüter, P./Klassmann, F./Nienhaus, M. (2014): Do Voluntary Reviews of Interim Financial Statements Improve the Quality and Information Content of Quarterly Earnings?, Working Paper, University of Münster.

Kajüter, P./Nienhaus, M. (2013): The Impact of IFRS 8 Adoption on the Value Relevance of Segment Reports, Working Paper, University of Münster.

Kang, H./Grey, S. J. (2012): Segment Reporting Practices in Australia: Has IFRS 8 Made a Difference?, Working Paper, The University of New South Wales.

Kaplan, R. S./Atkinson, A. A. (1998): Advanced Management Accounting, 3rd ed., Upper Saddle River 1998.

Kassarjian, H. H. (1977): Content Analysis in Consumer Research, in: Journal of Consumer Research, 4 (1), pp. 8–18.

Kim, O./Verrecchia, R. E. (1991): Trading Volume and Price Reactions to Public Announcements, in: Journal of Accounting Research, 29 (2), pp. 302–321.

Kinney, W. R. (1971): Predicting Earnings: Entity versus Subentity Data, in: Journal of Accounting Research, 9 (1), pp. 127–136.

Kinney, W. R. (1986): Empirical Accounting Research Design for Ph. D. Students, in: The Accounting Review, 61 (2), pp. 338–350.

Kirsch, H.-J./Koelen, P./Köhling, K. (2010): Möglichkeiten und Grenzen des management approach - Eine Analyse unter besonderer Berücksichtigung des Nutzungswerts des IAS 36, in: Zeitschrift für internationale und kapitalmarktorientierte Rechnungslegung, 10 (4), pp. 200–207.

Knutson, P. (1993): Financial Reporting in the 1990s and Beyond. A Position Paper of the Association for Investment Management and Research, Charlottesville 1993.

Kochanek, R. F. (1974): Segmental Financial Disclosure by Diversified Firms and Security Prices, in: The Accounting Review, 49 (2), pp. 245–258.

Köhle, I. (2006): Segmentberichterstattung: Eine theoretische, regulatorische und empirische Analyse zu Erstellung einer ausgewogenen Segmentberichterstattung in der Schweiz, Zürich 2006.

Kornmeier, M. (2007): Wissenschaftstheorie und wissenschaftliches Arbeiten – Eine Einführung für Wirtschaftswissenschaftler, Heidelberg 2007.

KPMG (2010): The Application of IFRS: Segment Reporting, London 2010.

Kräkel, M. (2007): Organisation und Management, 3rd ed., Tübingen 2007.

Küting, K./Lorson, P. (1998): Konvergenz von internem und externem Rechnungswesen: Anmerkungen zu Strategien und Konfliktfeldern, in: Die Wirtschaftsprüfung, 51 (11), pp. 483–493.

Küting, K./Pilhofer, J. (1999): Die neuen Vorschriften zur Segmentberichterstattung nach US-GAAP – Schließung der Regelungslücke in § 279 Abs. 1 HGB durch Adaption internationaler Standards? (Teil II), in: Deutsches Steuerrecht, 37 (14), pp. 603–608.

L

Laffont, J. J./Maskin, E. S. (1990): The Efficient Market Hypothesis and Insider Trading on the Stock Market, in: The Journal of Political Economy, 98 (1), pp. 70–93.

Lambert, R./Leuz, C./Verrecchia, R. E. (2007): Accounting Information, Disclosure, and the Cost of Capital, in: Journal of Accounting Research, 45 (2), pp. 385–420.

Lamont, O. (1997): Cash Flow and Investment: Evidence from Internal Capital Markets, in: The Journal of Finance, 52 (1), pp. 83–109.

Lang, M./Lundholm, R. (1993): Cross-Sectional Determinants of Analyst Ratings of Corporate Disclosures, in: Journal of Accounting Research, 31 (2), pp. 246–271.

Lang, M./Maffett, M. (2010): Economic Effects of Transparency in International Equity Markets: A Review and Suggestions for Future Research, in: Foundations and Trends in Accounting, 5 (3), pp. 175–241.

Lang, M. H./Lundholm, R. J. (1996): Corporate Disclosure Policy and Analyst Behavior, in: The Accounting Review, 71 (4), pp. 467–492.

Lee, C./Ng, D./Bhaskaran, S. (2009): Testing International Asset Pricing Models Using Implied Costs of Capital, in: Journal of Financial and Quantitative Analysis, 44 (2), pp. 307–335.

Leuz, C./Schrand, C. (2009): Disclosure and the Cost of Capital: Evidence From Firms' Responses to the Enron Shock, Working Paper, National Bureau of Economic Research.

Leuz, C./Verrecchia, R. E. (2000): The Economic Consequences of Increased Disclosure, in: Journal of Accounting Research, 38 (Suppl.), pp. 91–124.

Leuz, C./Wysocki, P. D. (2008): Economic Consequences of Financial Reporting and Disclosure Regulation: A Review and Suggestions for Future Research, Working Paper, University of Chicago.

Levitt, A. (1998): The Importance of High Quality Accounting Standards, in: Accounting Horizons, 12 (1), pp. 79–82.

Lindemann, J. (2004): Rechnungslegung und Kapitalmarkt: eine theoretische und empirische Analyse, Dissertation Universität Gießen, Lohmar 2004.

Lingnau, V. (1995): Kritischer Rationalismus und Betriebswirtschaftslehre, in: Wirtschaftswissenschaftliches Studium, 24 (3), pp. 124–129.

Lombardo, D./Pagano, M. (2002): Law and Equity Markets: A Simple Model, CSEF Working Paper, University of Salerno.

Lundholm, R. J. (1991): Public Signals and the Equilibrium Allocation of Private Information, in: Journal of Accounting Research, 29 (2), pp. 322–349.

M

Madhavan, A. (2000): Market Microstructure: A Survey, in: Journal of Financial Markets, 3 (3), pp. 205–258.

Maier, M. T. (2008): Der Management Approach: Herausforderungen für Controller und Abschlußprüfer im Kontext der IFRS-Finanzberichterstattung, Dissertation Universität Gießen, Frankfurt/Main 2008.

Maines, L. A./McDaniel, L. S./Harris, M. S. (1997): Implications of Proposed Segment Reporting Standards for Financial Analysts' Investment Judgements, in: Journal of Accounting Research, 35, pp. 1–24.

Mardini, G. H./Crawford, L./Power, D. M. (2012): The Impact of IFRS 8 on Disclosure Practices of Jordanian Listed Companies, in: Journal of Accounting in Emerging Economies, 2 (1), pp. 67–90.

Martin, P. (1997): The Management Approach, in: CA-magazine (11), pp. 29–30.

Matova, M. R./Pelger, C. (2010): Integration von interner und externer Segmentergebnisrechnung – Eine empirische Untersuchung auf Basis der Segmentberichterstattung nach IFRS 8, in: Zeitschrift für internationale und kapitalmarktorientierte Rechnungslegung, 10 (10), pp. 494–500.

Maury, B./Pajuste, A. (2005): Multiple Large Shareholders and Firm Value, in: Journal of Banking & Finance, 29 (7), pp. 1813–1834.

McConnel, P./Pacter, P. (1995): IASC and FASB Proposals Would Enhance Segment Reporting, in: The CPA Journal, pp. 32–51.

Meinhövel, H. (2005): Grundlagen der Principal-Agent-Theorie, in: Horsch, A./Meinhövel, H./Paul, S. (eds.), Institutionenökonomie und Betriebswirtschaftslehre, München 2005, pp. 65–80.

Melcher, W. (2002): Konvergenz von internem und externem Rechnungswesen: Umstellung des traditionellen Rechnungswesens und Einführung eines abgestimmten vertikalen und horizontalen Erfolgsspaltungskonzepts, Dissertation Unversität Rostock, Hamburg 2002.

Merschdorf, M. (2012): Der Management Approach in der IFRS-Rechnungslegung – Implikationen für Unternehmen und Investoren, Dissertation Westfälische Wilhelms-Universität Münster, Frankfurt 2012.

Merton, R. C. (1987): A Simple Model of Capital Market Equilibrium with Incomplete Information, in: The Journal of Finance, 42 (3), pp. 483–510.

Meyer, C./Weiss, S. (2010): IFRS 8 Operating Segments – Eine Untersuchung der erstmaligen Anwendung in der Schweiz, in: Der Schweizer Treuhänder, 84 (12), pp. 848–855.

Miller, M. C./Scott, M. R. (1980): Financial Reporting by Segments, Melbourne 1980.

Modigliani, F./Miller, M. H. (1958): The Cost of Capital, Corporation Finance and the Theory of Investment, in: The American Economic Review, 48 (3), pp. 261–297.

Möller, H. P. (1985): Die Informationseffizienz des deutschen Aktienmarktes – eine Zusammenfassung und Analyse empirischer Untersuchungen, in: Zeitschrift für betriebswirtschaftliche Forschung, 37 (6), pp. 500–518.

Müller, S./Ordemann, T./Pampel, J. R. (2005): Handlungsempfehlungen für die Anwendung der IFRS im Controlling mittelständischer Unternehmen, in: BetriebsBerater, 60 (39), pp. 2119–2125.

Müller, S./Peskes, M. (2006): Konsequenzen der geplanten Änderungen der Segmentberichterstattung nach IFRS für Abschlusserstellung und Unternehmenssteuerung, in: BetriebsBerater, 61 (15), pp. 819–825.

N

Naumann, T. K. (1999): Standardentwurf zur Segmentberichterstattung, in: BetriebsBerater, 54 (44), pp. 2288–2291.

Neal, R./Wheatley, S. M. (1998): Adverse Selection and Bid–Ask Spreads: Evidence From Closed-End Funds, in: Journal of Financial Markets, 1 (1), pp. 121–149.

Newey, W. K./West, K. D. (1987): A Simple, Positive Semi-Definite, Heteroskedasticity and Autocorrelation Consistent Covariance Matrix, in: Econometrica, 55 (3), pp. 703–708.

Nichols, N. B./Street, D. L./Cereola, S. J. (**2012**)**:** An Analysis of the Impact of Adopting IFRS 8 on the Segment Disclosures of European Blue Chip Companies, in: Journal of International Accounting, Auditing and Taxation, 21 (2), pp. 79–105.

Nichols, N. B./Street, D. L./Gray, S. J. (**2000**)**:** Geographic Segment Disclosures in the United States: Reporting Practices Enter A New Era, in: Journal of International Accounting, Auditing and Taxation, 9 (1), pp. 59–82.

North, D. C. (**1990**)**:** Institutions, Institutional Change and Economic Performance, Cambridge 1990.

O

OECD (**1990**)**:** Segmented Financial Information, Paris 1990.

Ohlson, J. A./Juettner-Nauroth, B. E. (**2005**)**:** Expected EPS and EPS Growth as Determinants of Value, in: Review of Accounting Studies, 10 (2-3), pp. 349–365.

P

Pacter, P. (**1993**)**:** Reporting Disaggregated Information, Norwalk 1993.

Park, J. C. (**2011**)**:** The Effect of SFAS 131 on the Stock Market's Ability to Predict Industry-Wide and Firm-Specific Components of Future Earnings, in: Accounting & Finance, 51 (2), pp. 575–607.

Paul, J. W./Largay III, J. A. (**2005**)**:** Does the "management approach" contribute to segment reporting transparency?, in: Business Horizons, 48 (4), pp. 303–310.

Pejic, P. (**1998**)**:** Segmentberichterstattung im externen Jahresabschluß – internationale Normierungspraxis und Informationsbedürfnisse der Adressaten, Dissertation European Business School Schloß Reichartshausen, Oestrich-Winkel, Wiesbaden 1998.

Peskes, M. (**2004**)**:** Zukunftsorientierte Segmentberichterstattung – Adressatenkonforme Segmentierung und Segmentabgrenzung im Rahmen der Segmentberichterstattung insbesondere zur Erfüllung des Erfordernisses der Zukunftsorientiertheit, Hamburg 2004.

Petersen, M. A. (**2008**)**:** Estimating Standard Errors in Finance Panel Data Sets: Comparing Approaches, in: Review of Financial Studies, 22 (1), pp. 435–480.

Pfaff, D./Zweifel, P. (**1998**)**:** Die Principal-Agent Theorie. Ein fruchtbarer Beitrag der Wirtschaftstheorie zur Praxis, in: Wirtschaftswissenschaftliches Studium, 27 (4), pp. 184–190.

Pisano, S./Landriana, L. (2012): The Determinants of Segment Disclosure: An Empirical Analysis on Italian Listed Companies, in: Financial Reporting, 1 (1), pp. 113–132.

Popper, K. (1935): Logik der Forschung – Zur Erkenntnistheorie der modernen Naturwissenschaft, 1ˢᵗ ed., Wien 1935.

Popper, K. (2005): Logik der Forschung, 11ᵗʰ ed., Tübingen 2005.

Preinreich, G. D. (1938): Annual Survey of Economic Theory: The Theory of Depreciation, in: Econometrica, 6 (3), pp. 219–241.

Prodhan, B. K. (1986): Geographical Segment Disclosure and Multinational Risk Profile, in: Journal of Business Finance & Accounting, 13 (1), pp. 15–37.

Prodhan, B. K./Harris, M. C. (1989): Systematic Risk and the Discretionary Disclosure of Geographical Segments: An Empirical Investigation of US Multinationals, in: Journal of Business Finance & Accounting, 16 (4), pp. 467–485.

R

Radebaugh, L. H./Gray, S. J./Black, E. L. (2006): International Accounting and Multinational Enterprises, 6ᵗʰ ed., Hoboken 2006.

Reinke, J. (2009): Impairment Test nach IAS 36 – Grundlagen, Durchführung, abschlusspolitisches Potenzial, Dissertation Helmut-Schmidt-Universität Hamburg, Berlin 2009.

Richter, R./Furubotn, E. G. (2010): Neue Institutionenökonomik, 4ᵗʰ ed., Tübingen 2010.

Roberts, C. B. (1989): Forecasting Earnings Using Geographical Segment Data: Some UK Evidence, in: Journal of International Financial Management & Accounting, 1 (2), pp. 130–151.

Rogler, S. (2009): Segmentberichterstattung nach IFRS 8 im Fokus von Bilanzpolitik und Bilanzanalyse (Teil 1), in: Zeitschrift für internationale und kapitalmarktorientierte Rechnungslegung, 9 (9), pp. 500–505.

Ross, S. A. (1973): The Economic Theory of Agency: The Principal's Problem, in: The American Economic Review, 63 (2), pp. 134–139.

S

Salamon, G. L./Dhaliwal, D. S. (1980): Company Size and Financial Disclosure Requirements With Evidence From the Segmental Reporting Issue, in: Journal of Business Finance & Accounting, 7 (4), pp. 555–568.

Sandleben, H.-M./Schmidt, J. (2010): Aktuelles zu IFRS 8 – Segmentberichterstattung, in: Zeitschrift für Internationale Rechnungslegung, 5 (2), pp. 48–50.

Schildbach, T. (1986): Jahresabschluß und Markt, Berlin 1986.

Schildbach, T. (1997): Cost accounting in Germany, in: Management Accounting Research, 8 (3), pp. 261–276.

Schipper, K. (1991): Analysts' Forecasts, in: Accounting Horizons, 5 (4), pp. 105–121.

Schweitzer, M. (1978): Auffassungen und Wissenschaftsziele der Betriebswirtschaftslehre, Darmstadt 1978.

SEC (1998a): In the Matter of Sony Corporation and Sumio Sano, Respondents, Accounting and Auditing Enforcement Release No. 1061.

SEC (1998b): Securities Exchange Commission V. Sony Corporation, Accounting and Auditing Enforcement Release No. 1062.

SEC (2004a): SEC Charges Richard A. Causey, Former Enron Chief Accounting Officer, with Fraud, Accounting and Auditing Enforcement Release No. 1947.

SEC (2004b): SEC Charges Jeffrey K. Skilling, Enron's Former President, Chief Executive Officer and Chief Operating Officer, with Fraud, Accounting and Auditing Enforcement Release No. 1959.

SEC (2004c): SEC Charges Kenneth L. Lay, Enron's Former Chairman and Chief Executive Officer, with Fraud and Insider Trading, Accounting and Auditing Enforcement Release No. 2051.

Shapiro, S. S./Wilk, M. B. (1965): An Analysis of Variance Test for Normality (Complete Samples), in: Biometrika, 52 (3-4), pp. 591–611.

Shin, H./Stulz, R. M. (1998): Are Internal Capital Markets Efficient?, in: Quarterly Journal of Economics, 113 (2), pp. 531–552.

Silhan, P. A. (1983): The Effects of Segmenting Quarterly Sales and Margins on Extrapolative Forecasts of Conglomerate Earnings: Extension and Replication, in: Journal of Accounting Research, 21 (1), pp. 341–347.

Spence, M. (1973): Job Market Signaling, in: The Quarterly Journal of Economics, 87 (3), pp. 355–374.

Spremann, K. (1990): Asymmetrische Information, in: Zeitschrift für Betriebswirtschaft, 60 (5-6), pp. 561–586.

Stiglitz, J. E. (1975): The Theory of "Screening", Education, and the Distribution of Income, in: The American Economic Review, 65 (3), pp. 283–300.

Stiglitz, J. E./Weiss, A. (1981): Credit Rationing in Markets with Imperfect Information, in: The American Economic Review, 71 (3), pp. 393–410.

Stoll, H. R. (1978a): The Pricing of Security Dealer Services: An Empirical Study of Nasdaq Stocks, in: The Journal of Finance, 33 (4), pp. 1153–1172.

Stoll, H. R. (1978b): The Supply of Dealer Services in Securities Markets, in: The Journal of Finance, 33 (4), pp. 1133–1151.

Street, D. L./Nichols, N. B. (2002): LOB and Geographic Segment Disclosures: An Analysis of the Impact of IAS 14 Revised, in: Journal of International Accounting, Auditing and Taxation, 11 (2), pp. 91–113.

Street, D. L./Nichols, N. B./Gray, S. J. (2000): Segment Disclosures under SFAS No. 131: Has Business Segment Reporting Improved?, in: Accounting Horizons, 14 (3), pp. 259–285.

Stubenrath, M. (2001): Kommunikation auf internationalen Kapitalmärkten – Eine informationsökonomische Analyse unter besonderer Berücksichtigung international heterogener Jahresabschlüsse, Dissertation, Lohmar 2001.

Stulz, R. M. (2009): Securities Laws, Disclosure, and National Capital Markets in the Age of Financial Globalization, in: Journal of Accounting Research, 47 (2), pp. 349–390.

Swaminathan, S. (1991): The Impact of SEC Mandated Segment Data on Price Variability and Divergence of Beliefs, in: The Accounting Review, 66 (1), pp. 23–41.

T

Trapp, R./Wolz, M. (2008): Segmentberichterstattung nach IFRS 8 – Konvergenz um jeden Preis?, in: Zeitschrift für Internationale Rechnungslegung, 3 (2), pp. 85–94.

U

Ulbrich, P. R. (2006): Segmentberichterstattung nach IAS 14 – Ein normativer Ansatz zur Neugestaltung auf der Grundlage des Beteiligungscontrollings, Dissertation Universität Eichstätt-Ingolstadt, Hamburg 2006.

V

Venkataraman, R. (2001): The Impact of SFAS 131 on Financial Analysts' Information Environment, Working Paper, Pennsylvania State University.

Venkatesh, P. C./Chiang, R. (1986): Information Asymmetry and the Dealer's Bid-Ask Spread: A Case Study of Earnings and Dividend Announcements, in: The Journal of Finance, 41 (5), pp. 1089–1102.

Véron, N. (2007): The Global Accounting Experiment, Brussels 2007.

Verrecchia, R. E. (1982): Information Acquisition in a Noisy Rational Expectations Economy, in: Econometrica, 50 (6), pp. 1415–1430.

Verrecchia, R. E. (1983): Discretionary disclosure, in: Journal of Accounting and Economics, 5 (1), pp. 179–194.

Verrecchia, R. E. (2001): Essays on disclosure, in: Journal of Accounting and Economics, 32 (1–3), pp. 97–180.

W

Wagenhofer, A. (2005): Internationale Rechnungslegungsstandards – IAS/IFRS, 5th ed., Frankfurt/Main 2005.

Wagenhofer, A. (2008): Konvergenz von intern und extern berichteten Ergebnisgrößen am Beispiel von Segmentergebnissen, in: Betriebswirtschaftliche Forschung und Praxis, 60 (2), pp. 161–176.

Wagenhofer, A./Ewert, R. (2007): Externe Unternehmensrechnung, 2nd ed., Berlin 2007.

Watrin, C. (2001): Internationale Rechnungslegung und Regulierungstheorie, Wiesbaden 2001.

Weber, M. (2006): Die Haftung des Analysten für fehlerhafte Wertpapieranalysen, Dissertation, Lohmar 2006.

Weiss, S. (2012): Segmentberichterstattung nach IFRS 8 - Analyse der Auswirkungen des Managementansatzes auf die Anwendung und die Qualität der Segmentberichterstattung in der Schweiz, Dissertation Universität Zürich, Zurich 2012.

Weißenberger, B. E./Franzen, N. (2011): Herausforderungen Management Approach – Theoretische und empirische Analyse der Segmentberichterstattung nach IFRS 8 in deutschen Unternehmen, in: Kajüter, P./Mindermann, T./Winkler, C. (eds.), Controlling und Rechnungslegung. Bestandsaufnahme, Schnittstellen, Perspektiven, Festschrift für Klaus-Peter Franz, Stuttgart 2011, pp. 323–352.

Weißenberger, B. E./Franzen, N./Pelster, F./Bremer, L. (2013): Verbessert sich unter IFRS 8 die Konsistenz von Segmentbericht und Lagebericht?, in: Zeitschrift für internationale und kapitalmarktorientierte Rechnungslegung, 13 (1), pp. 13–20.

Weißenberger, B. E./Maier, M. T. (2006): Der Management Approach in der IFRS-Rechnungslegung: Fundierung der Finanzberichterstattung durch Informationen aus dem Controlling, in: Der Betrieb, 59 (39), pp. 2077–2083.

Welker, M. (1995): Disclosure Policy, Information Asymmetry, and Liquidity in Equity Markets, in: Contemporary Accounting Research, 11 (2), pp. 801–827.

White, H. (1980): A Heteroskedasticity-Consistent Covariance Matrix Estimator and a Direct Test for Heteroskedasticity, in: Econometrica, 48 (4), pp. 817–838.

Williamson, O. E. (1975): Markets and Hierarchies: Analysis and Antitrust Implications: A Study in the Economics of Internal Organization, New York 1975.

Wooldridge, J. M. (2012): Introductory Econometrics: A Modern Approach, 5th ed., Cincinnati 2012.

Wulf, I./Jaeschke, C./Sackbrook, J. (2011): Nutzung der bilanzpolitischen Moglichkeiten beim goodwill impairment, in: Praxis der internationalen Rechnungslegung, 5 (4), pp. 96–103.

Münsteraner Schriften zur Internationalen Unternehmensrechnung

Herausgegeben von Peter Kajüter

www.peterlang.com